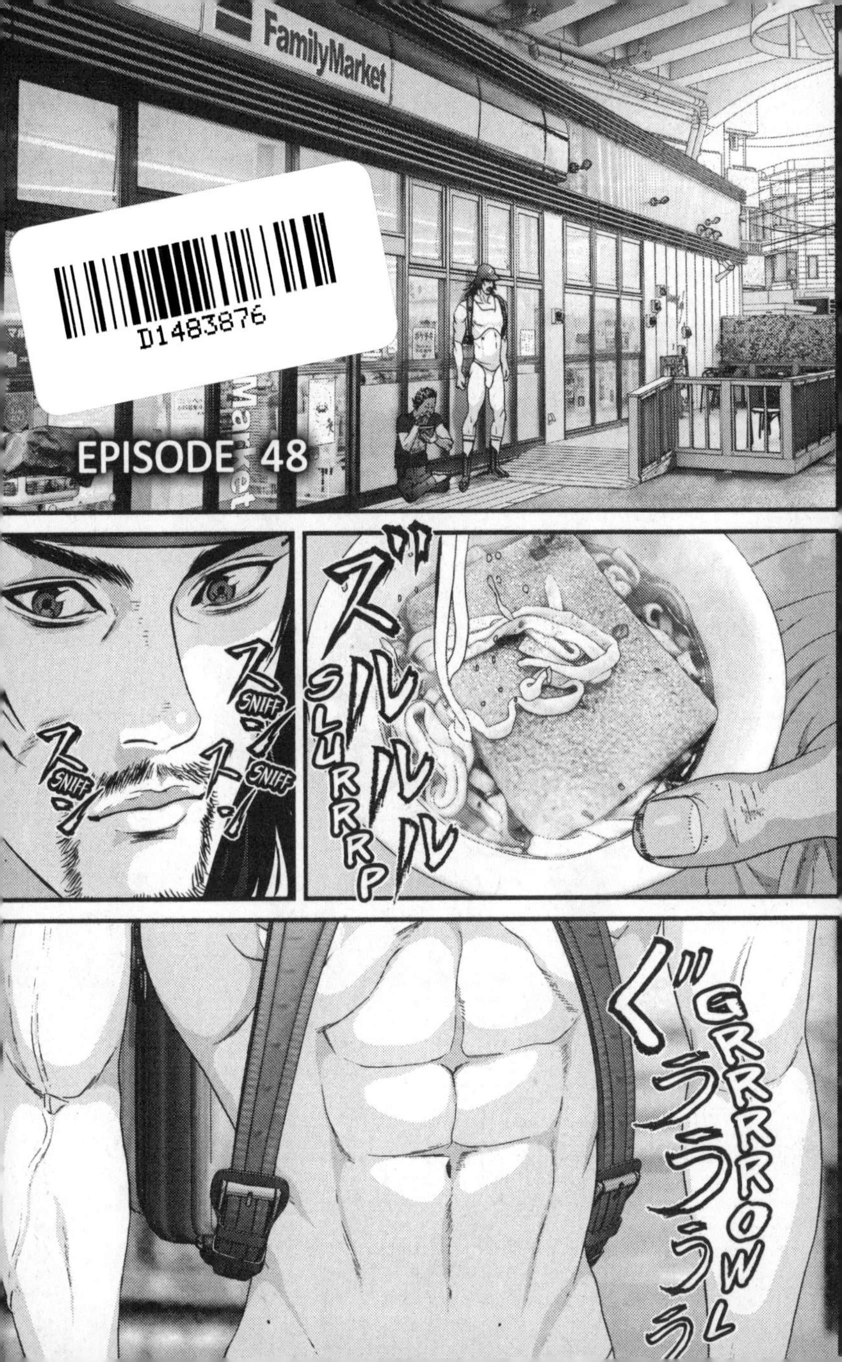
FamilyMarket
EPISODE 48
ズルルル
SLURRRP
スー
SNIFF
スー
SNIFF
スー
SNIFF
ぐうううう
GRRRROWL

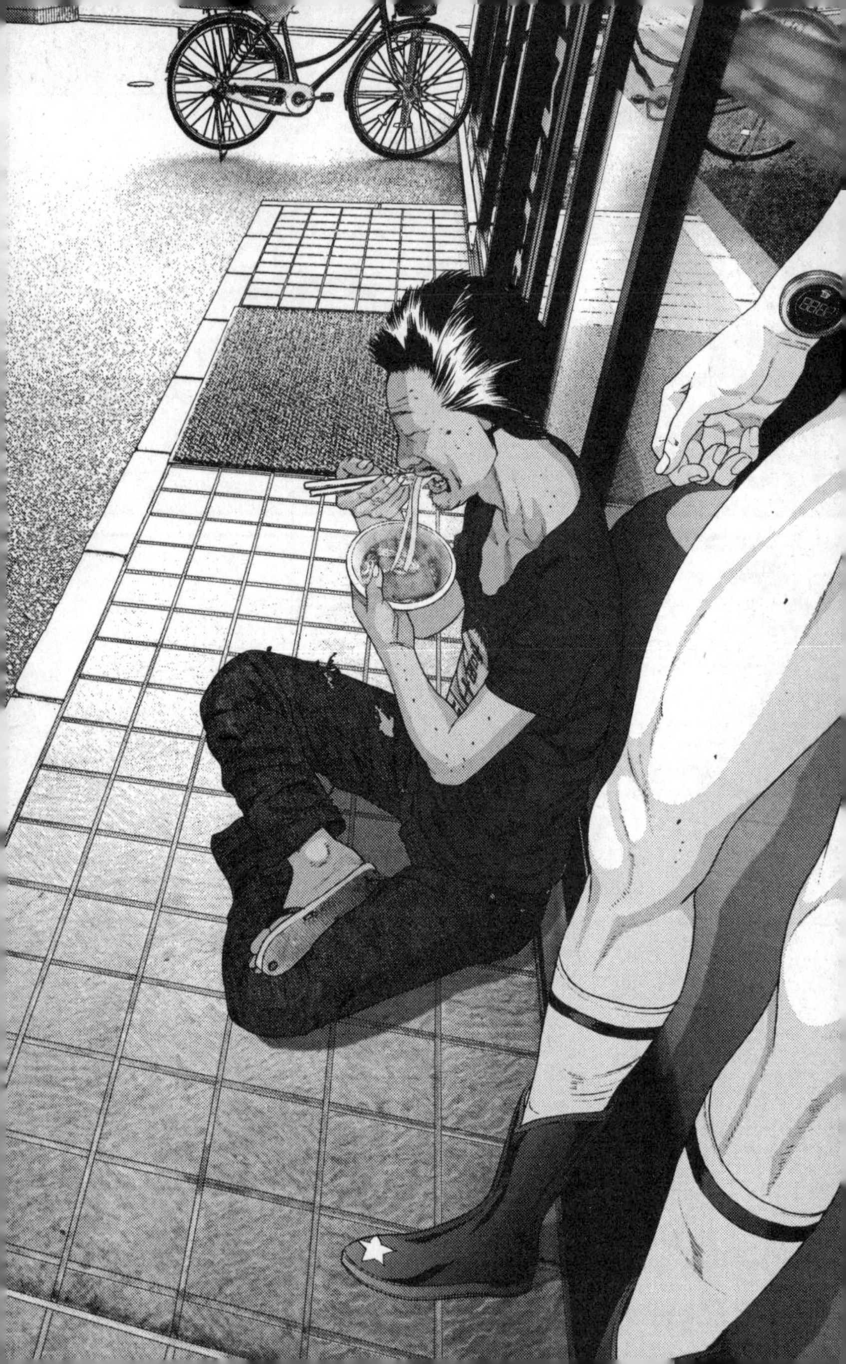

GIGANT

6

BY HIROYA OKU

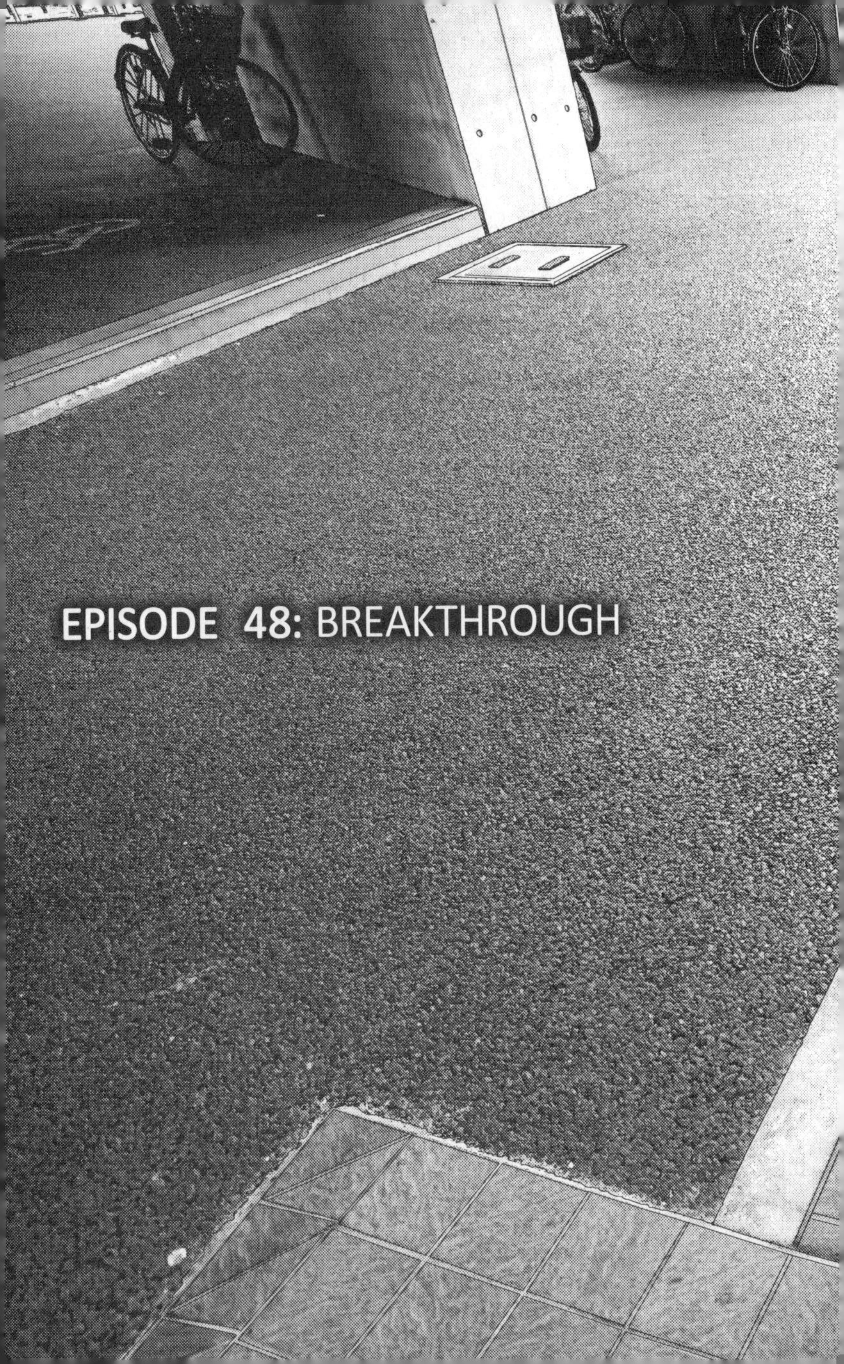
EPISODE 48: BREAKTHROUGH

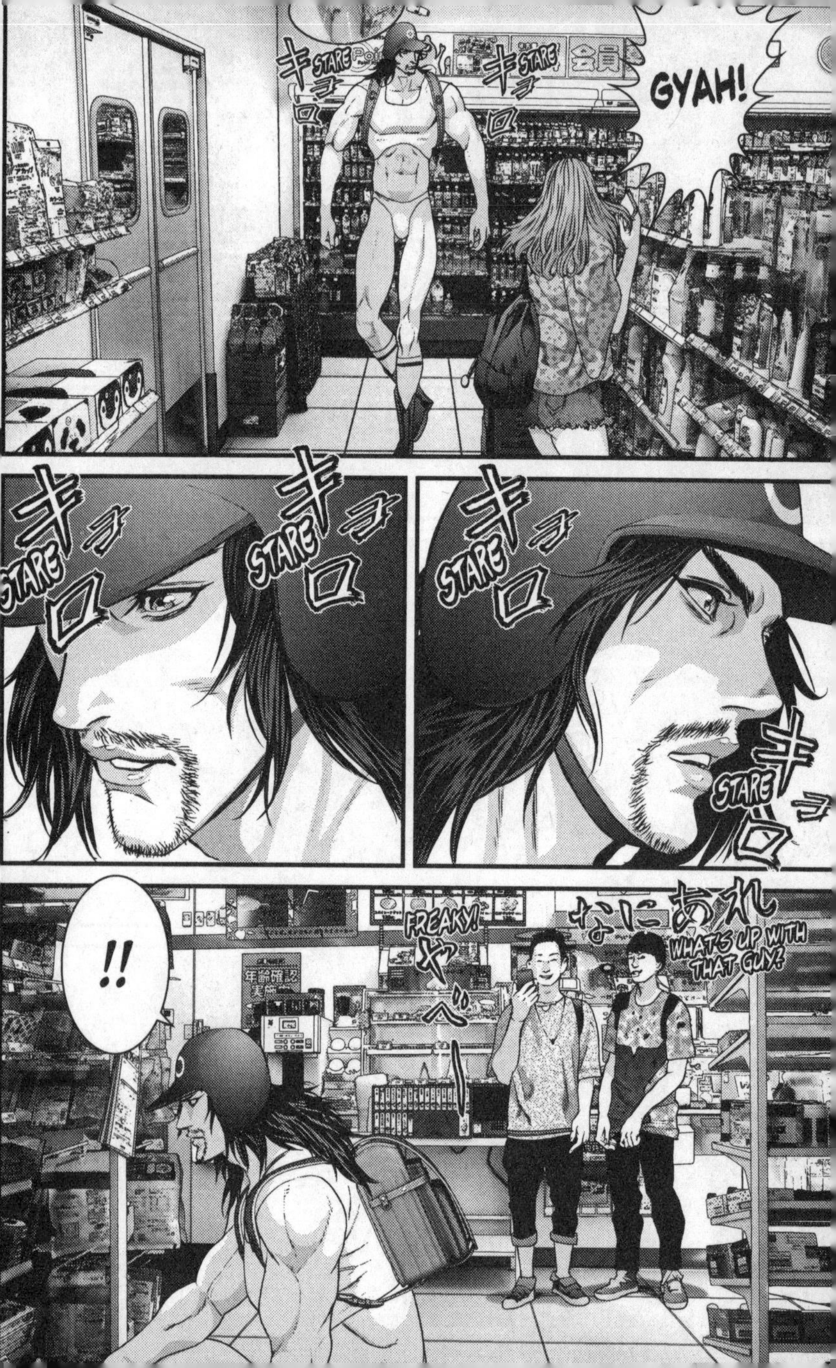
GYAH!
キョロ
STARE
キョロ
STARE
キョロ
STARE
キョロ
STARE
キョロ
STARE
キョロ
STARE
キョロ
STARE
なにあれ
WHAT'S UP WITH THAT GUY?
やべー
FREAKY!
!!

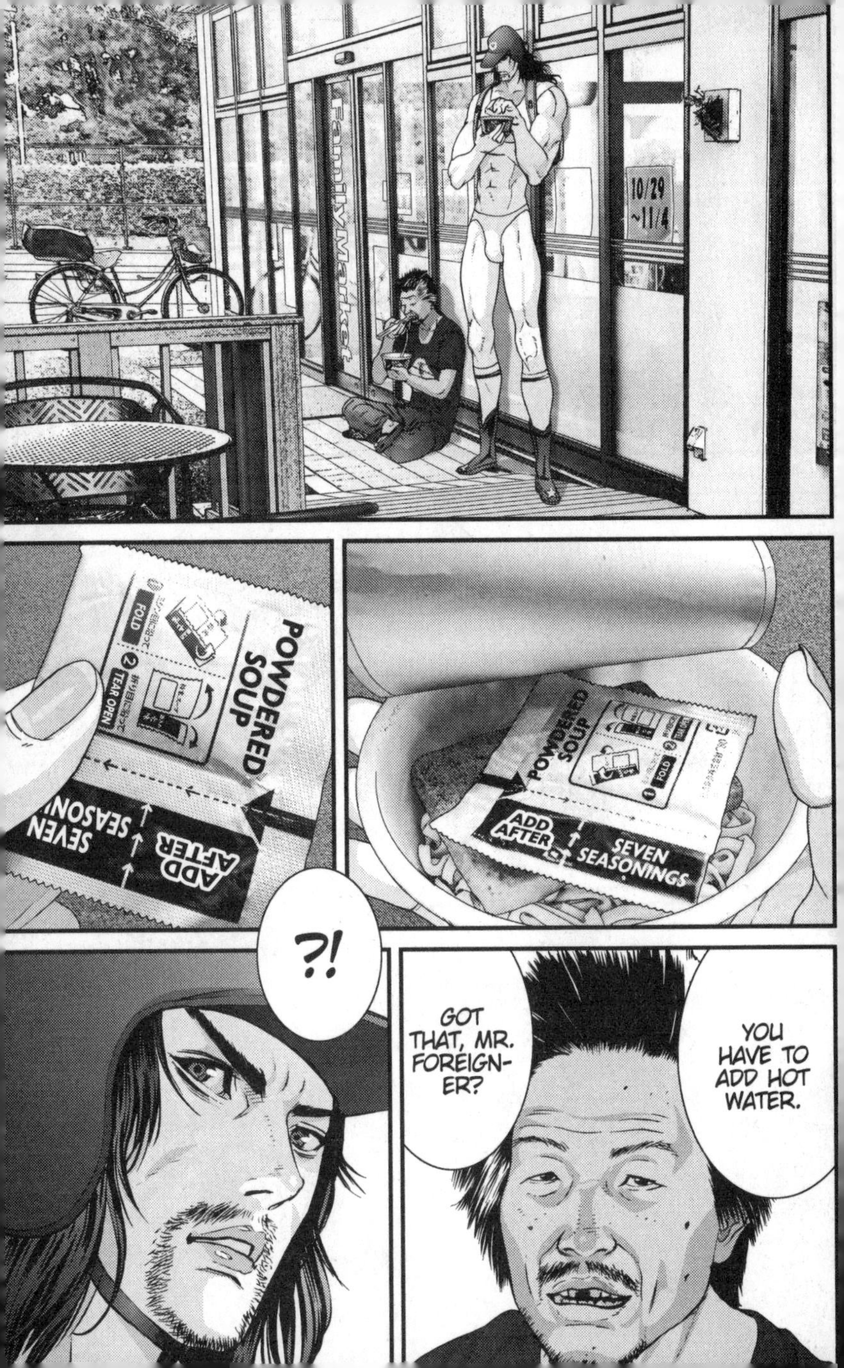
FamilyMarket
10/29 ~11/4
POWDERED SOUP
FOLD
ADD AFTER
SEVEN SEASONINGS
POWDERED SOUP
FOLD
TEAR OPEN
ADD AFTER
SEVEN
YOU HAVE TO ADD HOT WATER.
GOT THAT, MR. FOREIGNER?
?!

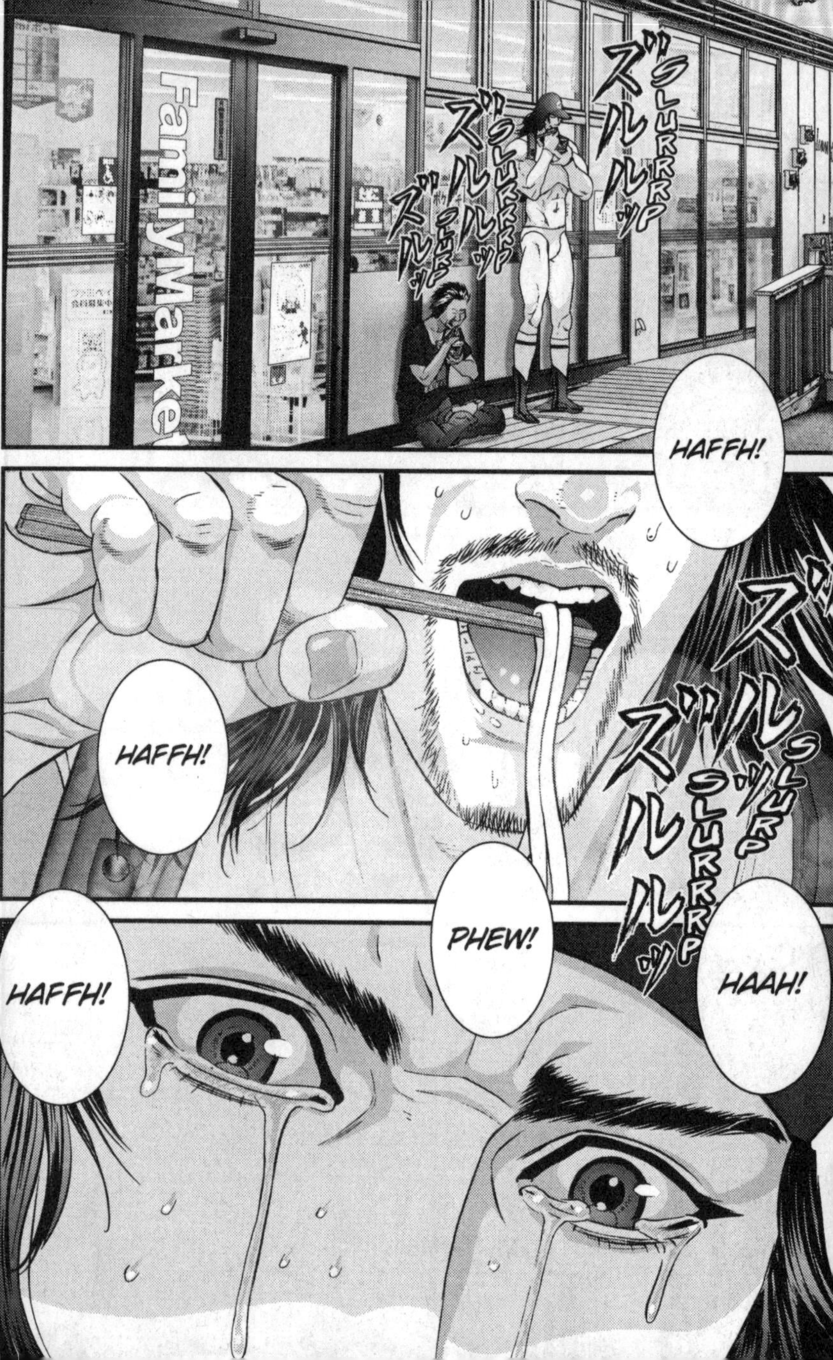

SLURRRP
SLURRRP
SLURP
HAFFH!
HAFFH!
SLURP
SLURRRP
HAAH!
PHEW!
HAFFH!

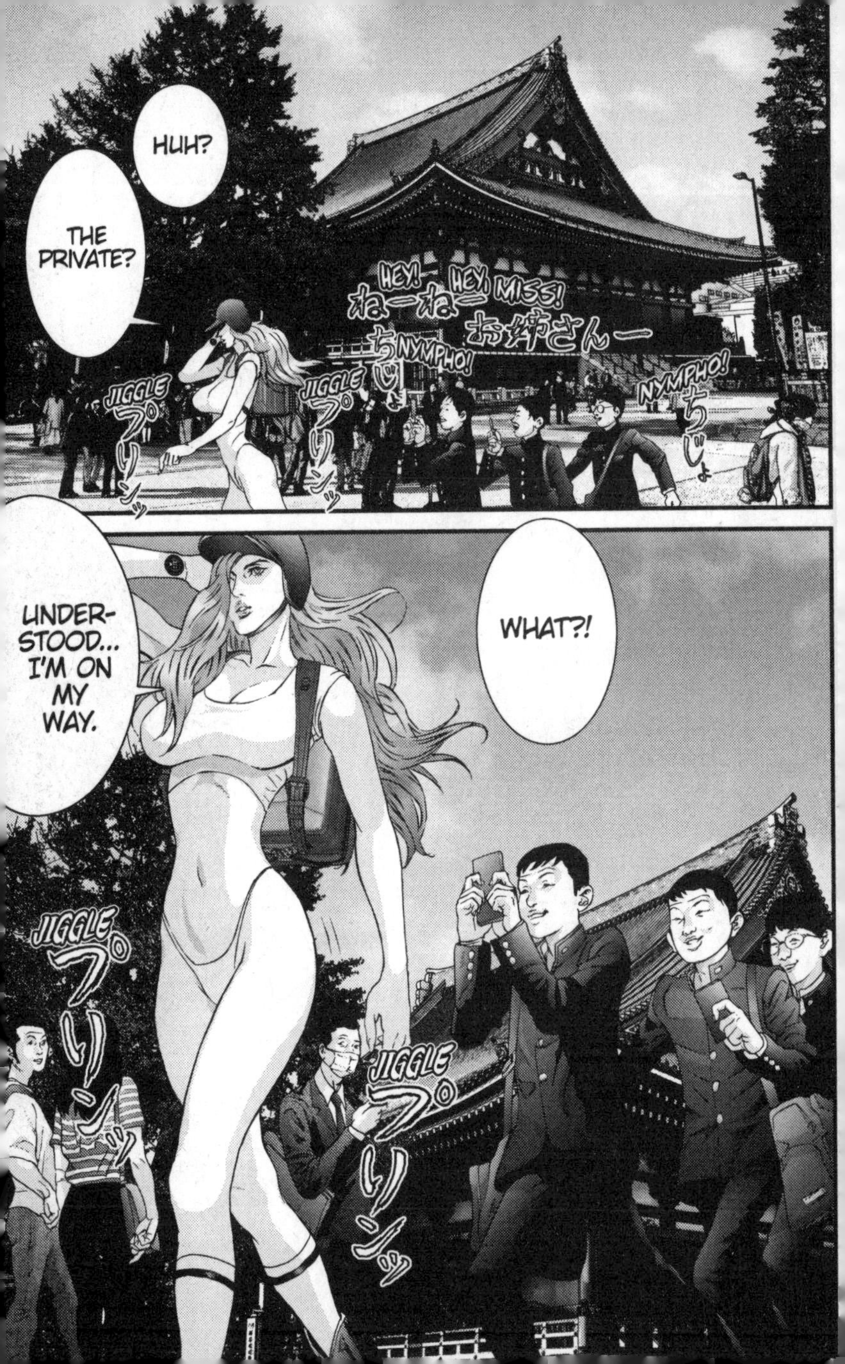
HEY! ねーね
HEY, MISS! お姉さんー
NYMPHO! ちじょ
NYMPHO! ちじょ
HUH?
THE PRIVATE?
JIGGLE プリンッ
JIGGLE プリンッ
WHAT?!
UNDER-STOOD... I'M ON MY WAY.
JIGGLE プリンッ
JIGGLE プリンッ

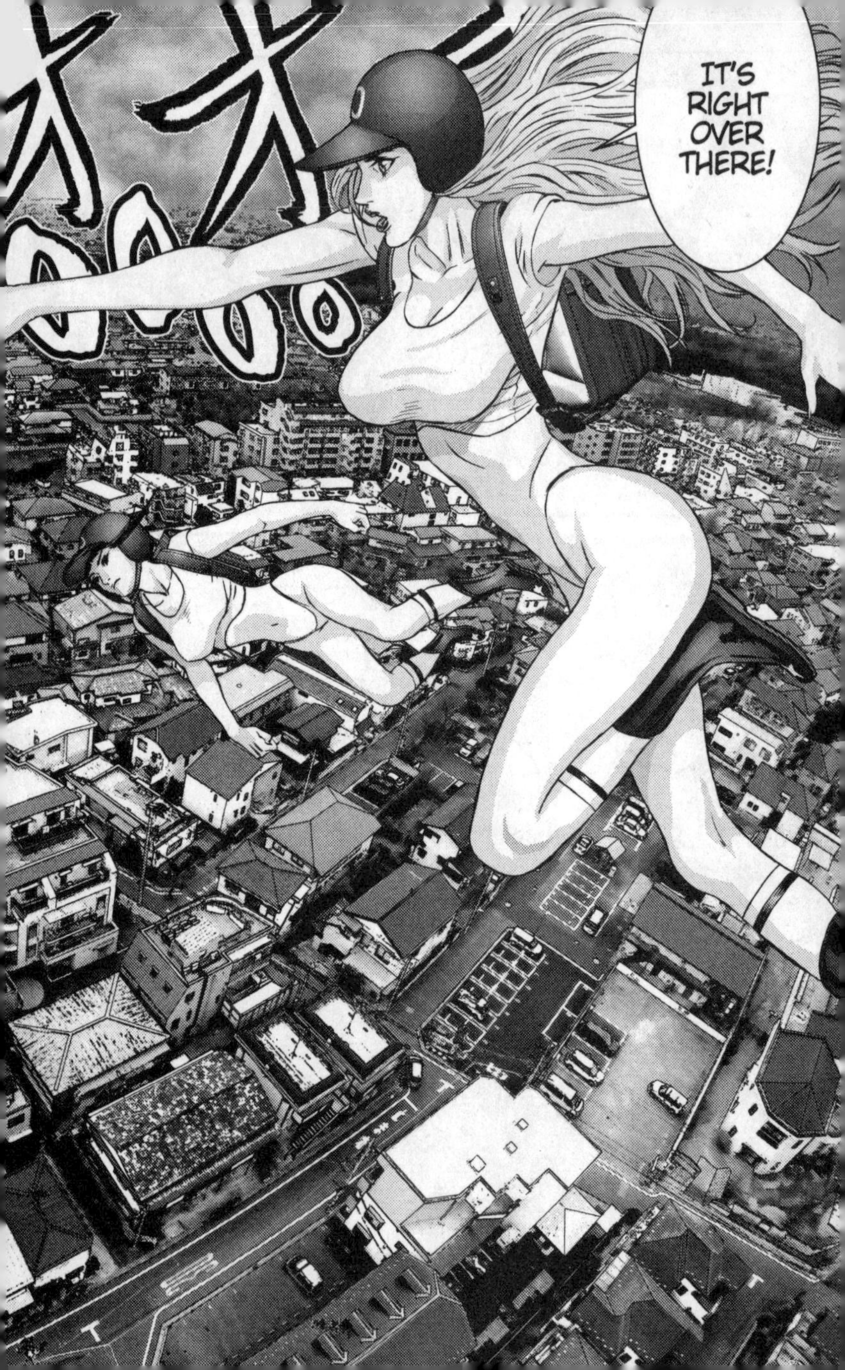
IT'S RIGHT OVER THERE!

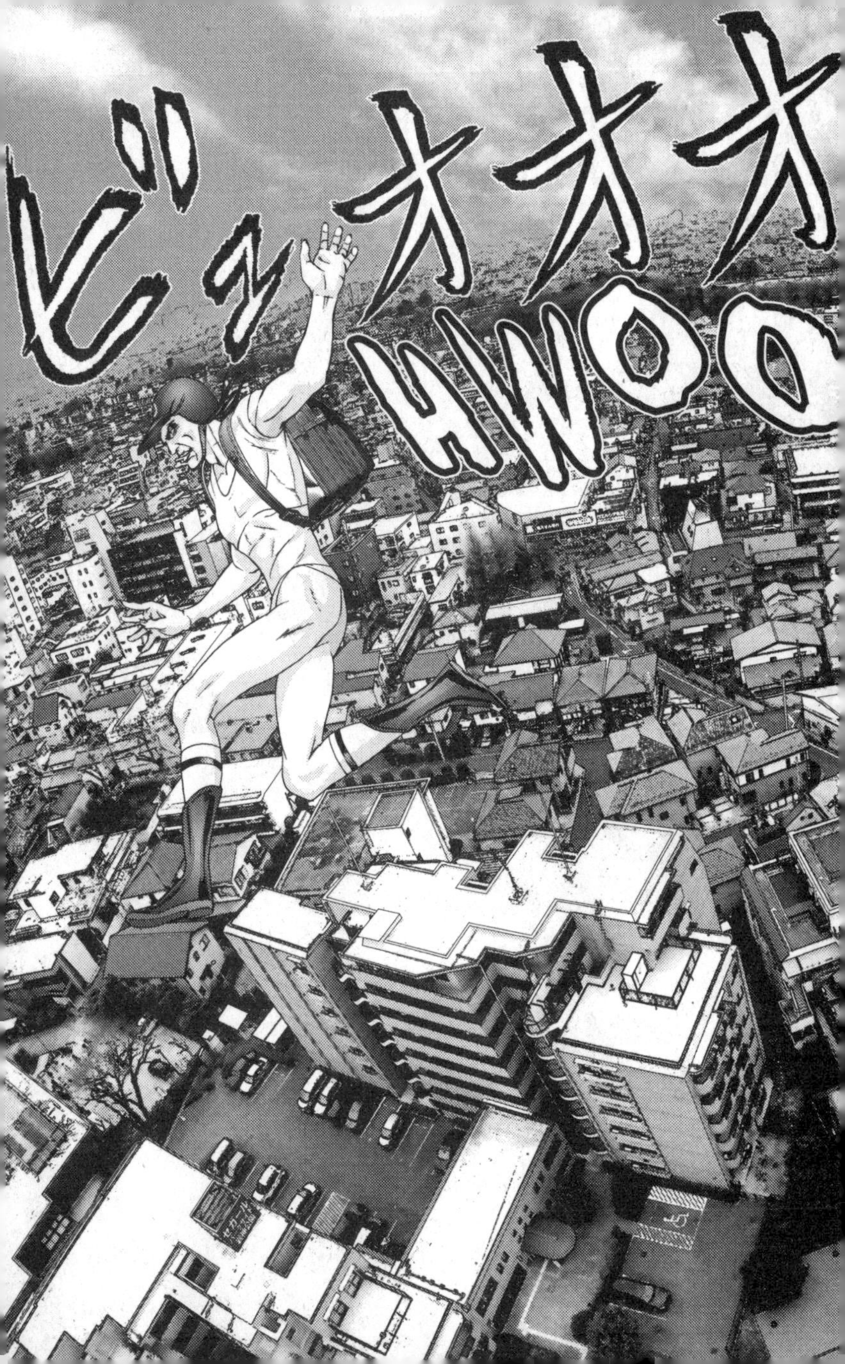
ビュオオオ
HWOO

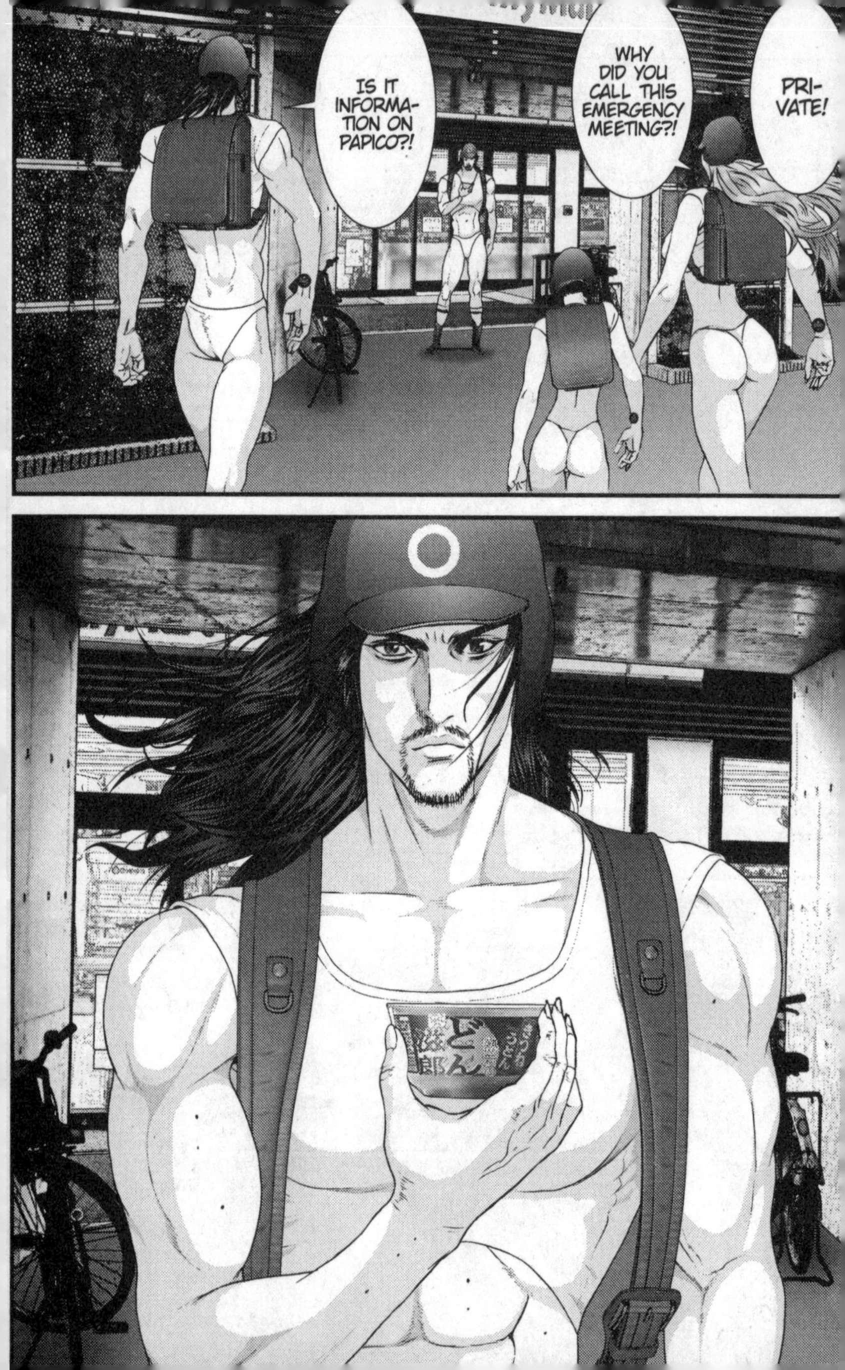
PRI-VATE!
WHY DID YOU CALL THIS EMERGENCY MEETING?!
IS IT INFORMATION ON PAPICO?!

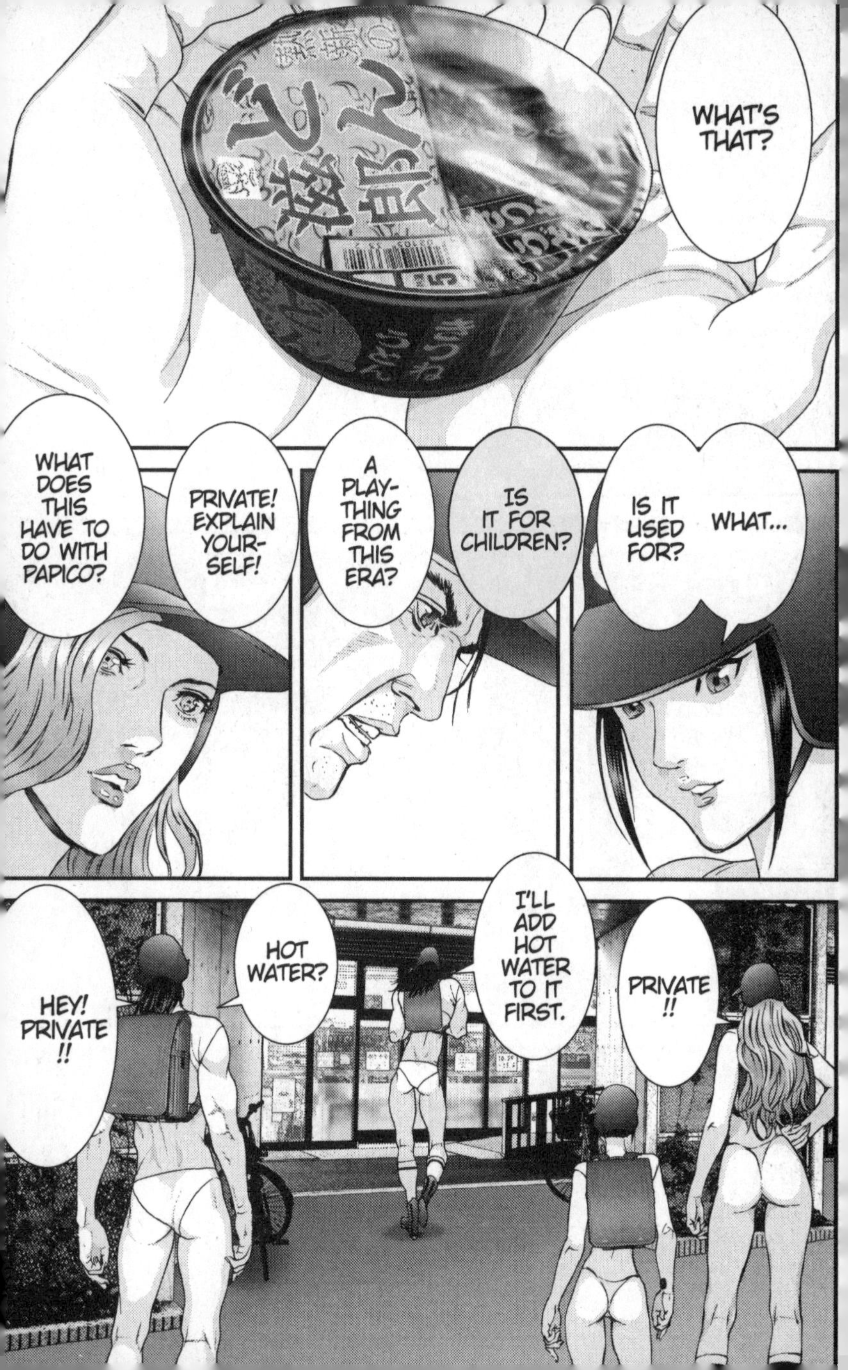
WHAT'S THAT?
WHAT...
IS IT USED FOR?
IS IT FOR CHILDREN?
A PLAY-THING FROM THIS ERA?
PRIVATE! EXPLAIN YOUR-SELF!
WHAT DOES THIS HAVE TO DO WITH PAPICO?
PRIVATE!!
I'LL ADD HOT WATER TO IT FIRST.
HOT WATER?
HEY! PRIVATE!!

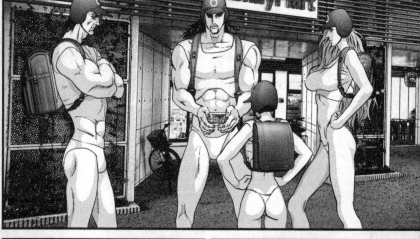

IT'S FOOD?

SNIFF
SNIFF
SNIFF

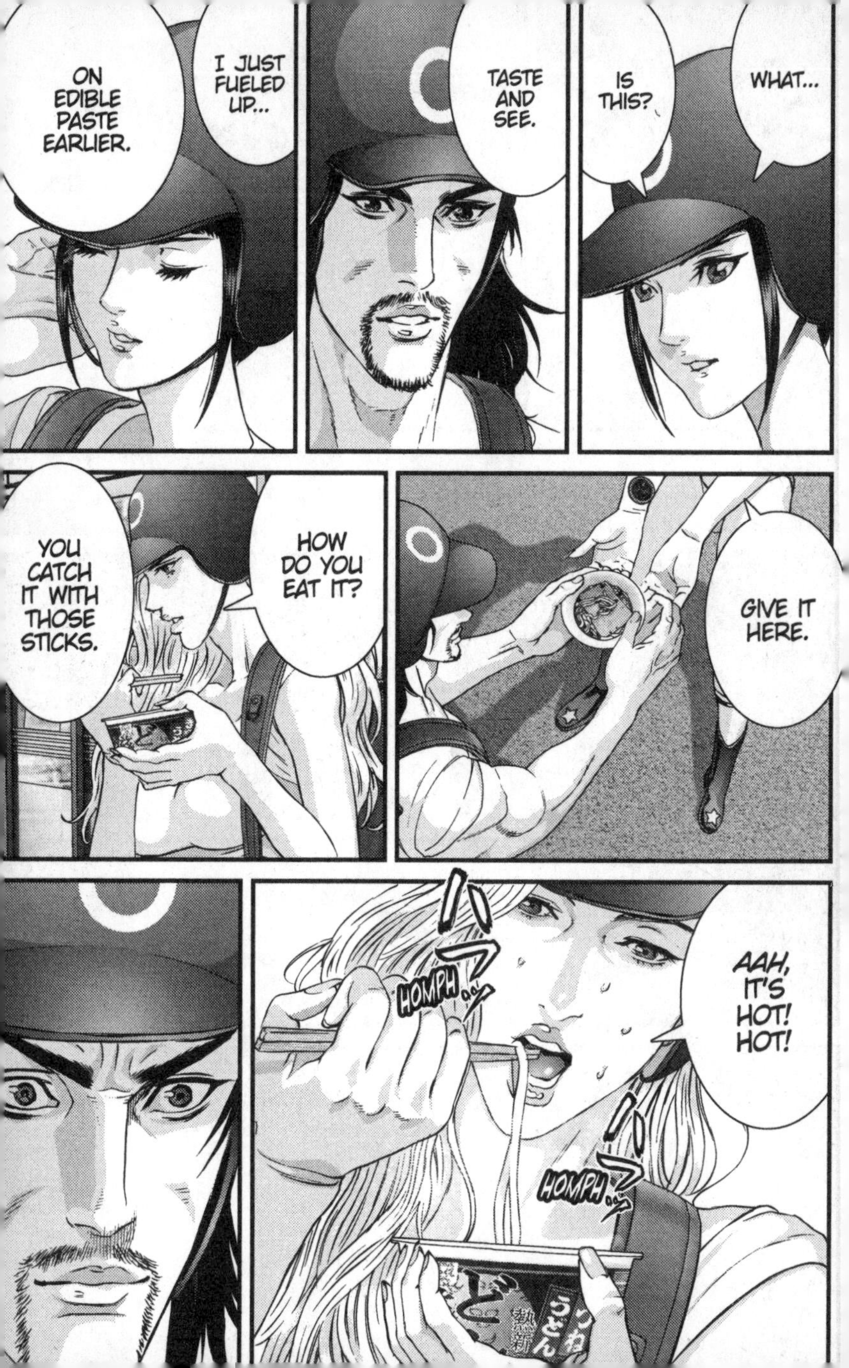
WHAT...
IS THIS?
TASTE AND SEE.
I JUST FUELED UP...
ON EDIBLE PASTE EARLIER.
GIVE IT HERE.
HOW DO YOU EAT IT?
YOU CATCH IT WITH THOSE STICKS.
AAH, IT'S HOT! HOT!
HOMPH
HOMPH

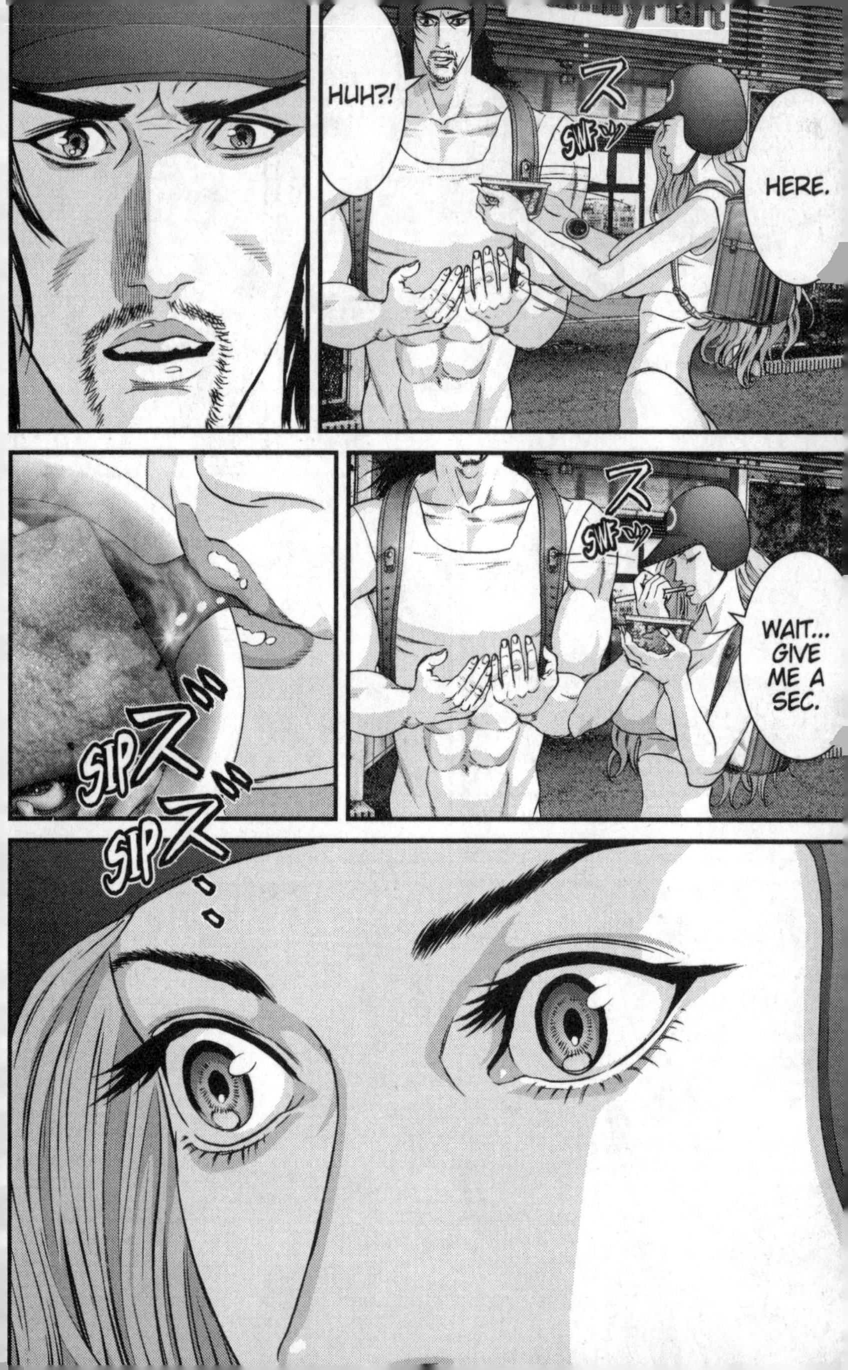
HUH?!
ス
SWF
HERE.
ス
SWF
WAIT... GIVE ME A SEC.
SIP スズ
SIP スズ

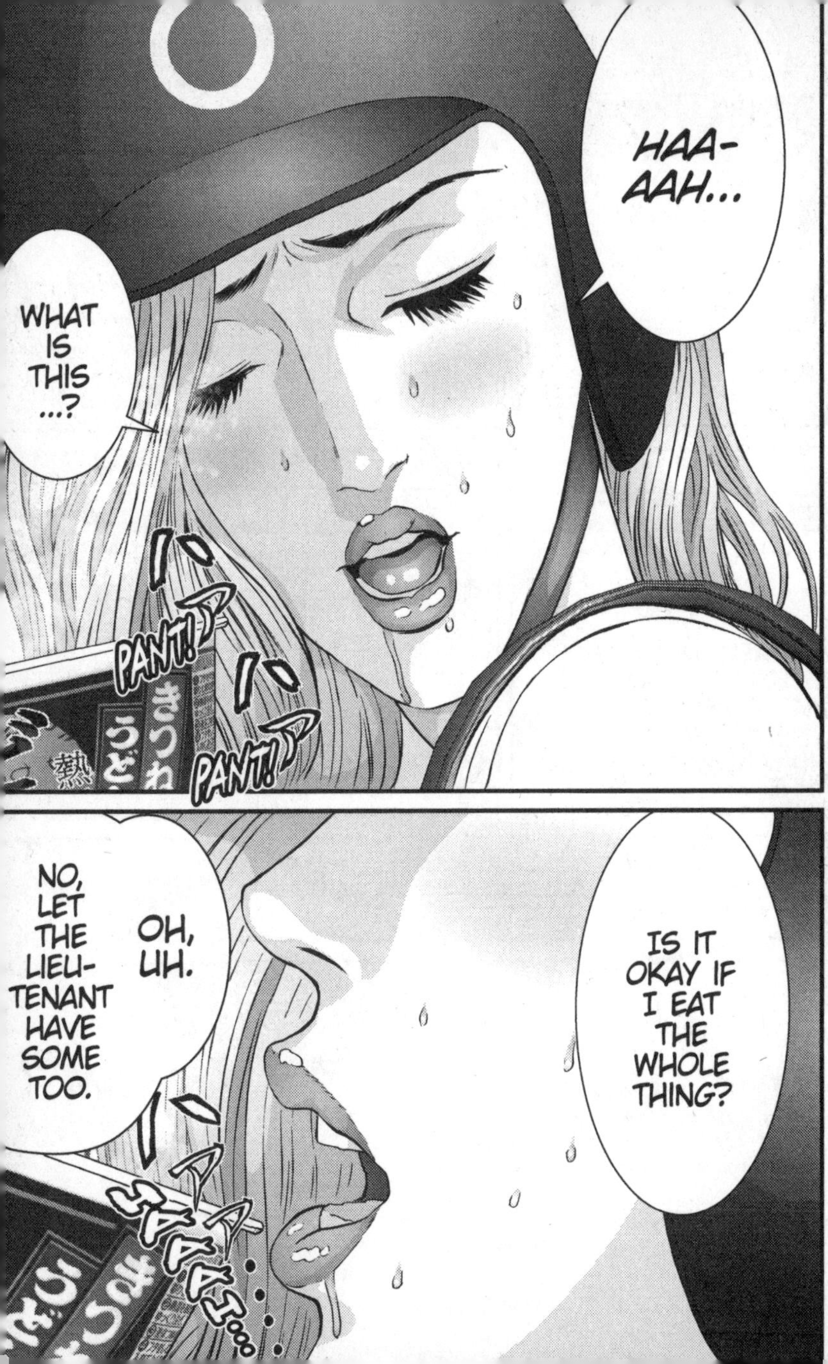
HAA-AAH...
WHAT IS THIS ...?
PANT!
PANT!
IS IT OKAY IF I EAT THE WHOLE THING?
OH, UH.
NO, LET THE LIEU-TENANT HAVE SOME TOO.

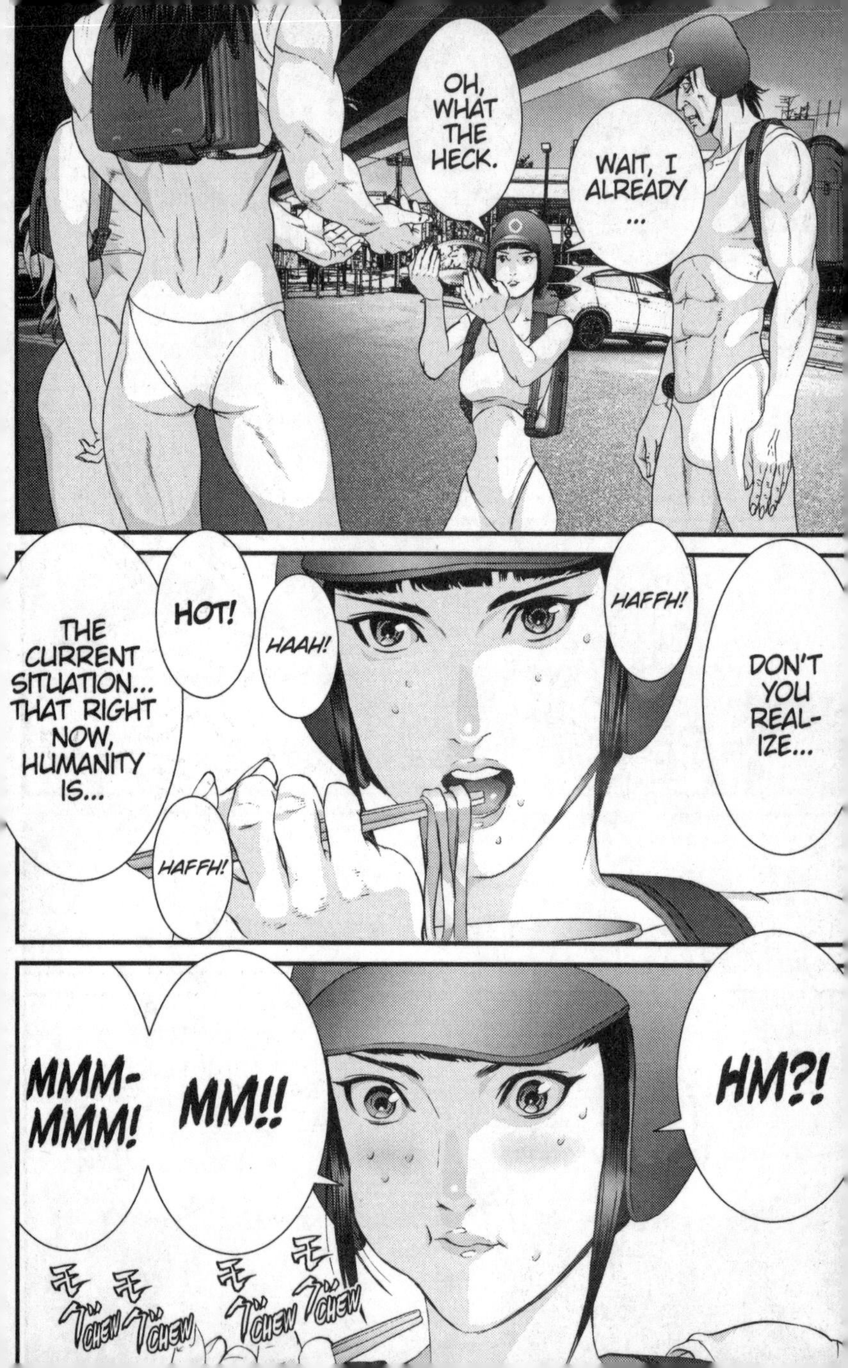
WAIT, I ALREADY ...
OH, WHAT THE HECK.
DON'T YOU REALIZE...
HAFFH!
HAAH!
HOT!
THE CURRENT SITUATION... THAT RIGHT NOW, HUMANITY IS...
HAFFH!
HM?!
MM!!
MMM-MMM!
CHEW
CHEW
CHEW
CHEW

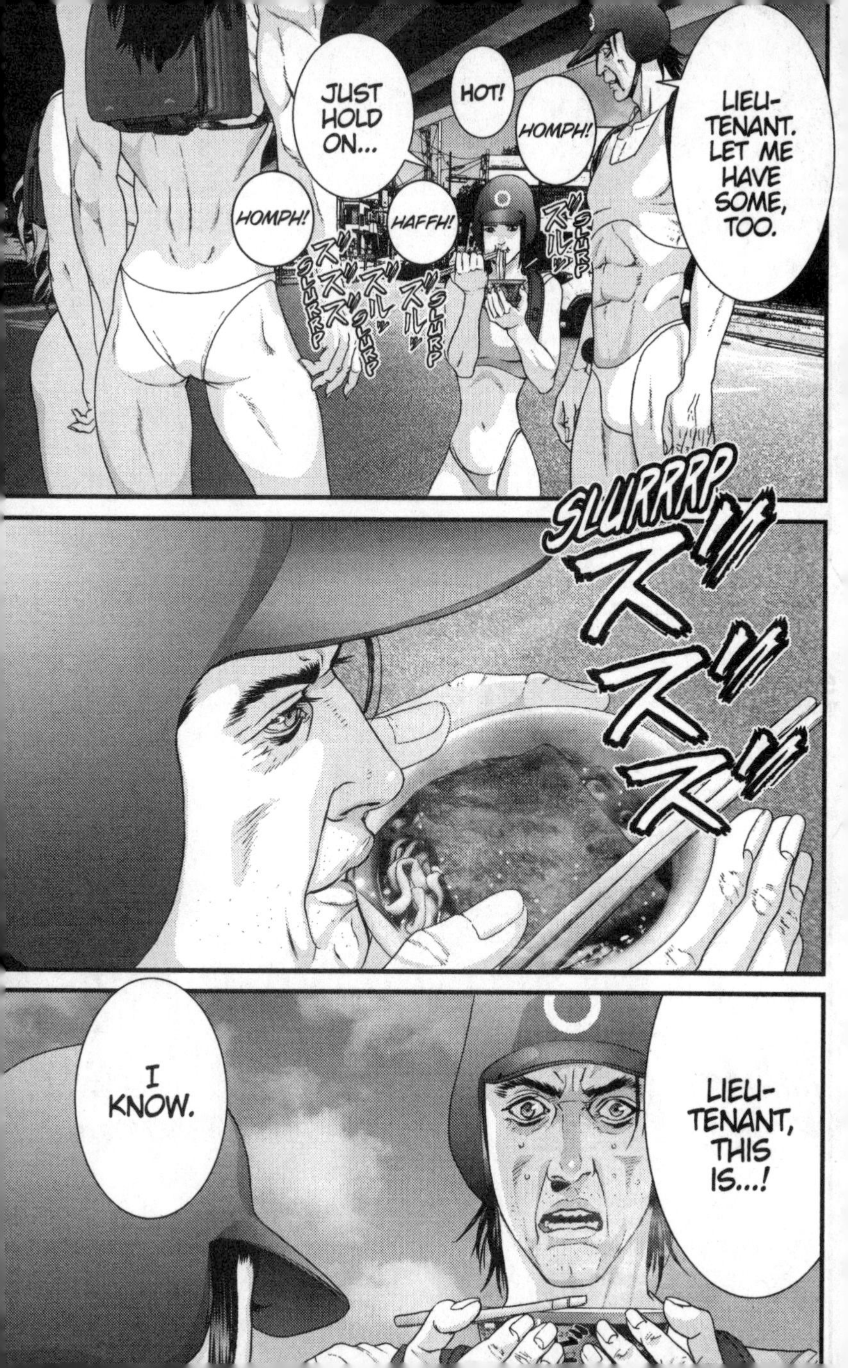

LIEU-TENANT. LET ME HAVE SOME, TOO.
HOMPH!
HOT!
JUST HOLD ON...
HAFFH!
HOMPH!
ズル SLURP
ズル SLURP
ズル SLURP
ズズズ SLURRP
SLURRRP
ズズズ
LIEU-TENANT, THIS IS...!
I KNOW.

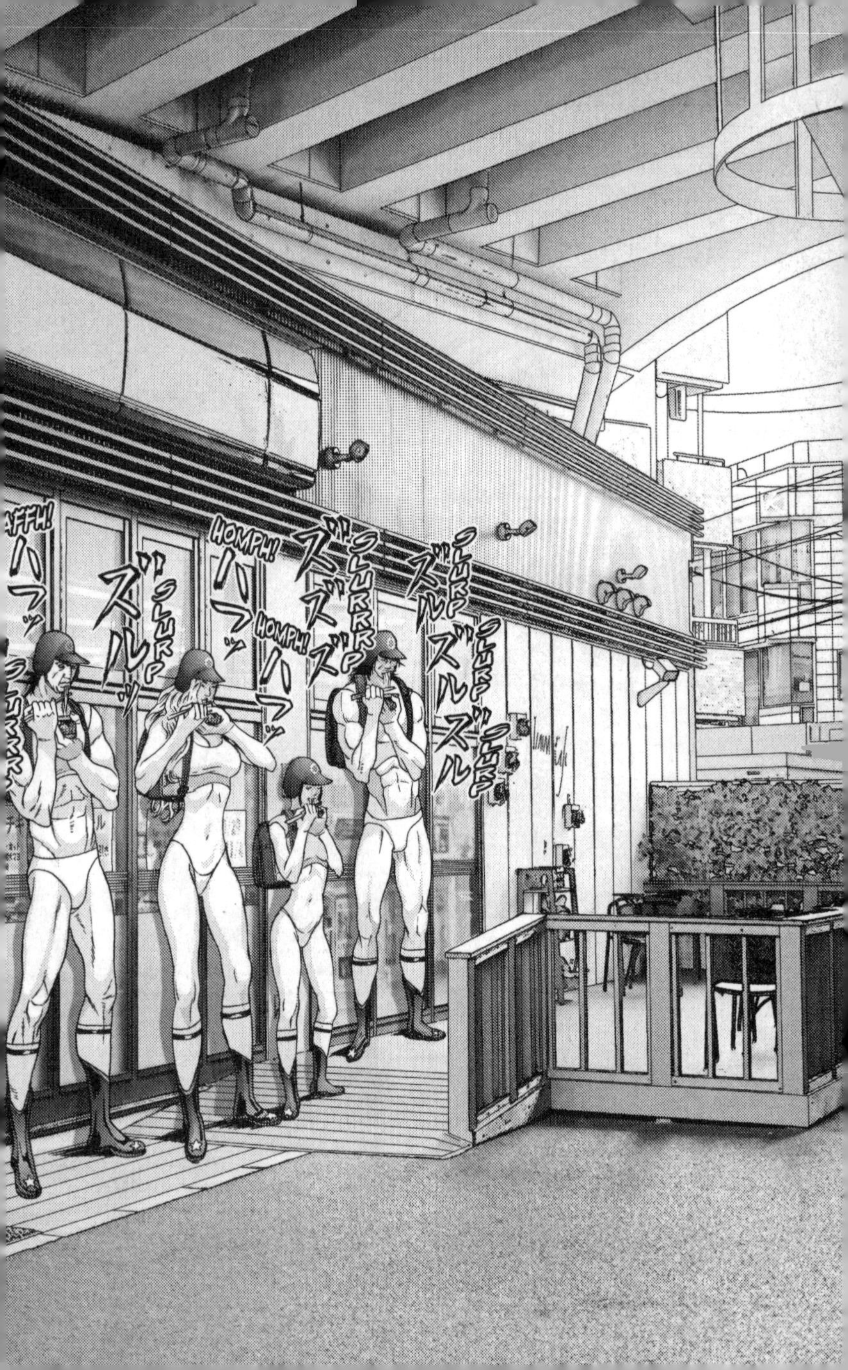
ズルッ
SLURP
ズルズル
SLURP
SLURP
ズズズ
SLURRRP
HOMPH!
ハフッ
HOMPH!
ハフッ
ズルッ
SLURP
AFFH!
ハフッ

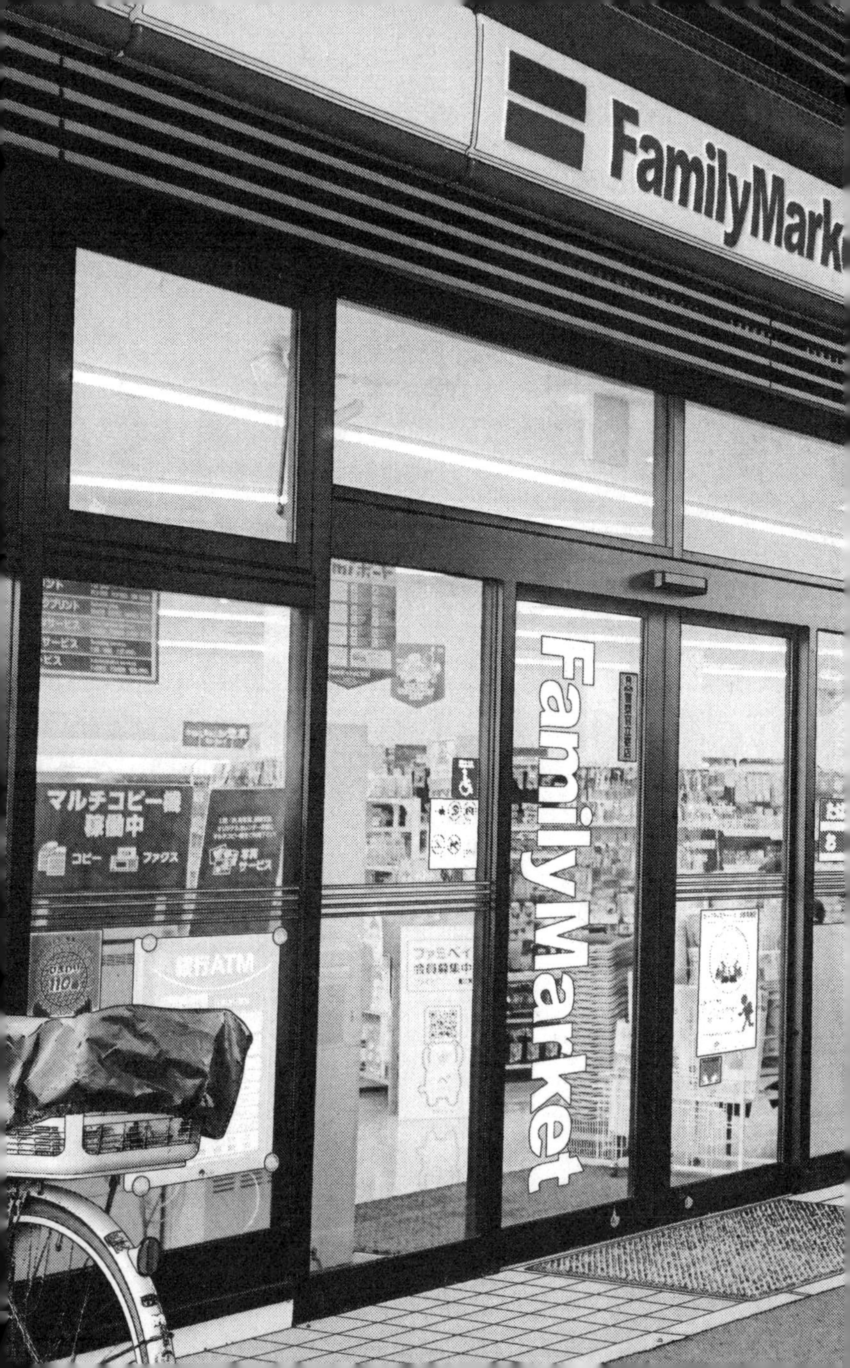
FamilyMark
FamilyMarket
マルチコピー機
稼働中
コピー
ファクス
銀行ATM
ファミペイ
会員募集中

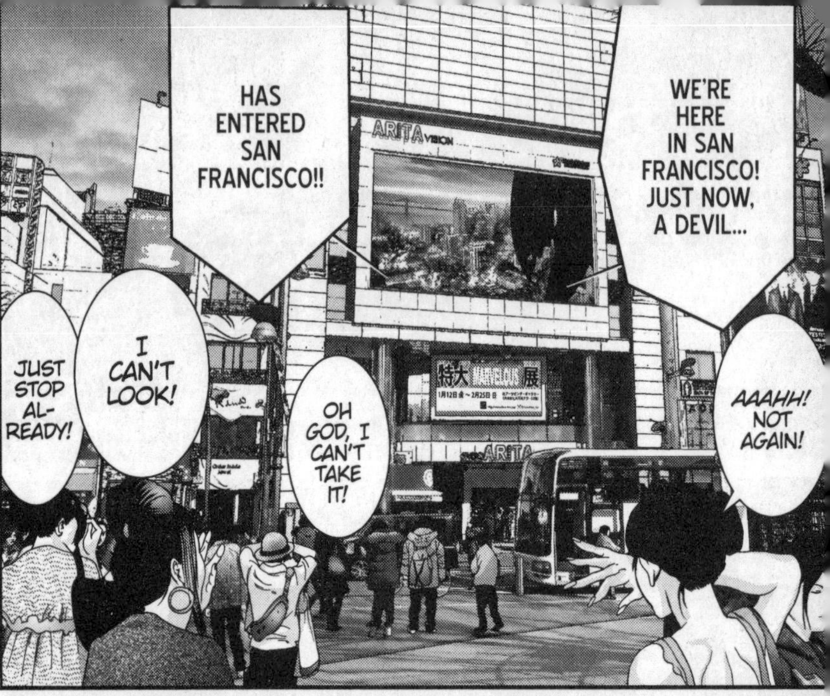
WE'RE HERE IN SAN FRANCISCO! JUST NOW, A DEVIL...
HAS ENTERED SAN FRANCISCO!!
AAAHH! NOT AGAIN!
OH GOD, I CAN'T TAKE IT!
I CAN'T LOOK!
JUST STOP AL-READY!

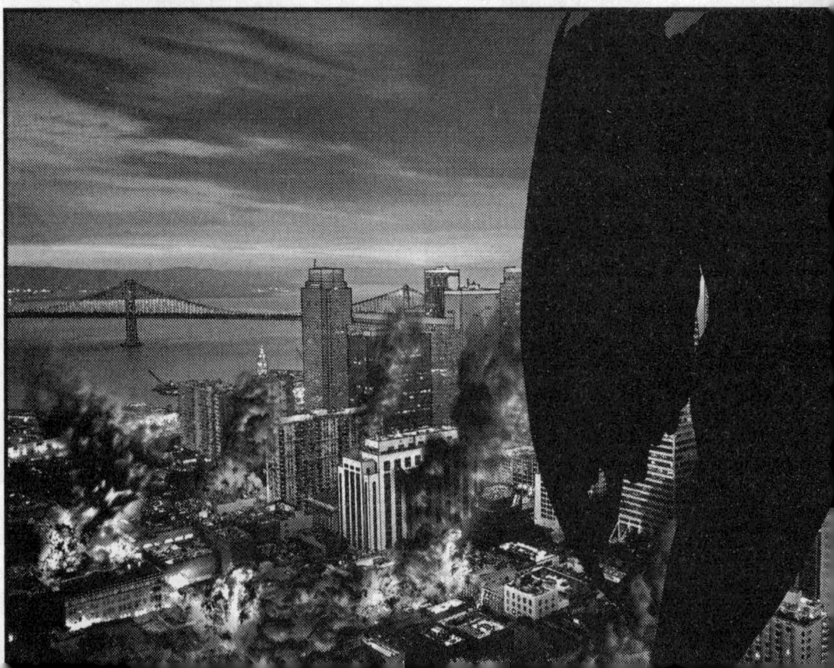

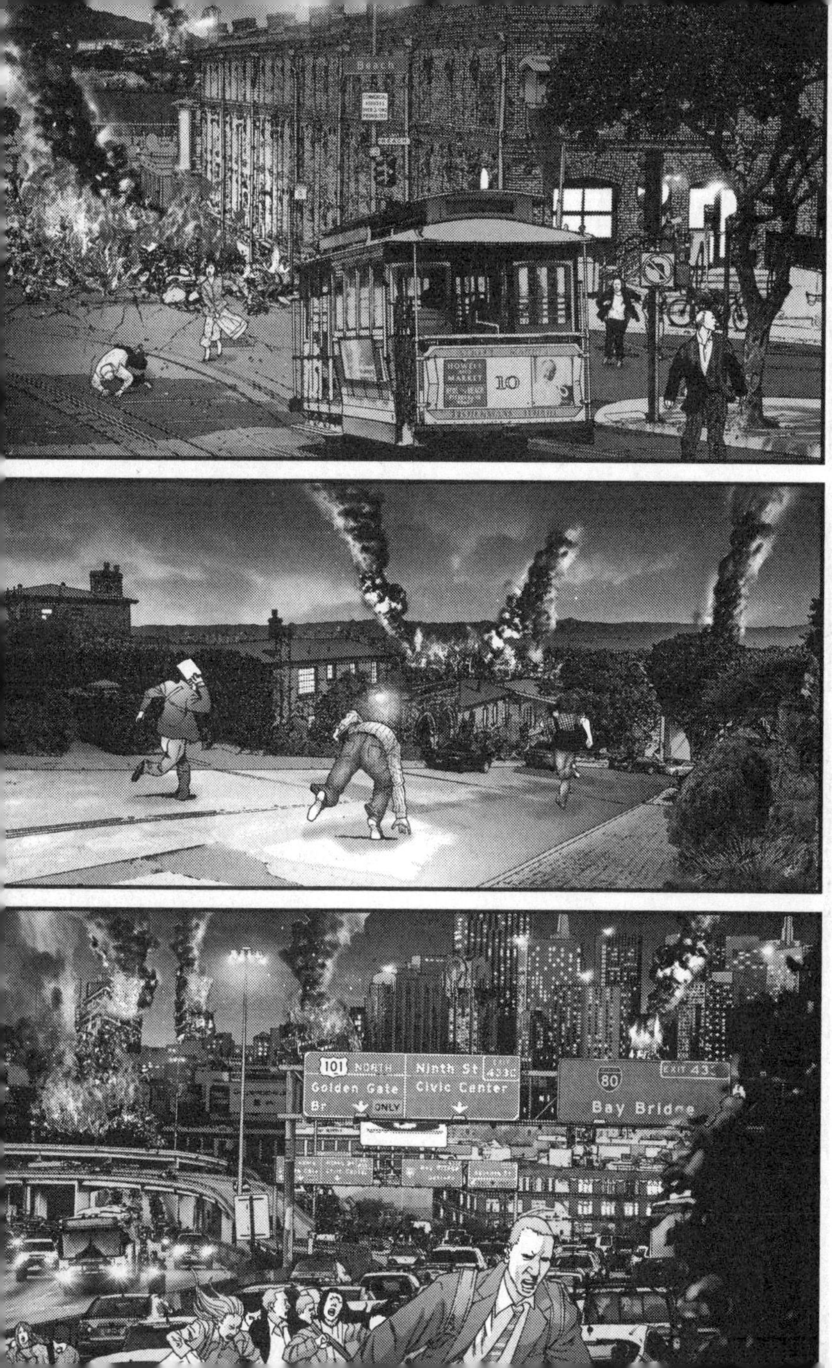
Beach
10
101 NORTH
Golden Gate
Br
ONLY
Ninth St
Civic Center
80
Bay Bridge

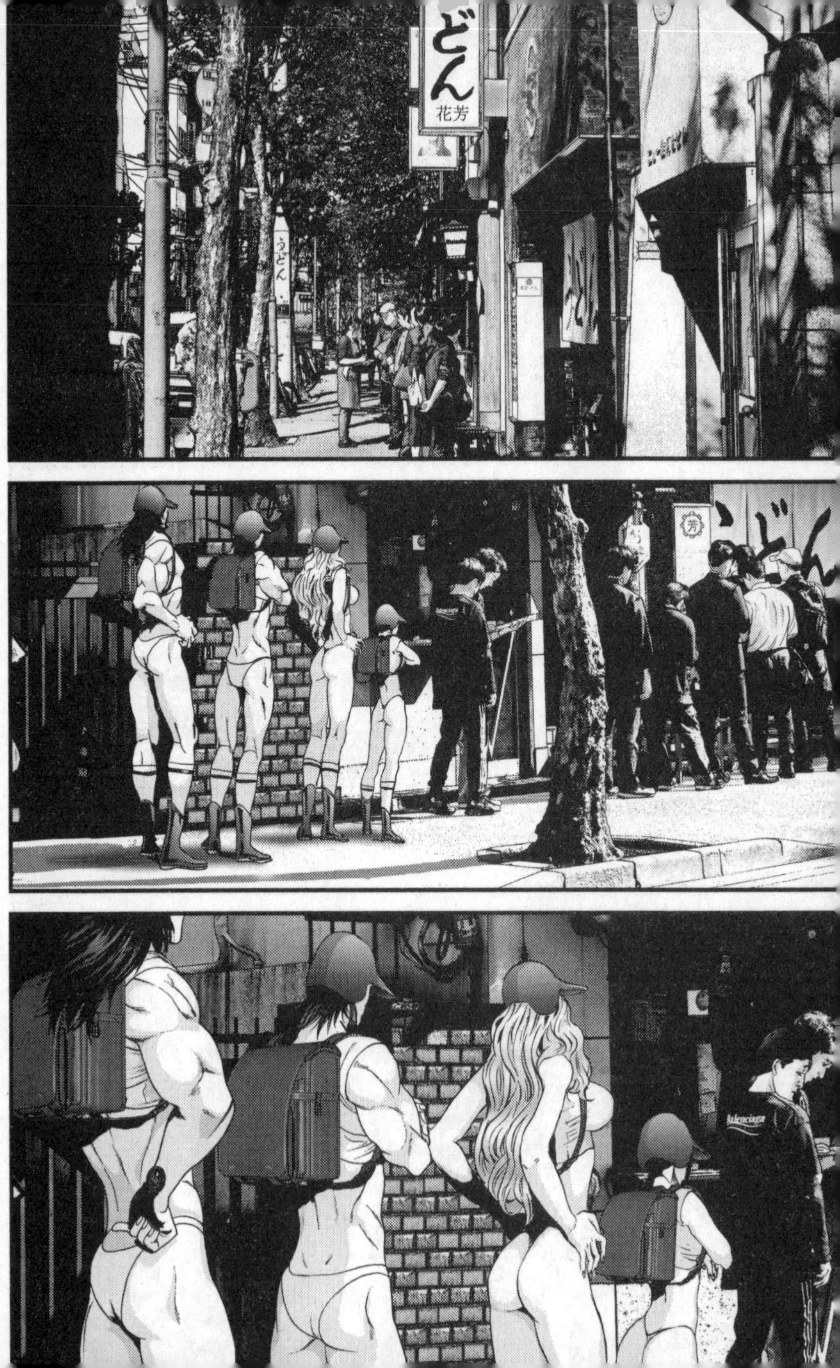
どん
花芳
うどん
芳
Balenciaga

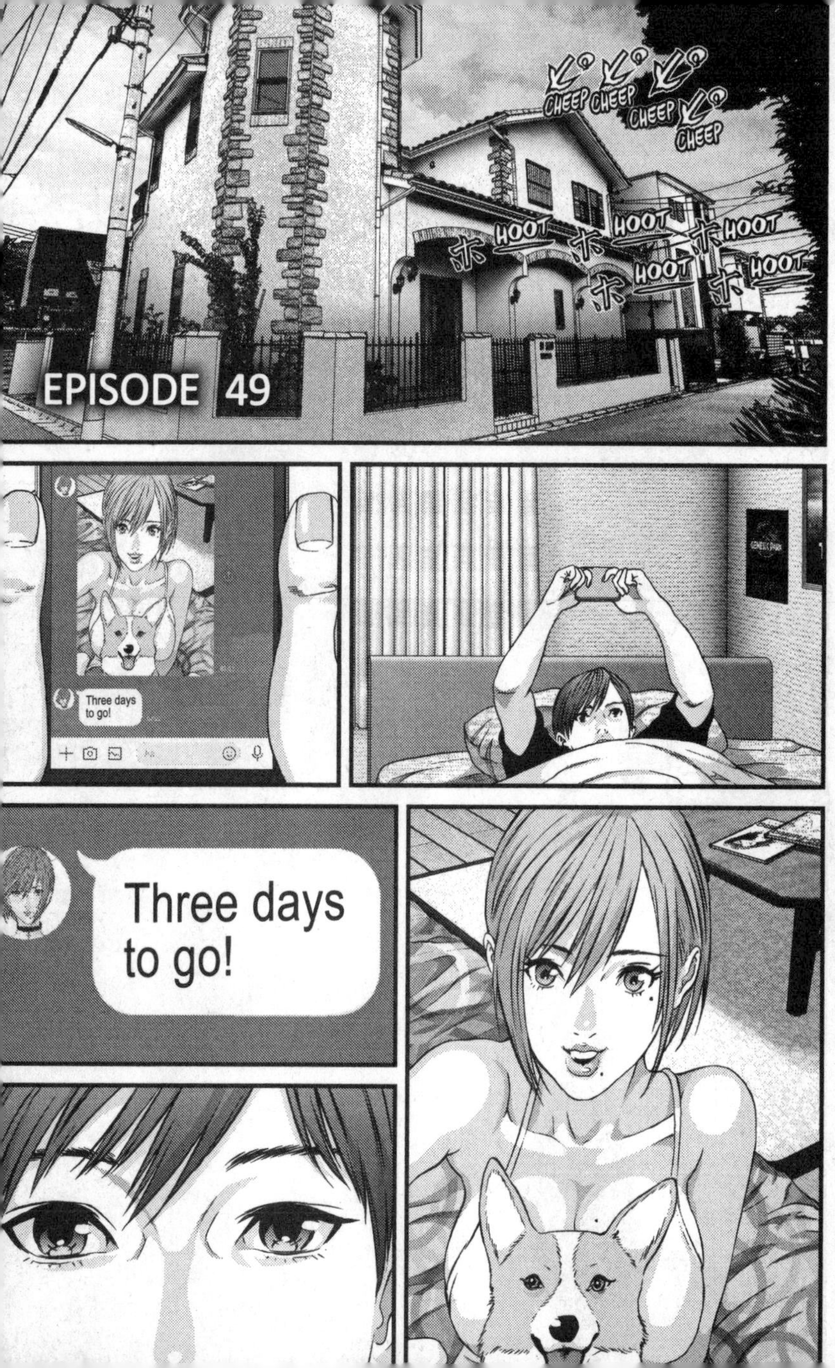
CHEEP CHEEP CHEEP CHEEP
HOOT HOOT HOOT HOOT HOOT HOOT
EPISODE 49
Three days to go!
Three days to go!

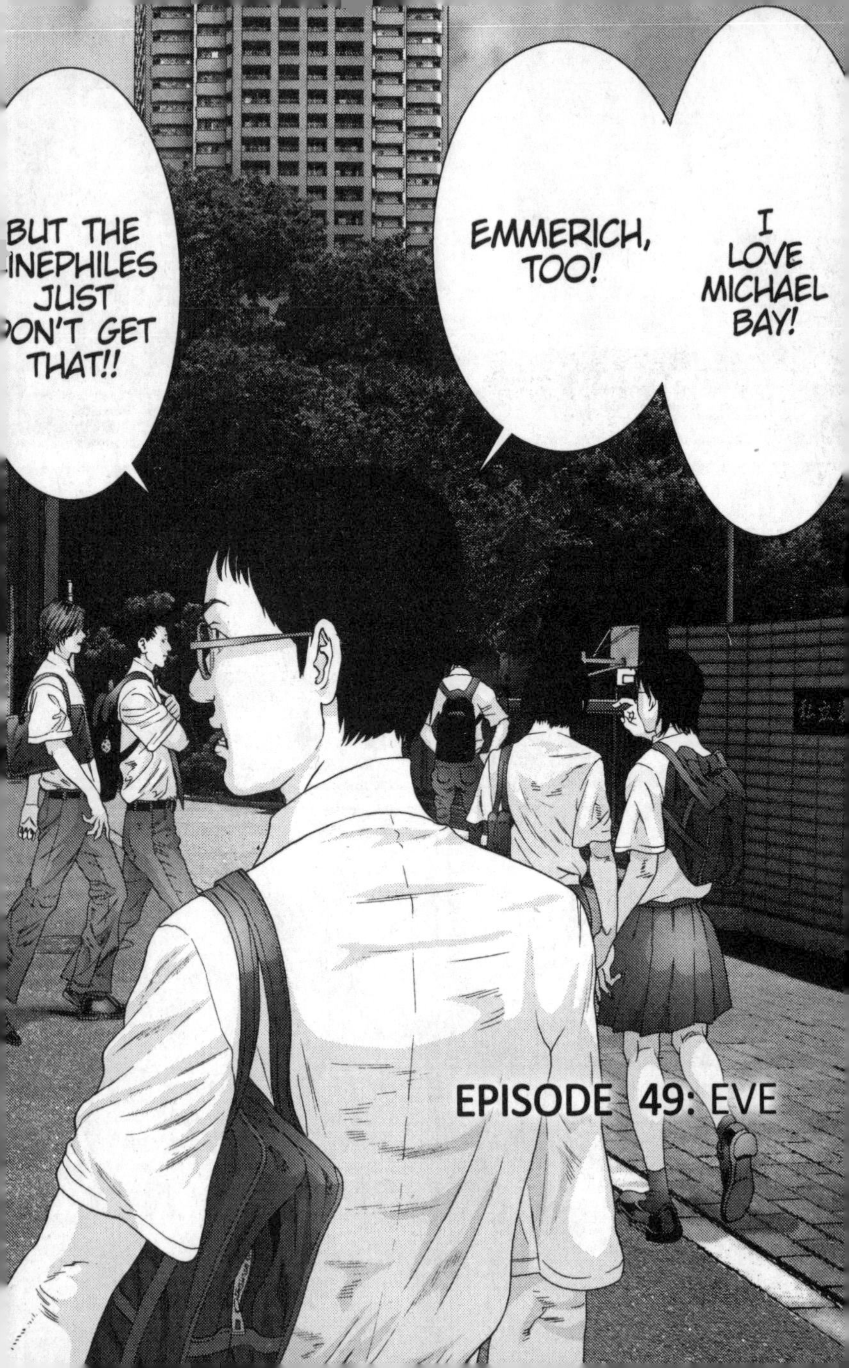
I LOVE MICHAEL BAY!
EMMERICH, TOO!
BUT THE INEPHILES JUST ON'T GET THAT!!
EPISODE 49: EVE

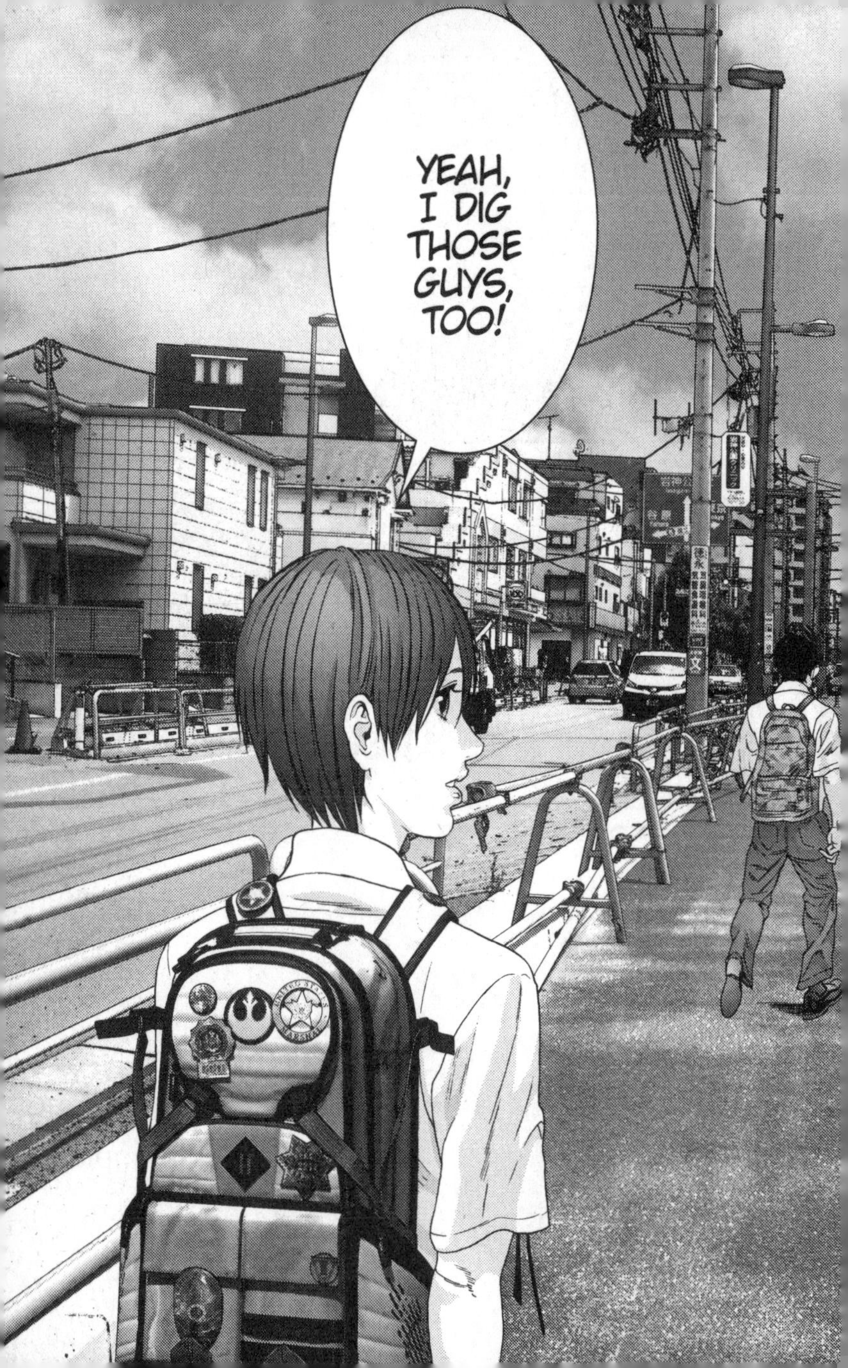
YEAH, I DIG THOSE GUYS, TOO!

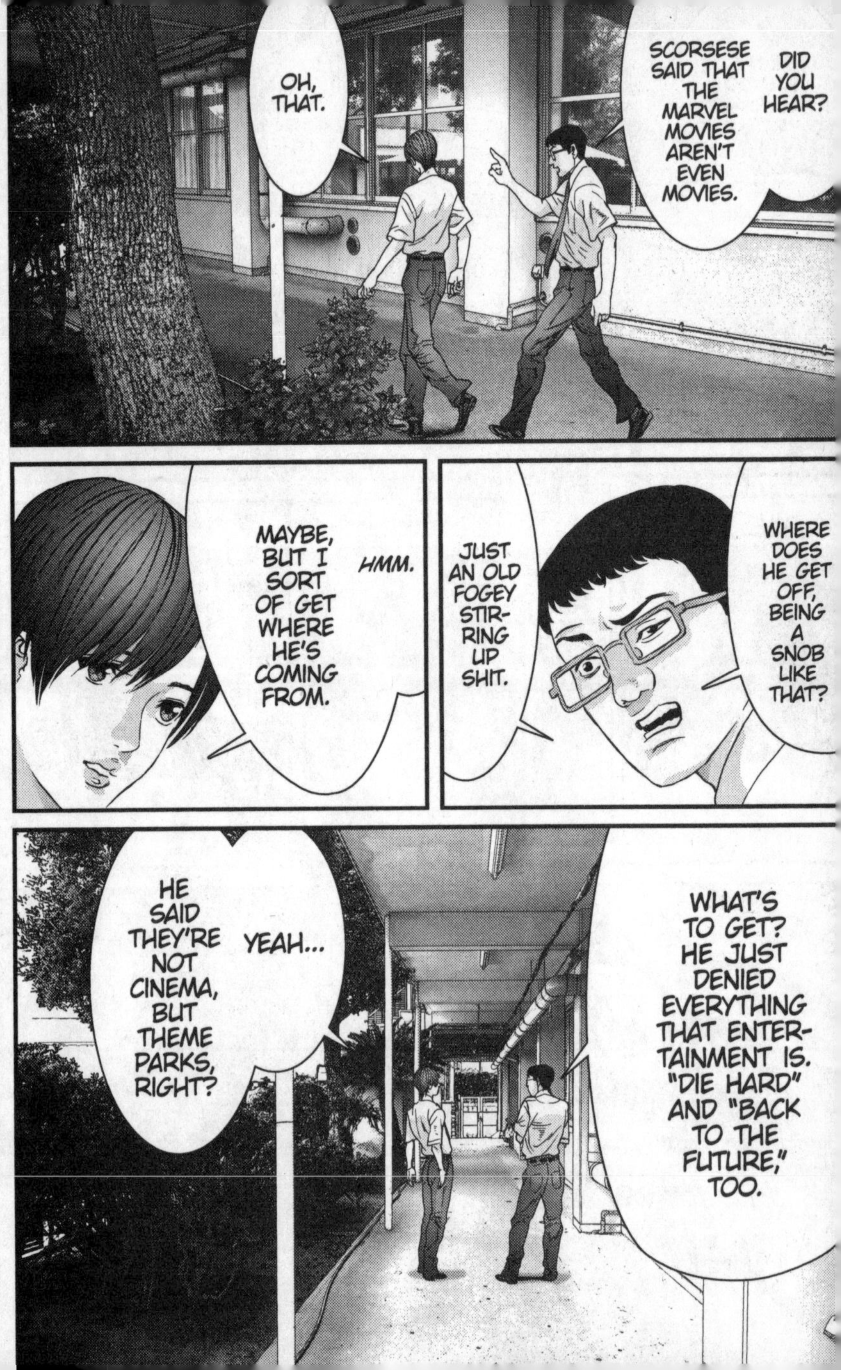
DID YOU HEAR?
SCORSESE SAID THAT THE MARVEL MOVIES AREN'T EVEN MOVIES.
OH, THAT.
WHERE DOES HE GET OFF, BEING A SNOB LIKE THAT?
JUST AN OLD FOGEY STIR-RING UP SHIT.
HMM.
MAYBE, BUT I SORT OF GET WHERE HE'S COMING FROM.
WHAT'S TO GET? HE JUST DENIED EVERYTHING THAT ENTER-TAINMENT IS. "DIE HARD" AND "BACK TO THE FUTURE," TOO.
YEAH...
HE SAID THEY'RE NOT CINEMA, BUT THEME PARKS, RIGHT?

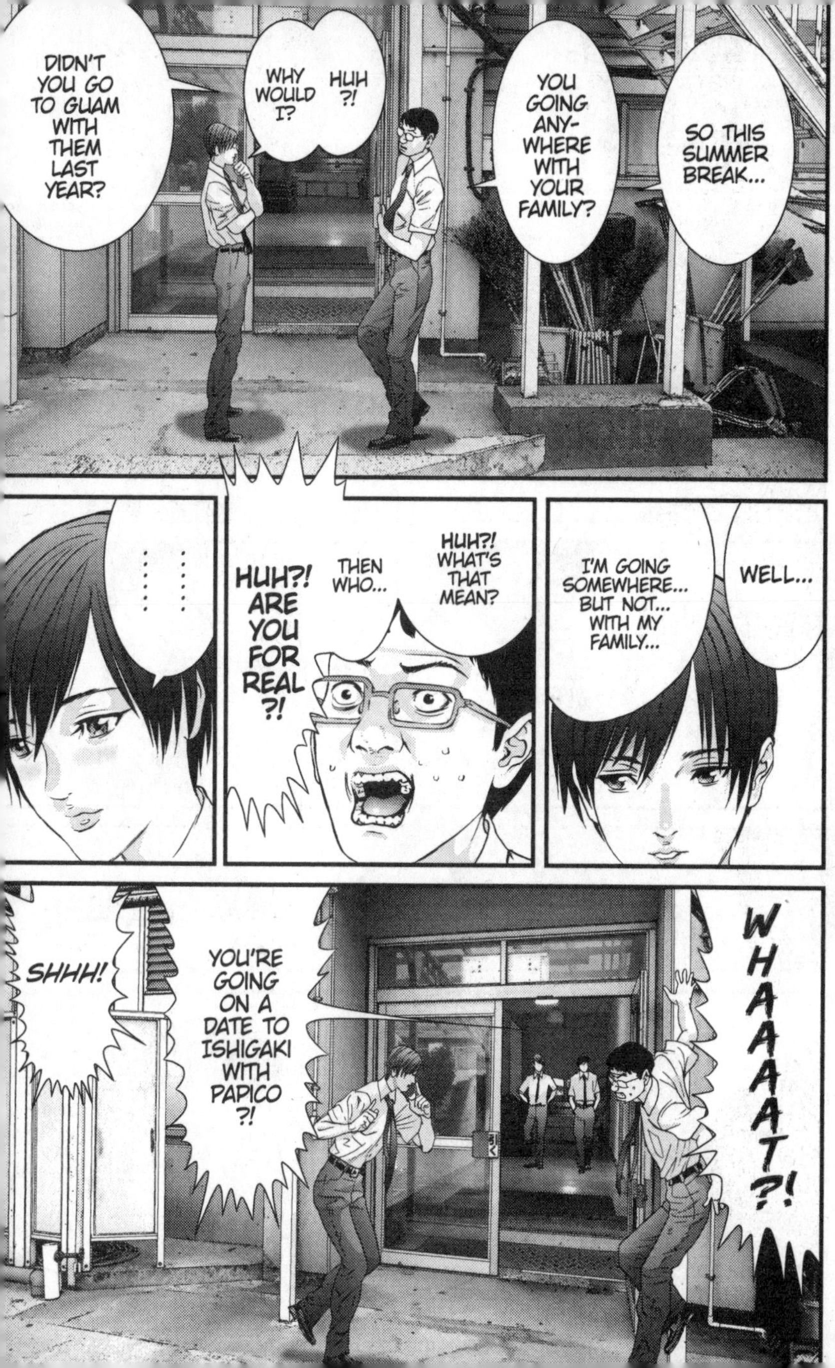
SO THIS SUMMER BREAK...
YOU GOING ANY-WHERE WITH YOUR FAMILY?
HUH ?!
WHY WOULD I?
DIDN'T YOU GO TO GUAM WITH THEM LAST YEAR?
WELL...
I'M GOING SOMEWHERE... BUT NOT... WITH MY FAMILY...
HUH?! WHAT'S THAT MEAN?
THEN WHO...
HUH?! ARE YOU FOR REAL ?!
......
WHAAAAAT?!
YOU'RE GOING ON A DATE TO ISHIGAKI WITH PAPICO ?!
SHHH!

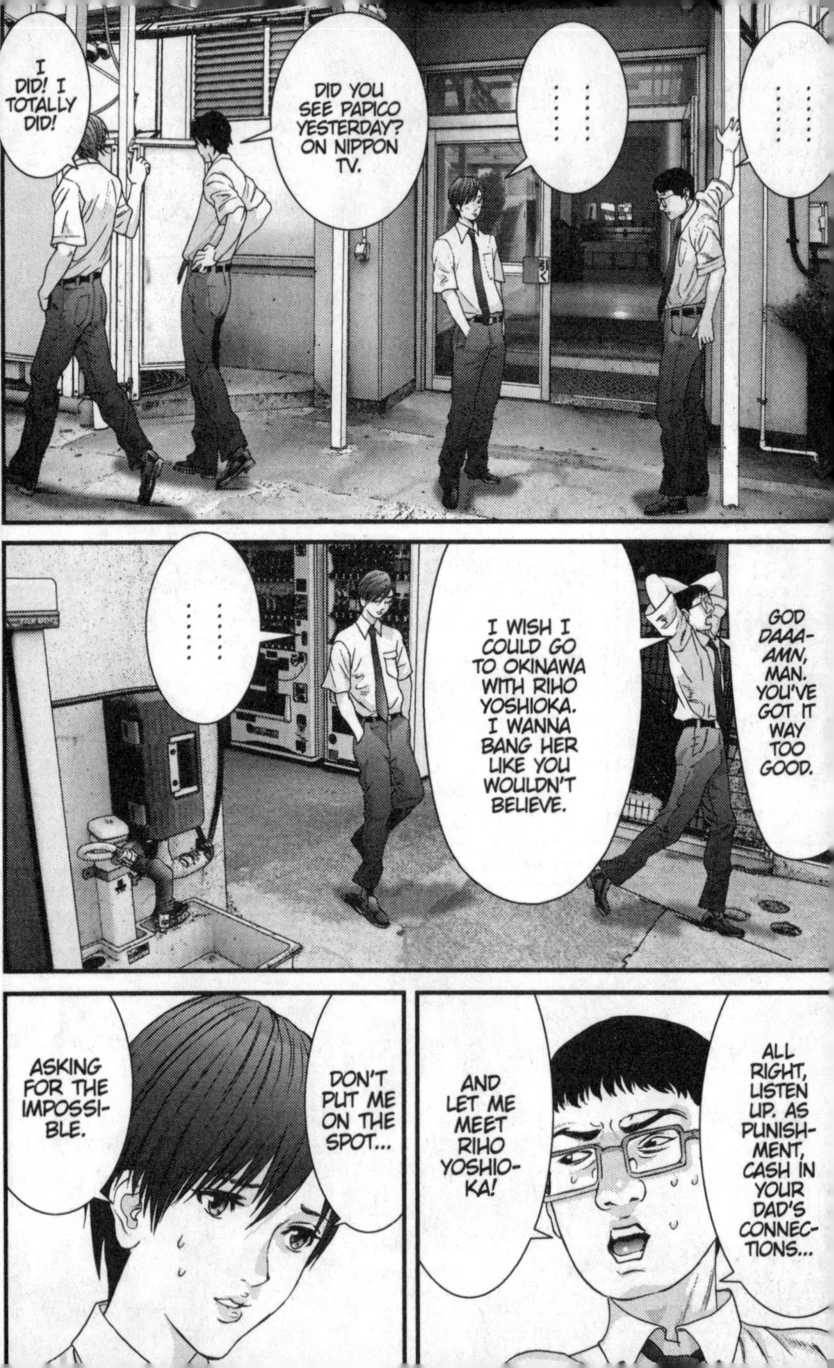
……
……
DID YOU SEE PAPICO YESTERDAY? ON NIPPON TV.
I DID! I TOTALLY DID!
GOD DAAA-AMN, MAN. YOU'VE GOT IT WAY TOO GOOD.
I WISH I COULD GO TO OKINAWA WITH RIHO YOSHIOKA. I WANNA BANG HER LIKE YOU WOULDN'T BELIEVE.
……
ALL RIGHT, LISTEN UP. AS PUNISHMENT, CASH IN YOUR DAD'S CONNECTIONS...
AND LET ME MEET RIHO YOSHIOKA!
DON'T PUT ME ON THE SPOT...
ASKING FOR THE IMPOSSIBLE.

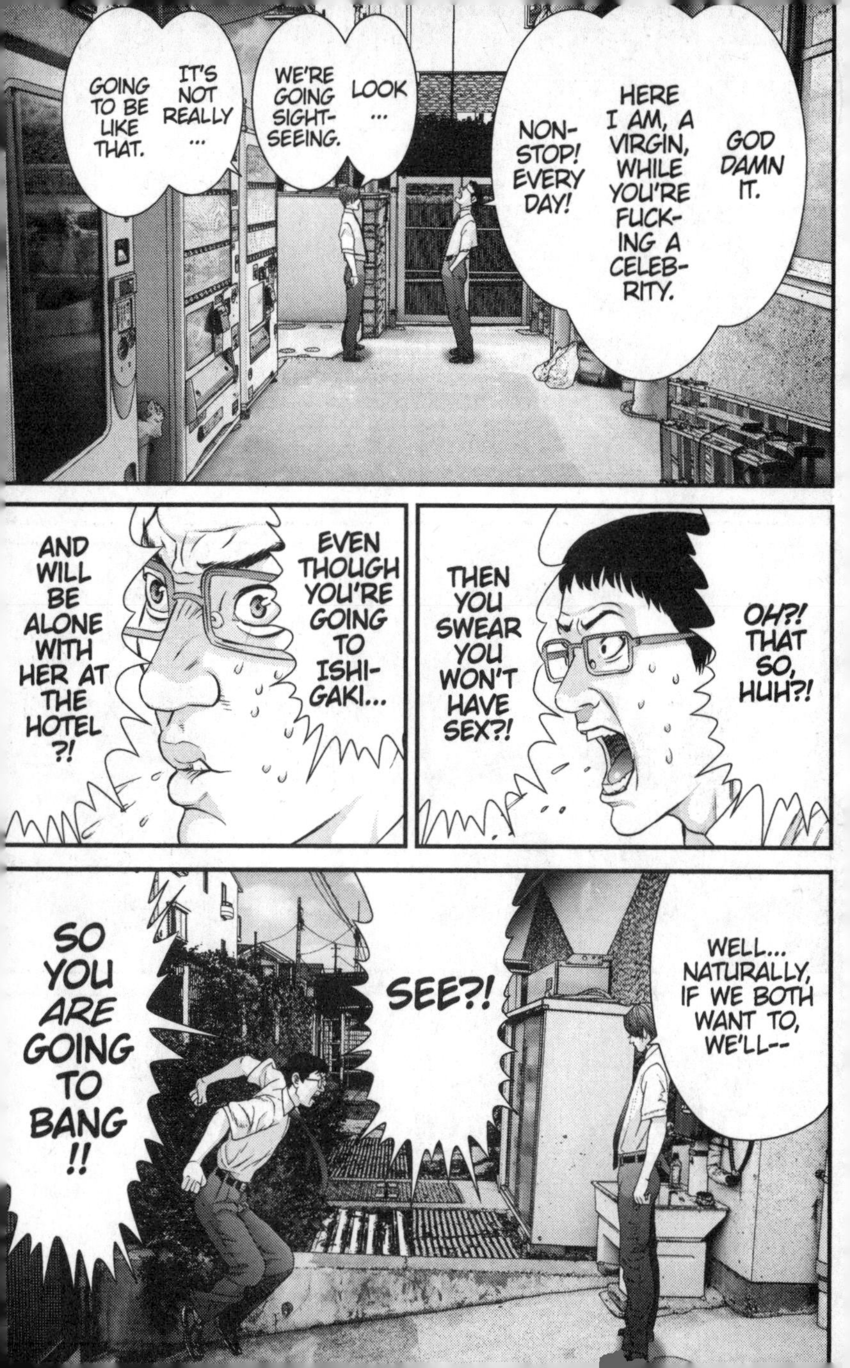
GOD DAMN IT.
HERE I AM, A VIRGIN, WHILE YOU'RE FUCKING A CELEBRITY.
NON-STOP! EVERY DAY!
LOOK...
WE'RE GOING SIGHT-SEEING.
IT'S NOT REALLY...
GOING TO BE LIKE THAT.
OH?! THAT SO, HUH?!
THEN YOU SWEAR YOU WON'T HAVE SEX?!
EVEN THOUGH YOU'RE GOING TO ISHIGAKI...
AND WILL BE ALONE WITH HER AT THE HOTEL?!
WELL... NATURALLY, IF WE BOTH WANT TO, WE'LL--
SEE?!
SO YOU ARE GOING TO BANG!!

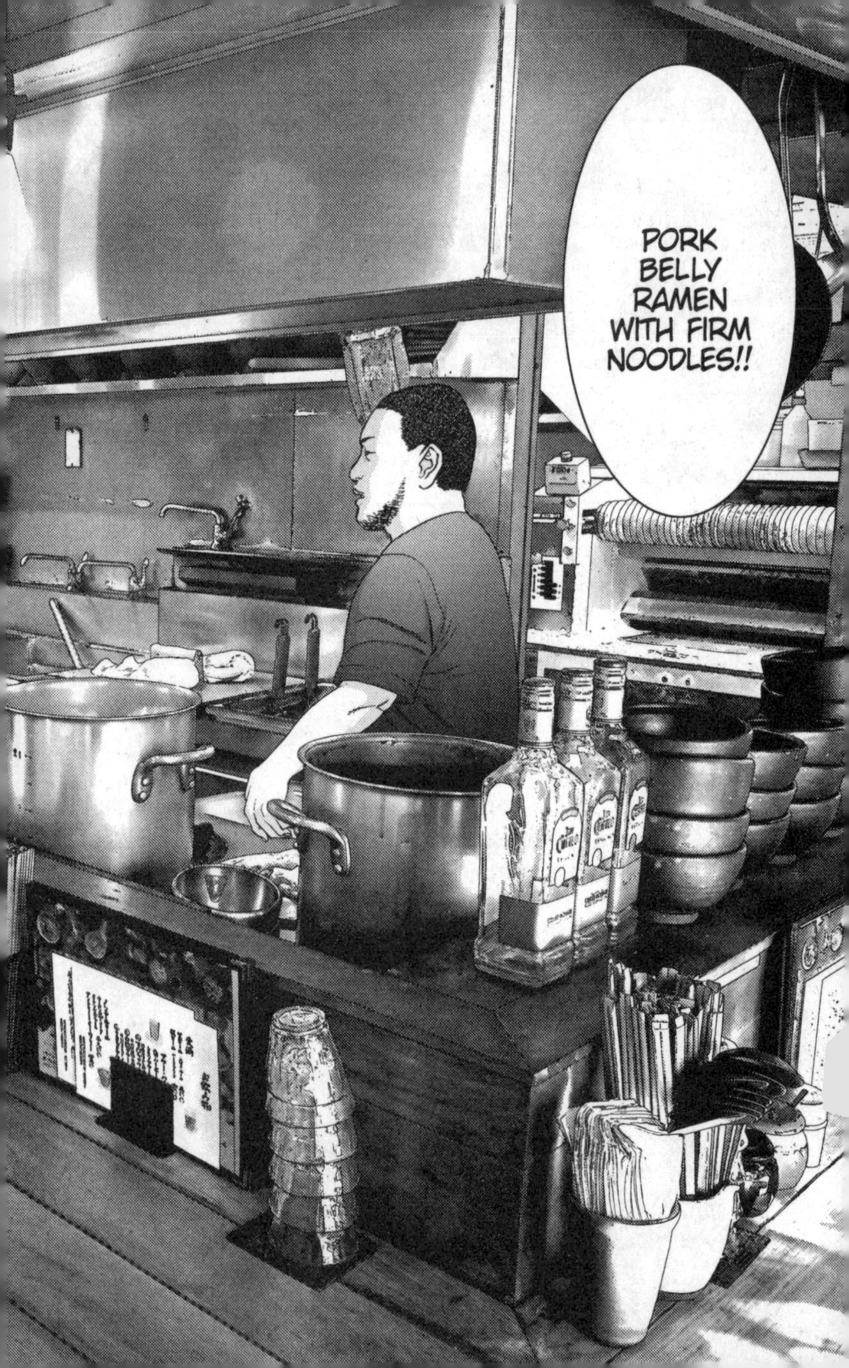
PORK BELLY RAMEN WITH FIRM NOODLES!!

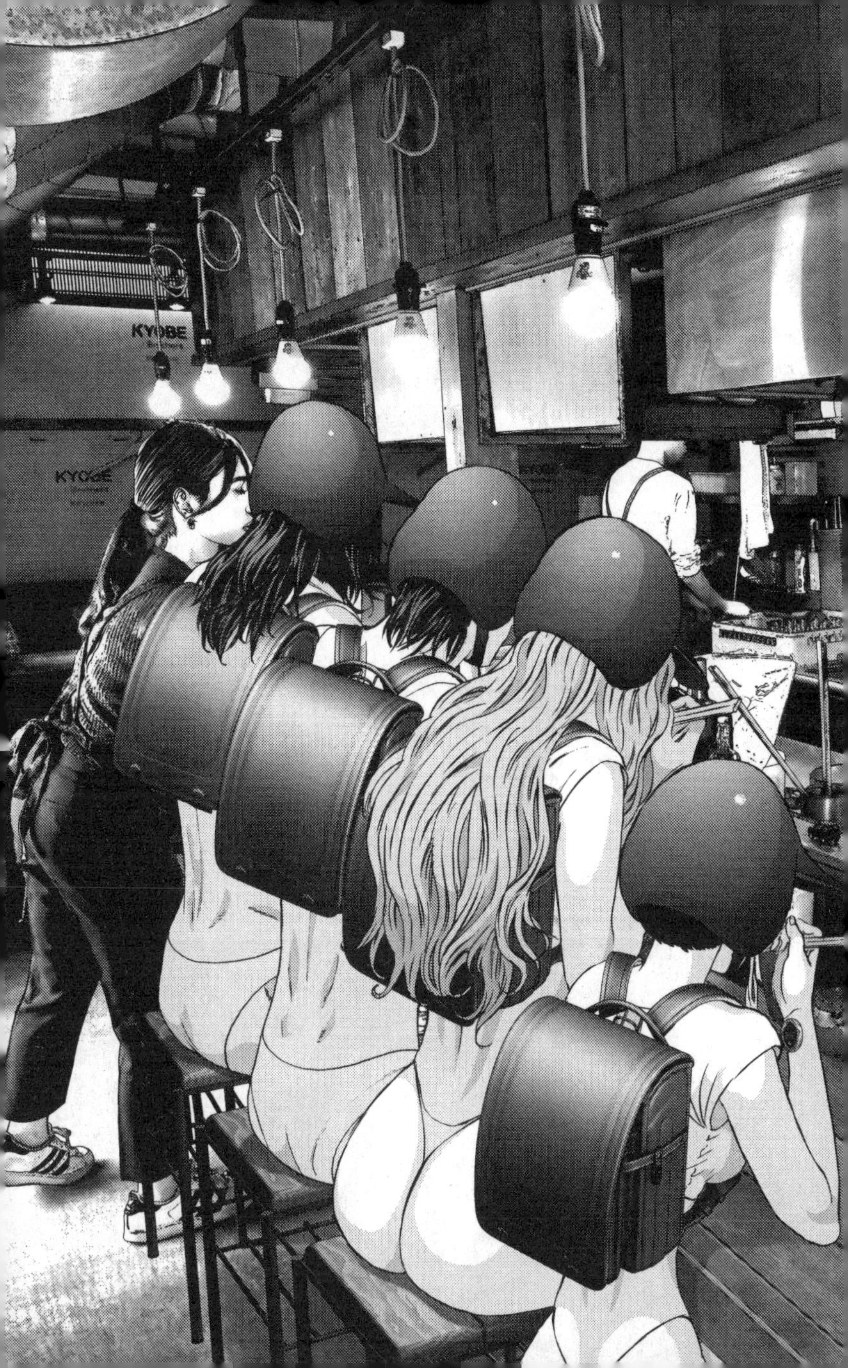
KYOBE
KYOBE

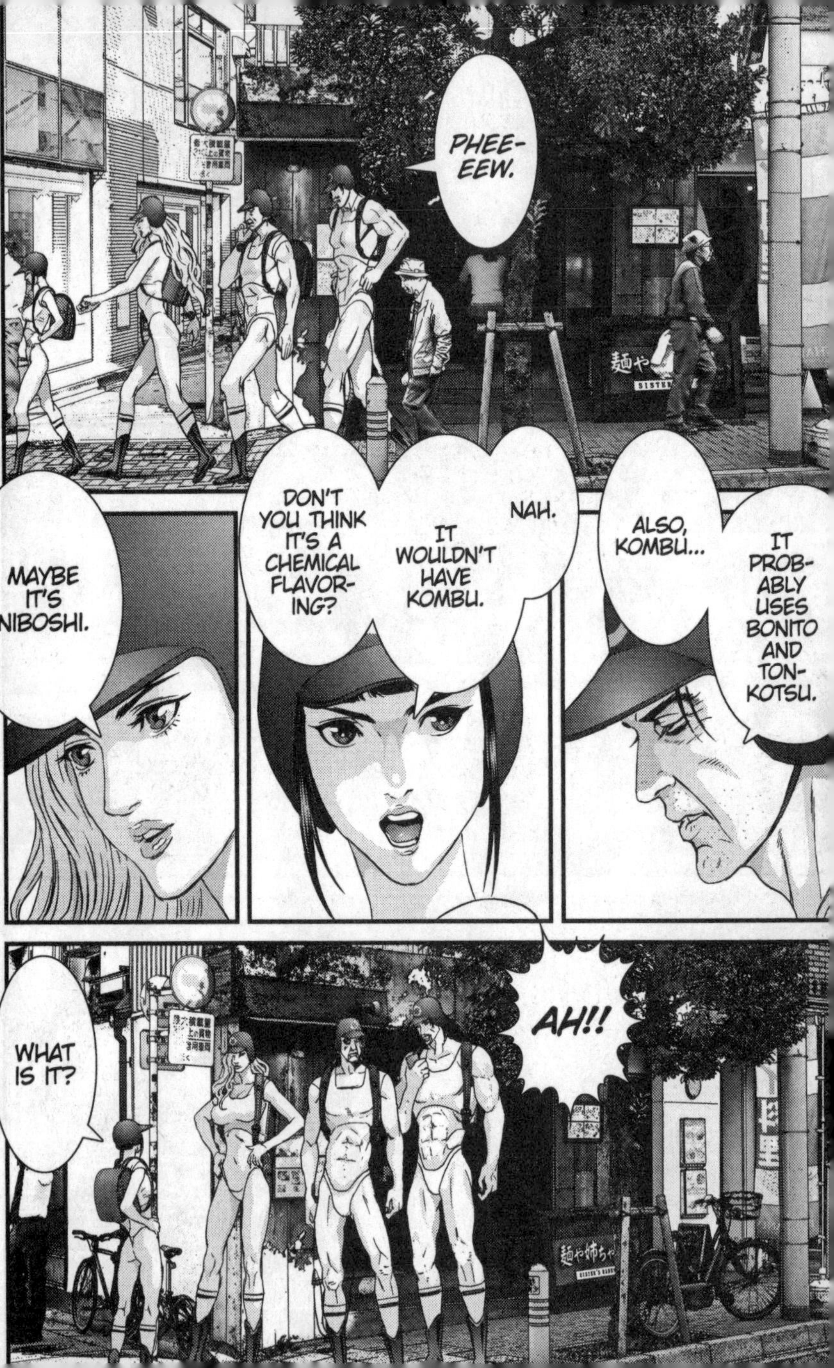
PHEEE-EEW.
IT PROBABLY USES BONITO AND TONKOTSU.
ALSO, KOMBU...
NAH.
IT WOULDN'T HAVE KOMBU.
DON'T YOU THINK IT'S A CHEMICAL FLAVORING?
MAYBE IT'S NIBOSHI.
AH!!
WHAT IS IT?

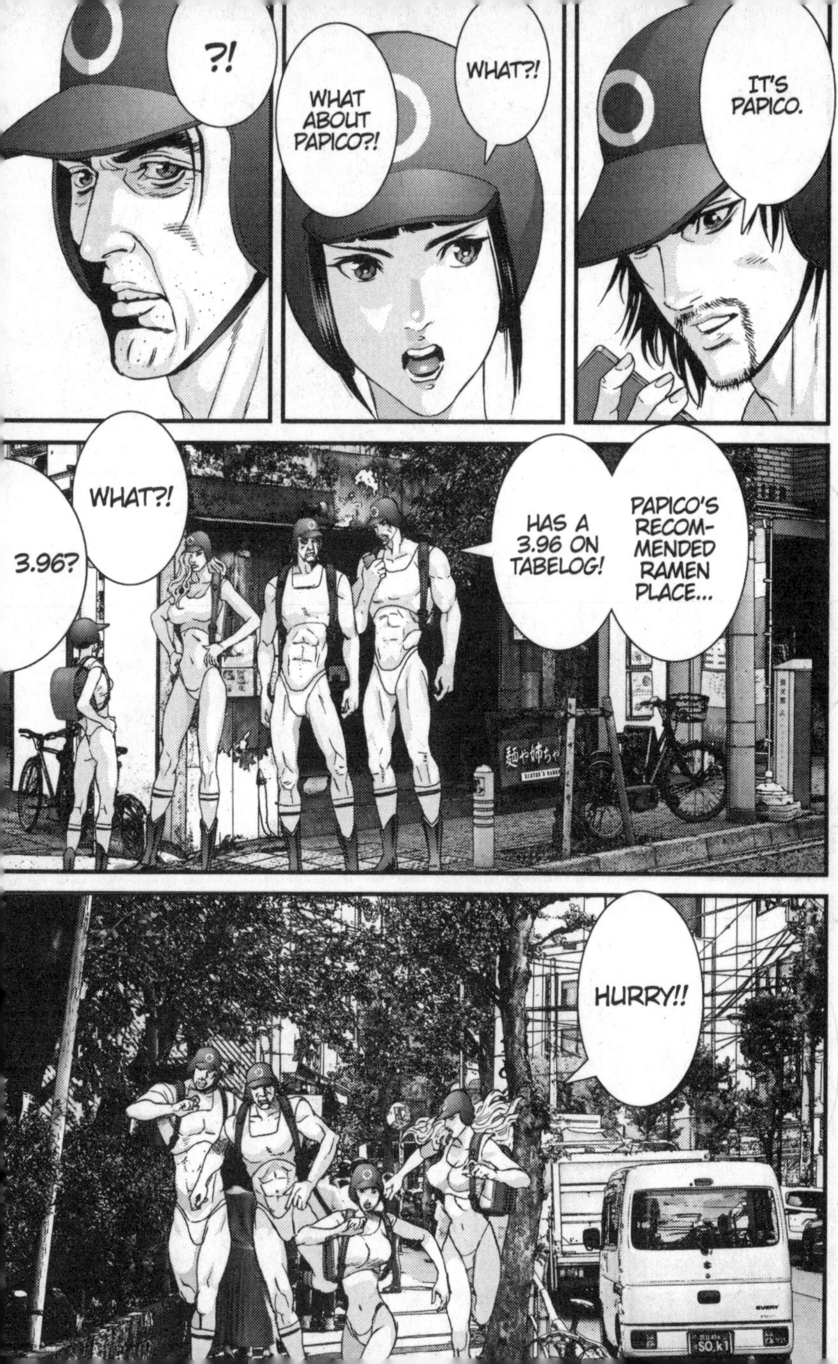
IT'S PAPICO.
WHAT?!
WHAT ABOUT PAPICO?!
?!
PAPICO'S RECOM-MENDED RAMEN PLACE...
HAS A 3.96 ON TABELOG!
WHAT?!
3.96?
HURRY!!

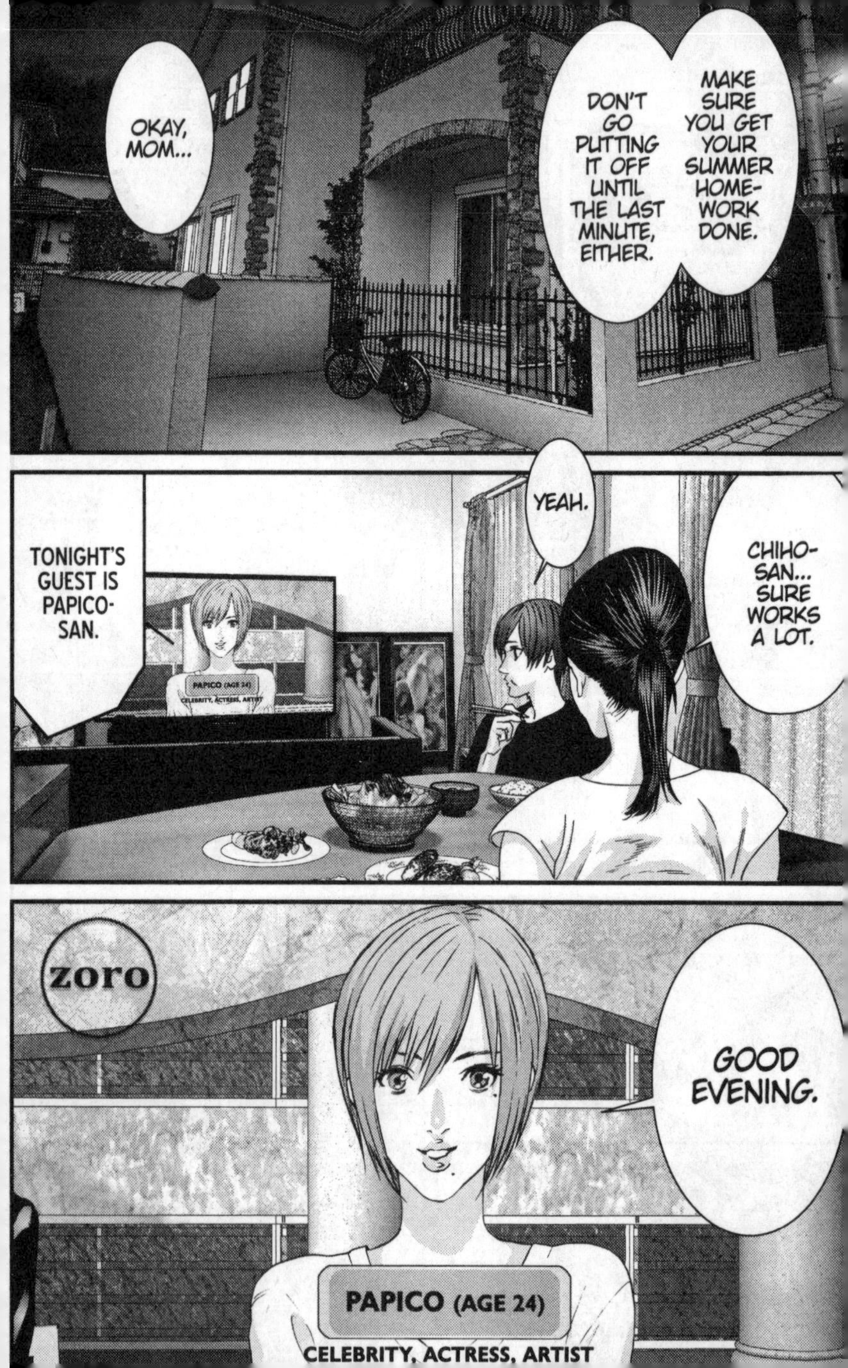
MAKE SURE YOU GET YOUR SUMMER HOME-WORK DONE.
DON'T GO PUTTING IT OFF UNTIL THE LAST MINUTE, EITHER.
OKAY, MOM...
CHIHO-SAN... SURE WORKS A LOT.
YEAH.
TONIGHT'S GUEST IS PAPICO-SAN.
GOOD EVENING.
zoro
PAPICO (AGE 24)
CELEBRITY, ACTRESS, ARTIST

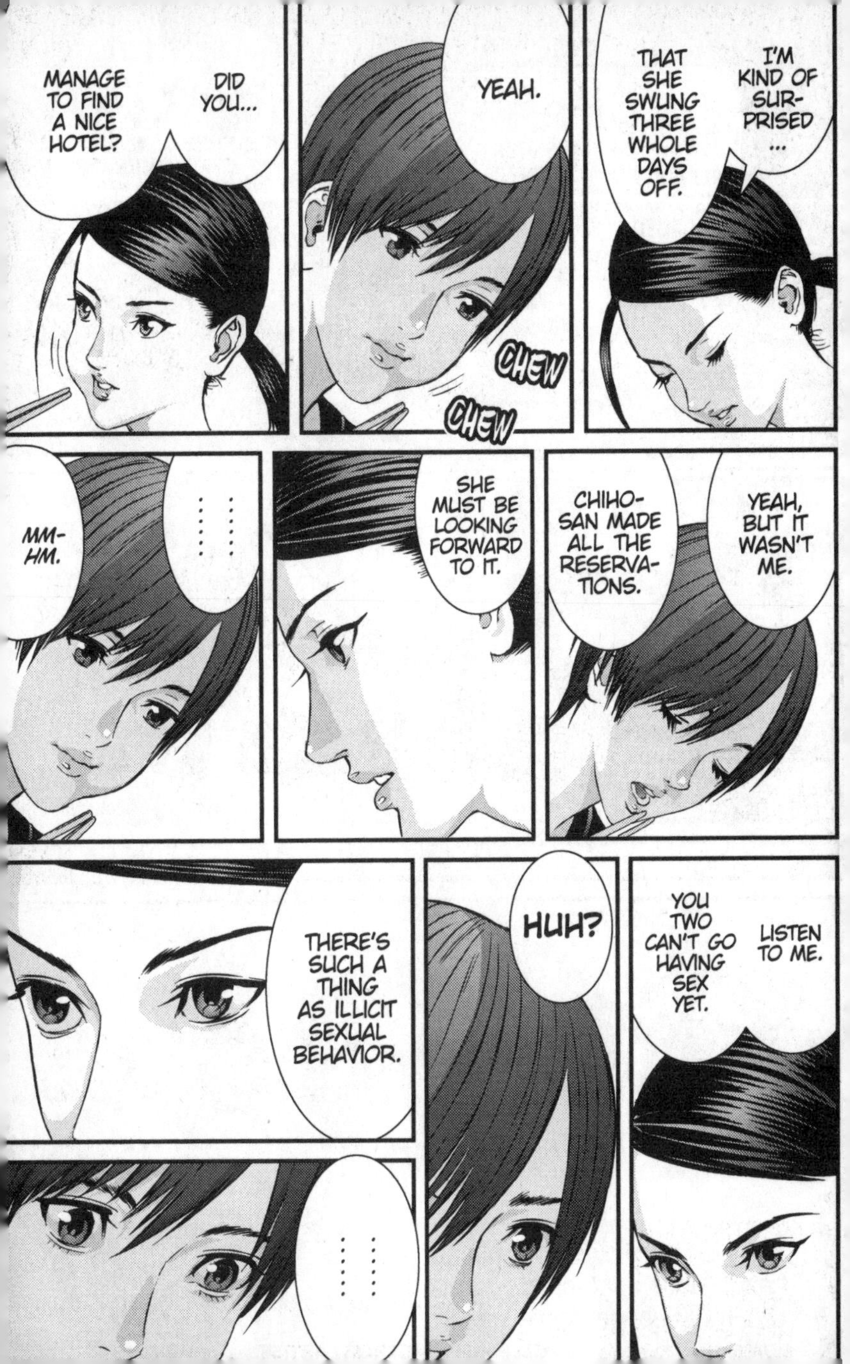
I'M KIND OF SUR-PRISED...
THAT SHE SWUNG THREE WHOLE DAYS OFF.
YEAH.
CHEW
CHEW
DID YOU...
MANAGE TO FIND A NICE HOTEL?
YEAH, BUT IT WASN'T ME.
CHIHO-SAN MADE ALL THE RESERVA-TIONS.
SHE MUST BE LOOKING FORWARD TO IT.
......
MM-HM.
LISTEN TO ME.
YOU TWO CAN'T GO HAVING SEX YET.
HUH?
THERE'S SUCH A THING AS ILLICIT SEXUAL BEHAVIOR.
......

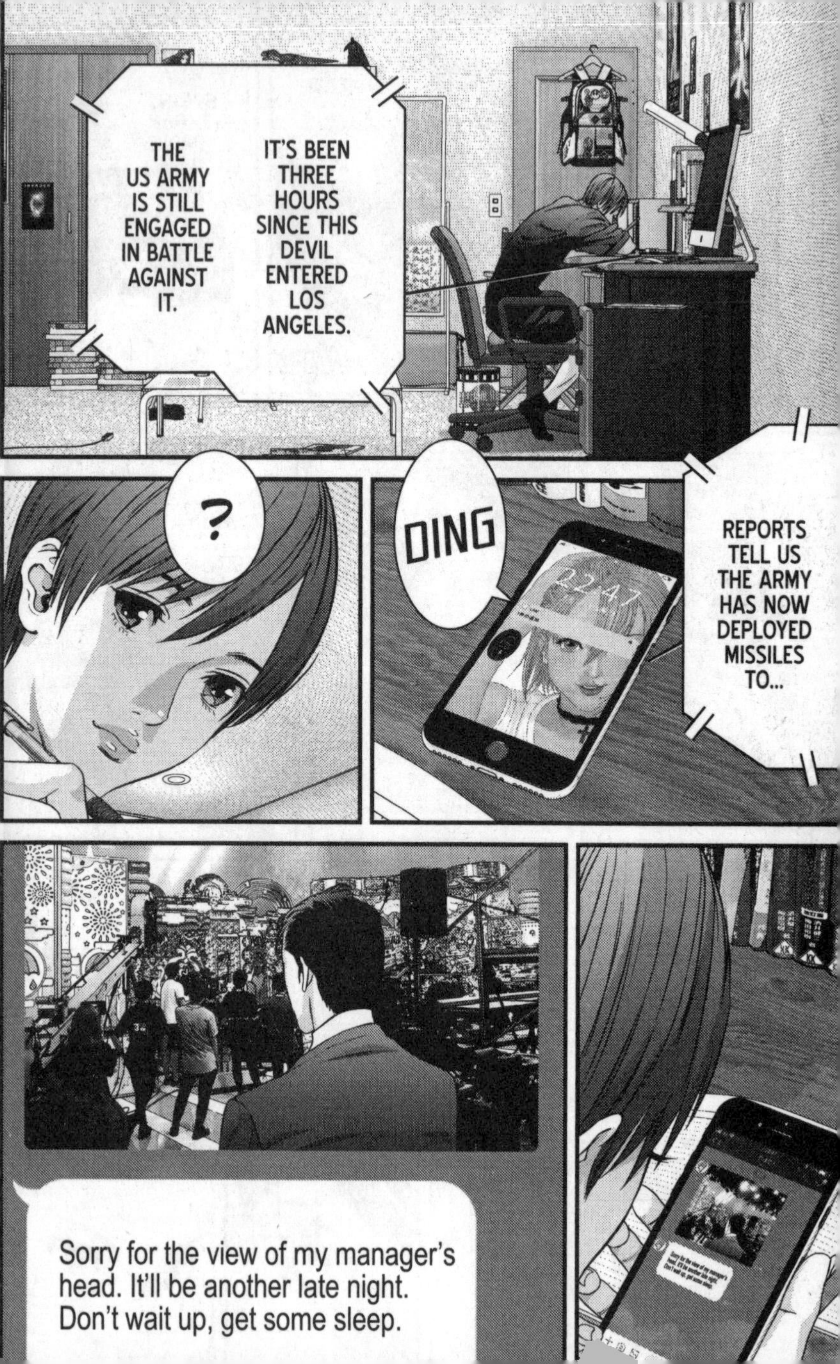
IT'S BEEN THREE HOURS SINCE THIS DEVIL ENTERED LOS ANGELES.
THE US ARMY IS STILL ENGAGED IN BATTLE AGAINST IT.
REPORTS TELL US THE ARMY HAS NOW DEPLOYED MISSILES TO...
DING
22:47
?
Sorry for the view of my manager's head. It'll be another late night. Don't wait up, get some sleep.

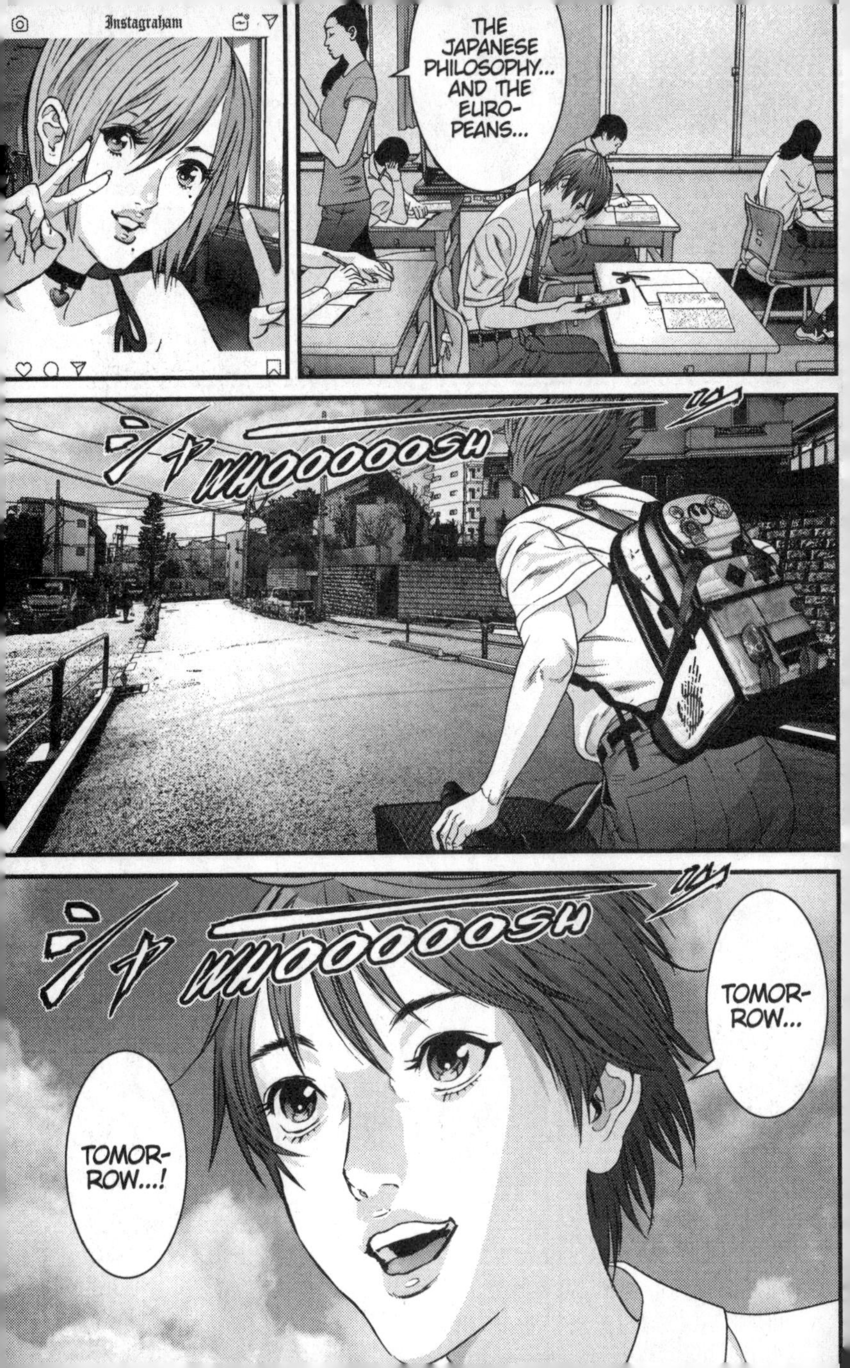
THE JAPANESE PHILOSOPHY... AND THE EUROPEANS...
Instagraham
シャ
WHOOOOOOSH
ッ
シャ
WHOOOOOOOSH
ッ
TOMOR-ROW...
TOMOR-ROW...!

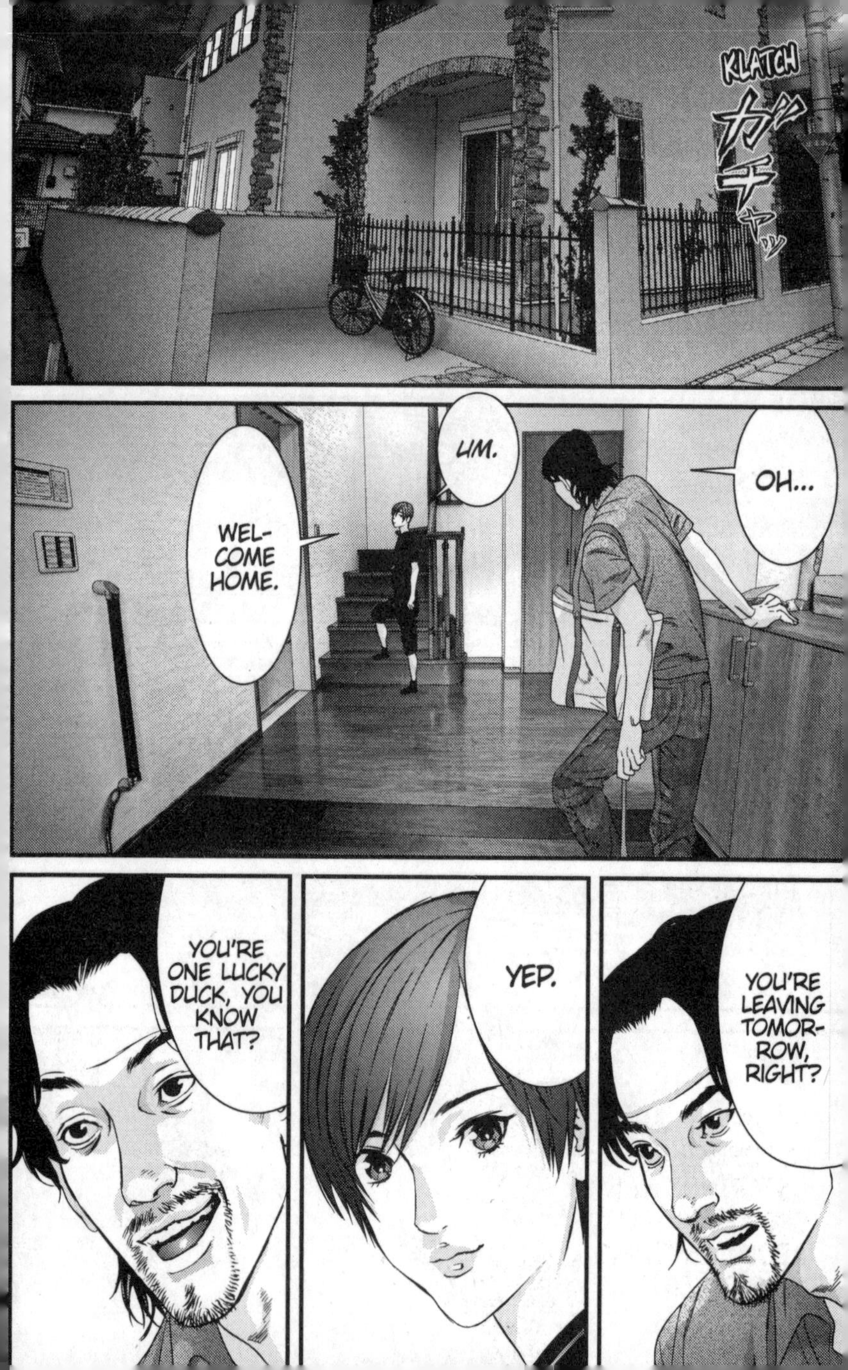
KLATCH
カチャッ
OH...
UM.
WEL-COME HOME.
YOU'RE LEAVING TOMOR-ROW, RIGHT?
YEP.
YOU'RE ONE LUCKY DUCK, YOU KNOW THAT?

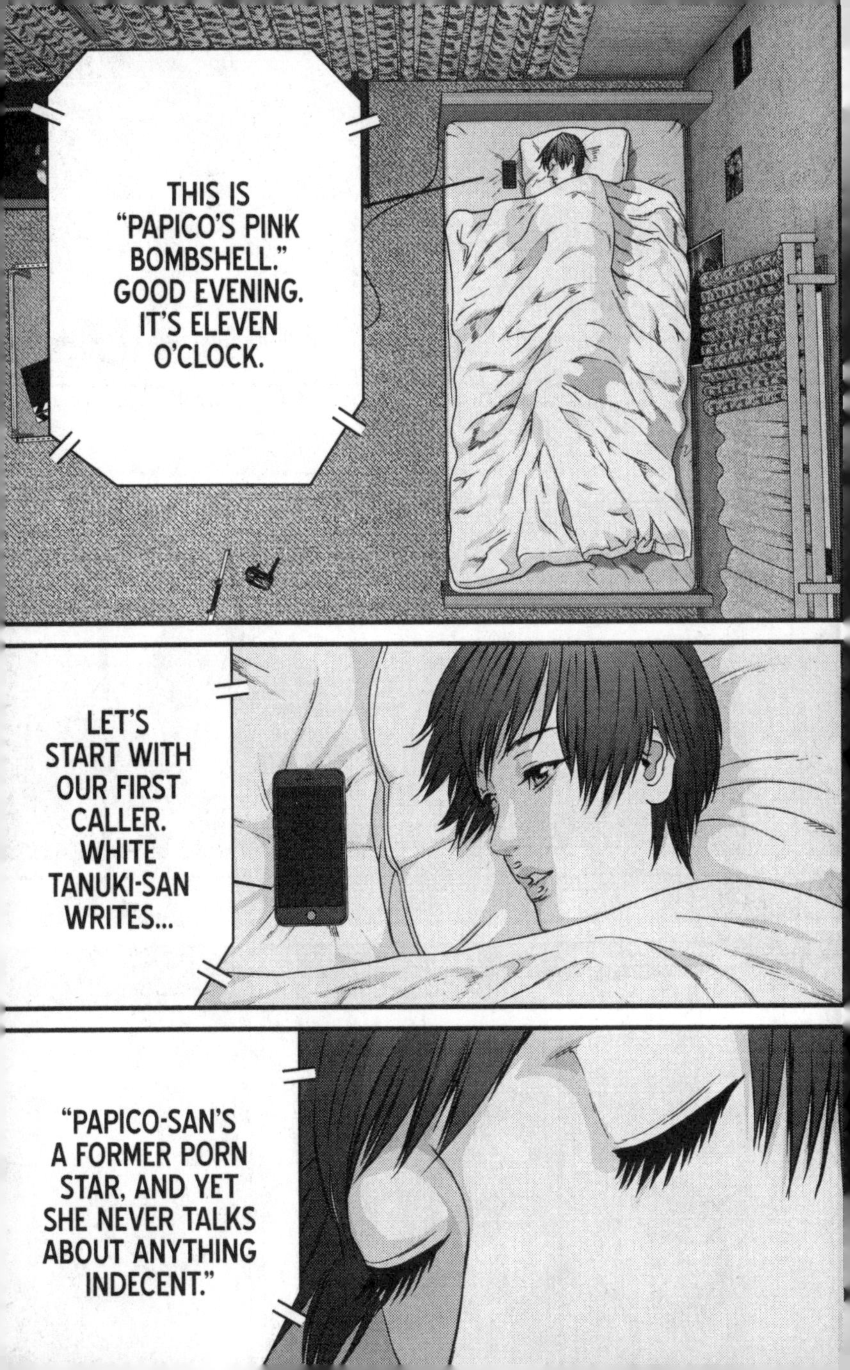
THIS IS "PAPICO'S PINK BOMBSHELL." GOOD EVENING. IT'S ELEVEN O'CLOCK.
LET'S START WITH OUR FIRST CALLER. WHITE TANUKI-SAN WRITES...
"PAPICO-SAN'S A FORMER PORN STAR, AND YET SHE NEVER TALKS ABOUT ANYTHING INDECENT."

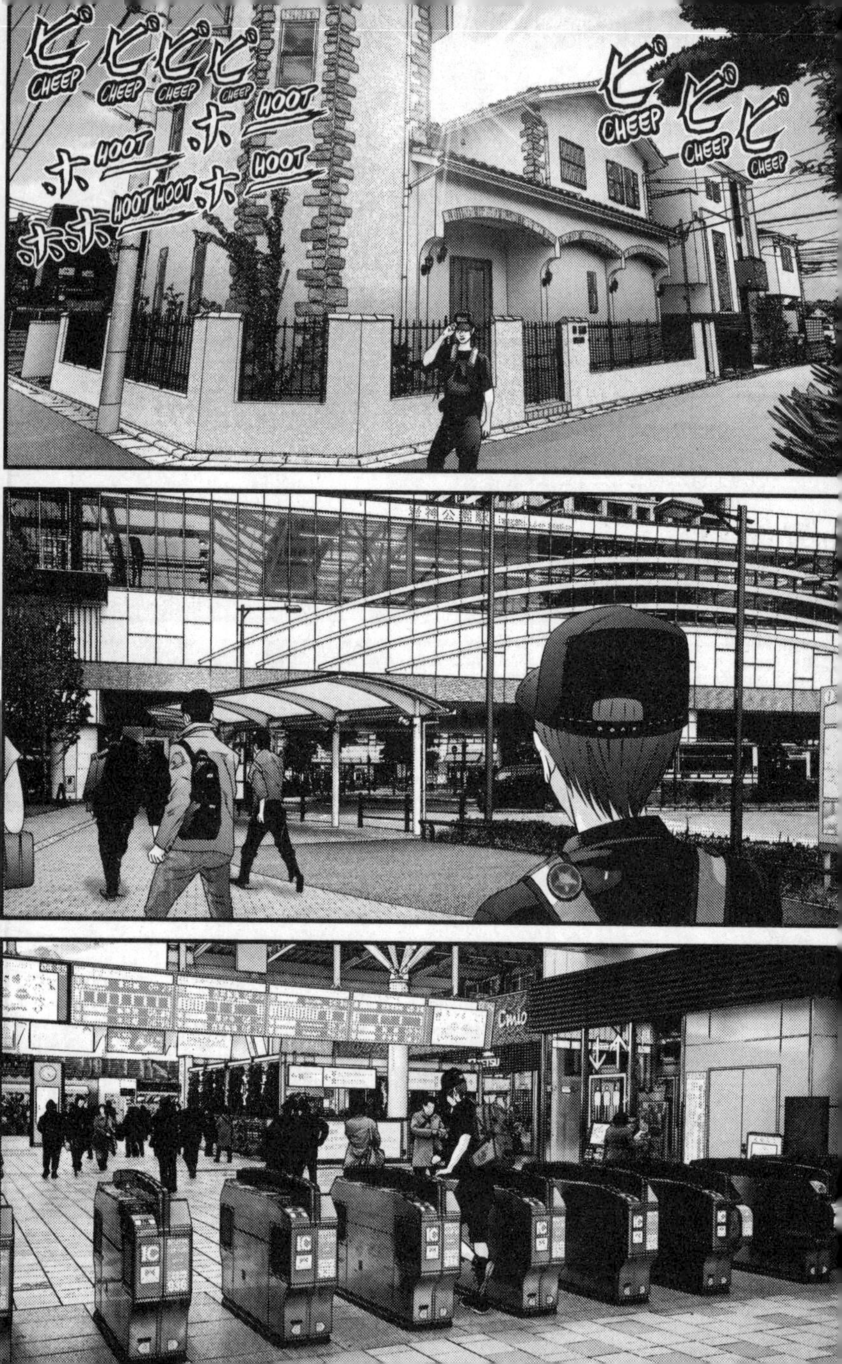
ピ CHEEP
ピ CHEEP
ピ CHEEP
ピ CHEEP
ピ CHEEP
ピ CHEEP
ピ CHEEP
ホ HOOT
ホ HOOT
ホ HOOT
ホホ HOOT HOOT
ホ HOOT

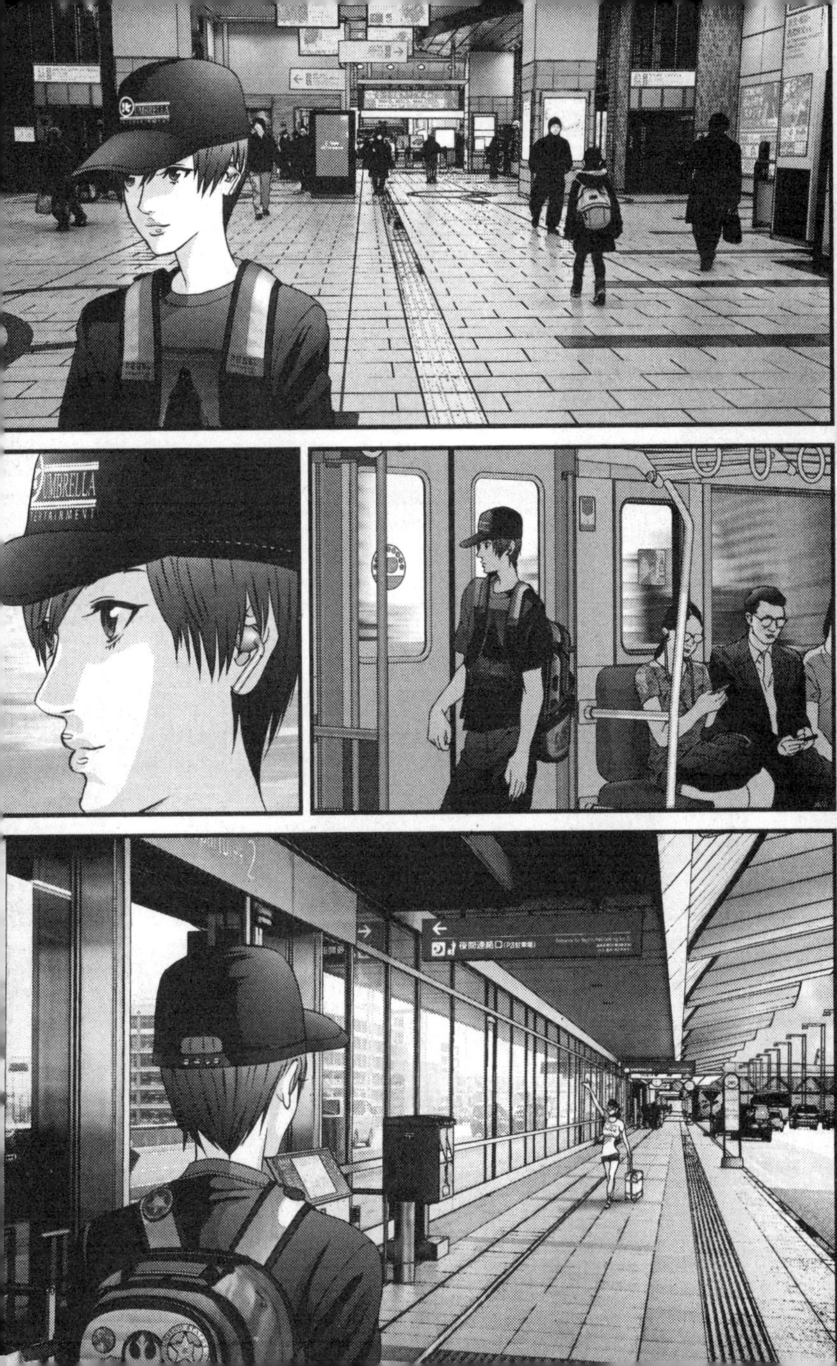
UMBRELLA

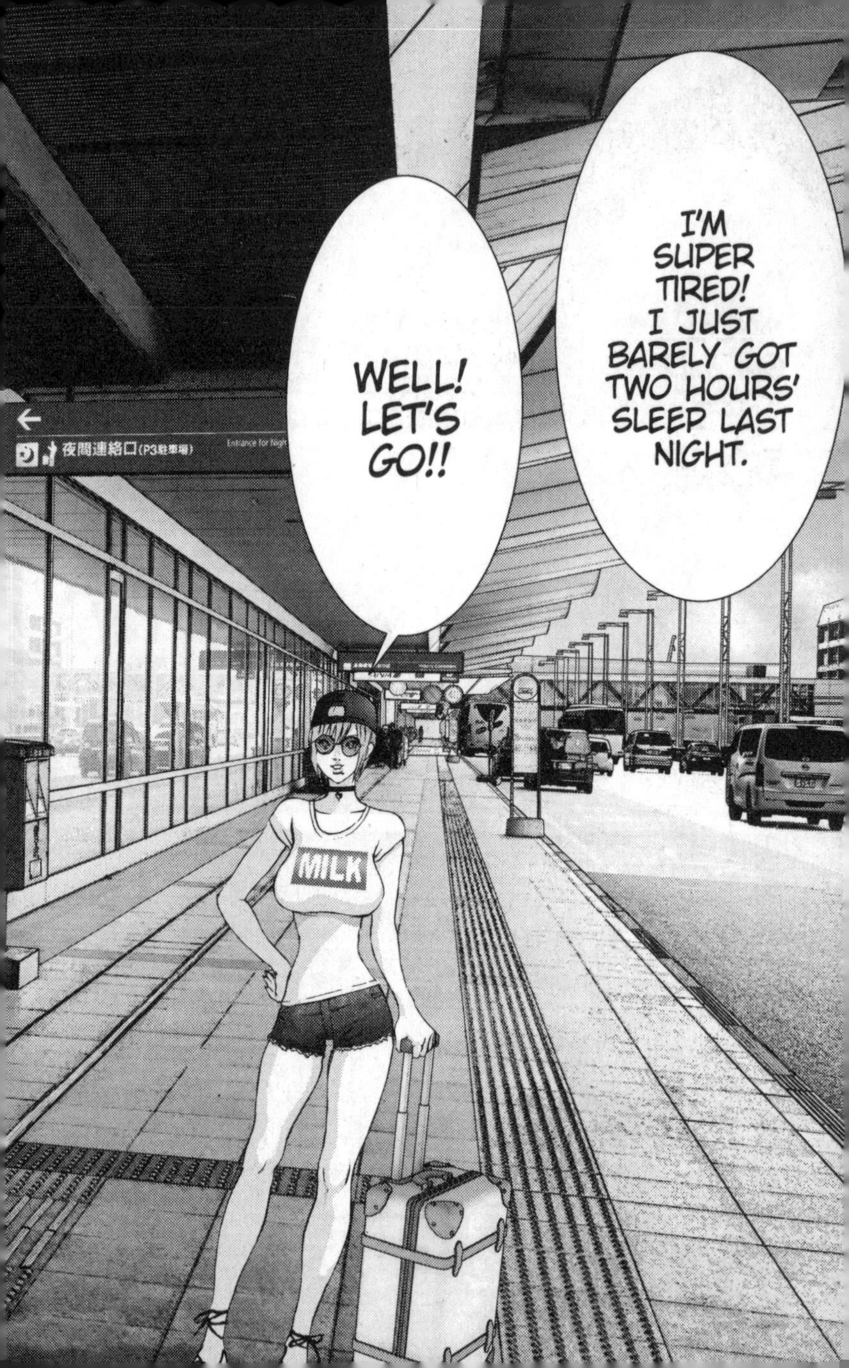
I'M SUPER TIRED! I JUST BARELY GOT TWO HOURS' SLEEP LAST NIGHT.
WELL! LET'S GO!!
夜間連絡口(P3駐車場)
MILK

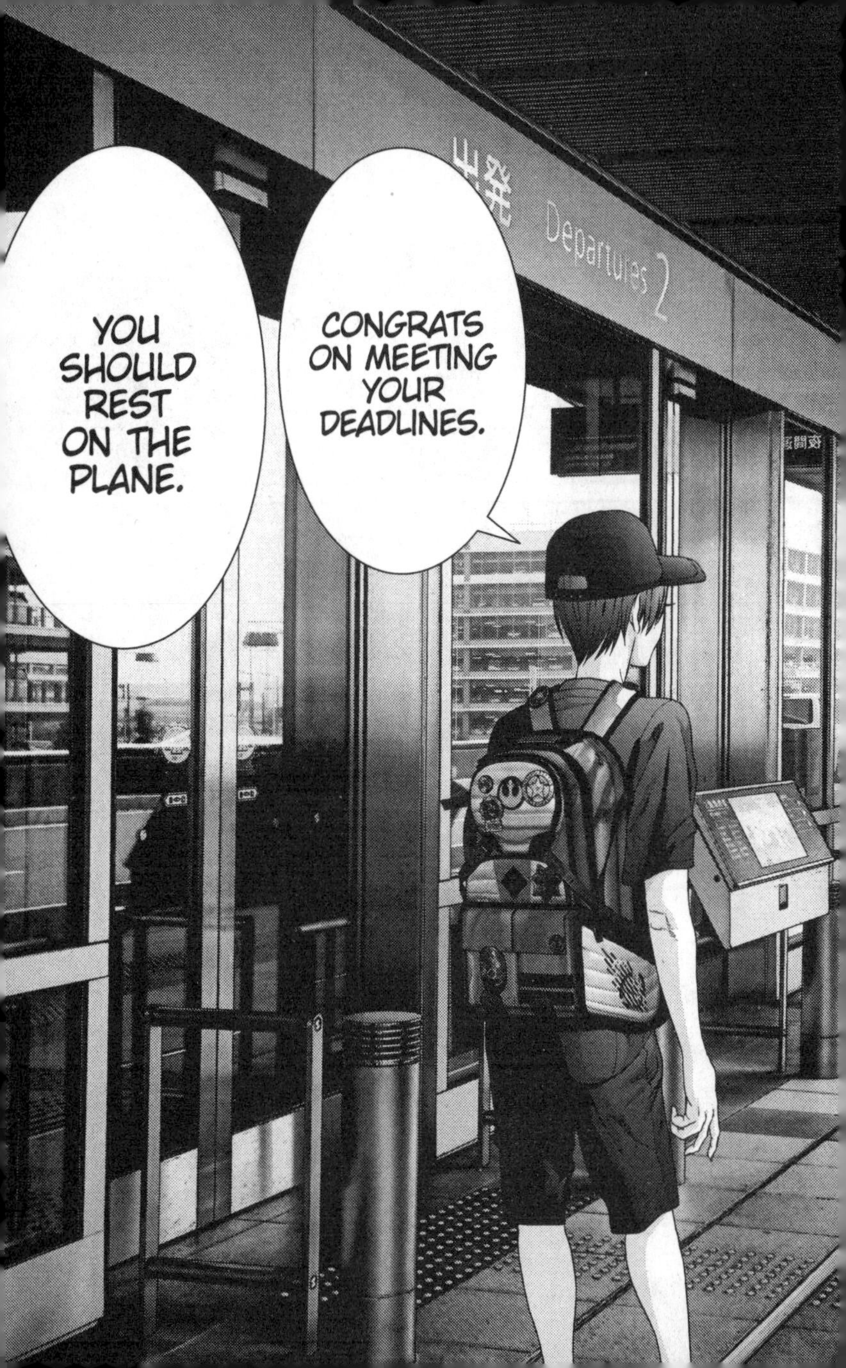
出発 Departures 2
CONGRATS ON MEETING YOUR DEADLINES.
YOU SHOULD REST ON THE PLANE.

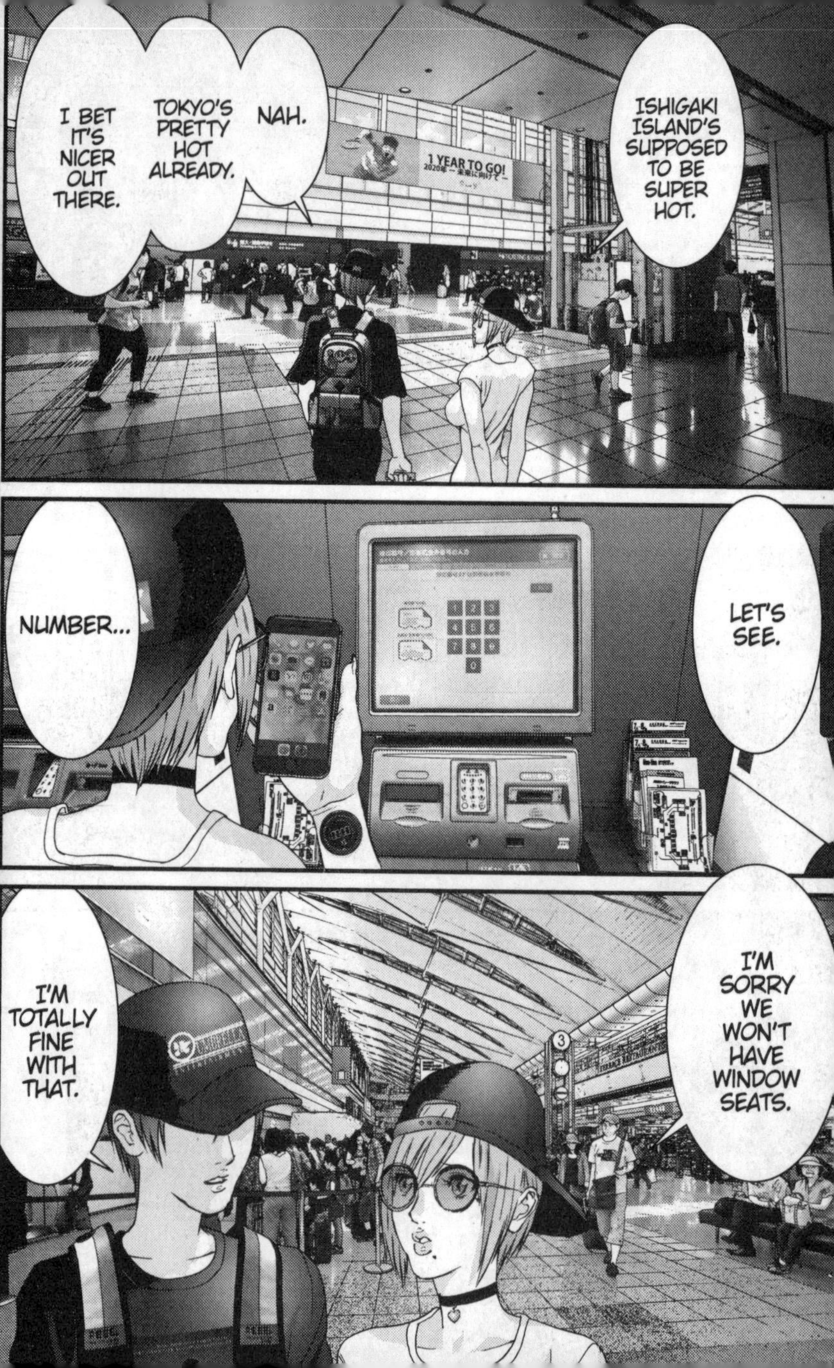
ISHIGAKI ISLAND'S SUPPOSED TO BE SUPER HOT.
1 YEAR TO GO!
NAH.
TOKYO'S PRETTY HOT ALREADY.
I BET IT'S NICER OUT THERE.
LET'S SEE.
NUMBER...
I'M SORRY WE WON'T HAVE WINDOW SEATS.
I'M TOTALLY FINE WITH THAT.

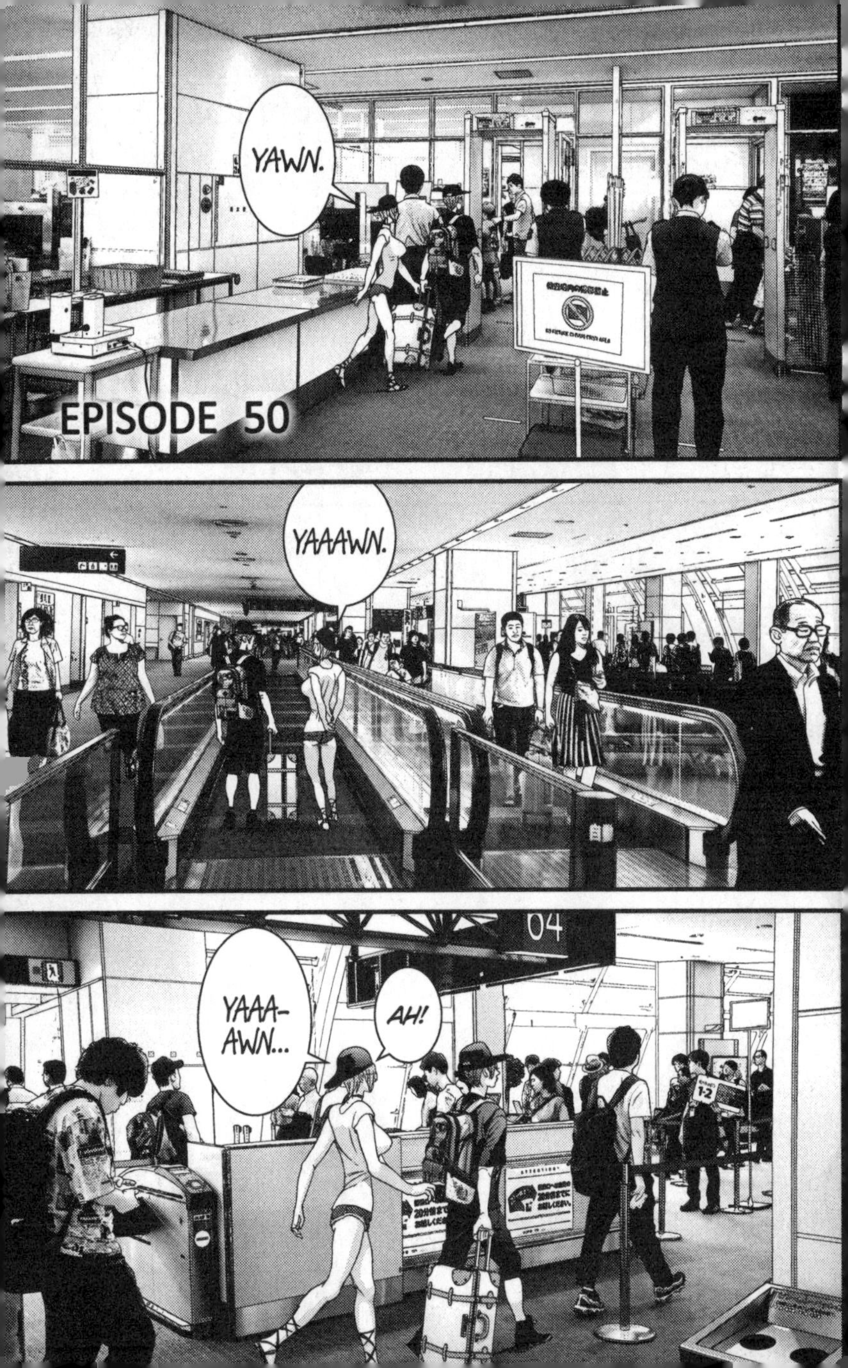
YAWN.
EPISODE 50
YAAAWN.
AH!
YAAA-AWN...

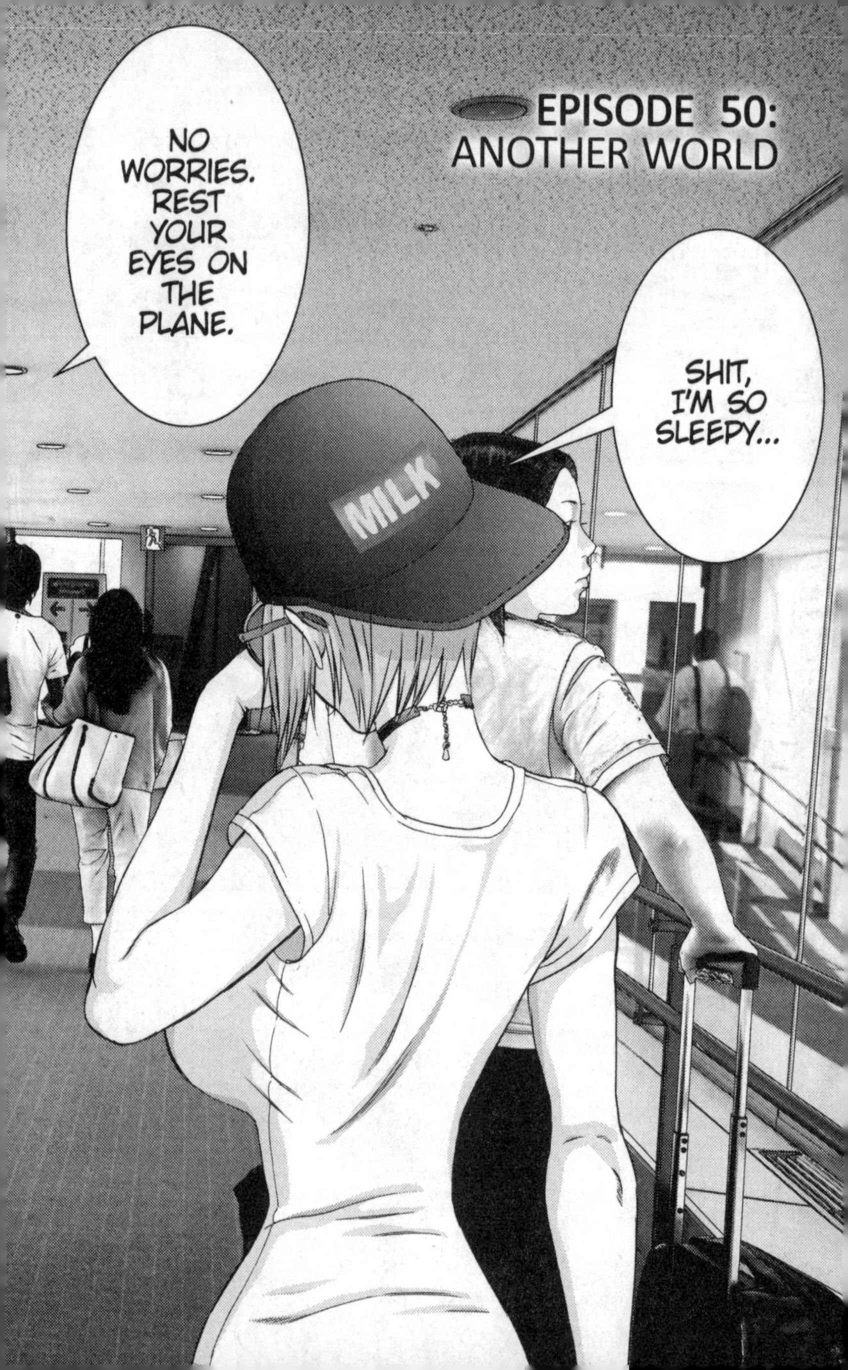
EPISODE 50: ANOTHER WORLD
SHIT, I'M SO SLEEPY...
NO WORRIES. REST YOUR EYES ON THE PLANE.
MILK

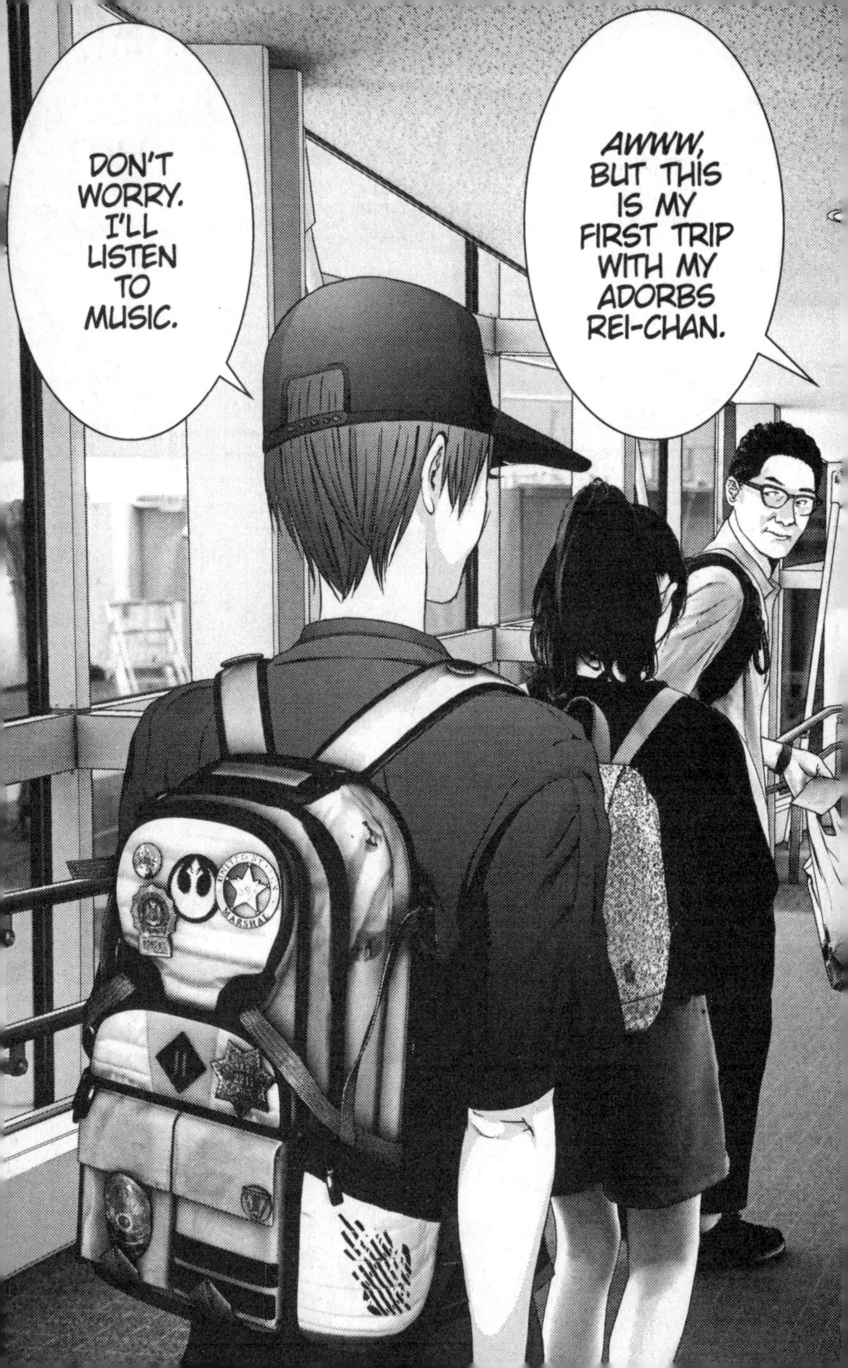
AWWW, BUT THIS IS MY FIRST TRIP WITH MY ADORBS REI-CHAN.
DON'T WORRY. I'LL LISTEN TO MUSIC.

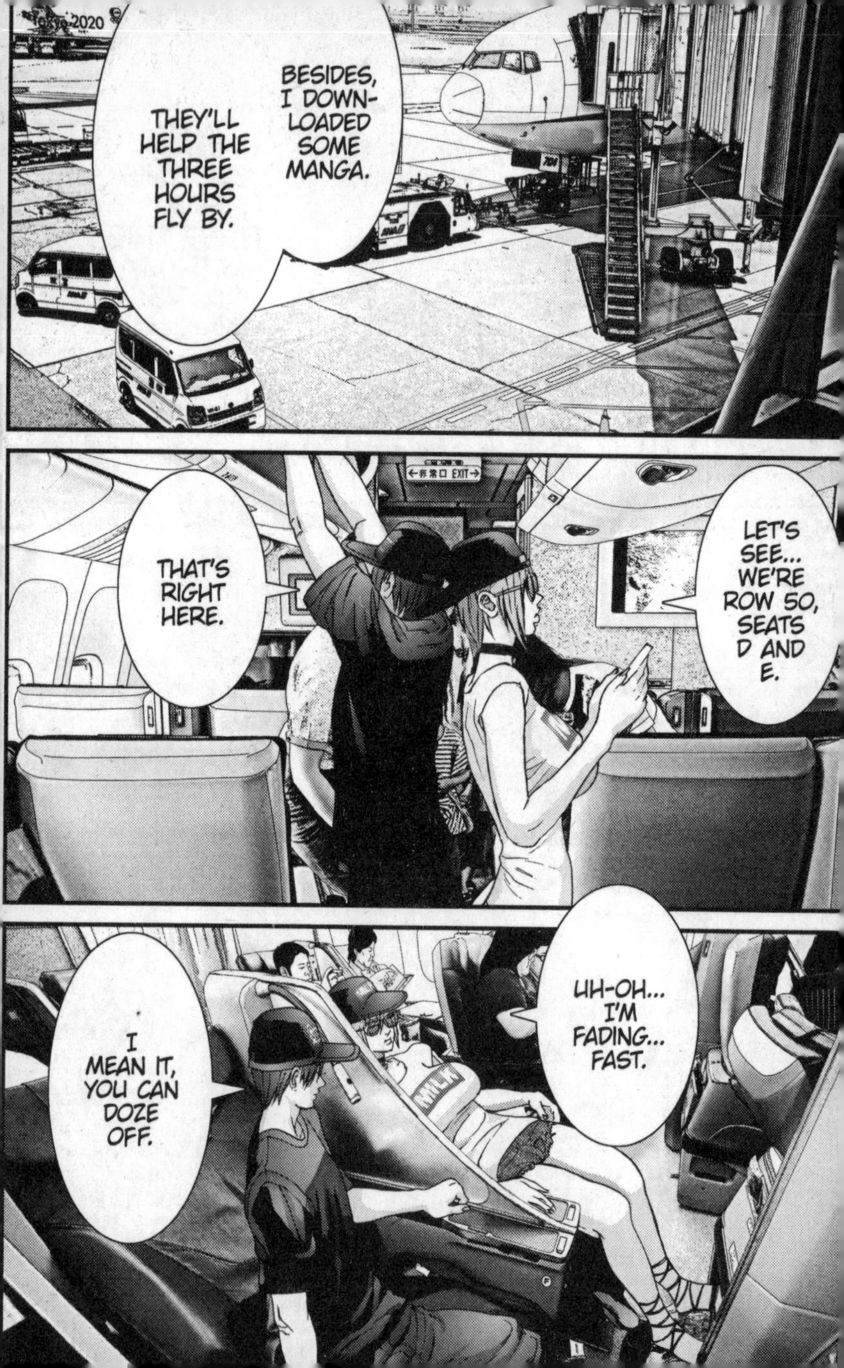
Tokyo 2020
BESIDES, I DOWN-LOADED SOME MANGA.
THEY'LL HELP THE THREE HOURS FLY BY.
非常口 EXIT
LET'S SEE... WE'RE ROW 50, SEATS D AND E.
THAT'S RIGHT HERE.
UH-OH... I'M FADING... FAST.
I MEAN IT, YOU CAN DOZE OFF.

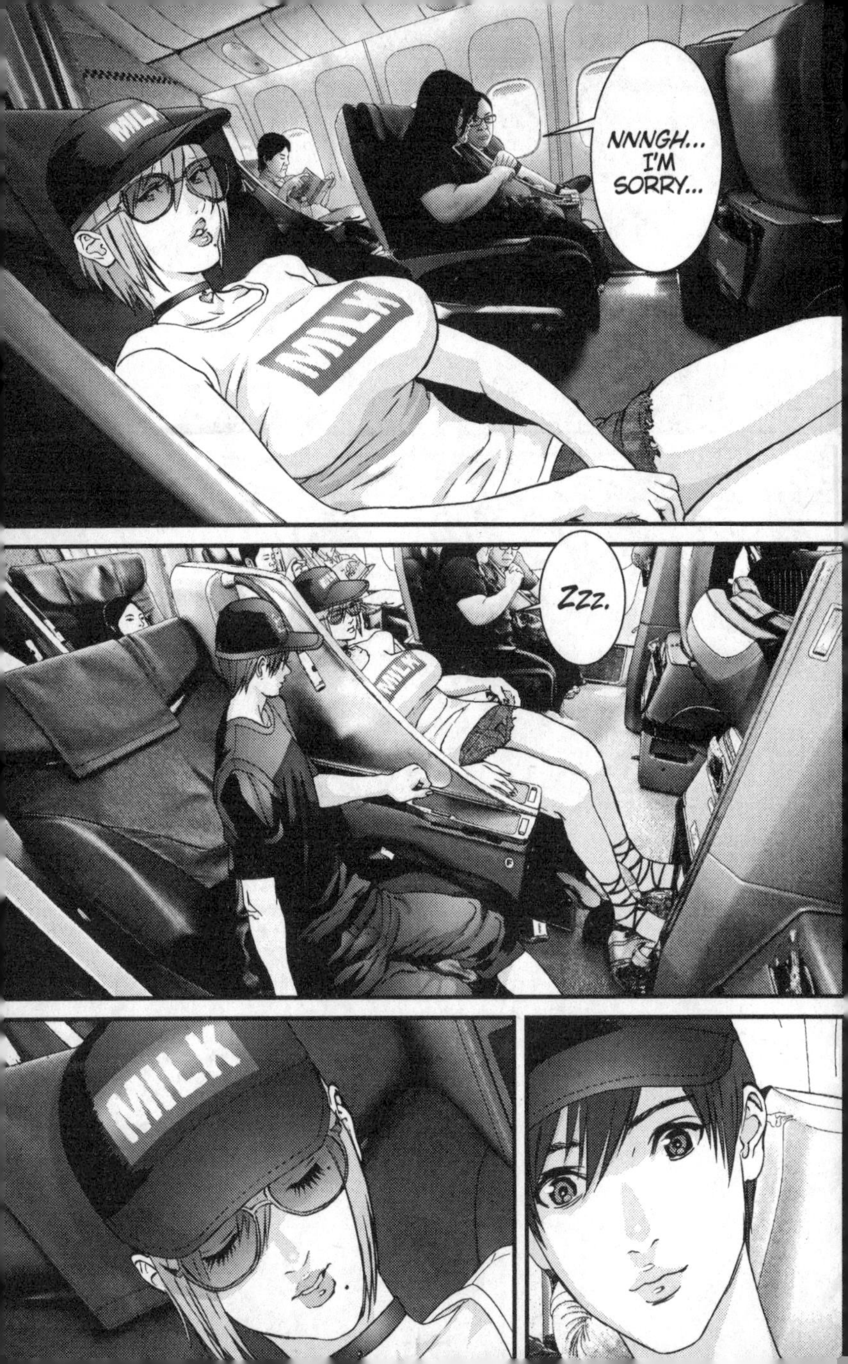
NNNGH... I'M SORRY...
Zzz.
MILK
MILK
MILK

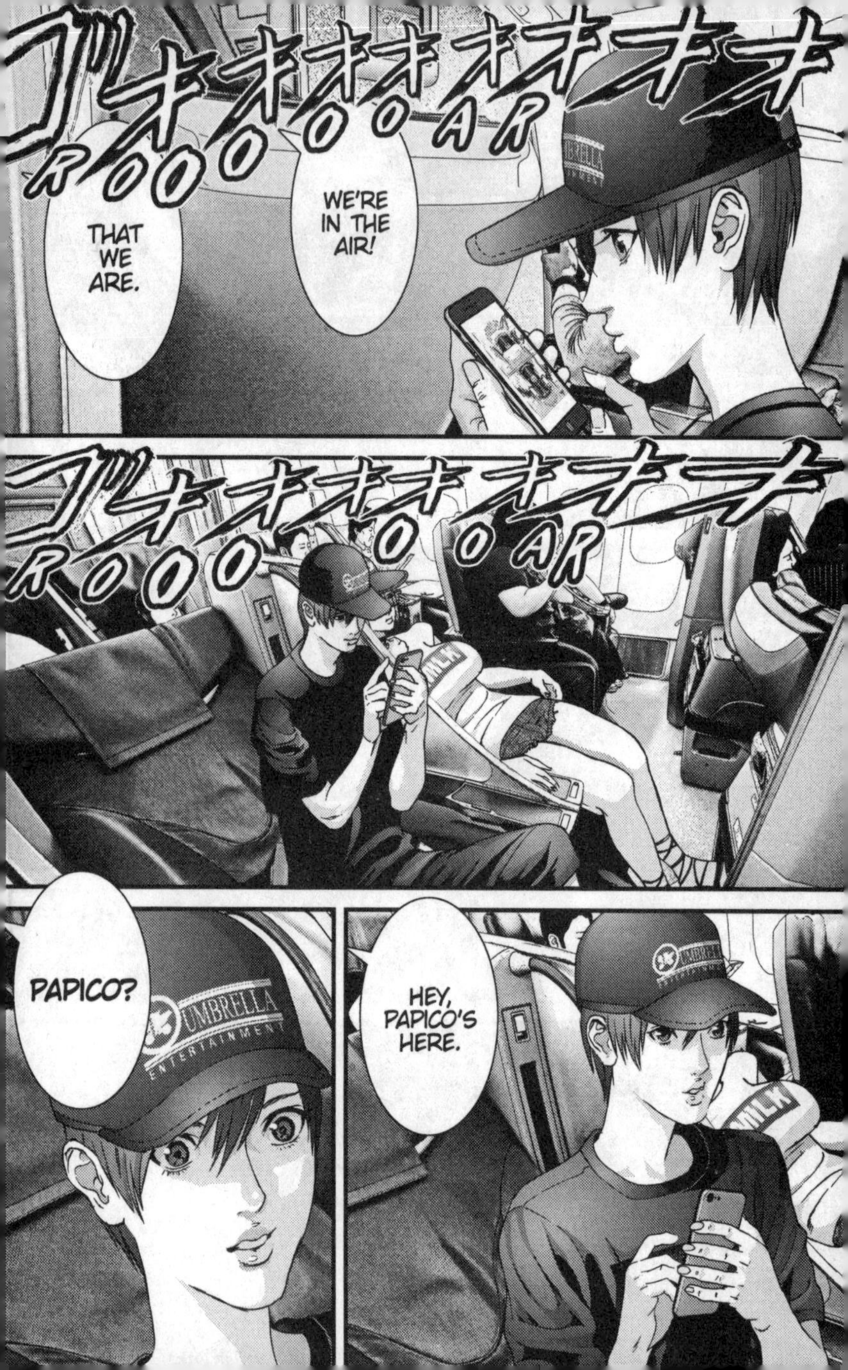
ROOOOOAR
WE'RE IN THE AIR!
THAT WE ARE.
ROOOOOAR
HEY, PAPICO'S HERE.
PAPICO?

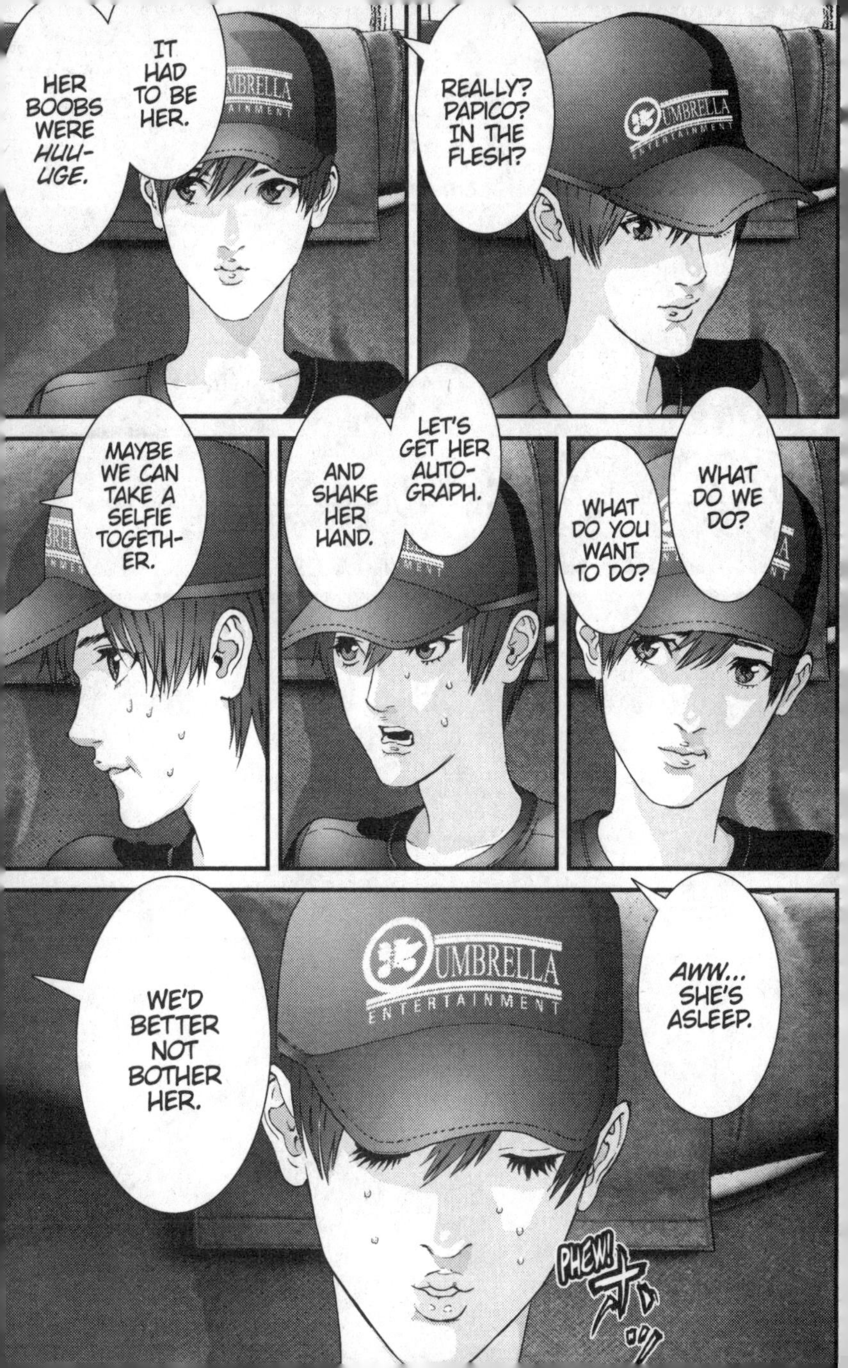
REALLY? PAPICO? IN THE FLESH?
IT HAD TO BE HER.
HER BOOBS WERE HUU-UGE.
WHAT DO WE DO?
WHAT DO YOU WANT TO DO?
LET'S GET HER AUTO-GRAPH.
AND SHAKE HER HAND.
MAYBE WE CAN TAKE A SELFIE TOGETH-ER.
AWW... SHE'S ASLEEP.
WE'D BETTER NOT BOTHER HER.
PHEW!

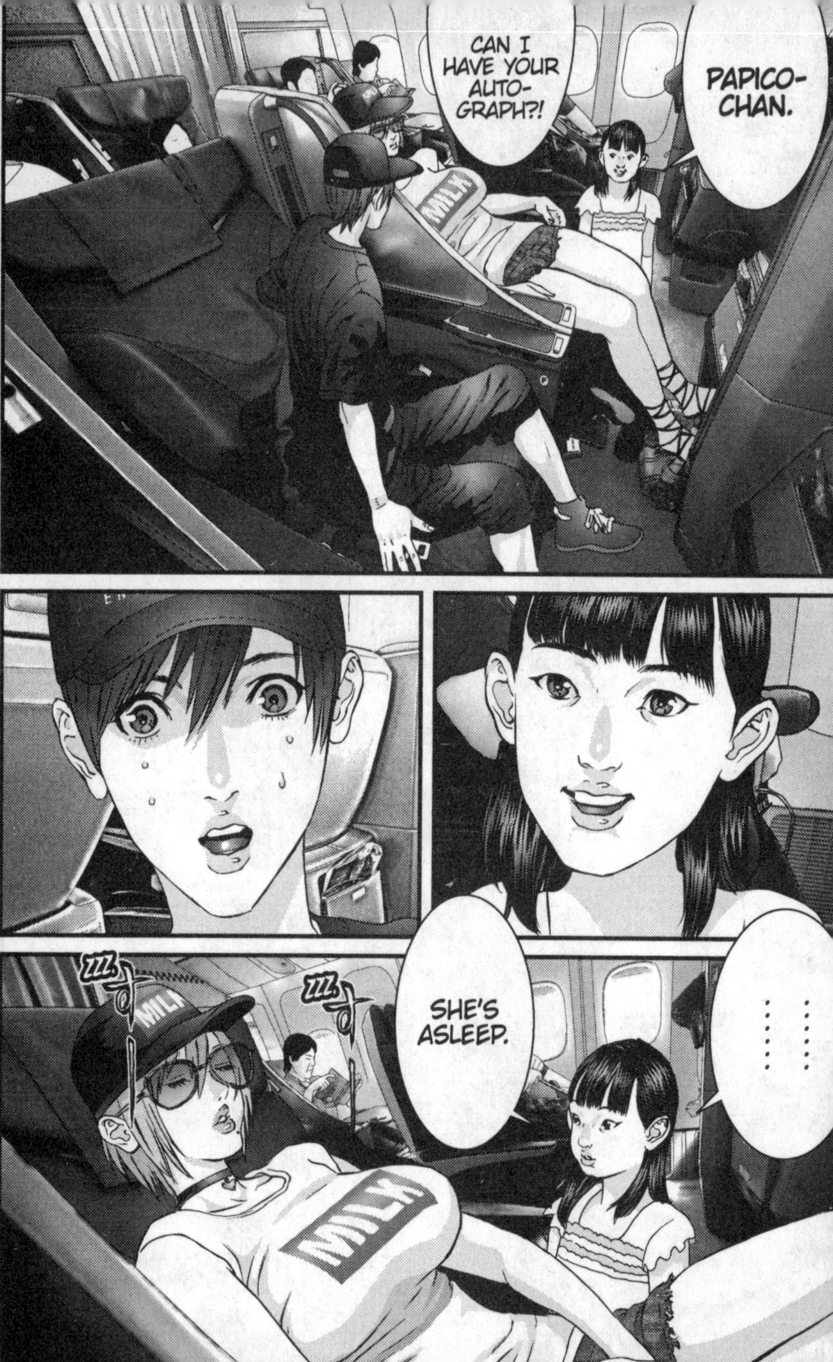

PAPICO-CHAN.
CAN I HAVE YOUR AUTO-GRAPH?!
......
SHE'S ASLEEP.
ZZZ.
ZZZ.

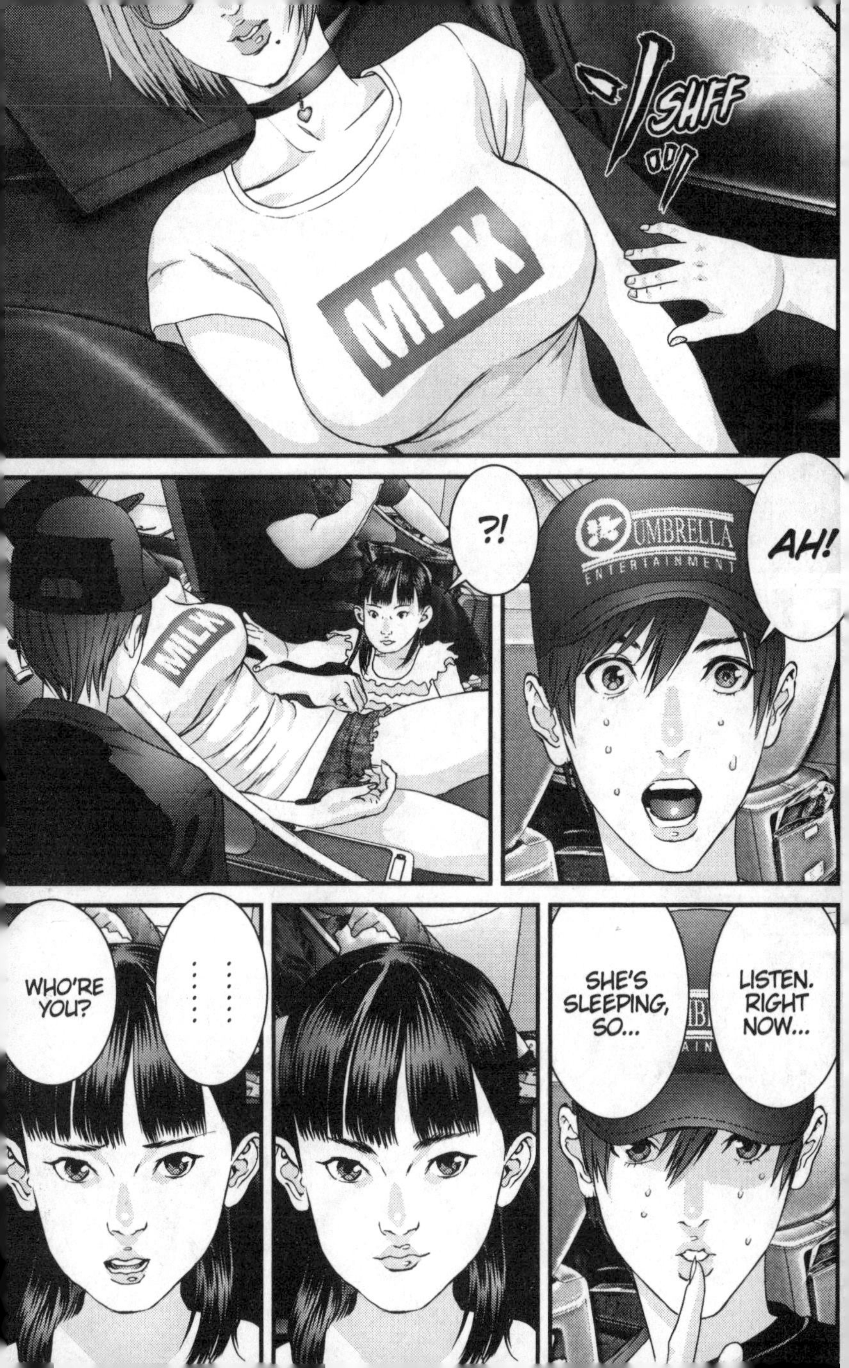

SHFF
MILK
AH!
UMBRELLA
ENTERTAINMENT
?!
MILK
LISTEN. RIGHT NOW...
SHE'S SLEEPING, SO...
......
WHO'RE YOU?

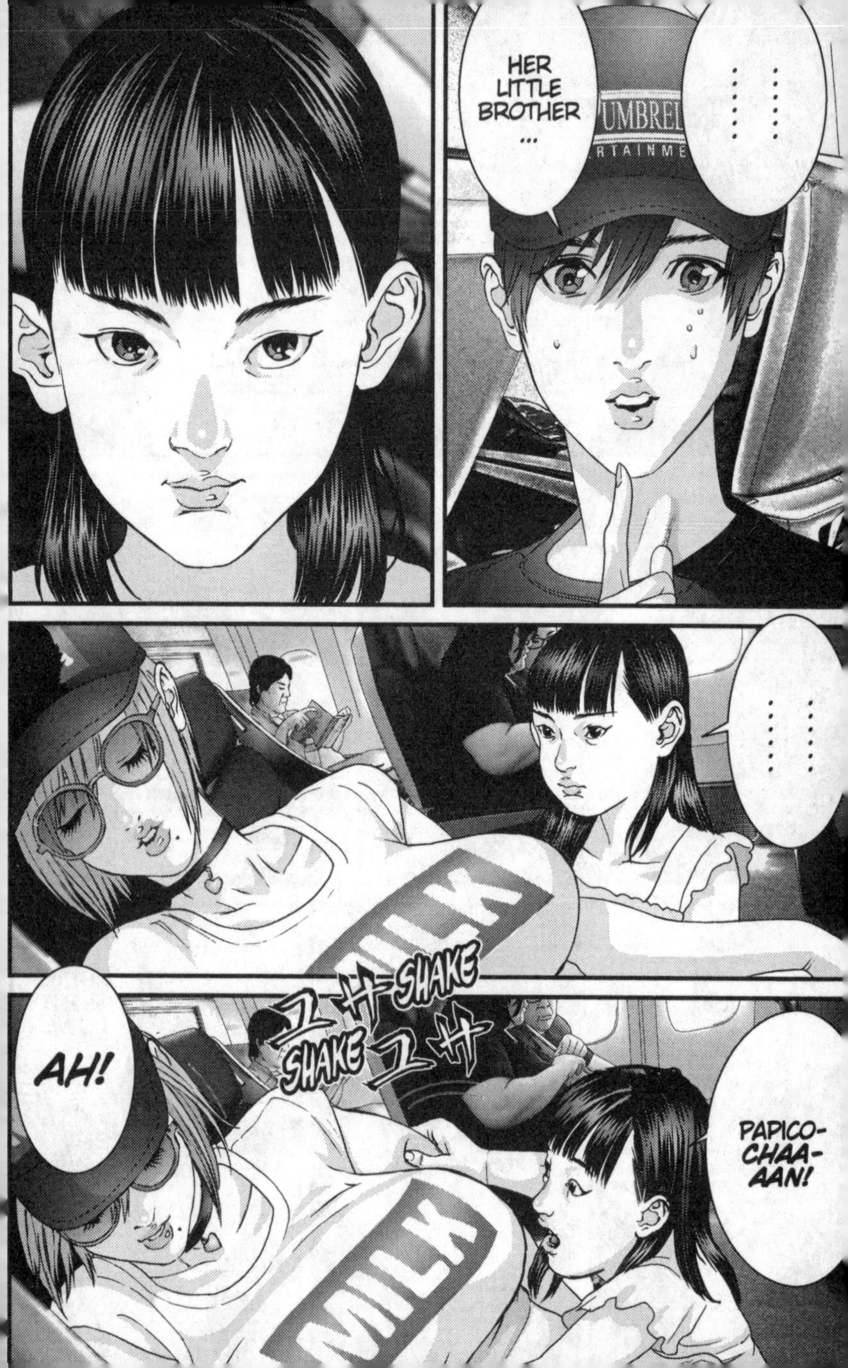
......
HER LITTLE BROTHER ...
......
PAPICO-CHAAA-AAN!
SHAKE
SHAKE
AH!

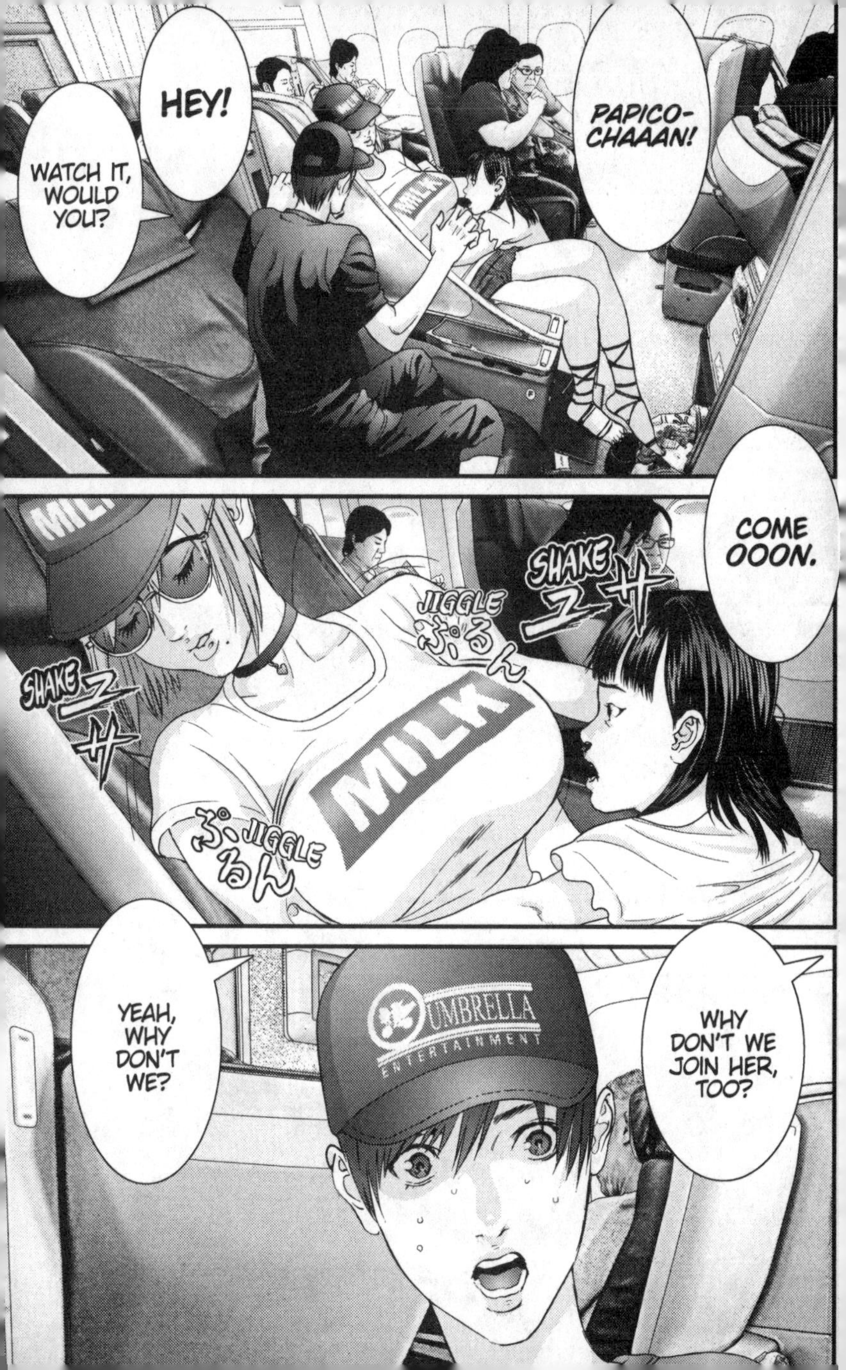
PAPICO-CHAAAN!
HEY!
WATCH IT, WOULD YOU?
MILK
COME OOON.
SHAKE ユサ
JIGGLE ぷるん
SHAKE ユサ
MILK
JIGGLE ぷるん
WHY DON'T WE JOIN HER, TOO?
UMBRELLA ENTERTAINMENT
YEAH, WHY DON'T WE?

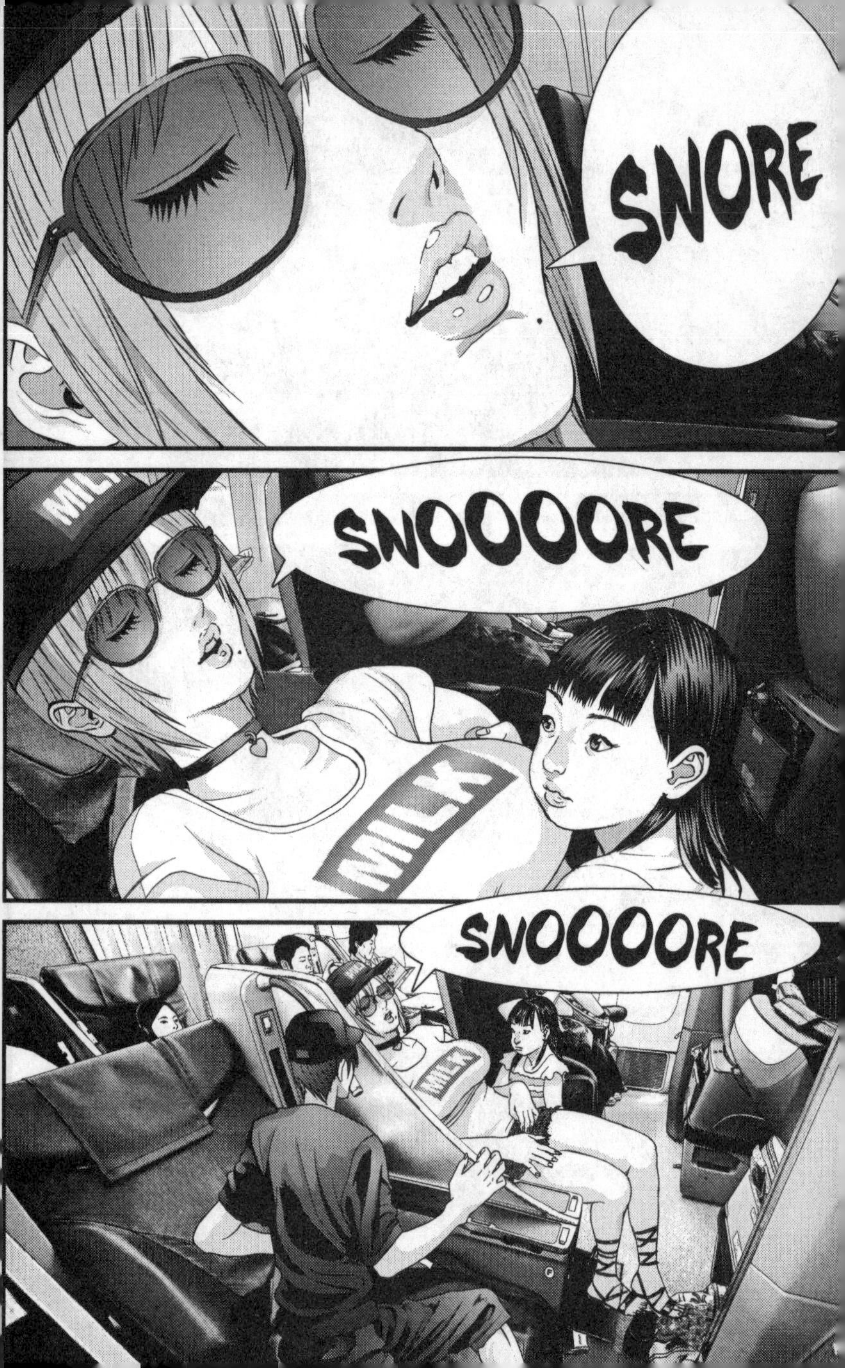
SNORE
SNOOOORE
MILK
SNOOOORE

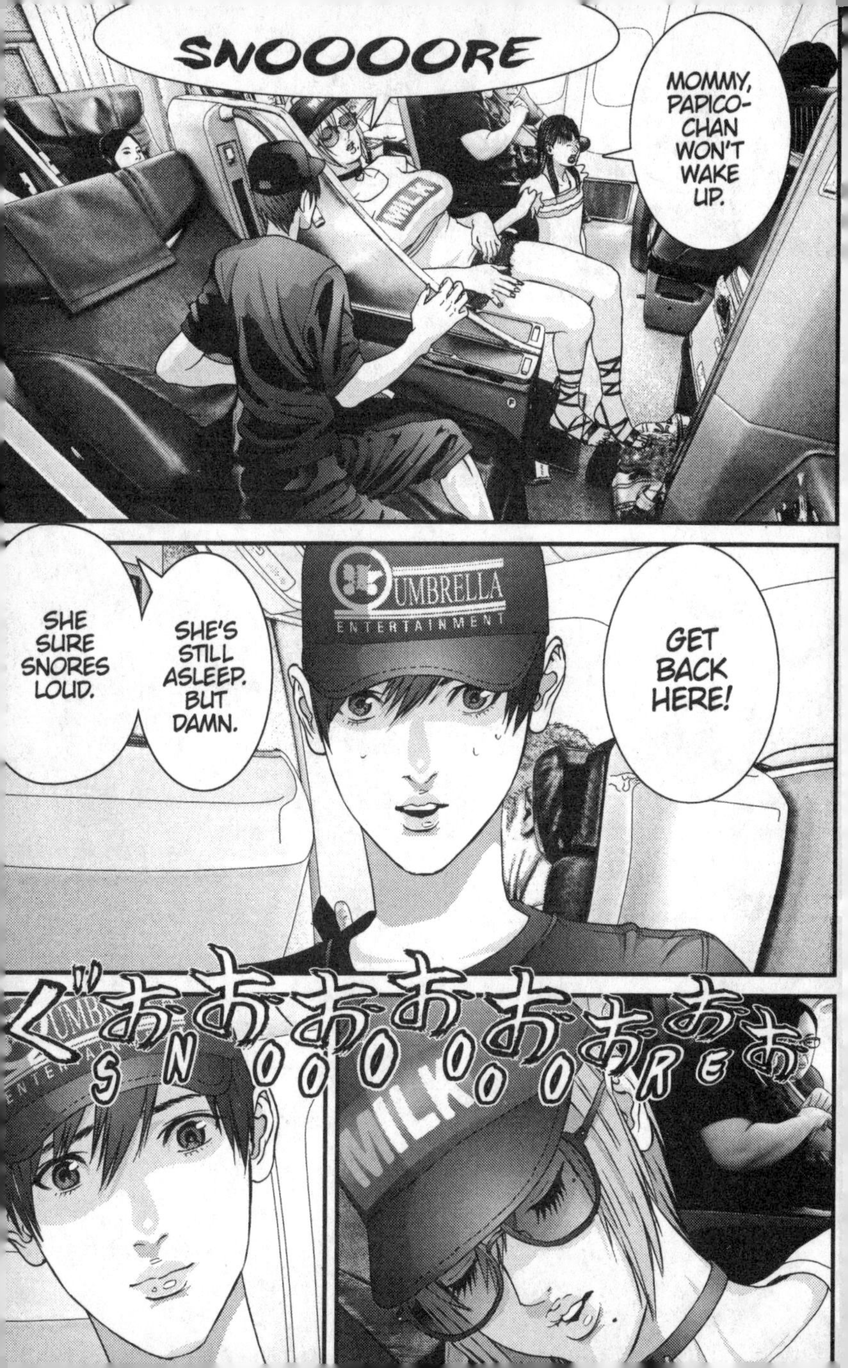
SNOOOORE
MOMMY, PAPICO-CHAN WON'T WAKE UP.
GET BACK HERE!
SHE'S STILL ASLEEP. BUT DAMN.
SHE SURE SNORES LOUD.
ぐおおおおおおおおお
SNOOOOOORE

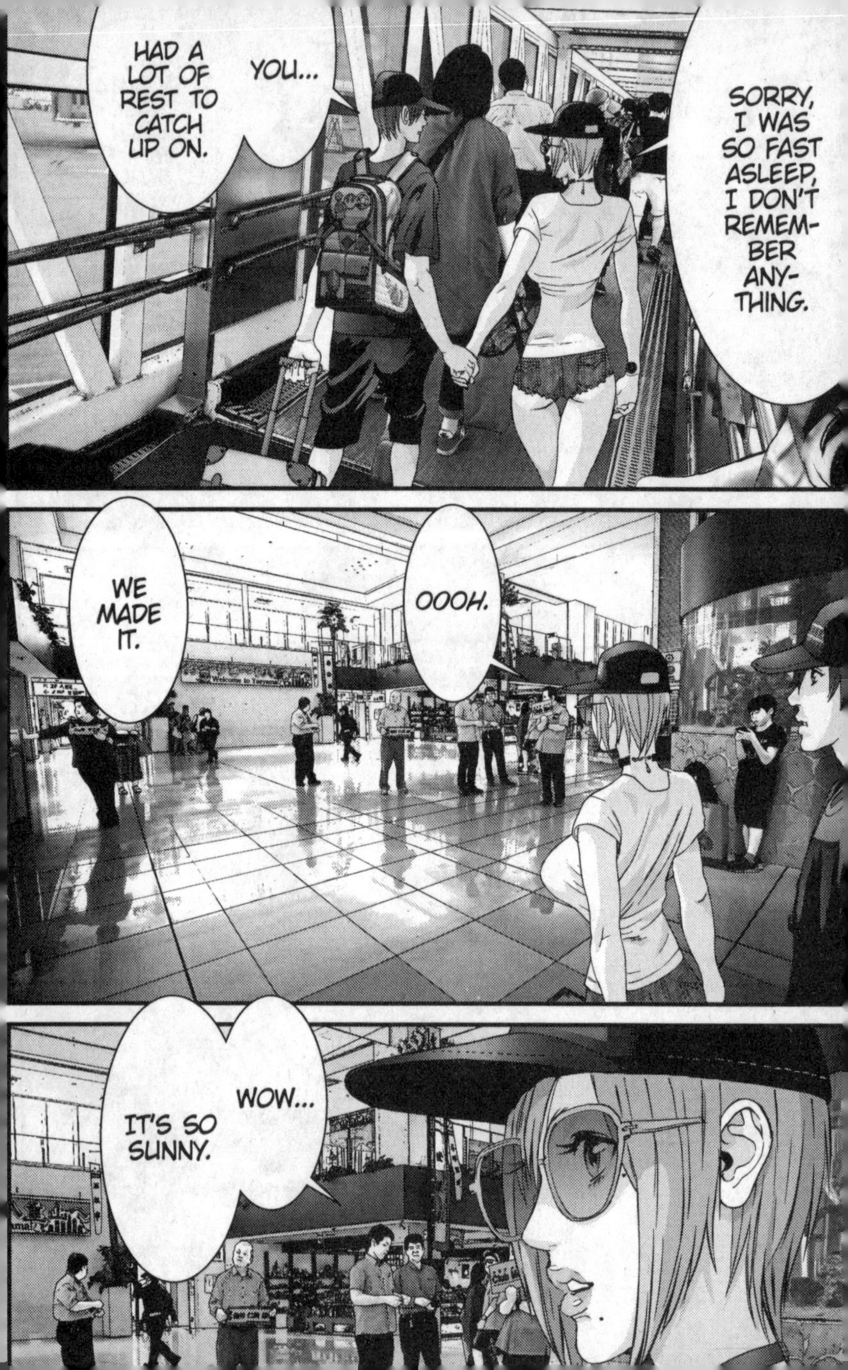
SORRY, I WAS SO FAST ASLEEP, I DON'T REMEMBER ANYTHING.
YOU... HAD A LOT OF REST TO CATCH UP ON.
OOOH.
WE MADE IT.
WOW... IT'S SO SUNNY.

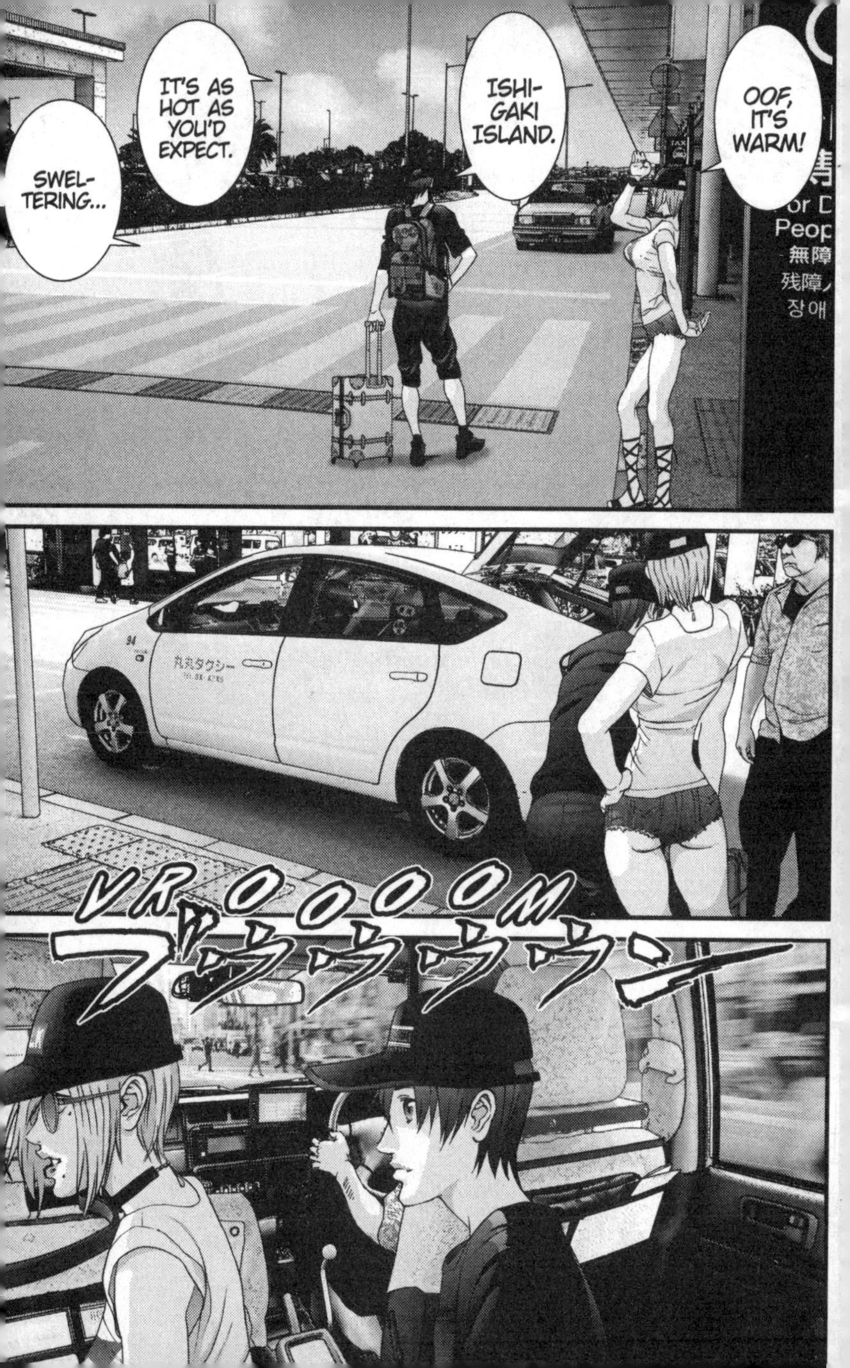
OOF, IT'S WARM!
ISHI-GAKI ISLAND.
IT'S AS HOT AS YOU'D EXPECT.
SWEL-TERING...
丸丸タクシー
VROOOOOM
ブウウウウン

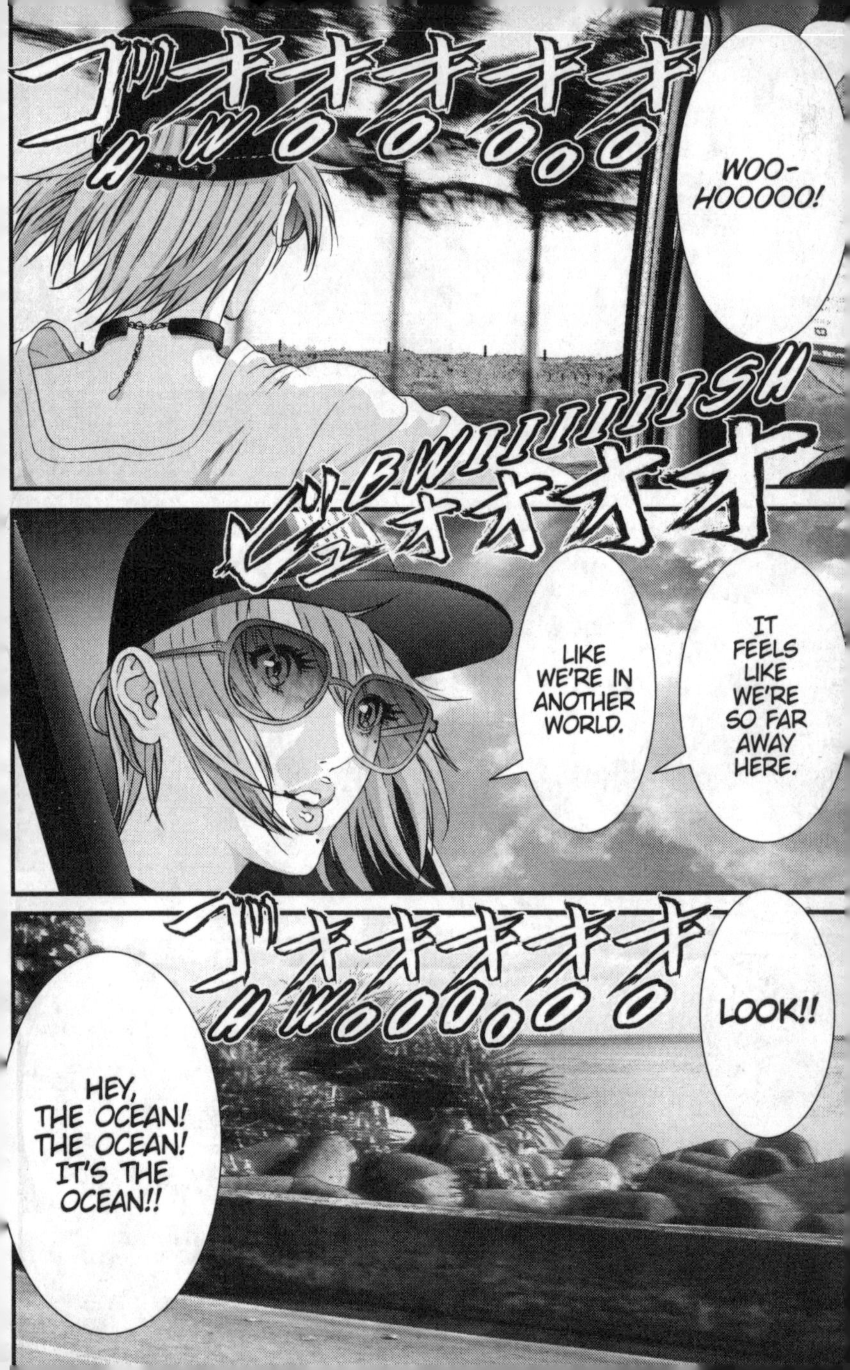
WOO-HOOOOO!
HWOOOOO
BWIIIIIIIISH
IT FEELS LIKE WE'RE SO FAR AWAY HERE.
LIKE WE'RE IN ANOTHER WORLD.
LOOK!!
HWOOOOOO
HEY, THE OCEAN! THE OCEAN! IT'S THE OCEAN!!

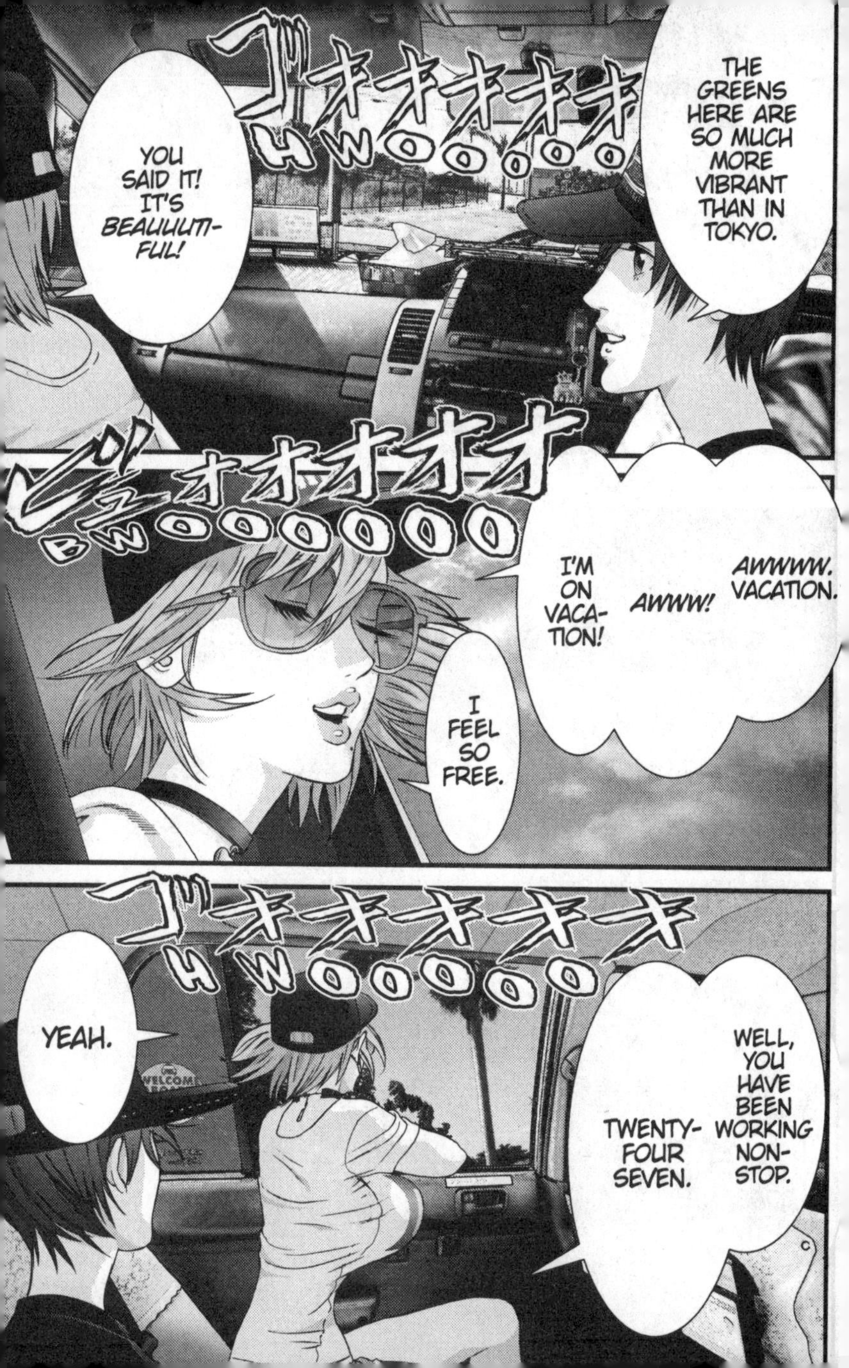
THE GREENS HERE ARE SO MUCH MORE VIBRANT THAN IN TOKYO.
ゴオオオオオ
HWOO.OOO
YOU SAID IT! IT'S BEAUUUTI-FUL!
ビュオオオオオ
BWOOOOOOO
AWWWW. VACATION.
AWWW!
I'M ON VACA-TION!
I FEEL SO FREE.
ゴオオオオオ
HWOOOOOO
WELL, YOU HAVE BEEN WORKING NON-STOP.
TWENTY-FOUR SEVEN.
YEAH.

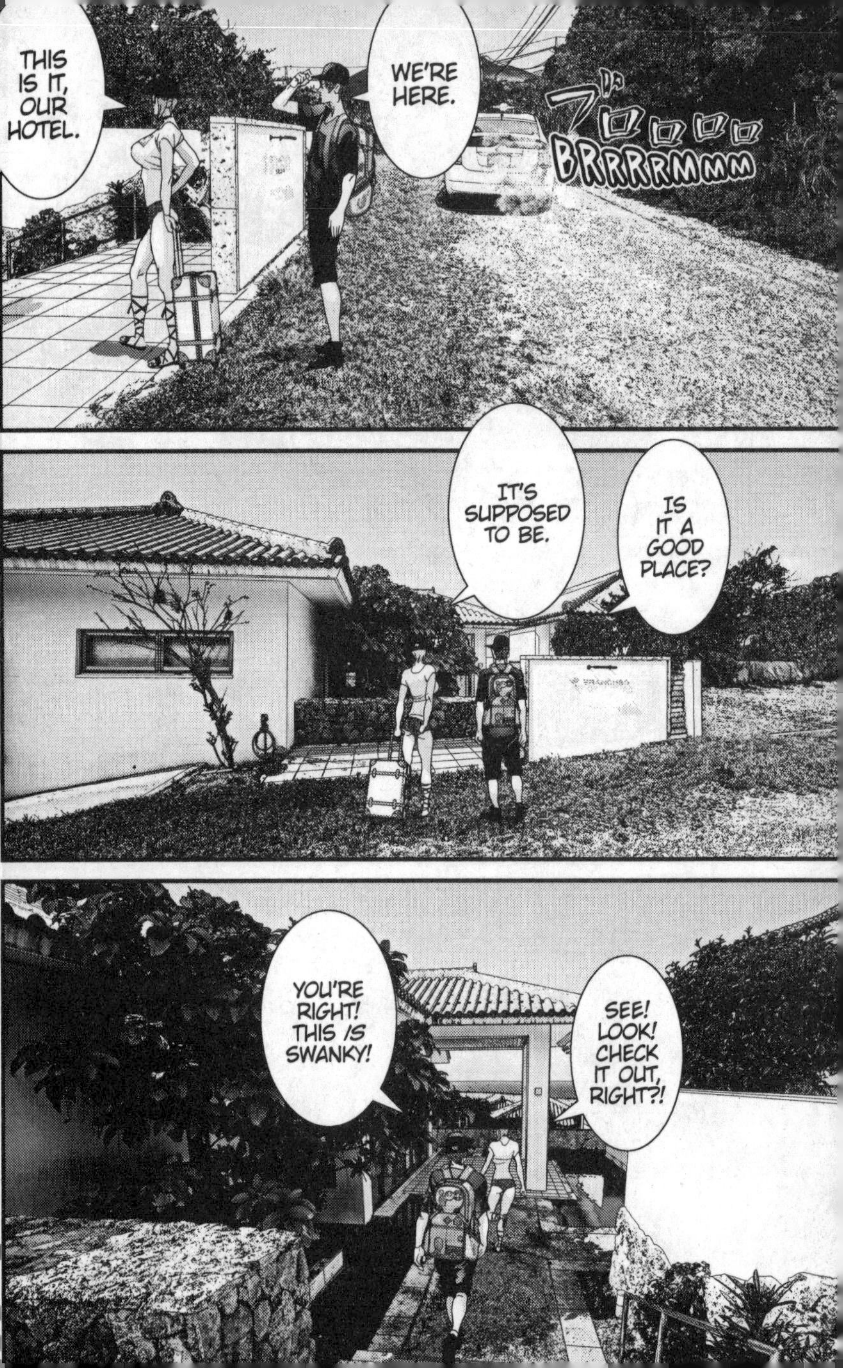
BRRRRMMM
WE'RE HERE.
THIS IS IT, OUR HOTEL.
IS IT A GOOD PLACE?
IT'S SUPPOSED TO BE.
SEE! LOOK! CHECK IT OUT, RIGHT?!
YOU'RE RIGHT! THIS *IS* SWANKY!

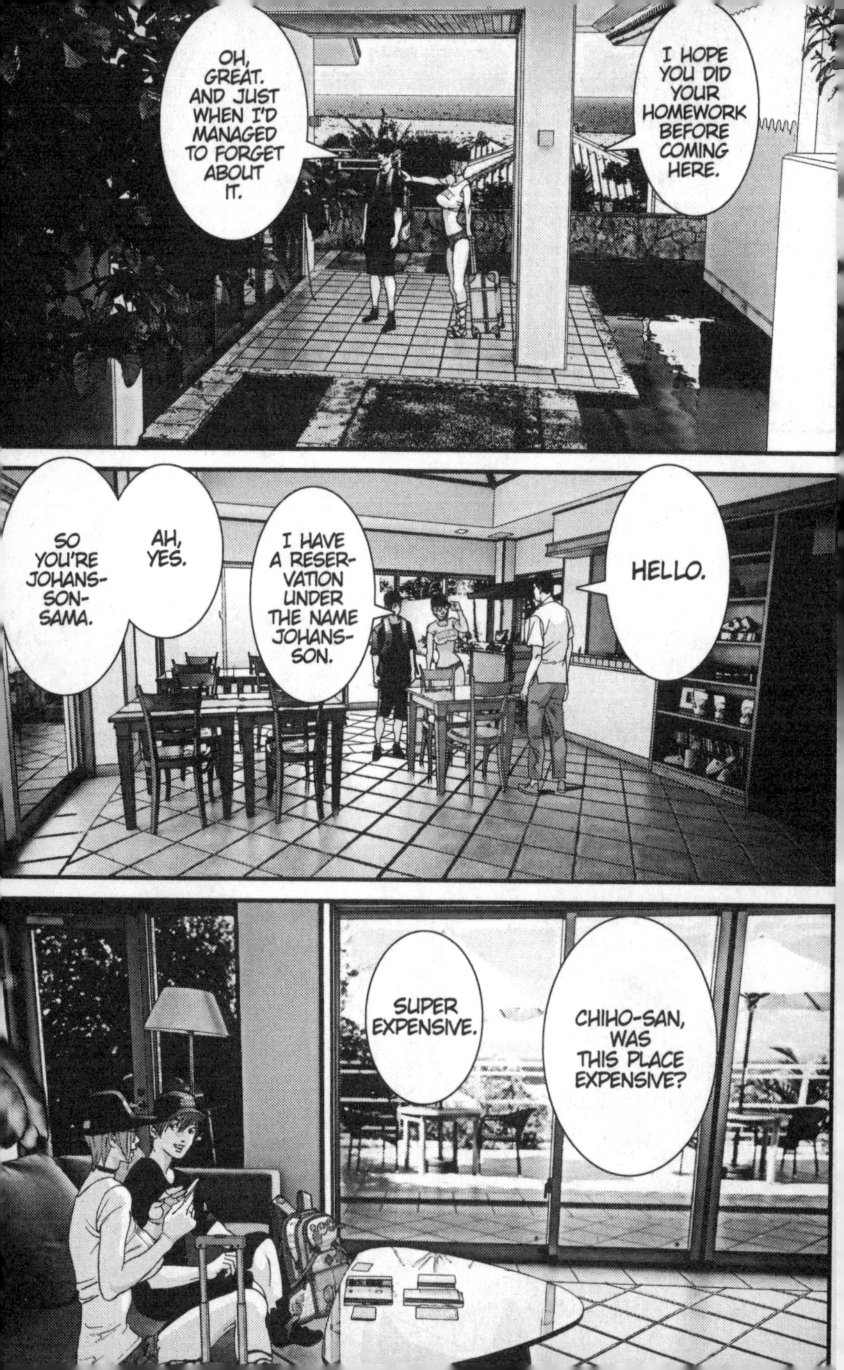
I HOPE YOU DID YOUR HOMEWORK BEFORE COMING HERE.
OH, GREAT. AND JUST WHEN I'D MANAGED TO FORGET ABOUT IT.
HELLO.
I HAVE A RESERVATION UNDER THE NAME JOHANSSON.
AH, YES.
SO YOU'RE JOHANSSON-SAMA.
CHIHO-SAN, WAS THIS PLACE EXPENSIVE?
SUPER EXPENSIVE.

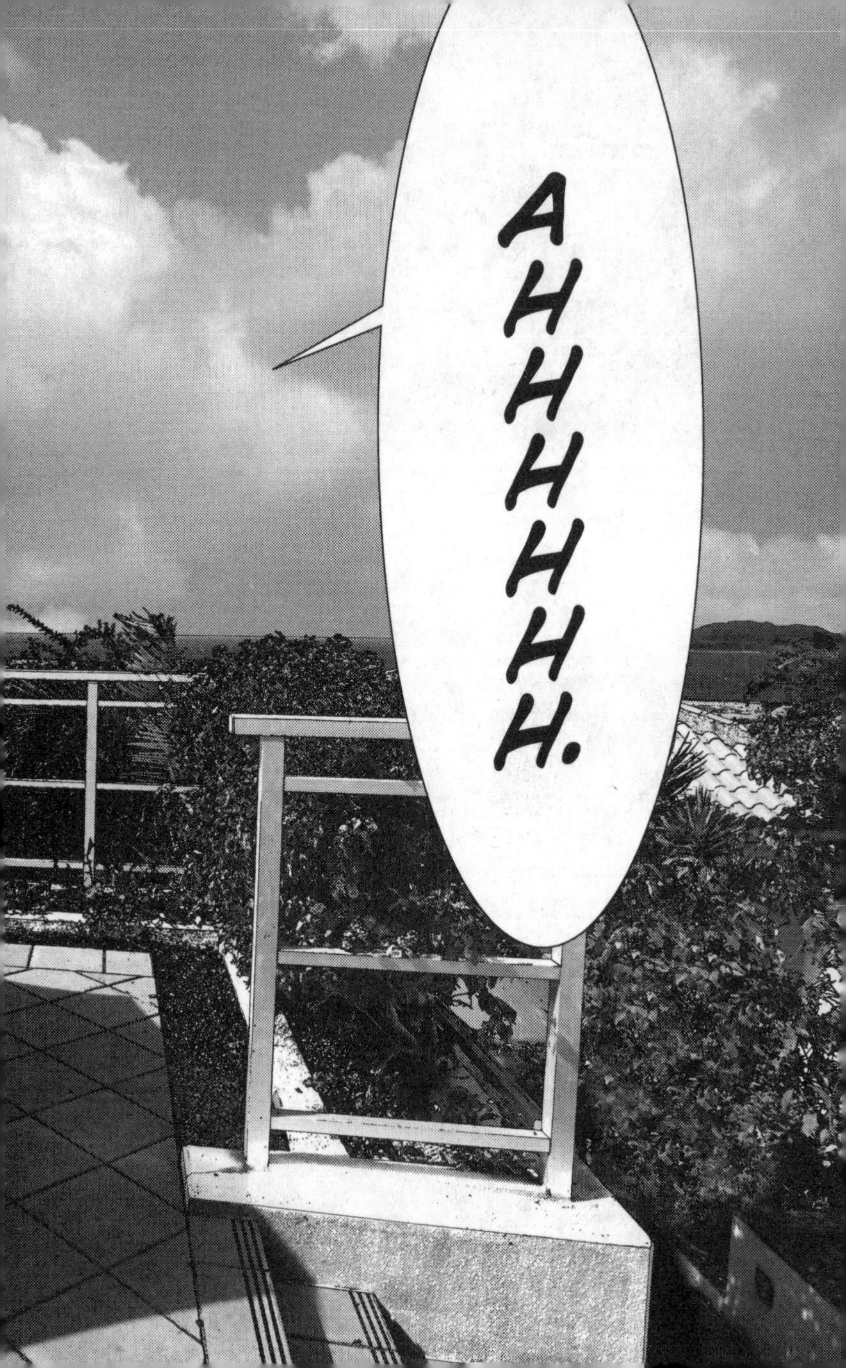
AHHHHHH.

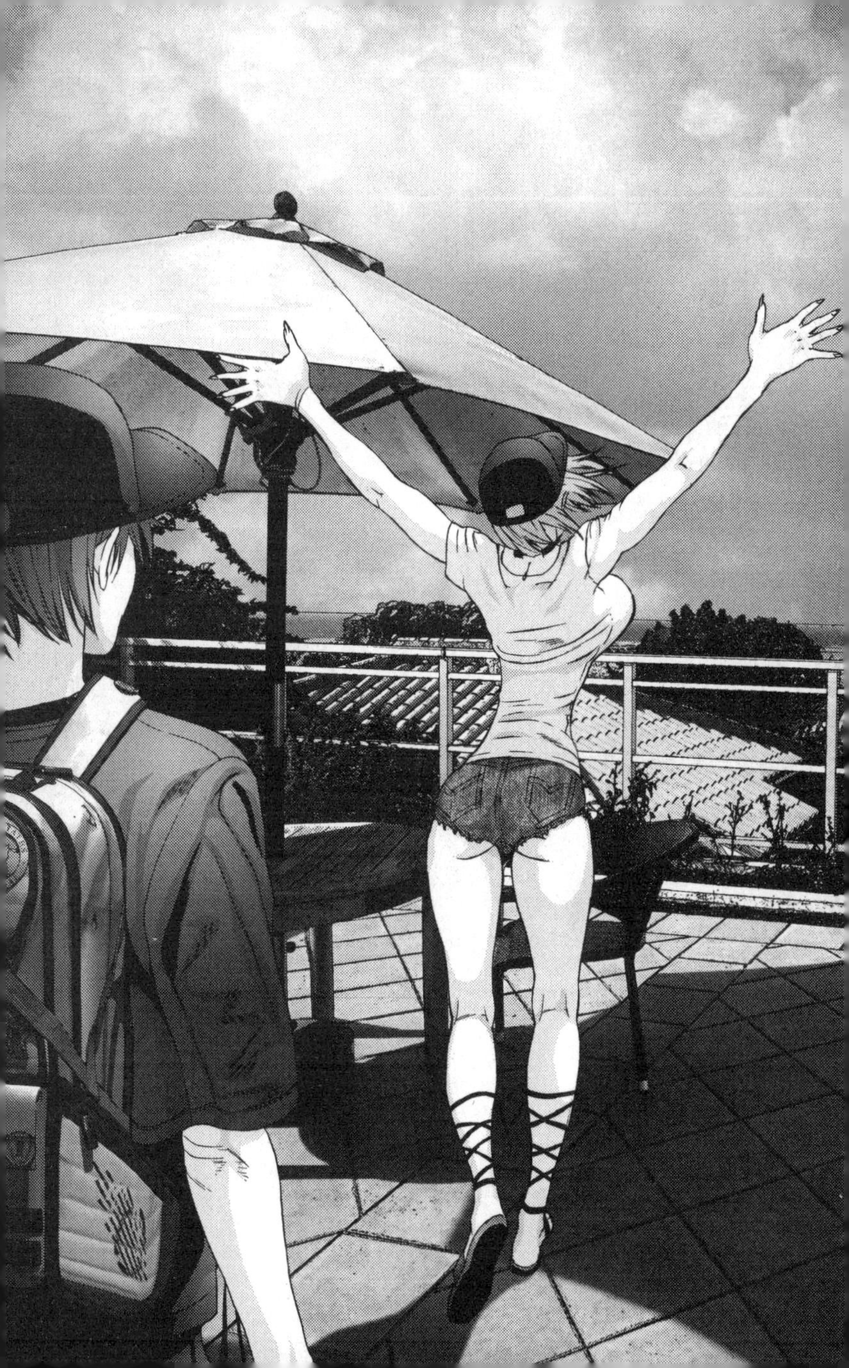

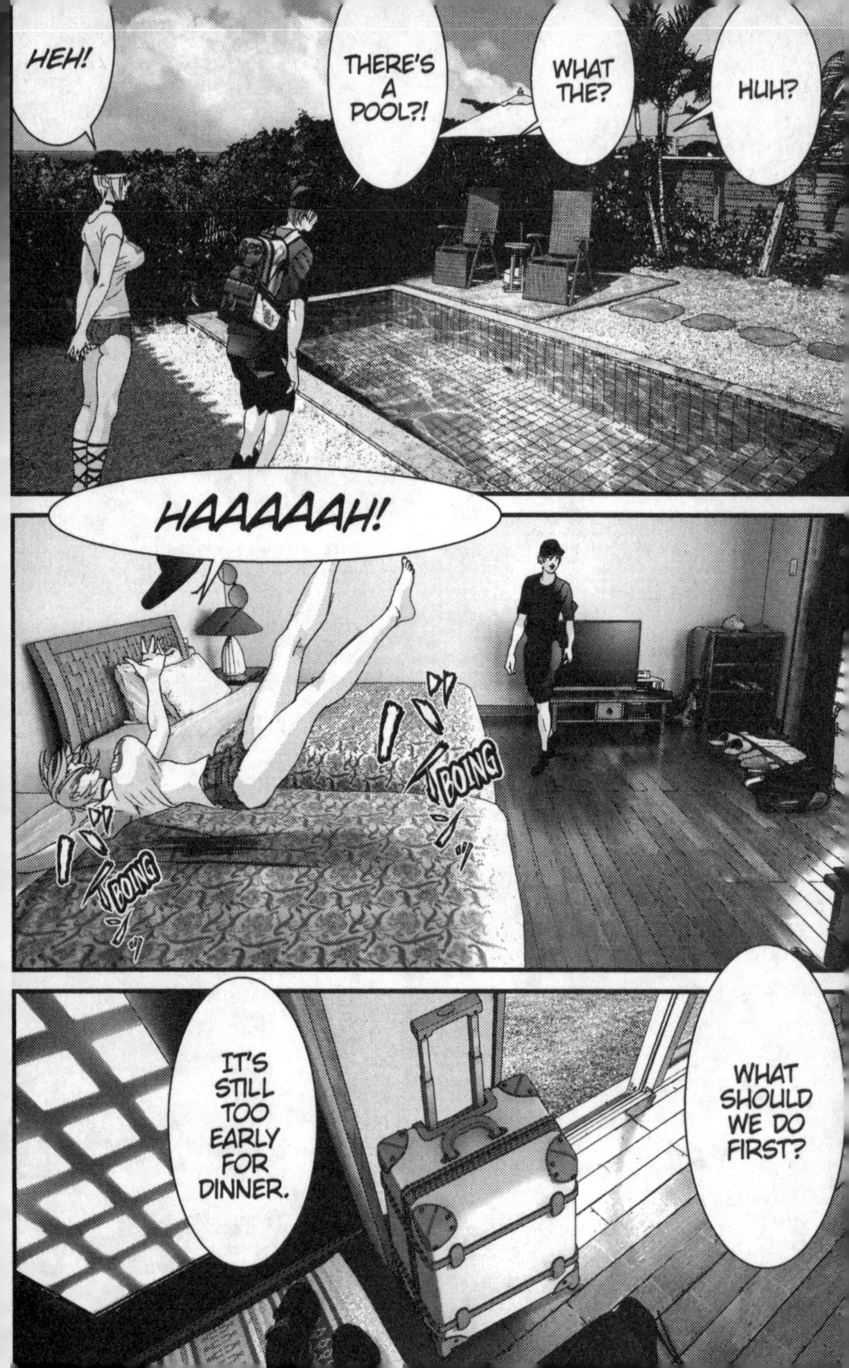
HUH?
WHAT THE?
THERE'S A POOL?!
HEH!
HAAAAAH!
BOING
BOING
WHAT SHOULD WE DO FIRST?
IT'S STILL TOO EARLY FOR DINNER.

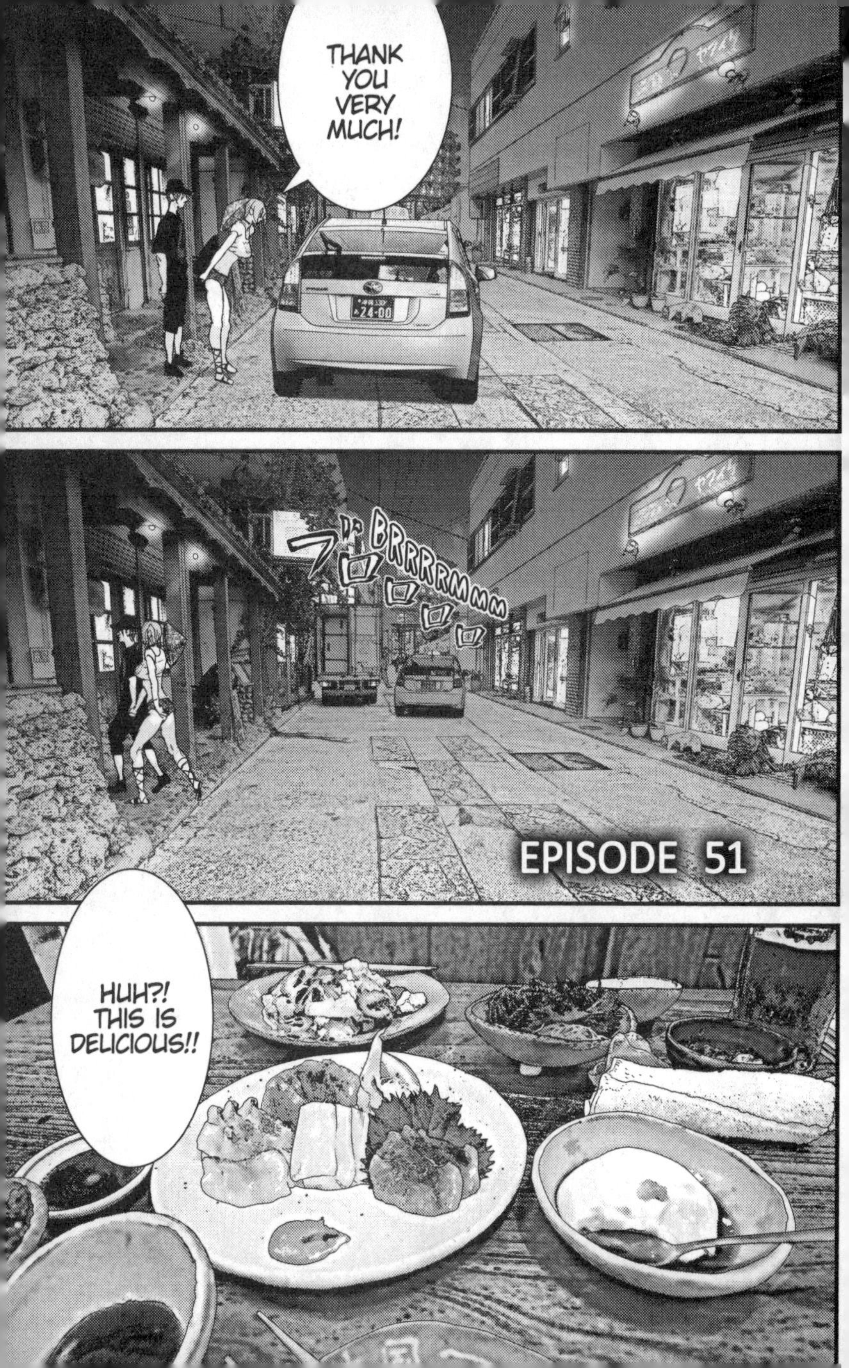
THANK YOU VERY MUCH!
BRRRRRMMM
EPISODE 51
HUH?! THIS IS DELICIOUS!!

EPISODE 51: POOL

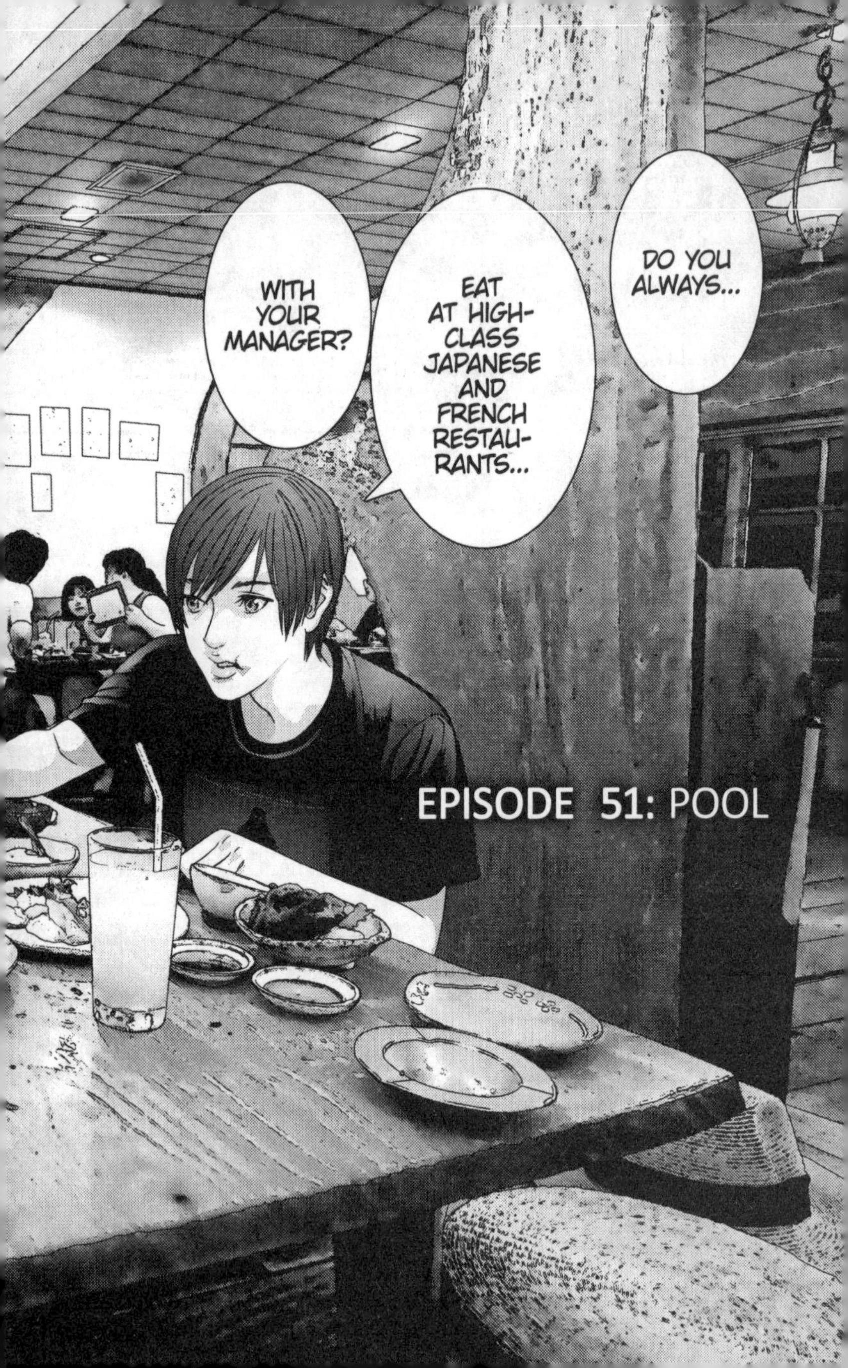
DO YOU ALWAYS...
EAT AT HIGH-CLASS JAPANESE AND FRENCH RESTAURANTS...
WITH YOUR MANAGER?

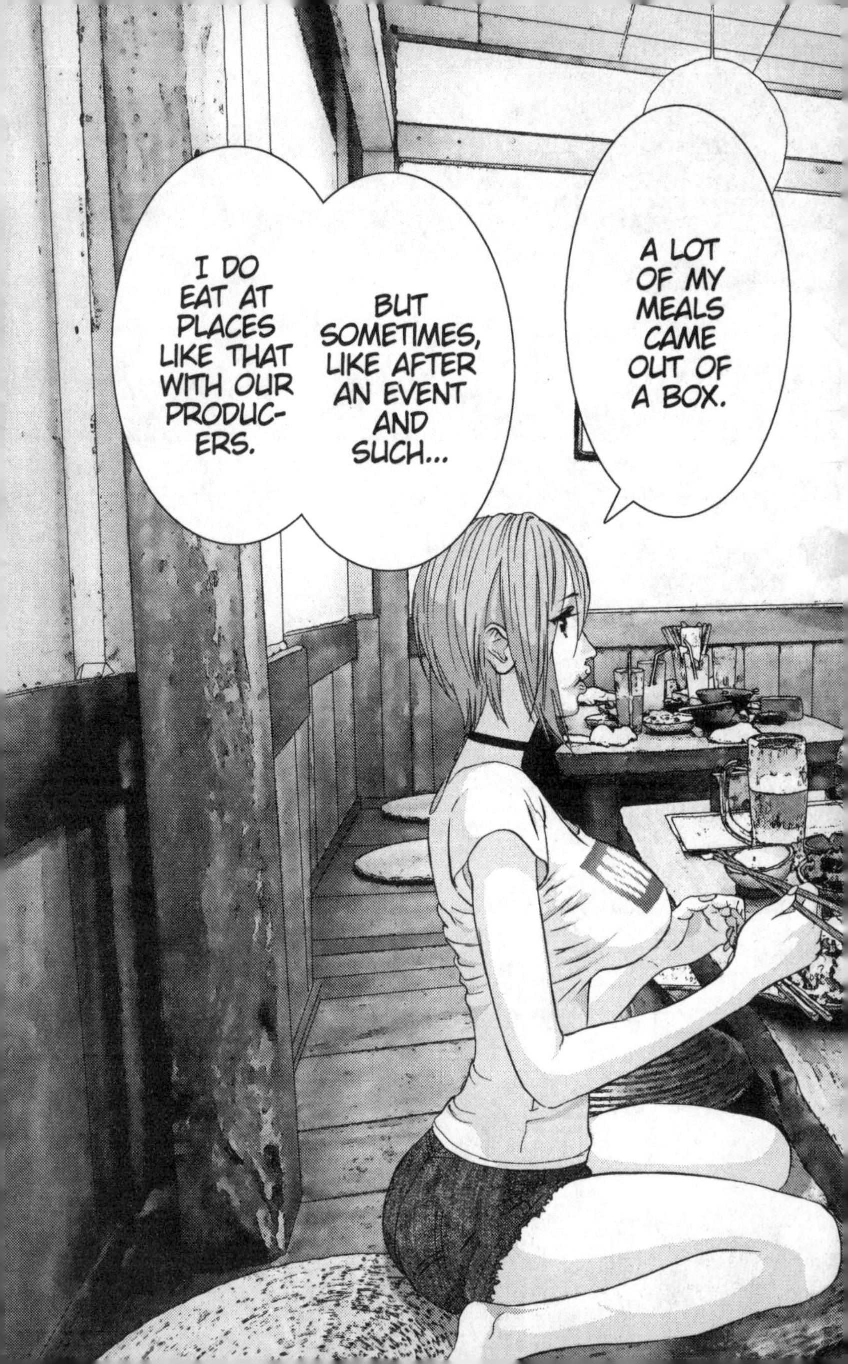
A LOT OF MY MEALS CAME OUT OF A BOX.
BUT SOMETIMES, LIKE AFTER AN EVENT AND SUCH...
I DO EAT AT PLACES LIKE THAT WITH OUR PRODUC-ERS.

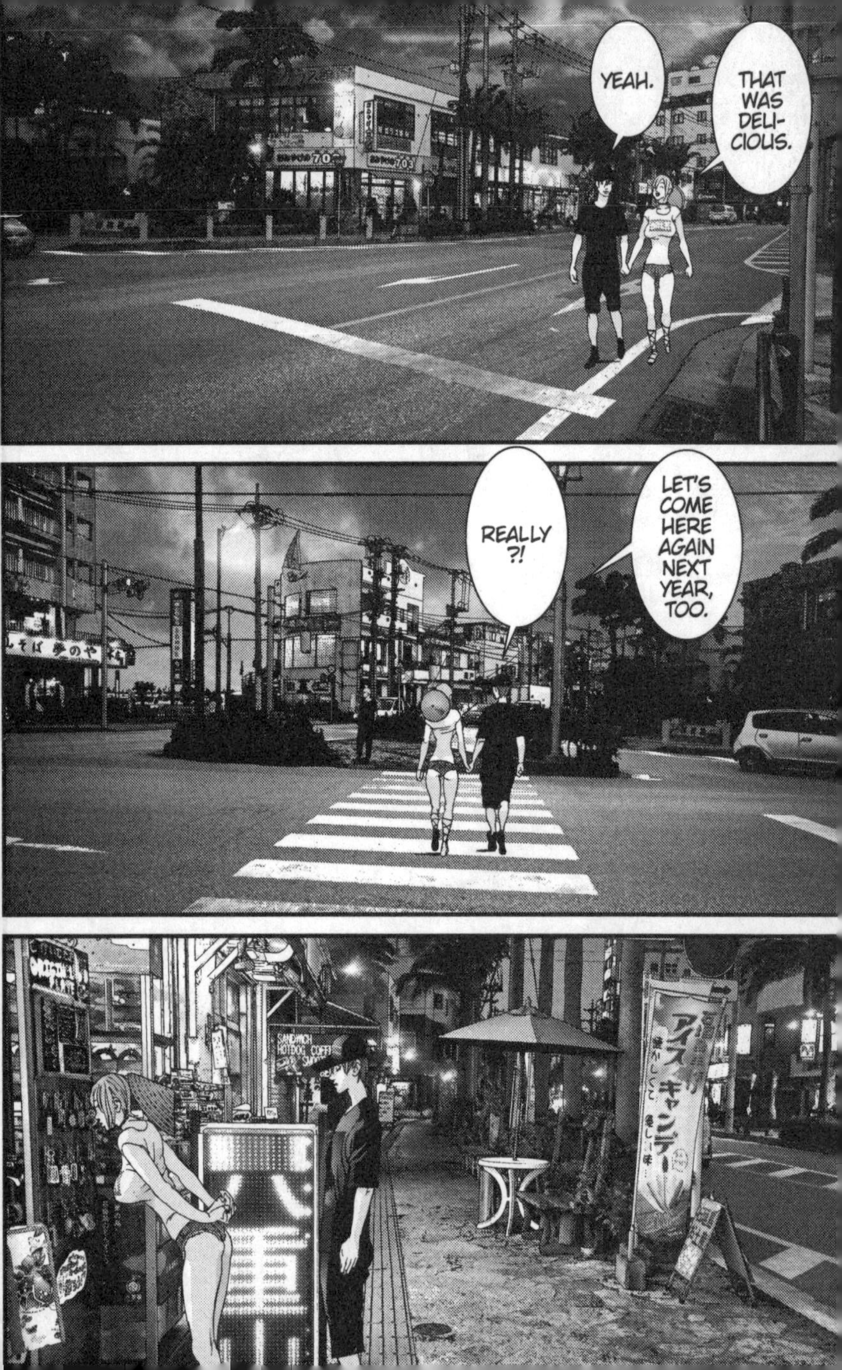
THAT WAS DELI-CIOUS.
YEAH.
LET'S COME HERE AGAIN NEXT YEAR, TOO.
REALLY ?!

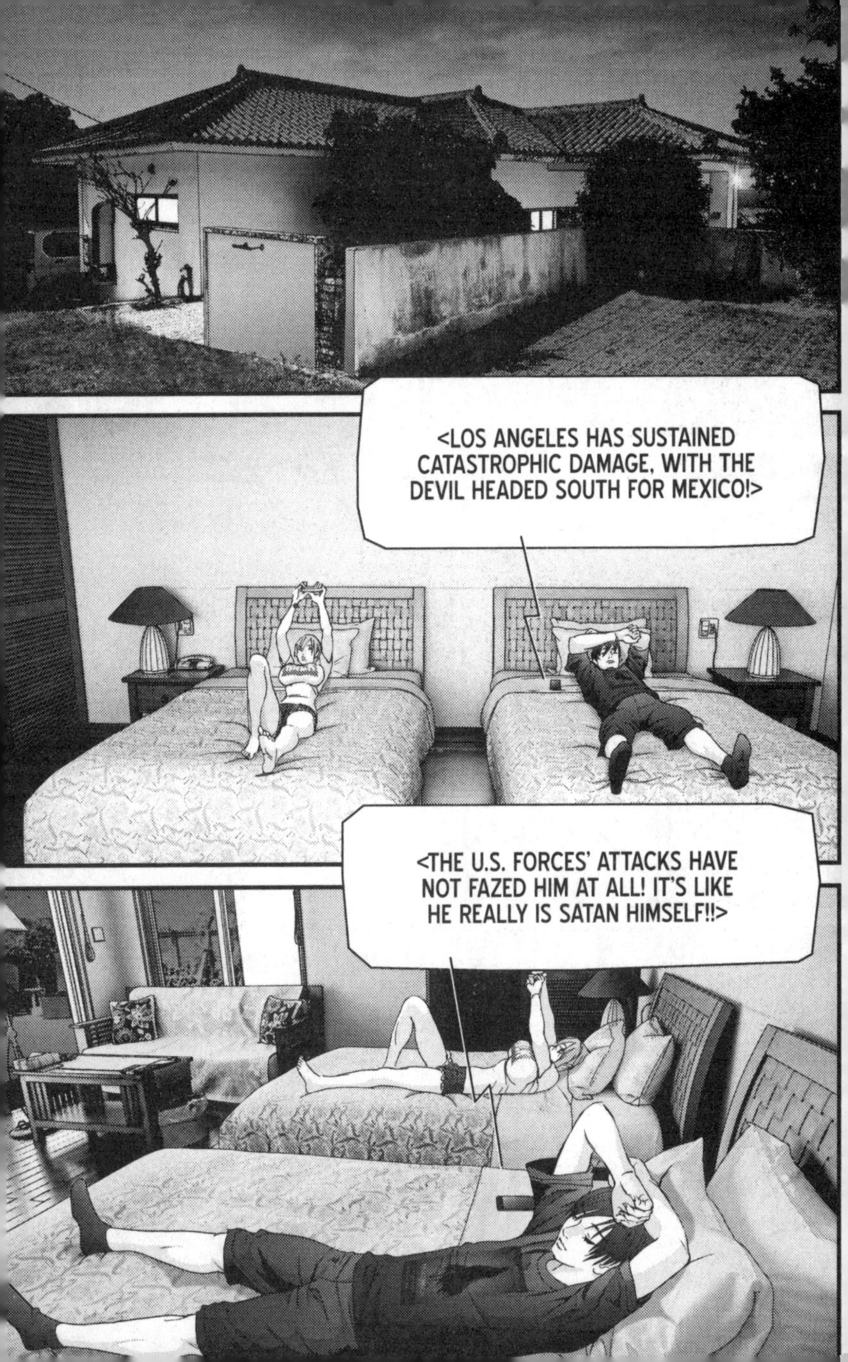
<LOS ANGELES HAS SUSTAINED CATASTROPHIC DAMAGE, WITH THE DEVIL HEADED SOUTH FOR MEXICO!>
<THE U.S. FORCES' ATTACKS HAVE NOT FAZED HIM AT ALL! IT'S LIKE HE REALLY IS SATAN HIMSELF!!>

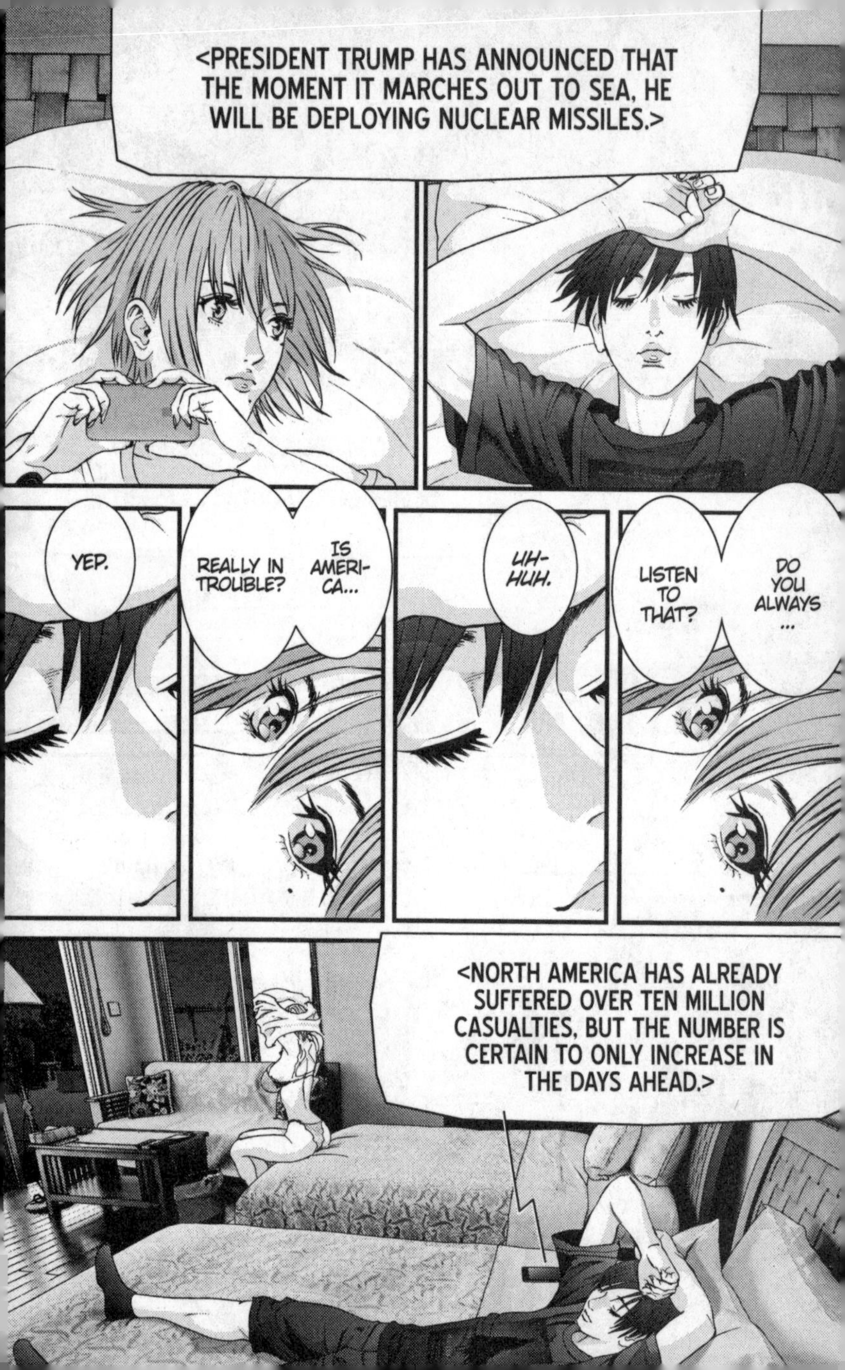
<PRESIDENT TRUMP HAS ANNOUNCED THAT THE MOMENT IT MARCHES OUT TO SEA, HE WILL BE DEPLOYING NUCLEAR MISSILES.>
DO YOU ALWAYS ...
LISTEN TO THAT?
UH-HUH.
IS AMERI-CA...
REALLY IN TROUBLE?
YEP.
<NORTH AMERICA HAS ALREADY SUFFERED OVER TEN MILLION CASUALTIES, BUT THE NUMBER IS CERTAIN TO ONLY INCREASE IN THE DAYS AHEAD.>

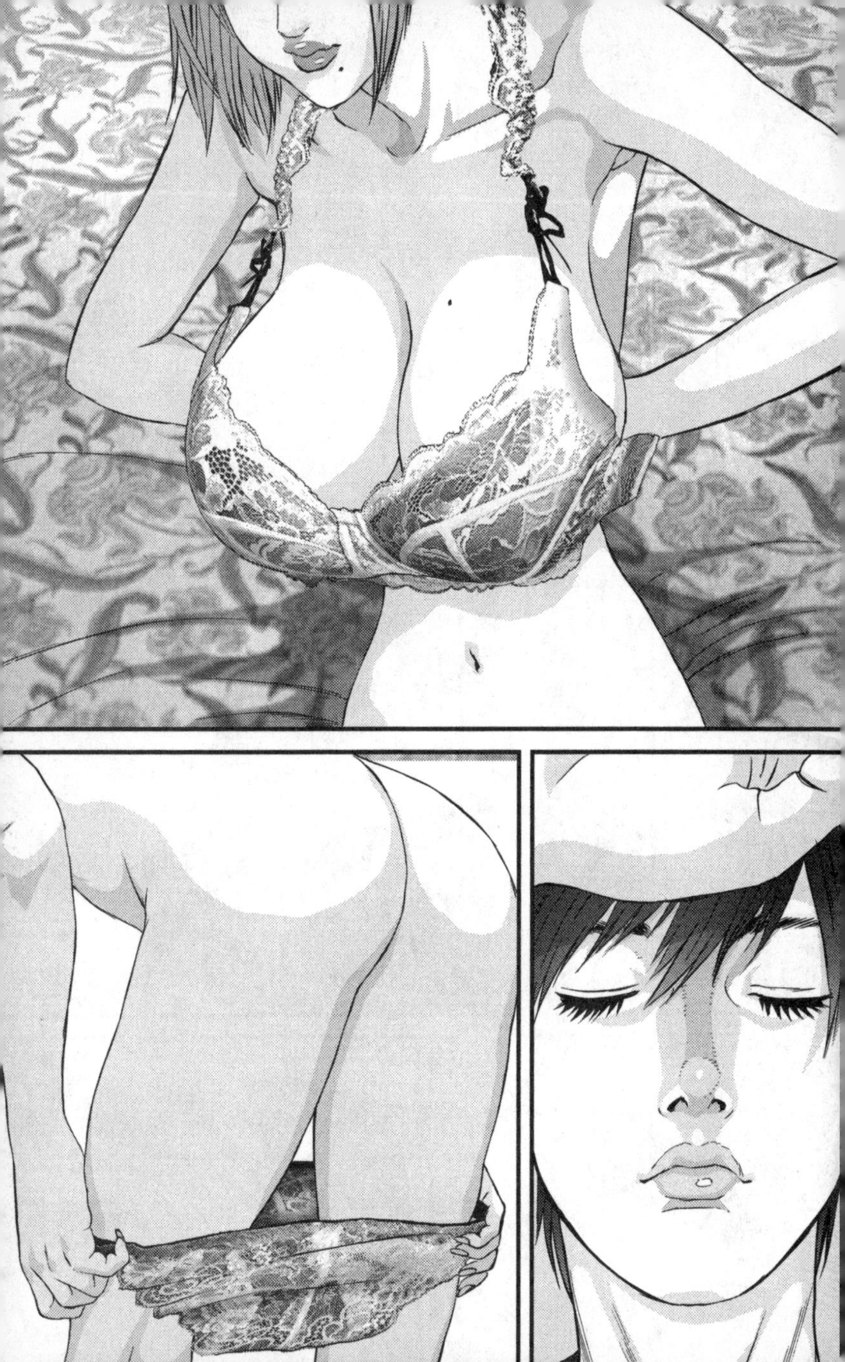

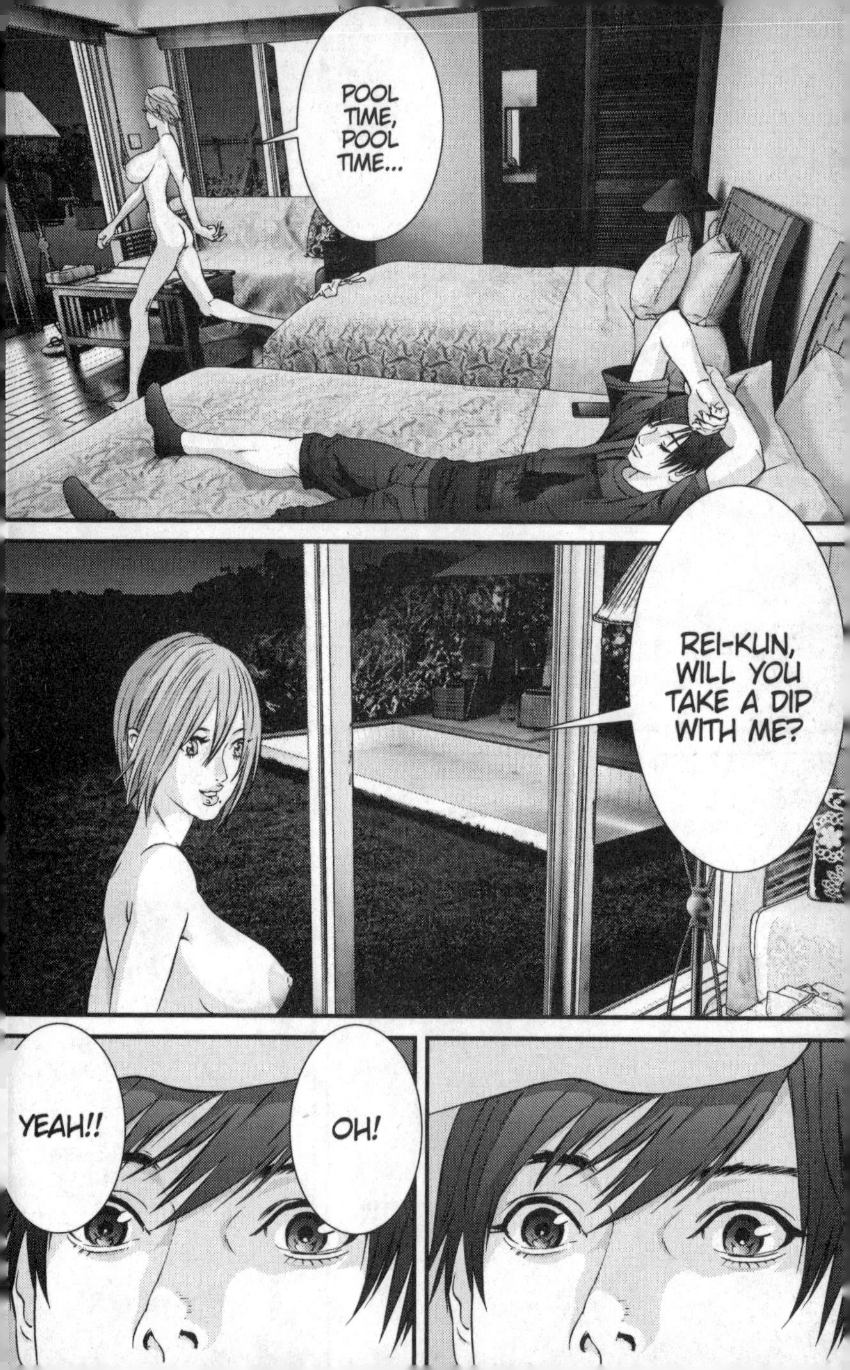
POOL TIME, POOL TIME...
REI-KUN, WILL YOU TAKE A DIP WITH ME?
OH!
YEAH!!

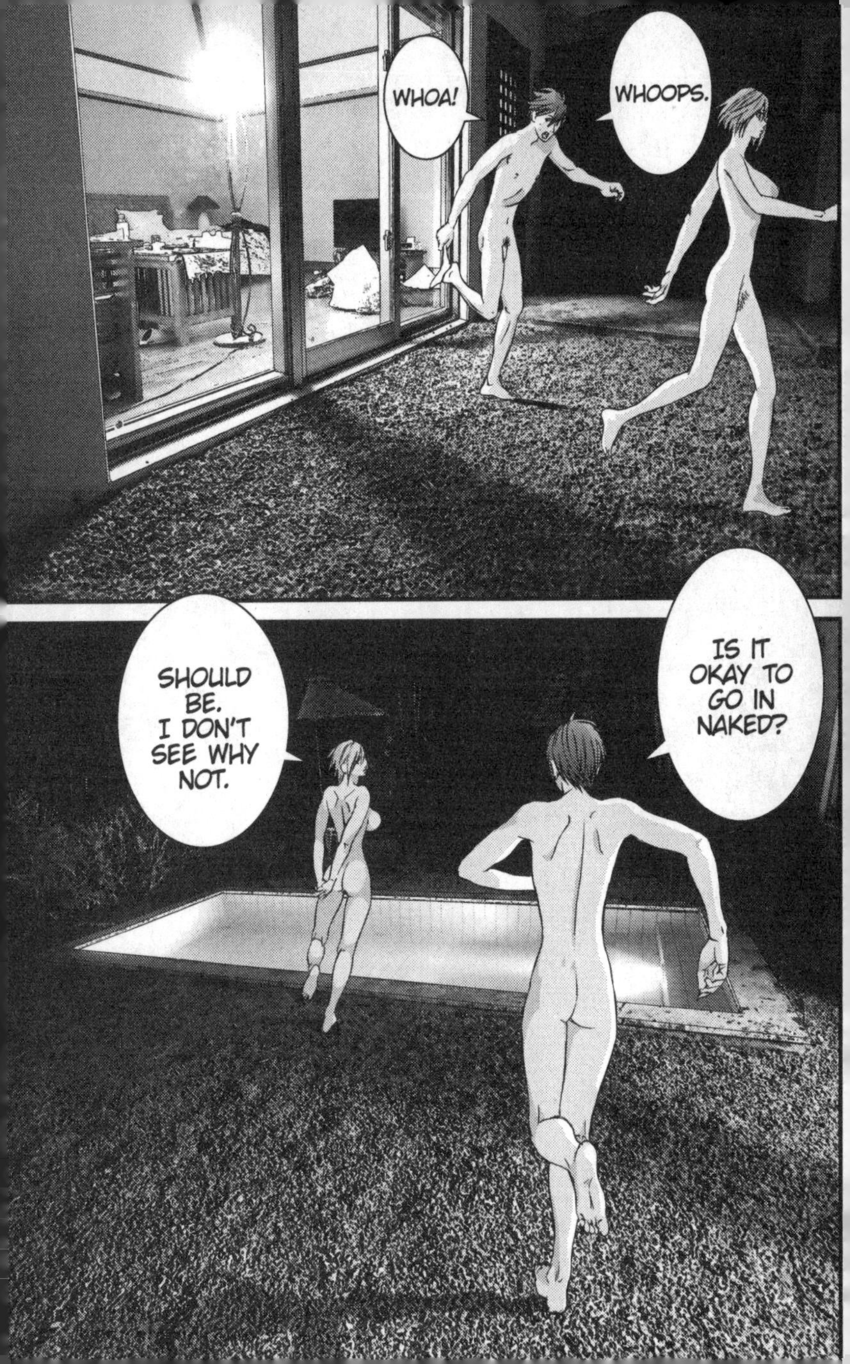
WHOOPS.
WHOA!
IS IT OKAY TO GO IN NAKED?
SHOULD BE. I DON'T SEE WHY NOT.

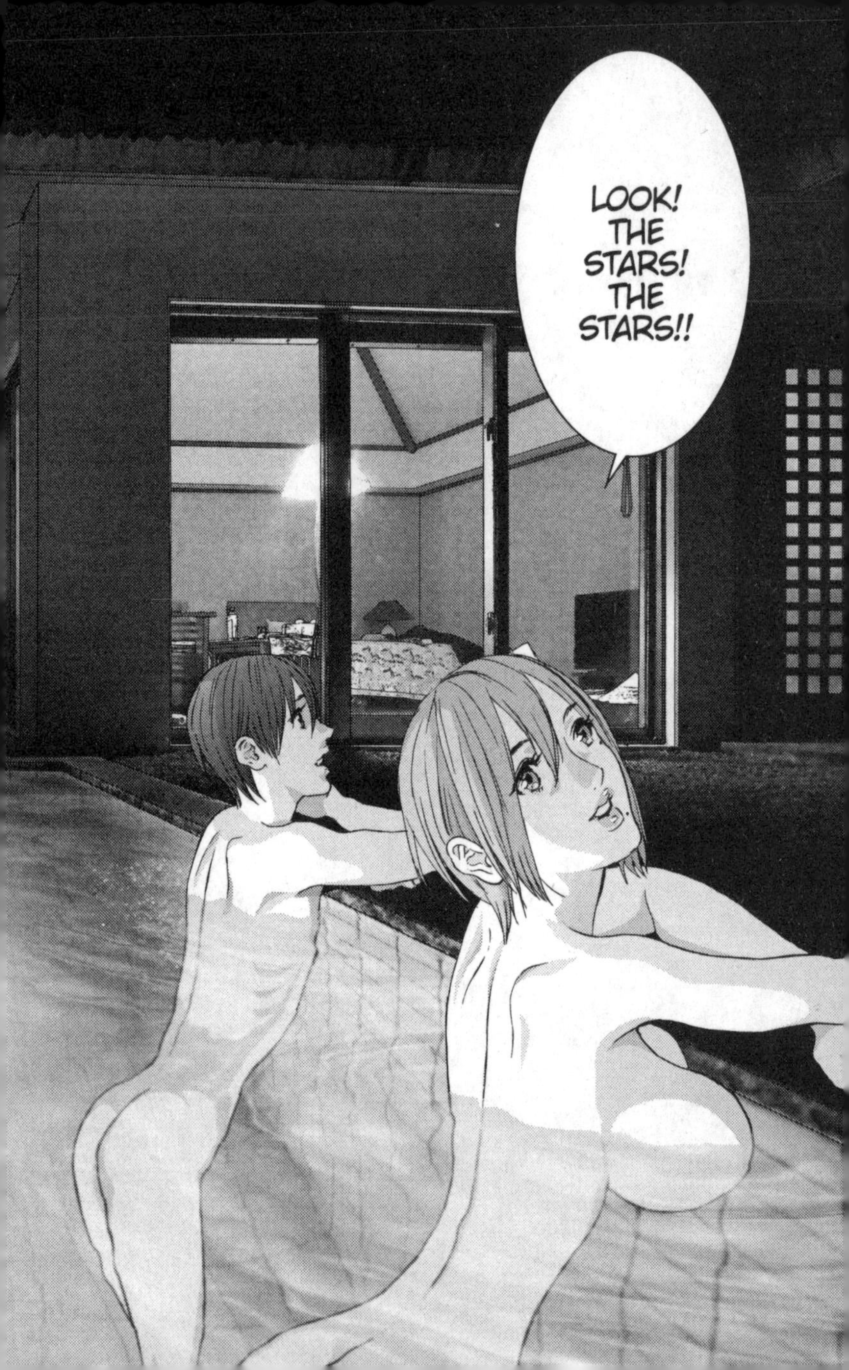
LOOK! THE STARS! THE STARS!!

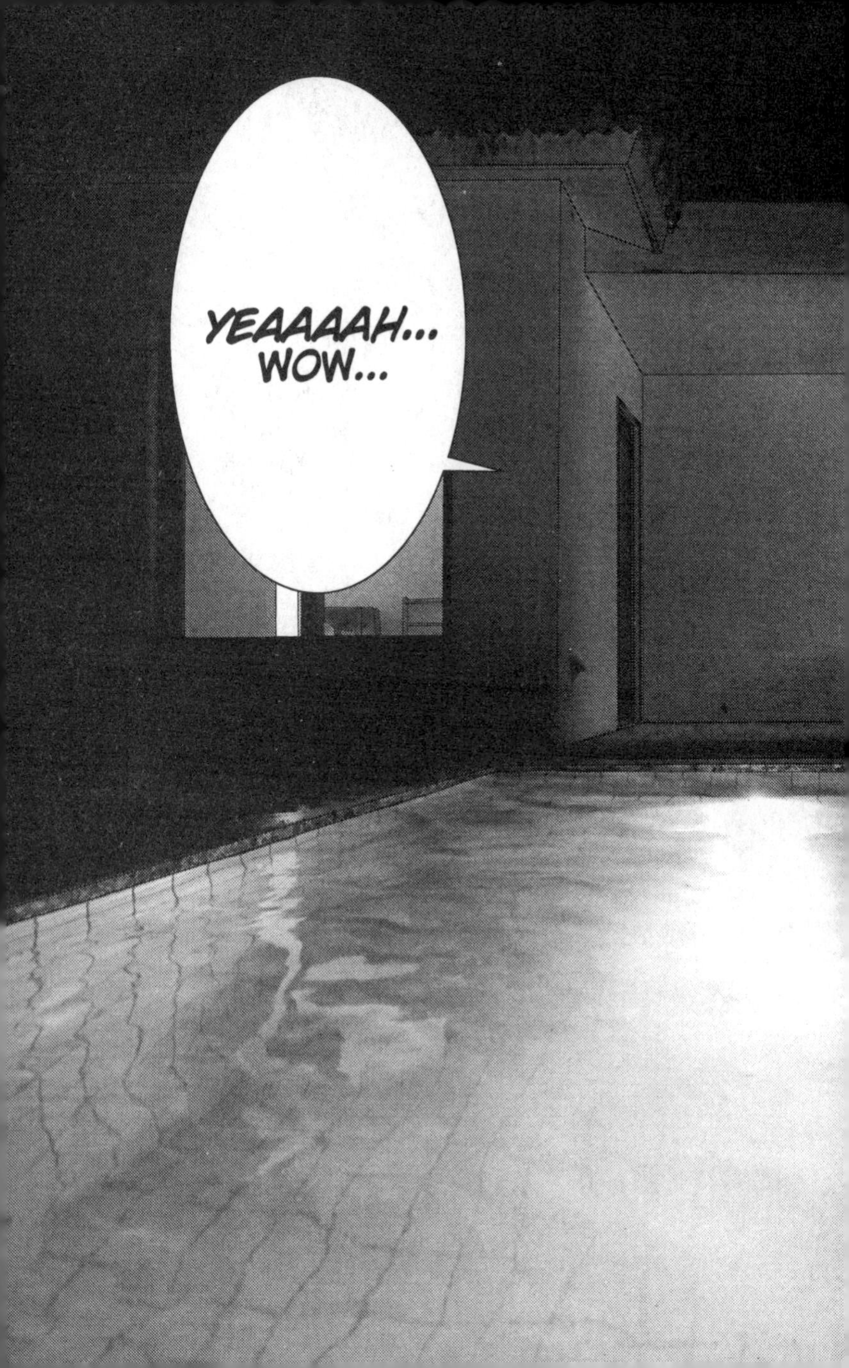
YEAAAAH... WOW...

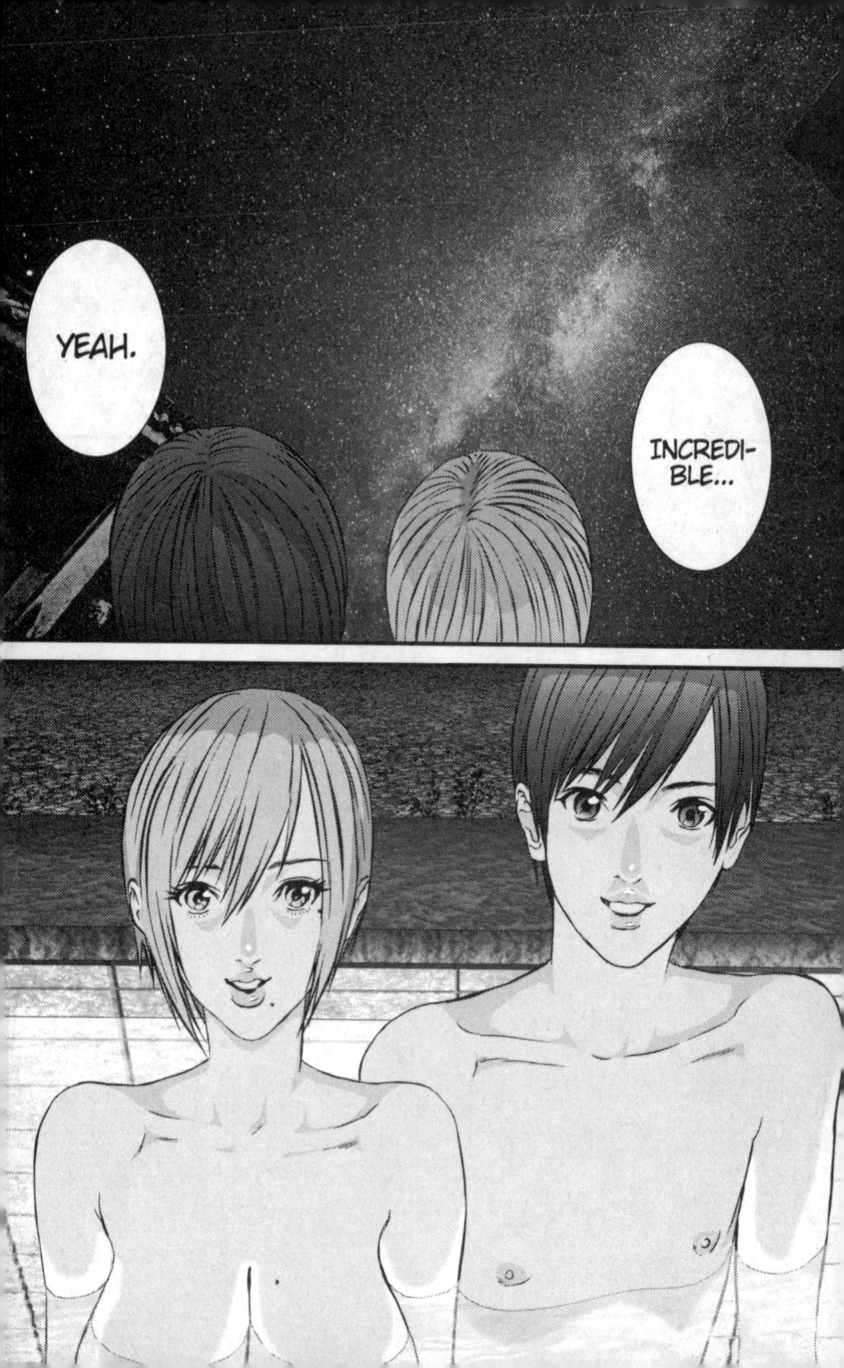
INCREDIBLE...
YEAH.

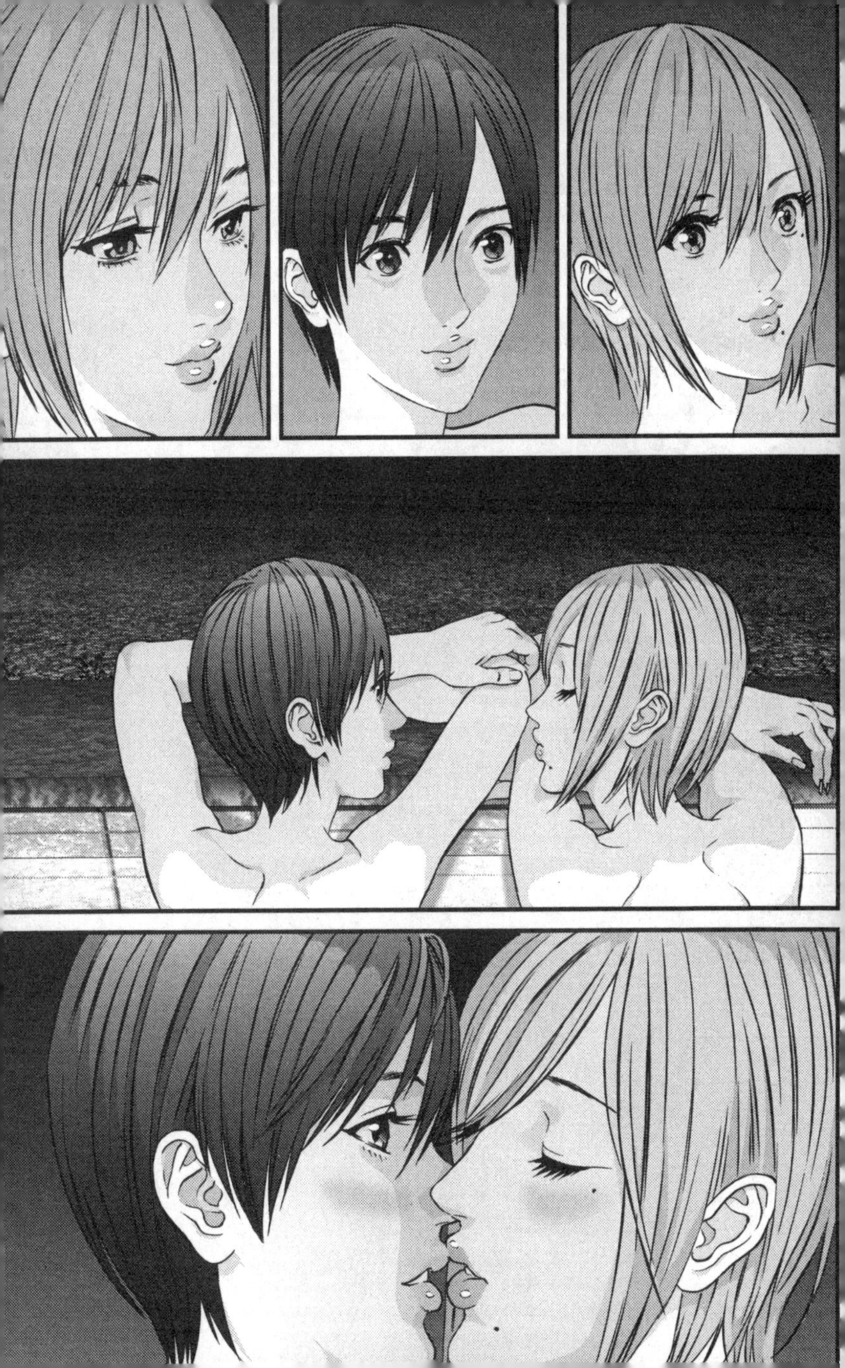

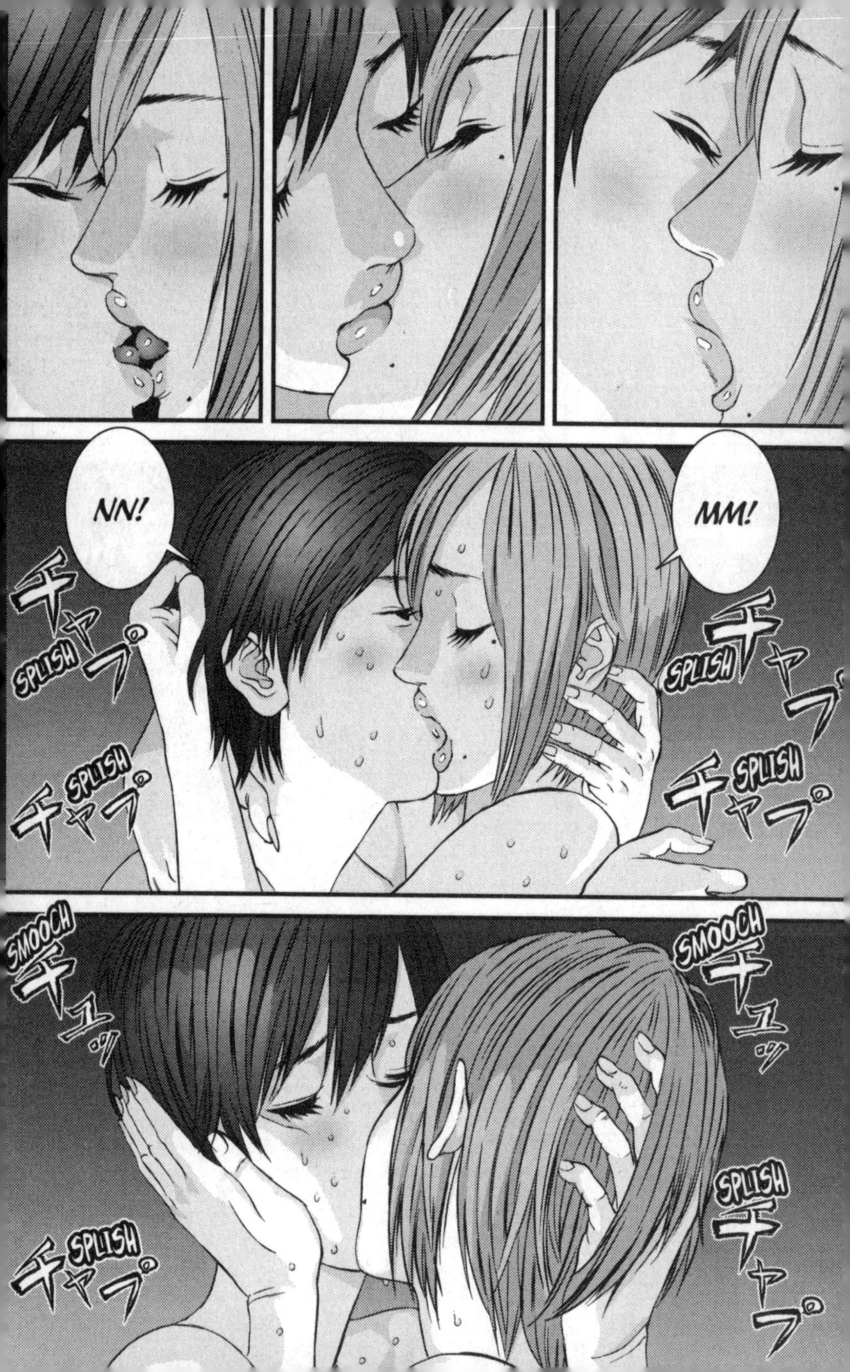
MM!
SPLISH
チャプ
SPLISH
チャプ
NN!
SPLISH
チャプ
SPLISH
チャプ
SMOOCH
チュッ
SPLISH
チャプ
SMOOCH
チュッ
SPLISH
チャプ

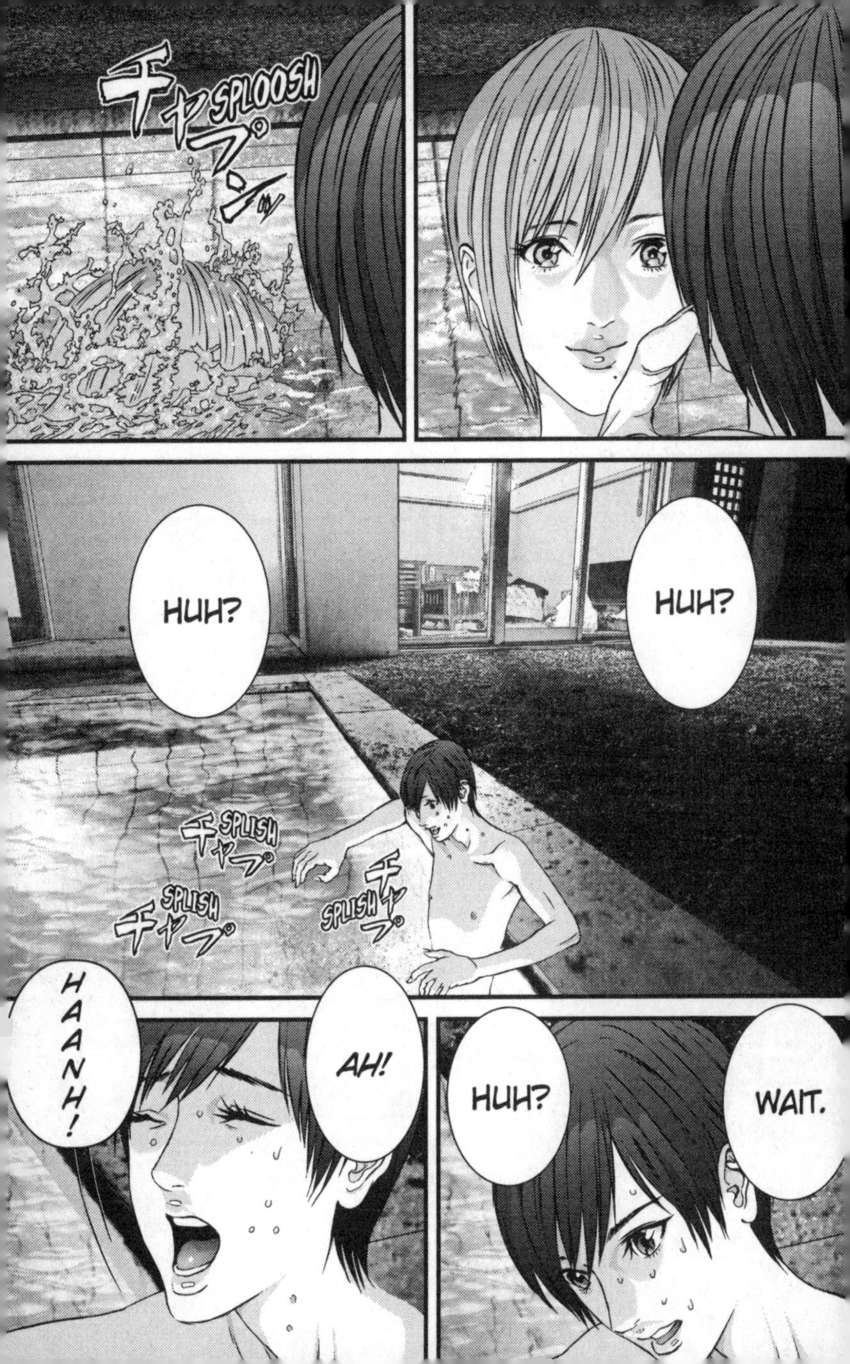

チャプン
SPLOOSH
HUH?
HUH?
チャプ
SPLISH
チャプ
SPLISH
チャプ
SPLISH
WAIT.
HUH?
AH!
HAAANH!

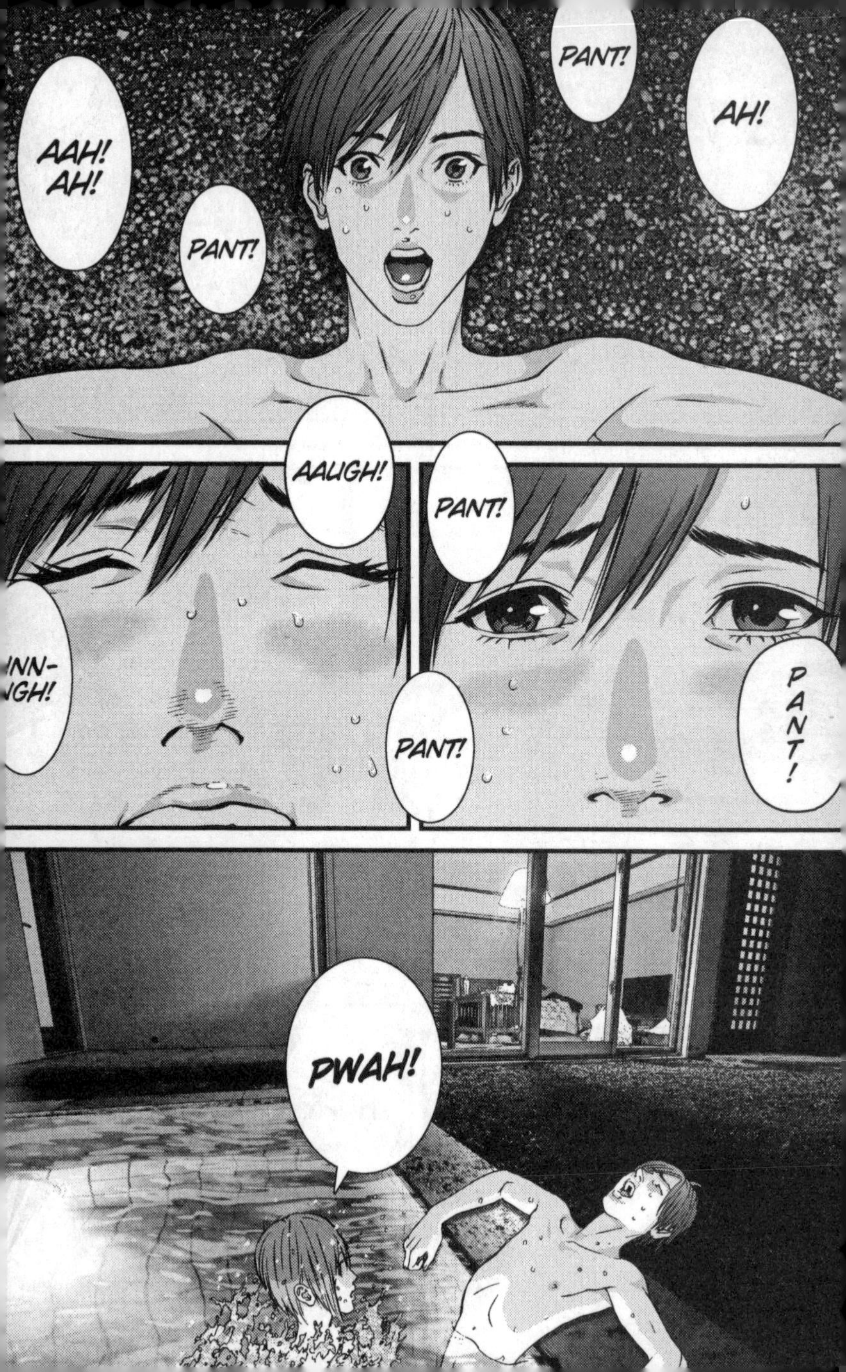
PANT!
AH!
AAH! AH!
PANT!
PANT!
PANT!
PANT!
AAUGH!
NN-NGH!
PWAH!

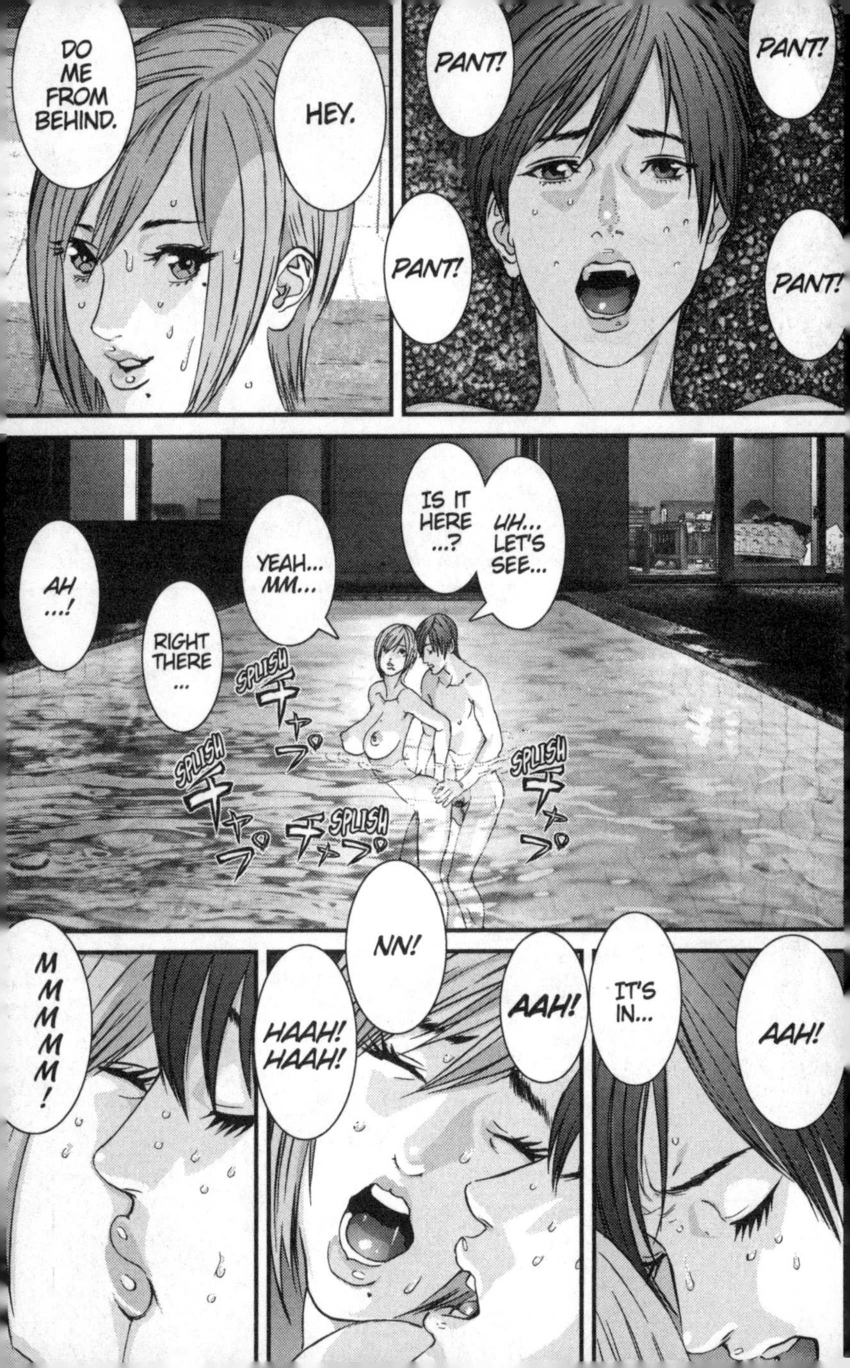
PANT!
PANT!
PANT!
PANT!
HEY.
DO ME FROM BEHIND.
UH... LET'S SEE...
IS IT HERE ...?
YEAH... MM...
SPLISH
SPLISH
SPLISH
RIGHT THERE ...
AH ...!
SPLISH
AAH!
IT'S IN...
AAH!
NN!
HAAH! HAAH!
MMMMMM!

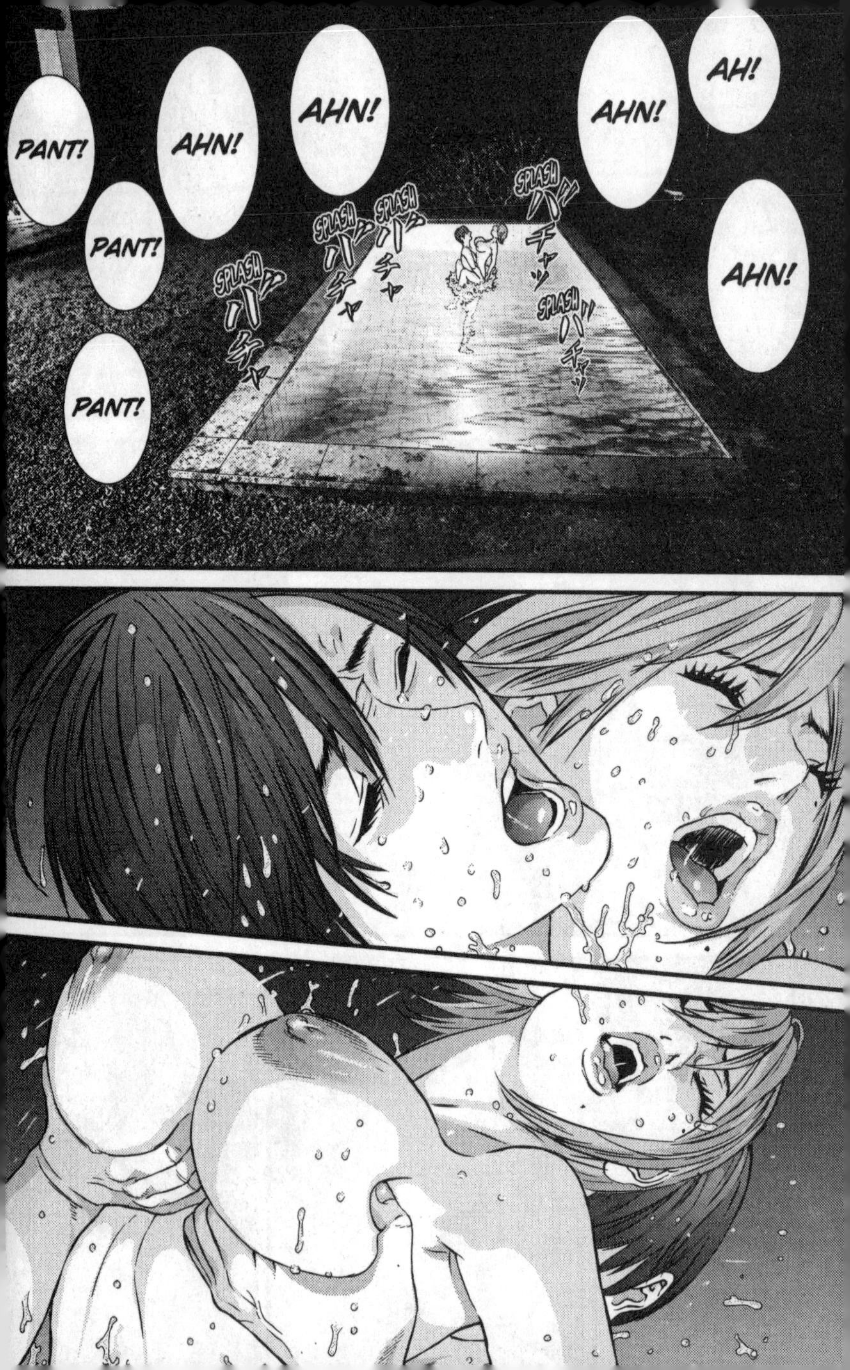

AH!
AHN!
AHN!
SPLASH
SPLASH
AHN!
SPLASH
SPLASH
AHN!
PANT!
PANT!
SPLASH
PANT!

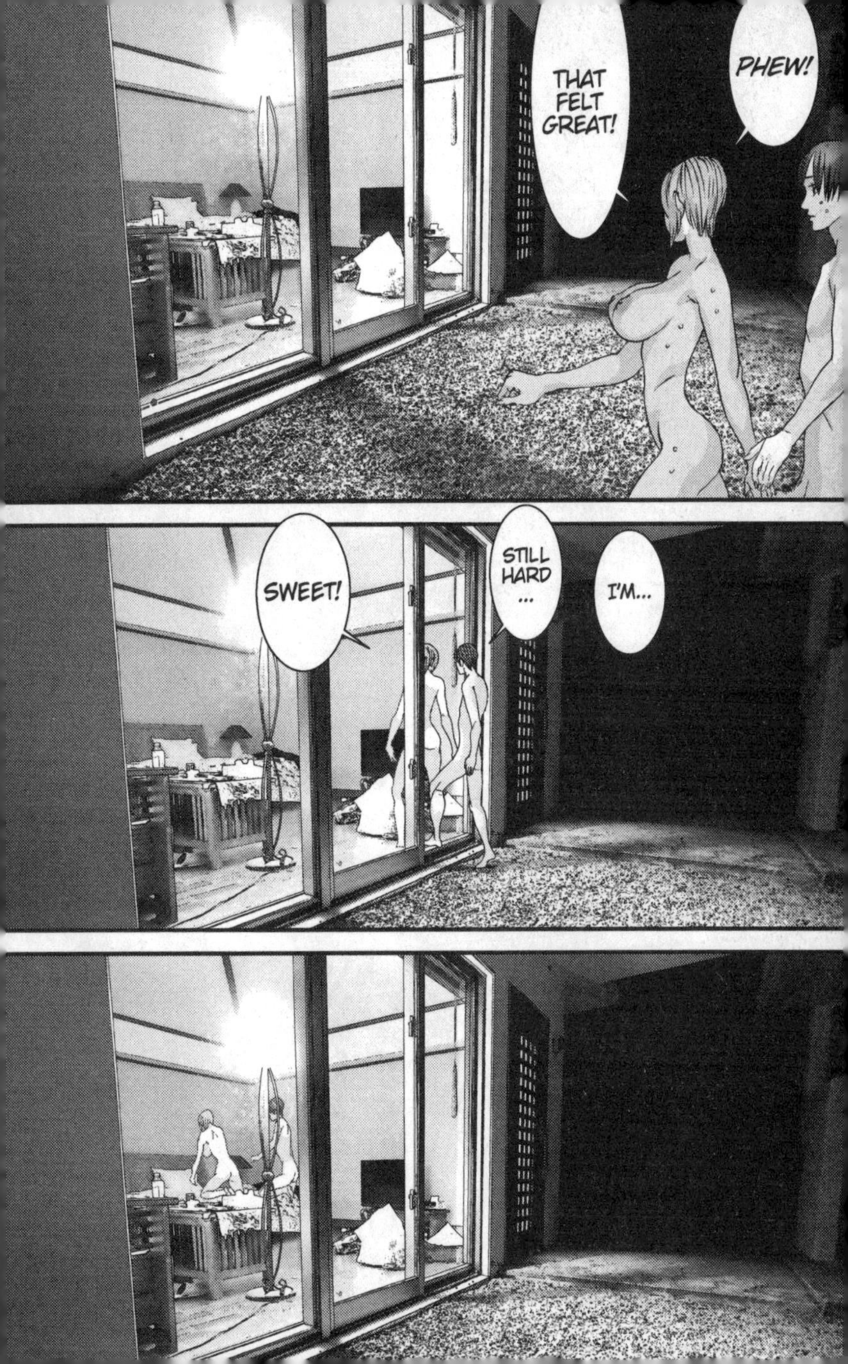
PHEW!
THAT FELT GREAT!
I'M...
STILL HARD ...
SWEET!

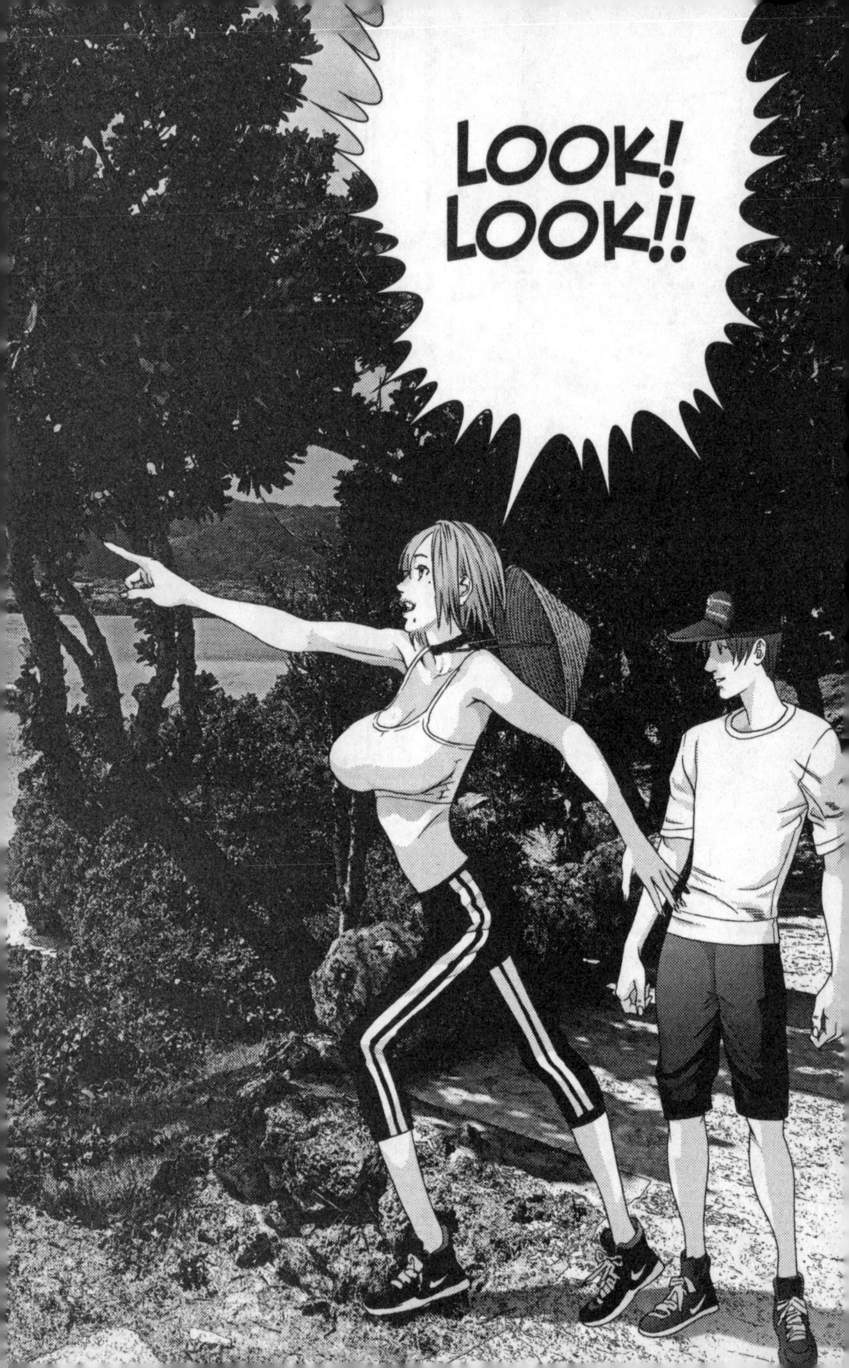
LOOK!
LOOK!!

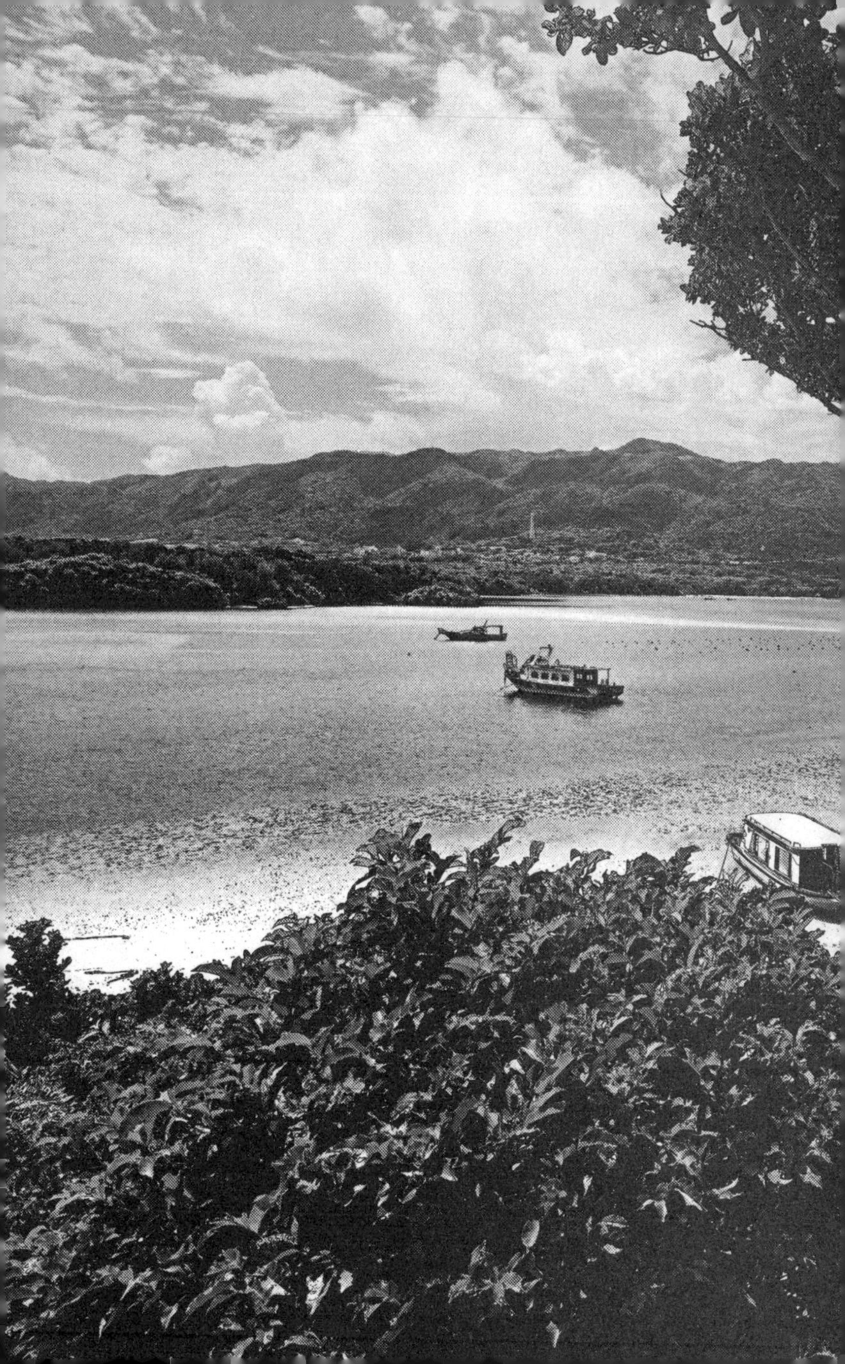

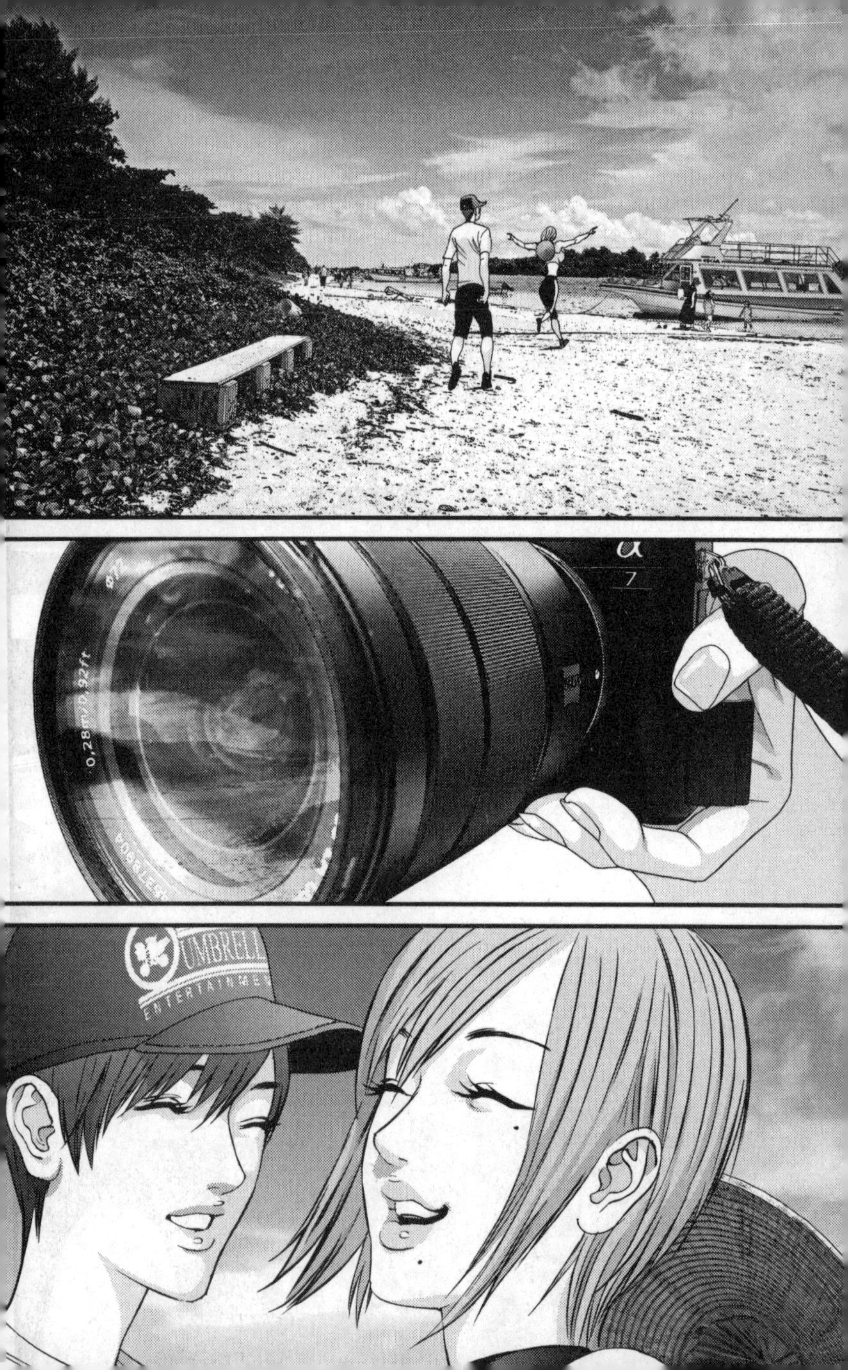

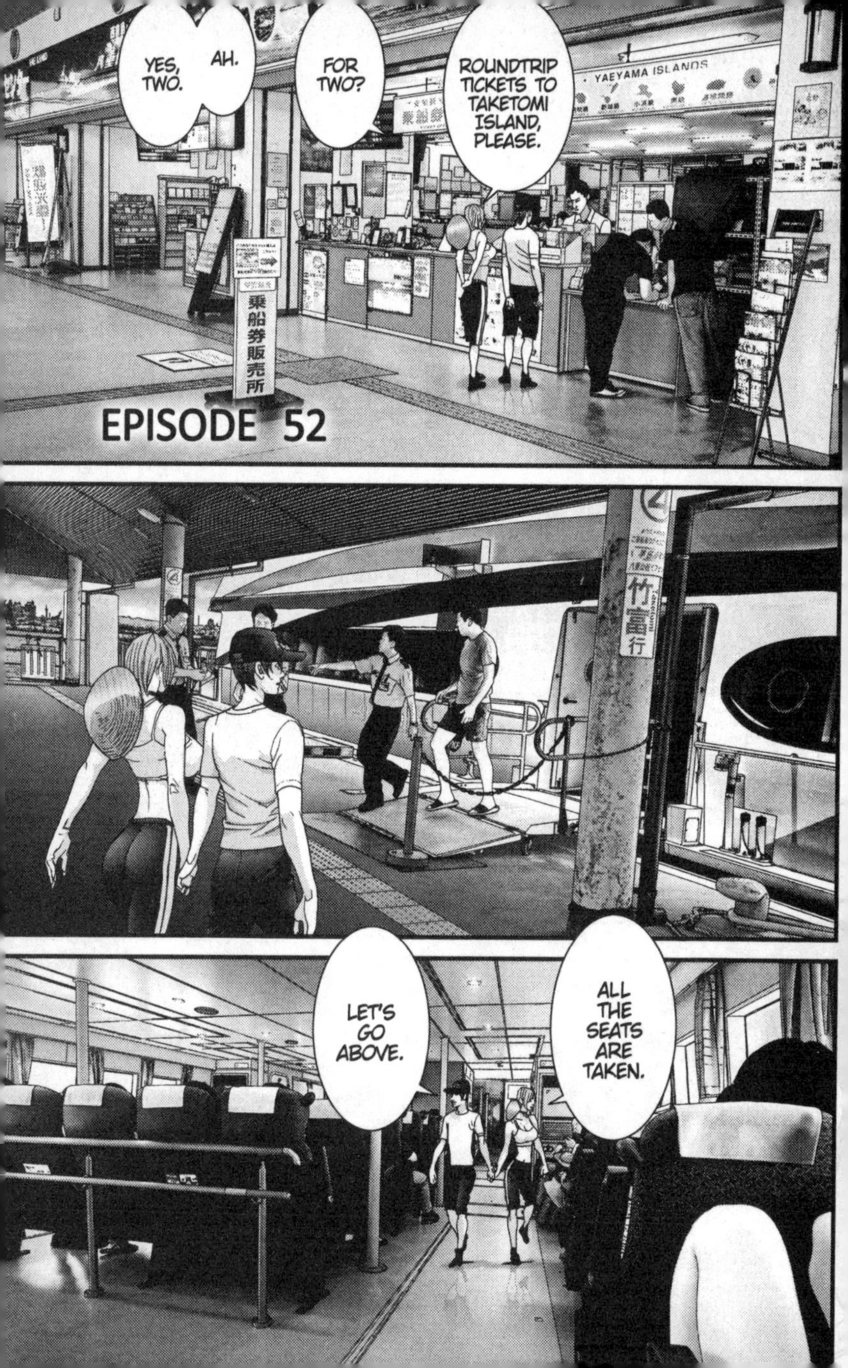
ROUNDTRIP TICKETS TO TAKETOMI ISLAND, PLEASE.
FOR TWO?
AH.
YES, TWO.
YAEYAMA ISLANDS
乗船券販売所
EPISODE 52
竹富行
ALL THE SEATS ARE TAKEN.
LET'S GO ABOVE.

EPISODE 52: CHIHO-SAN

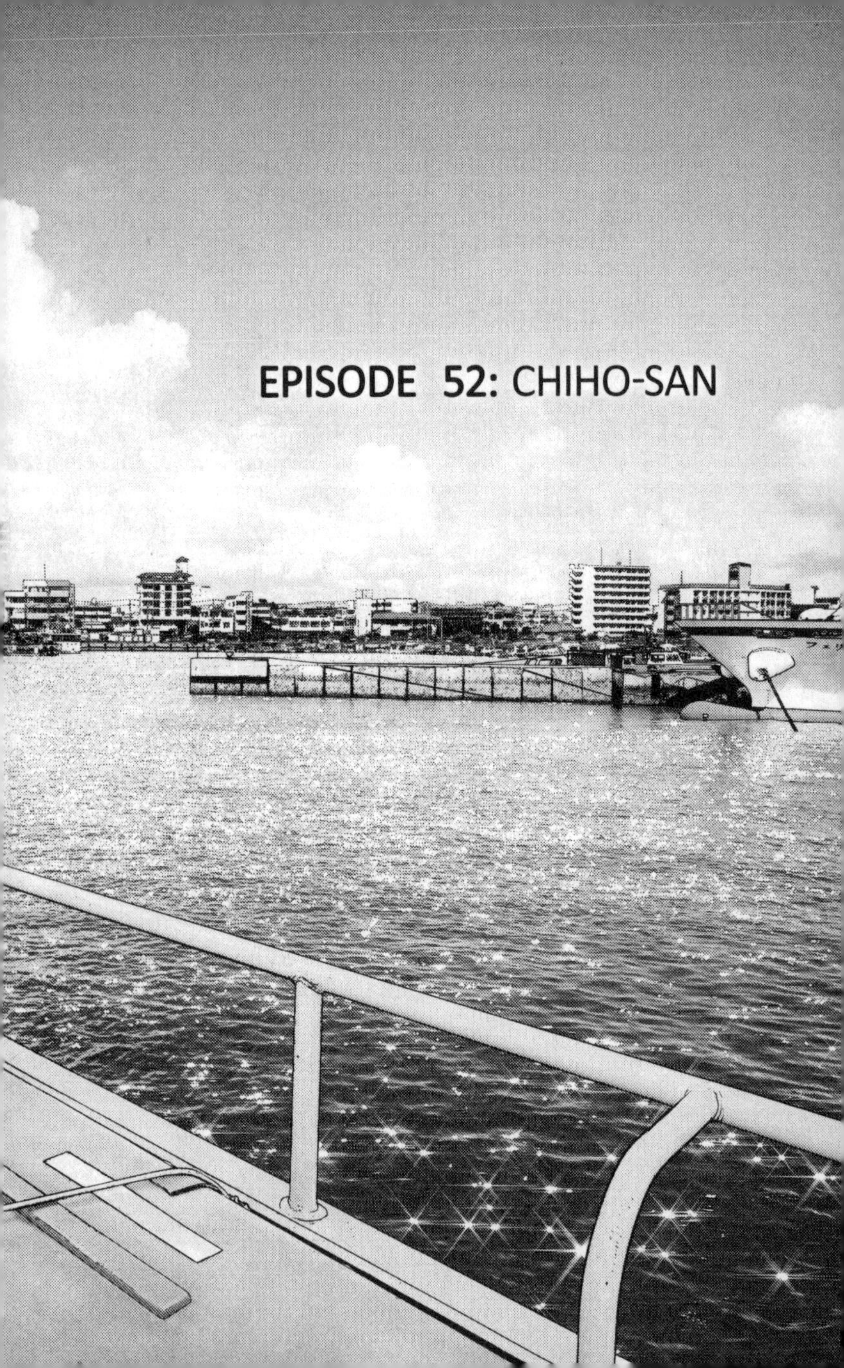

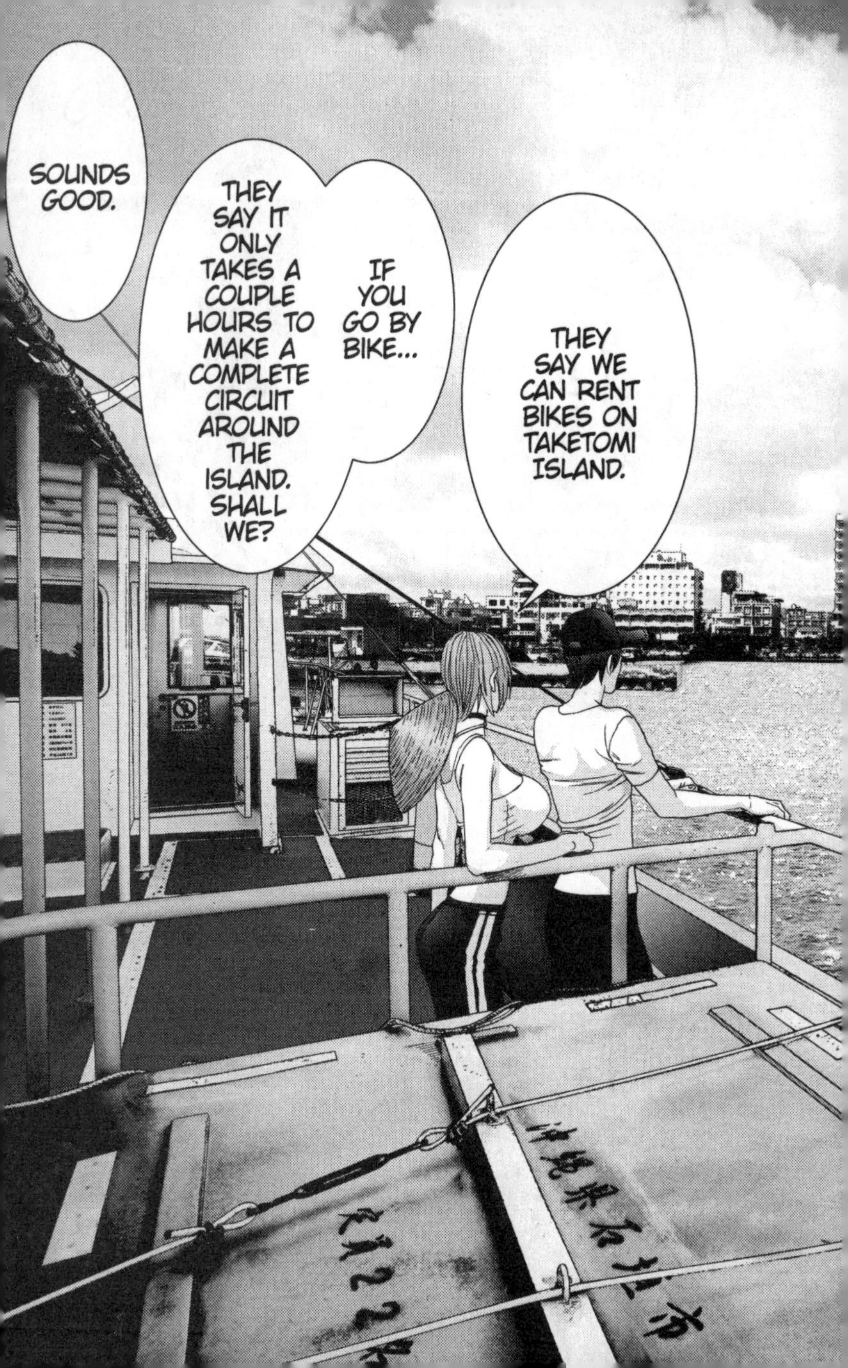
THEY SAY WE CAN RENT BIKES ON TAKETOMI ISLAND.
IF YOU GO BY BIKE...
THEY SAY IT ONLY TAKES A COUPLE HOURS TO MAKE A COMPLETE CIRCUIT AROUND THE ISLAND. SHALL WE?
SOUNDS GOOD.

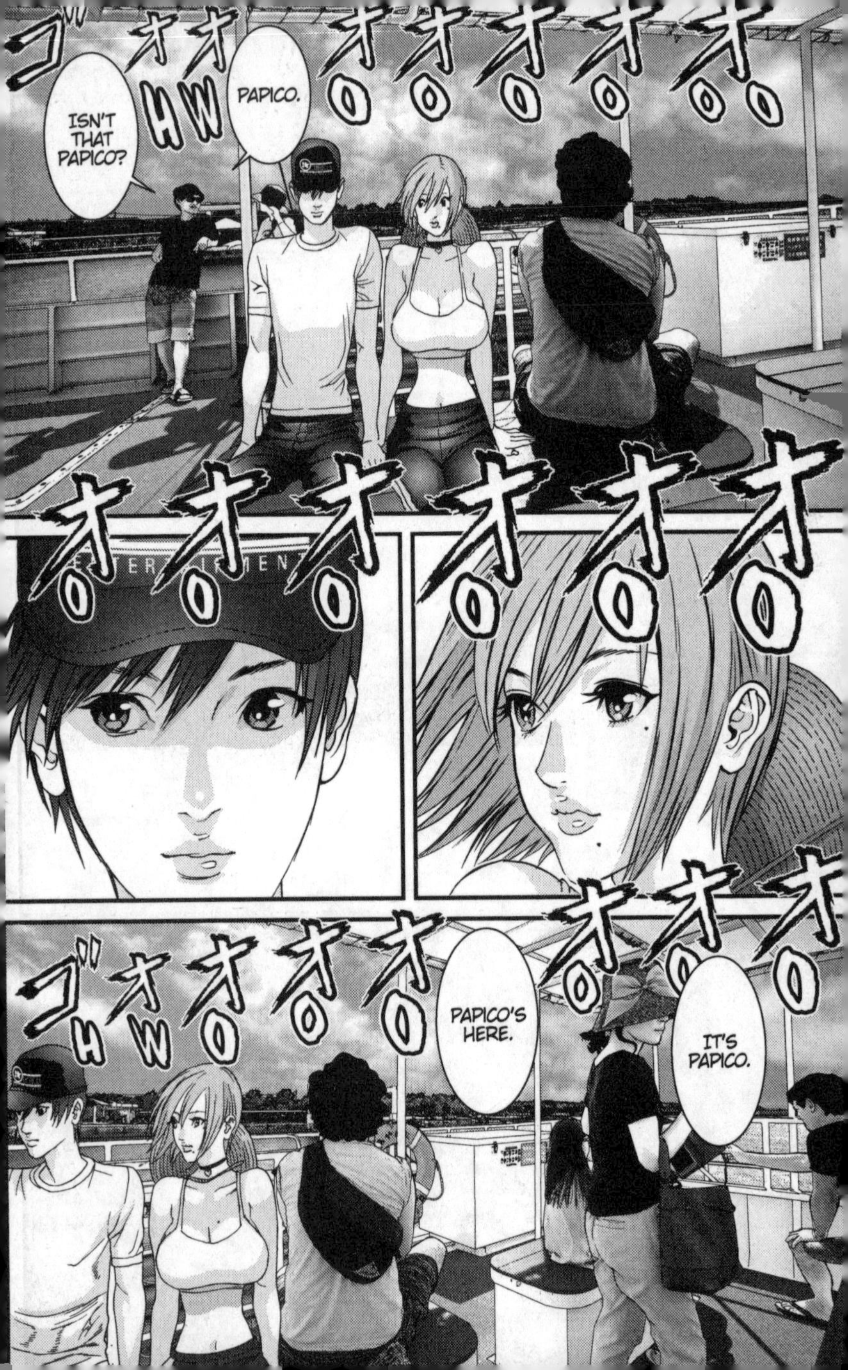

ゴォオオオオオオ
HWOOOOOO
PAPICO.
ISN'T THAT PAPICO?
オオオオオオ
OOOOOO
ゴォオオオオオオオ
HWOOOOOOO
IT'S PAPICO.
PAPICO'S HERE.

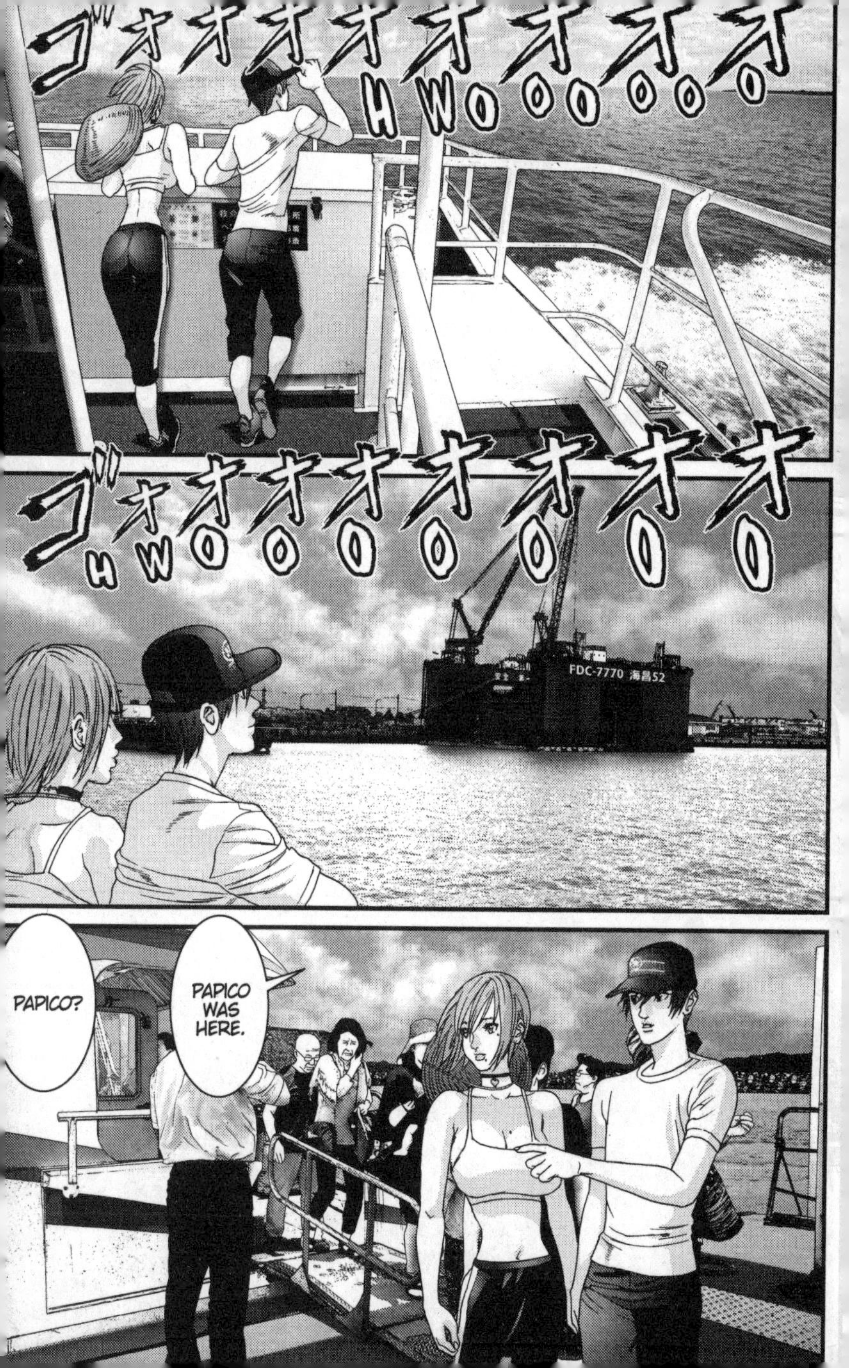
ゴォオオオオオオ
HWOOOOOO
ゴォオオオオオオオ
HWOOOOOOO
FDC-7770 海昌52
PAPICO WAS HERE.
PAPICO?

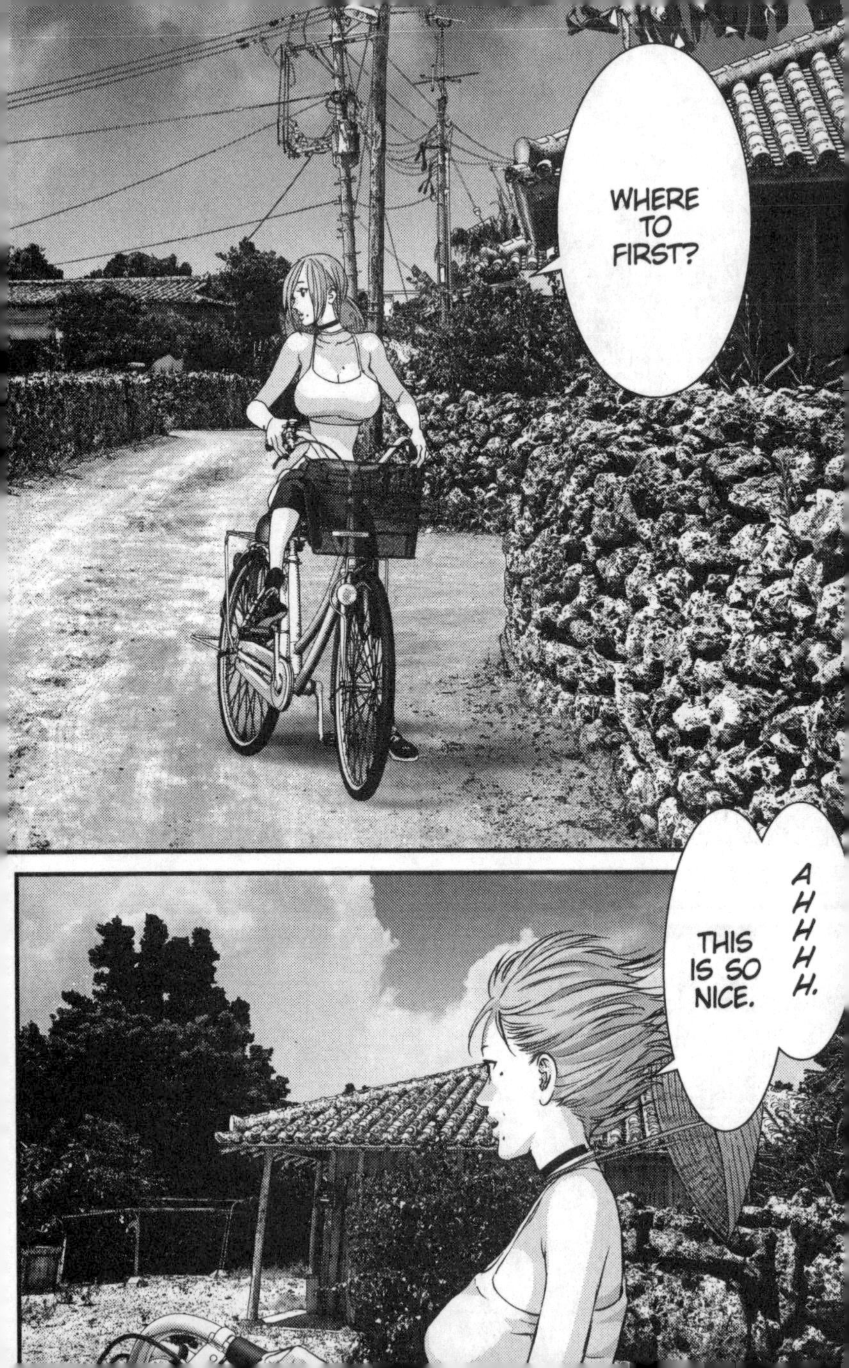
WHERE TO FIRST?
AHHHH.
THIS IS SO NICE.

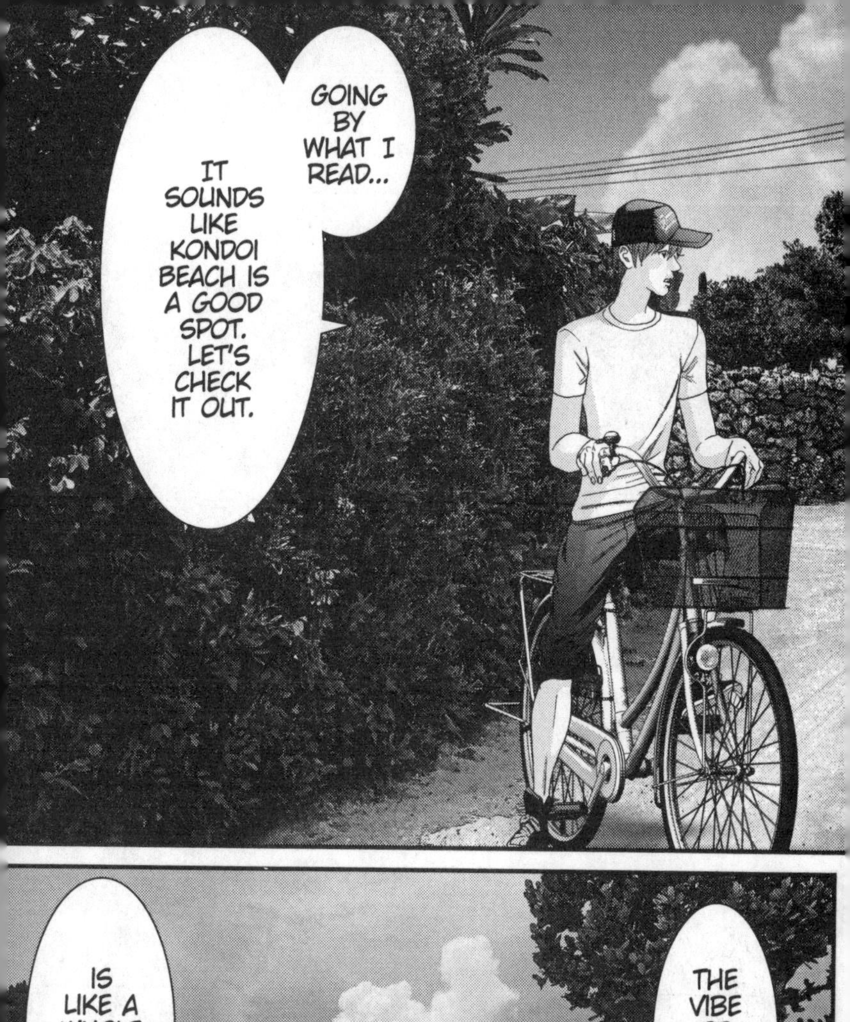
GOING BY WHAT I READ...
IT SOUNDS LIKE KONDOI BEACH IS A GOOD SPOT. LET'S CHECK IT OUT.

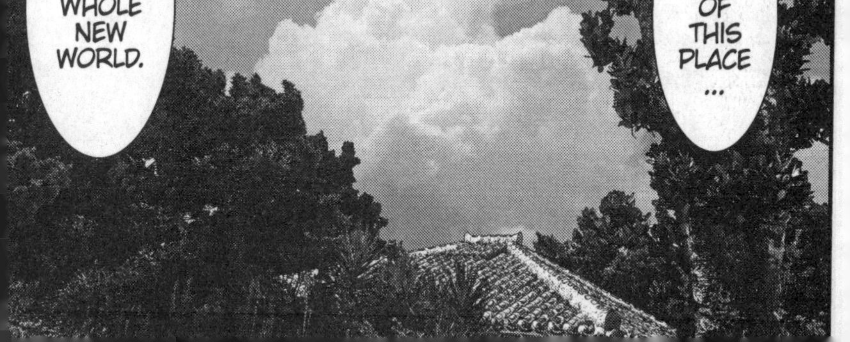
THE VIBE OF THIS PLACE ...
IS LIKE A WHOLE NEW WORLD.

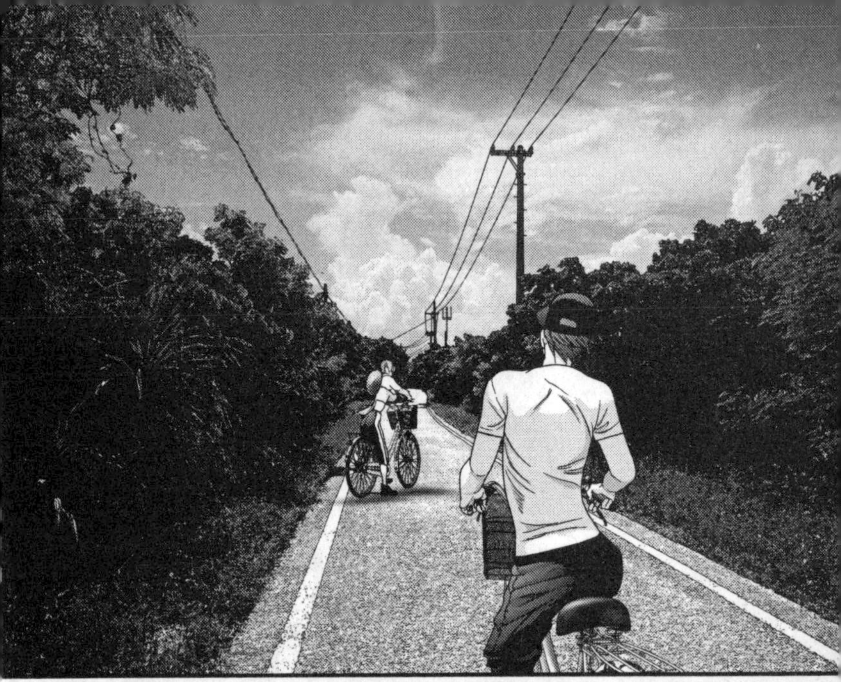

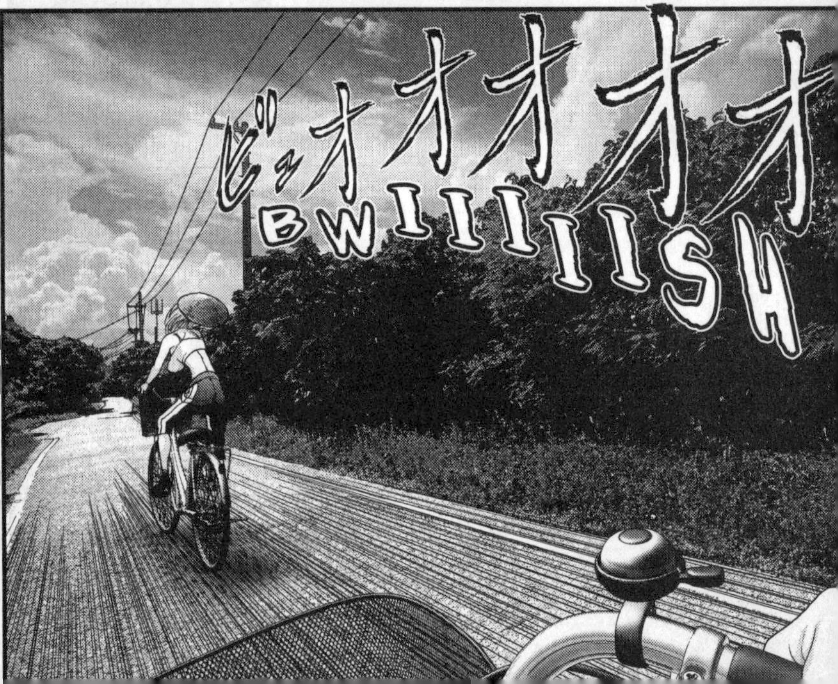
ビュオオオオオ
BWIIIIIISH

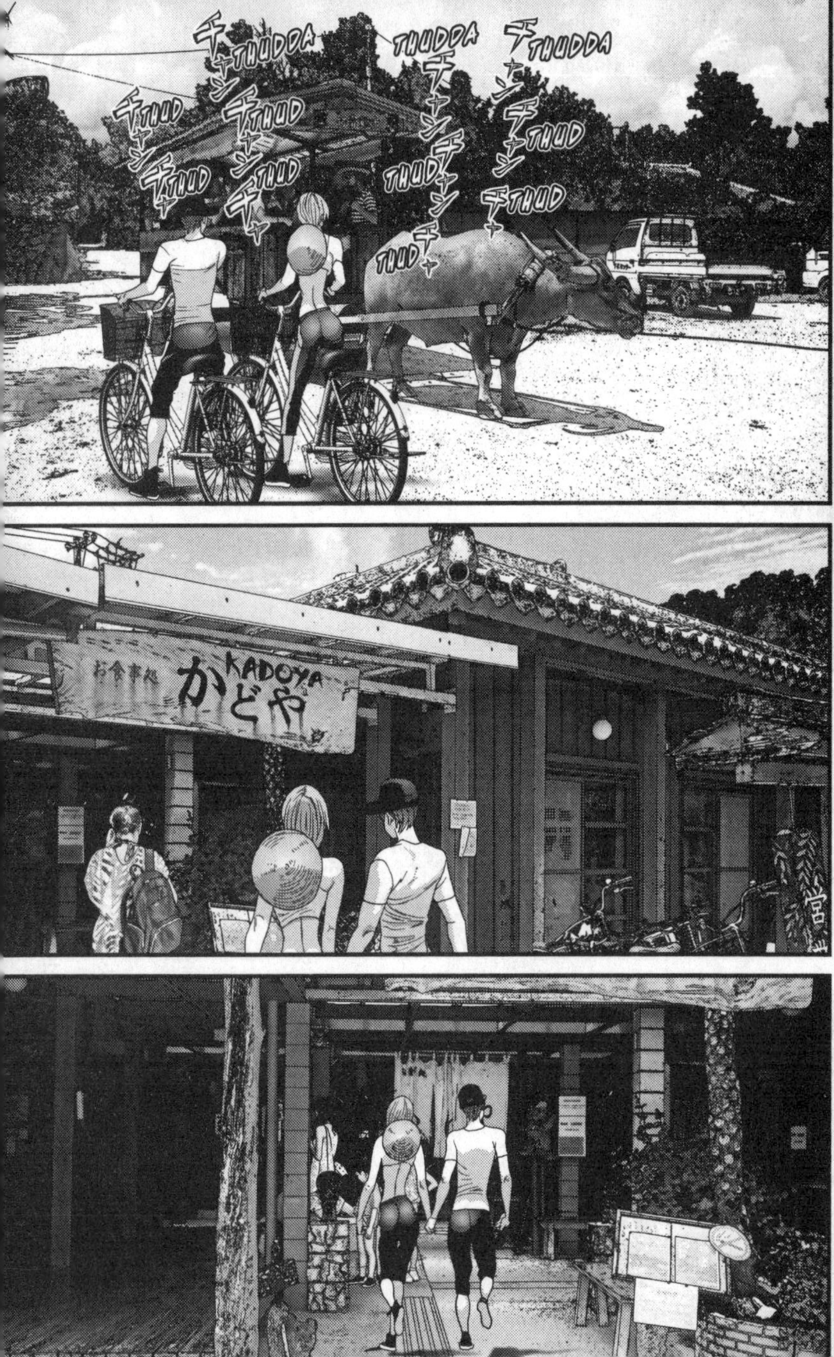

チャンチャンチャ
THUDDA
THUD
THUD
チャンチャンチャ
THUDDA
THUD
THUD
チャンチャンチャ
THUDDA
THUD
THUD
チャンチャ
THUD
THUD
お食事処
かどや
KADOYA

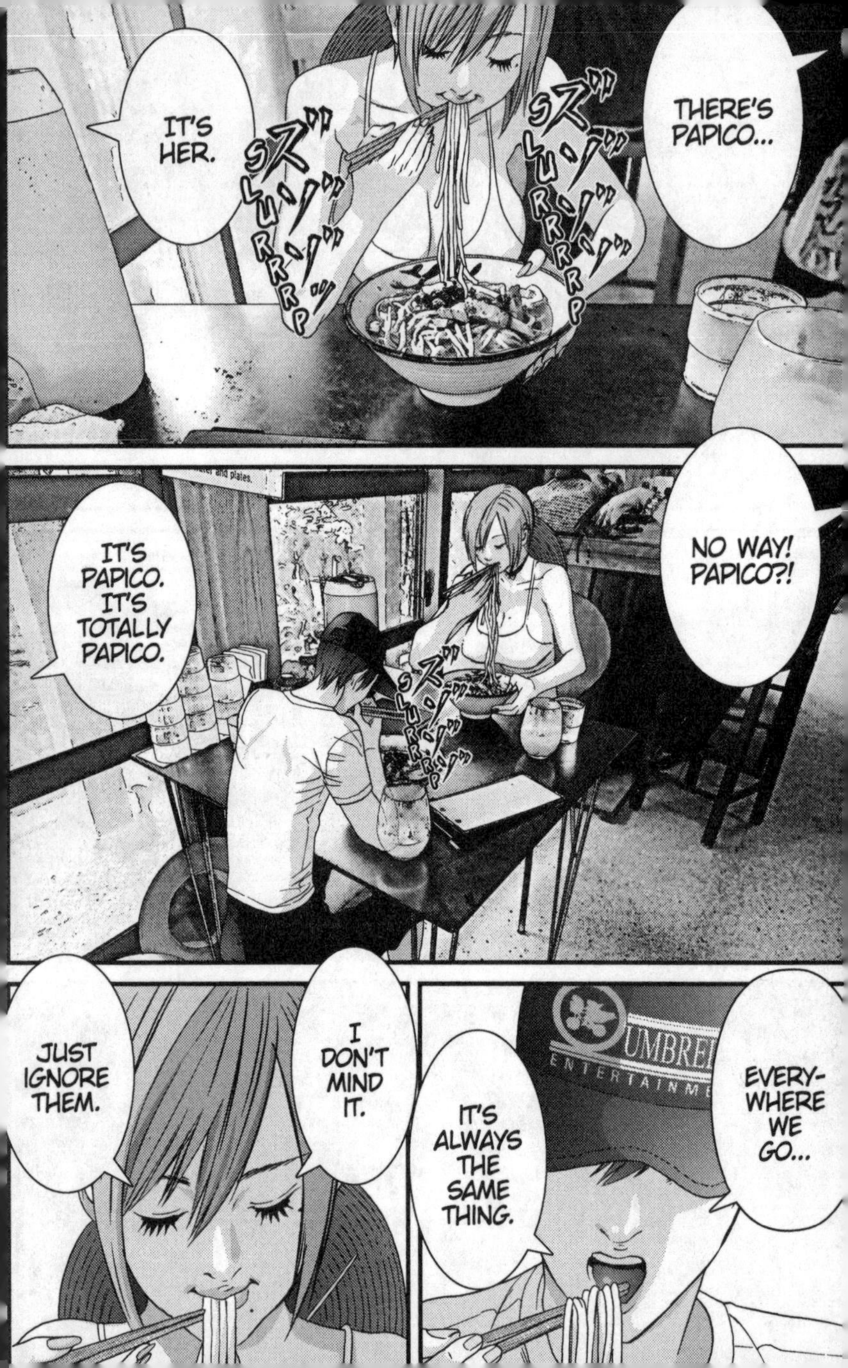
THERE'S PAPICO...
IT'S HER.
SLURRRRP
SLURRRRP
NO WAY! PAPICO?!
IT'S PAPICO. IT'S TOTALLY PAPICO.
SLURRRRP
EVERY-WHERE WE GO...
IT'S ALWAYS THE SAME THING.
I DON'T MIND IT.
JUST IGNORE THEM.

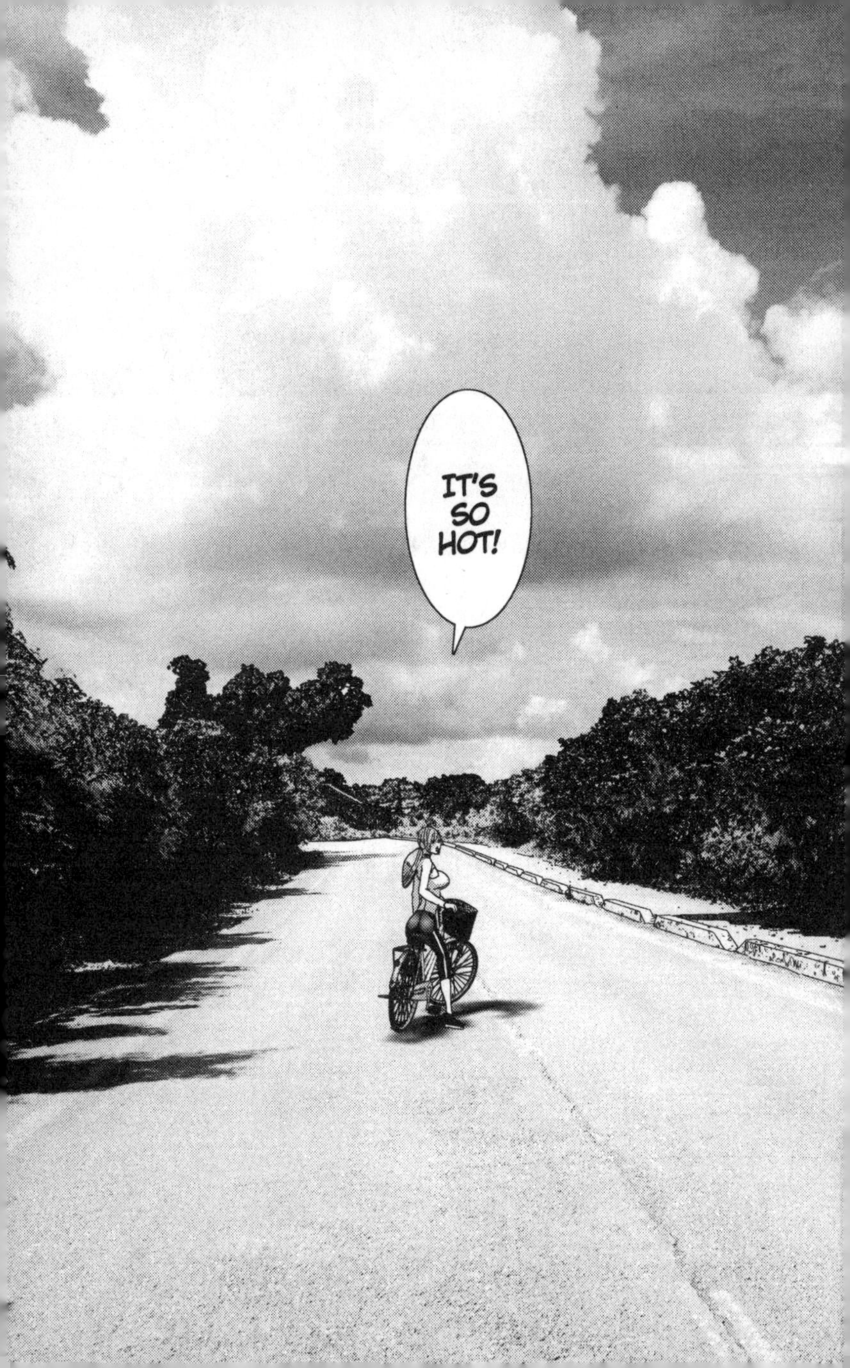
IT'S SO HOT!

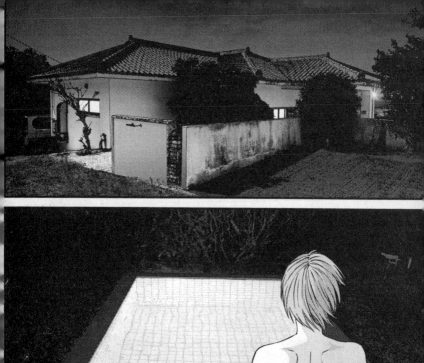

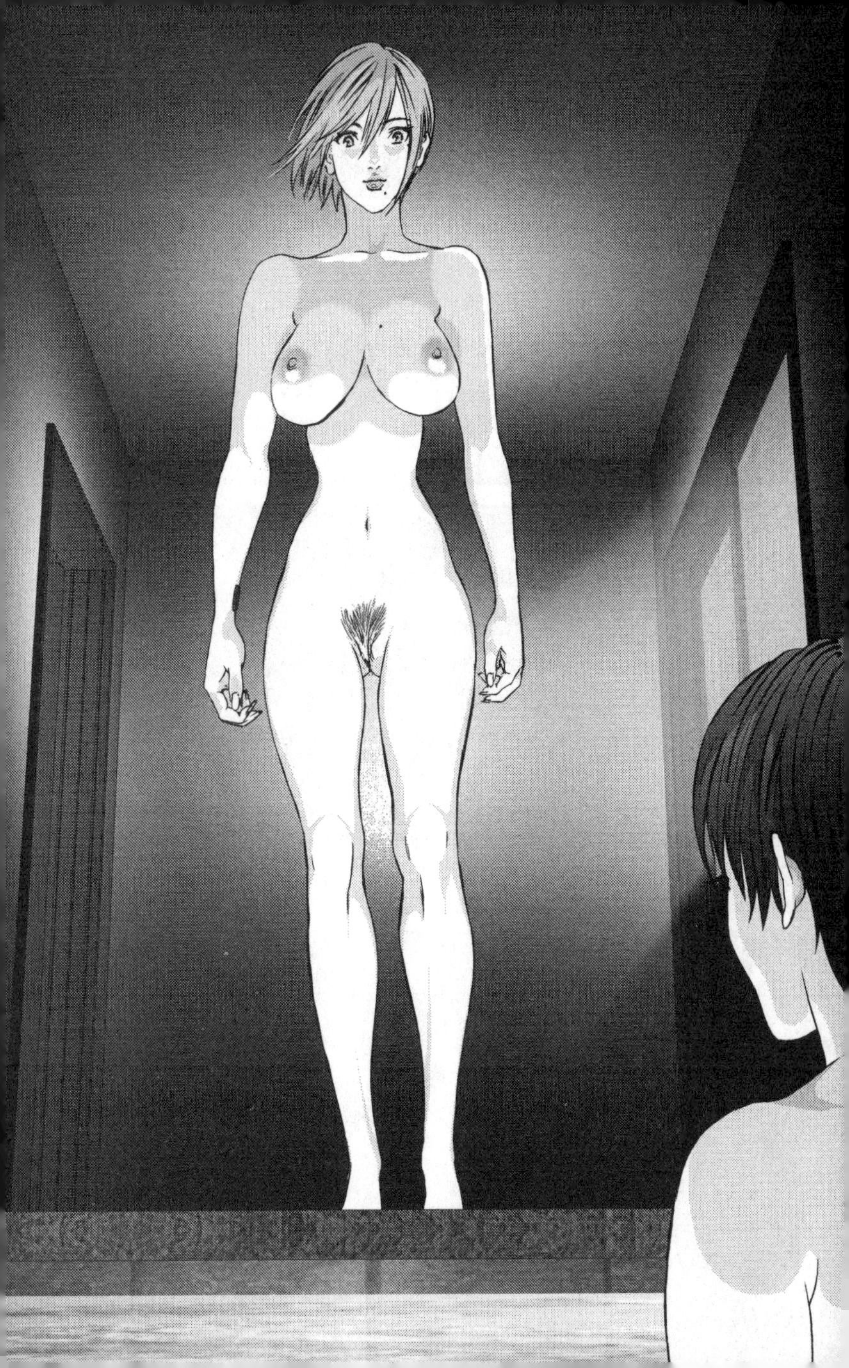

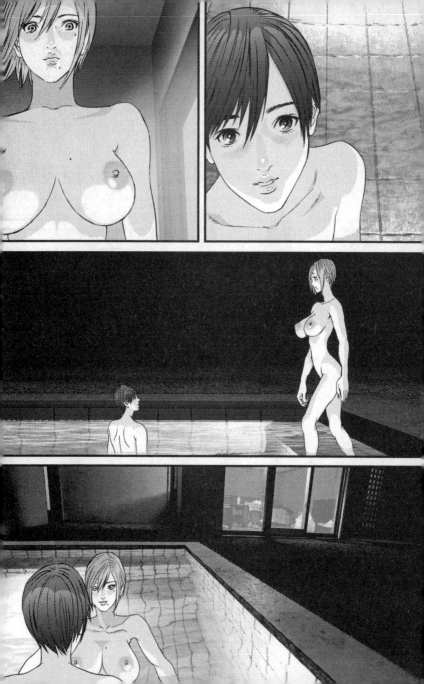

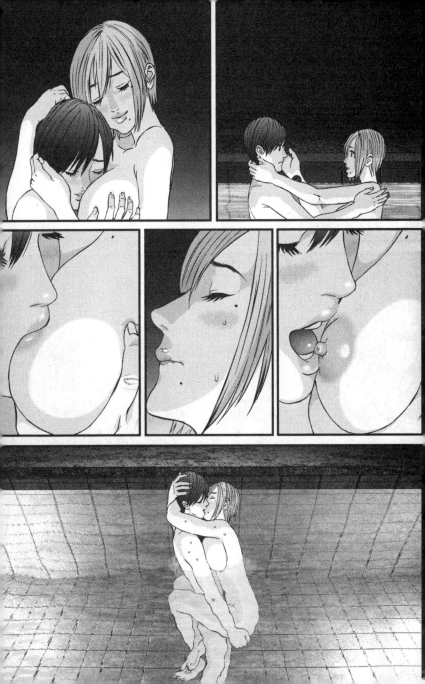

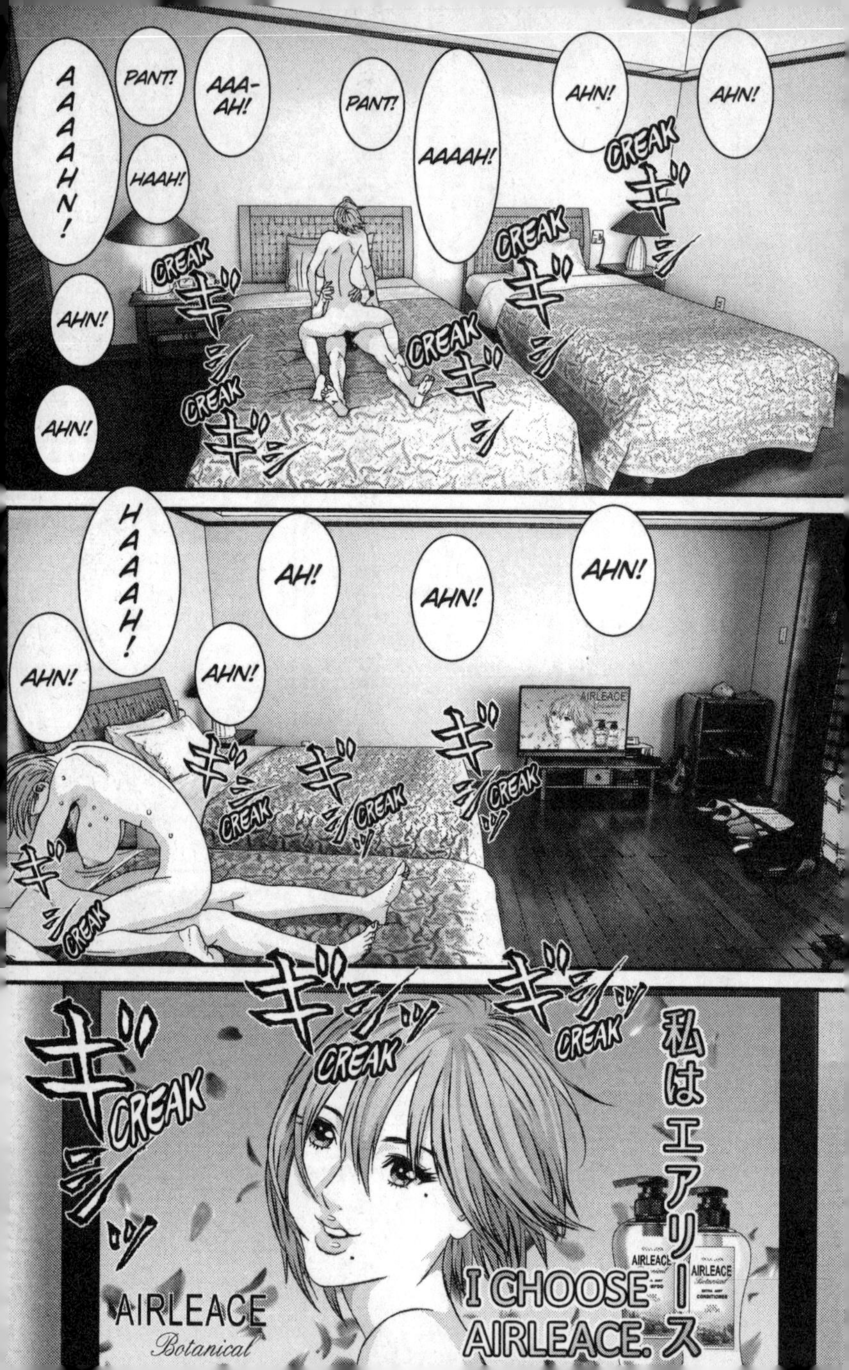
AHN!
AHN!
CREAK
ギシ
AAAAH!
PANT!
CREAK
ギシ
CREAK
ギシ
AAA-AH!
PANT!
AAAAAHN!
HAAH!
CREAK
ギシ
AHN!
CREAK
ギシ
AHN!
AHN!
AHN!
AH!
HAAAAH!
AHN!
AHN!
ギシ
CREAK
ギシ
CREAK
ギシ
CREAK
ギシ
CREAK
ギシ
CREAK
私はエアリース
ギシ
CREAK
ギシ
CREAK
ギシ
CREAK
AIRLEACE
I CHOOSE AIRLEACE.
AIRLEACE
Botanical

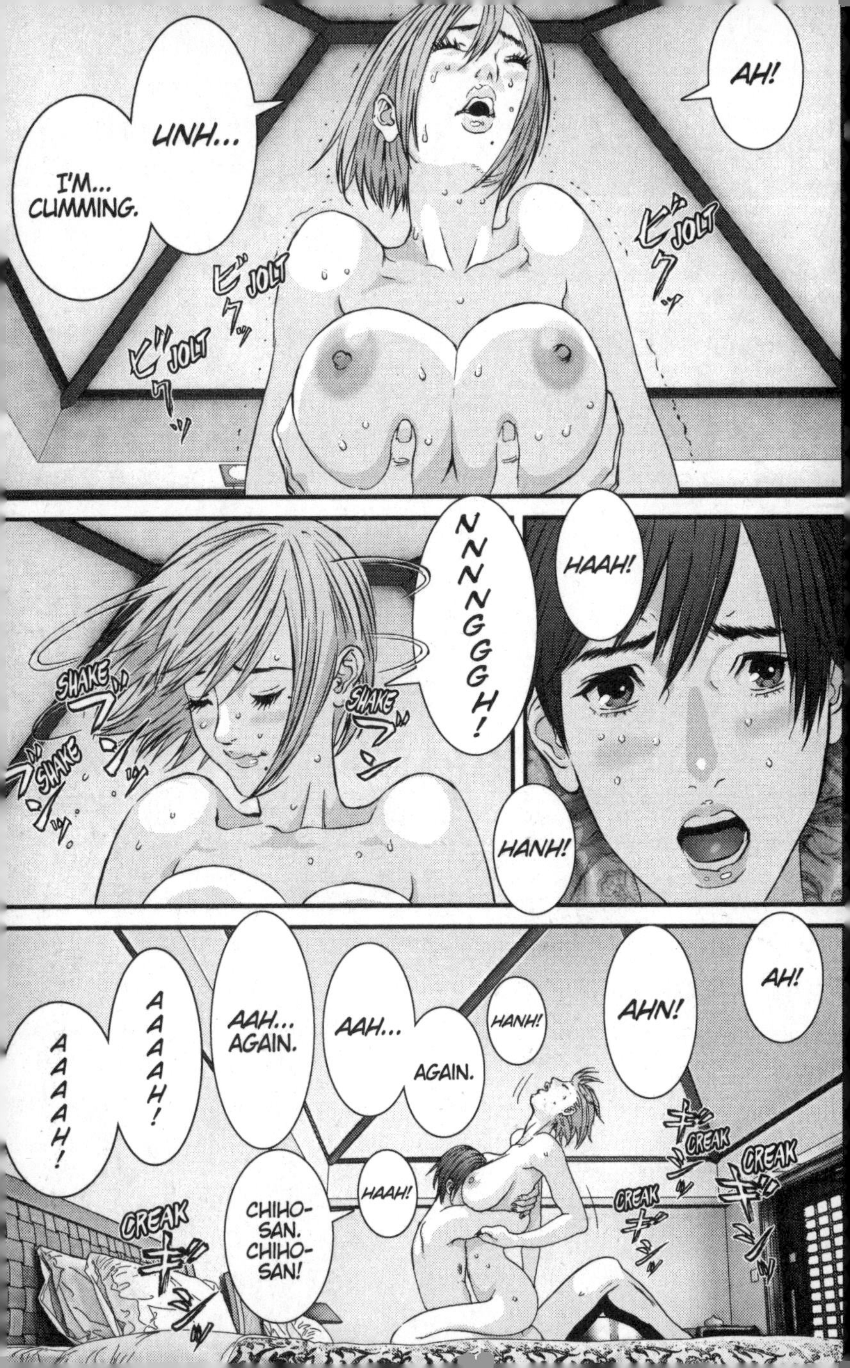
AH!
UNH...
I'M... CUMMING.
JOLT
JOLT
JOLT
HAAH!
HANH!
NNNNGGGH!
SHAKE
SHAKE
SHAKE
AH!
AHN!
HANH!
AAH...
AGAIN.
AAH... AGAIN.
AAAAAH!
AAAAAH!
CREAK
CREAK
CREAK
HAAH!
CHIHO-SAN. CHIHO-SAN!
CREAK

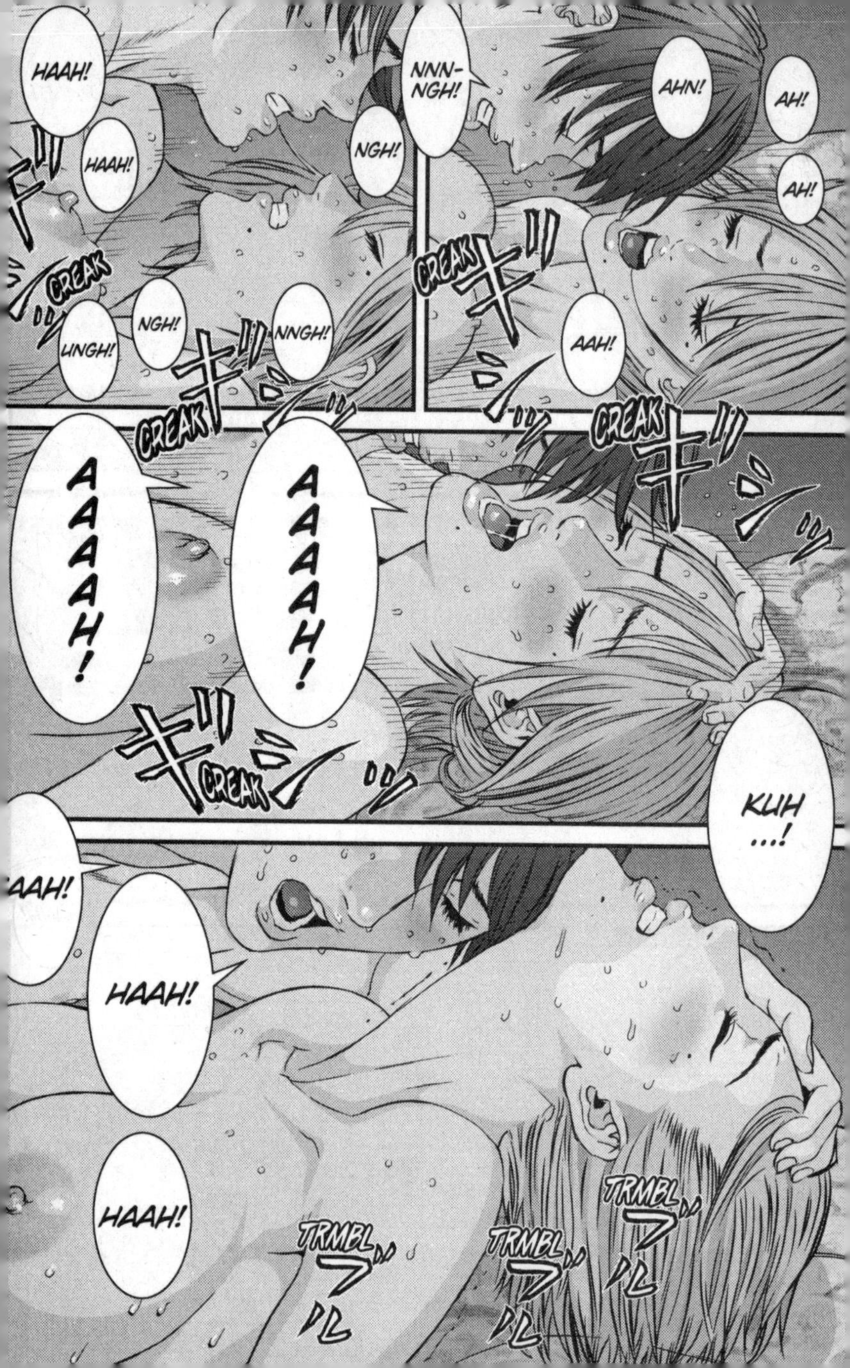
AH!
AH!
AHN!
CREAK
AAH!
NNN-NGH!
NGH!
HAAH!
HAAH!
CREAK
NNGH!
NGH!
UNGH!
CREAK
CREAK
AAAAAH!
AAAAAH!
CREAK
KUH...!
TRMBL
TRMBL
TRMBL
AAH!
HAAH!
HAAH!

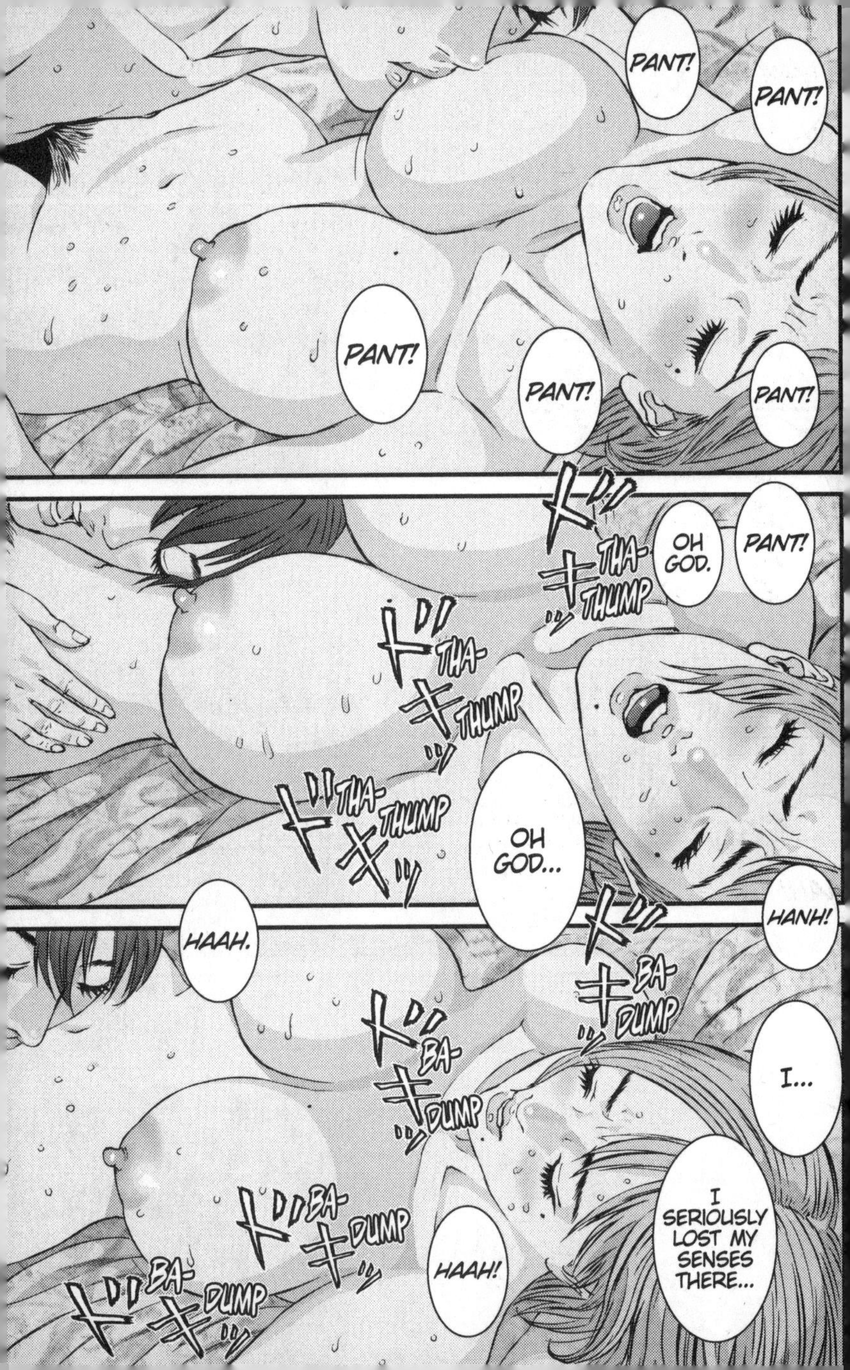
PANT!
PANT!
PANT!
PANT!
PANT!
PANT!
OH GOD.
ドキッ THA-THUMP
ドキッ THA-THUMP
ドキッ THA-THUMP
OH GOD...
HANH!
ドキッ BA-DUMP
HAAH.
I...
ドキッ BA-DUMP
I SERIOUSLY LOST MY SENSES THERE...
HAAH!
ドキッ BA-DUMP
ドキッ BA-DUMP

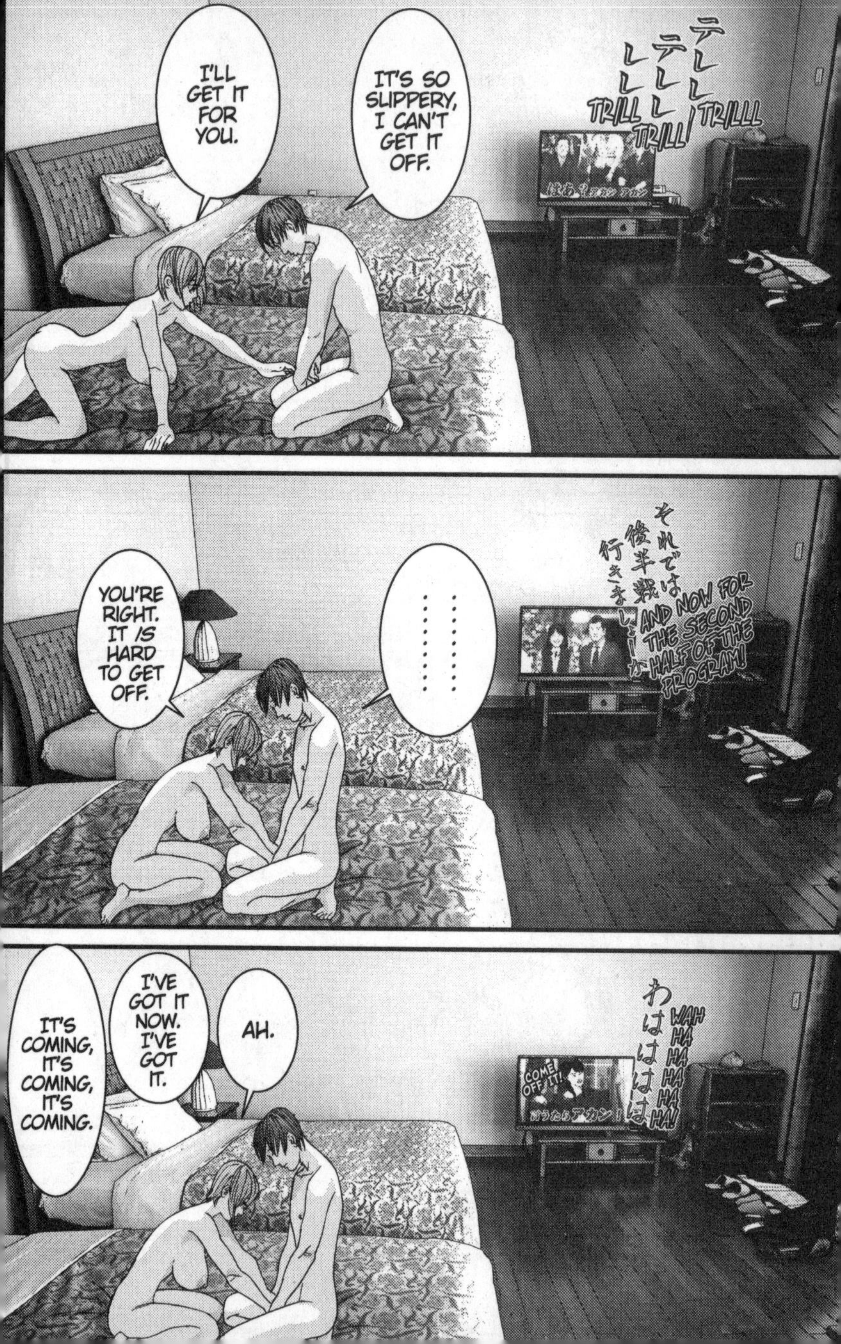
テレレ テレレ テレレ
TRILL TRILL TRILLL
IT'S SO SLIPPERY, I CAN'T GET IT OFF.
I'LL GET IT FOR YOU.
それでは後半戦は行きましょうか
AND NOW FOR THE SECOND HALF OF THE PROGRAM!
......
YOU'RE RIGHT. IT IS HARD TO GET OFF.
わはははは
WAH HA HA HA HA HA!
COME OFF IT!
AH.
I'VE GOT IT NOW. I'VE GOT IT.
IT'S COMING, IT'S COMING, IT'S COMING.

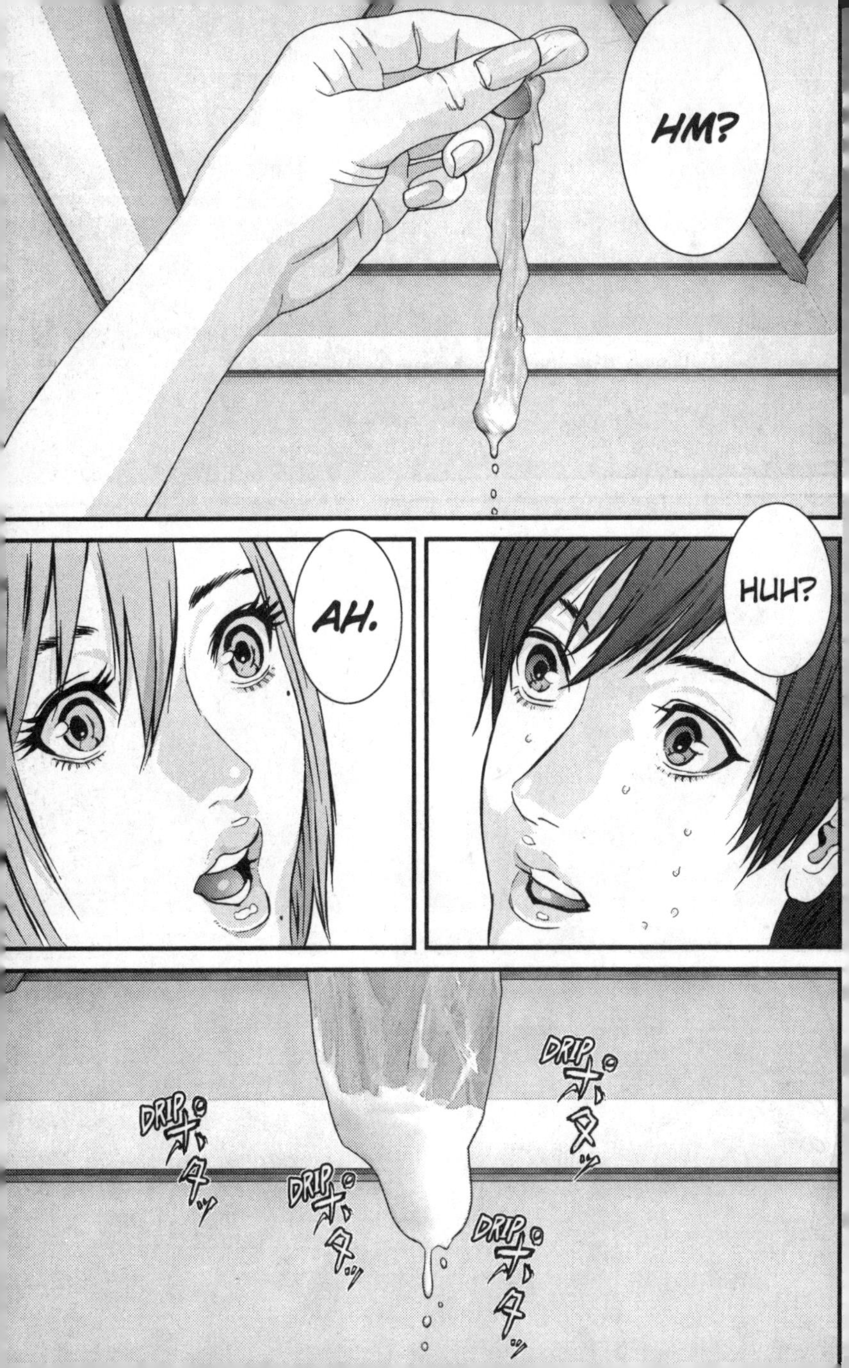
HM?
HUH?
AH.
DRIP ポタッ
DRIP ポタッ
DRIP ポタッ
DRIP ポタッ

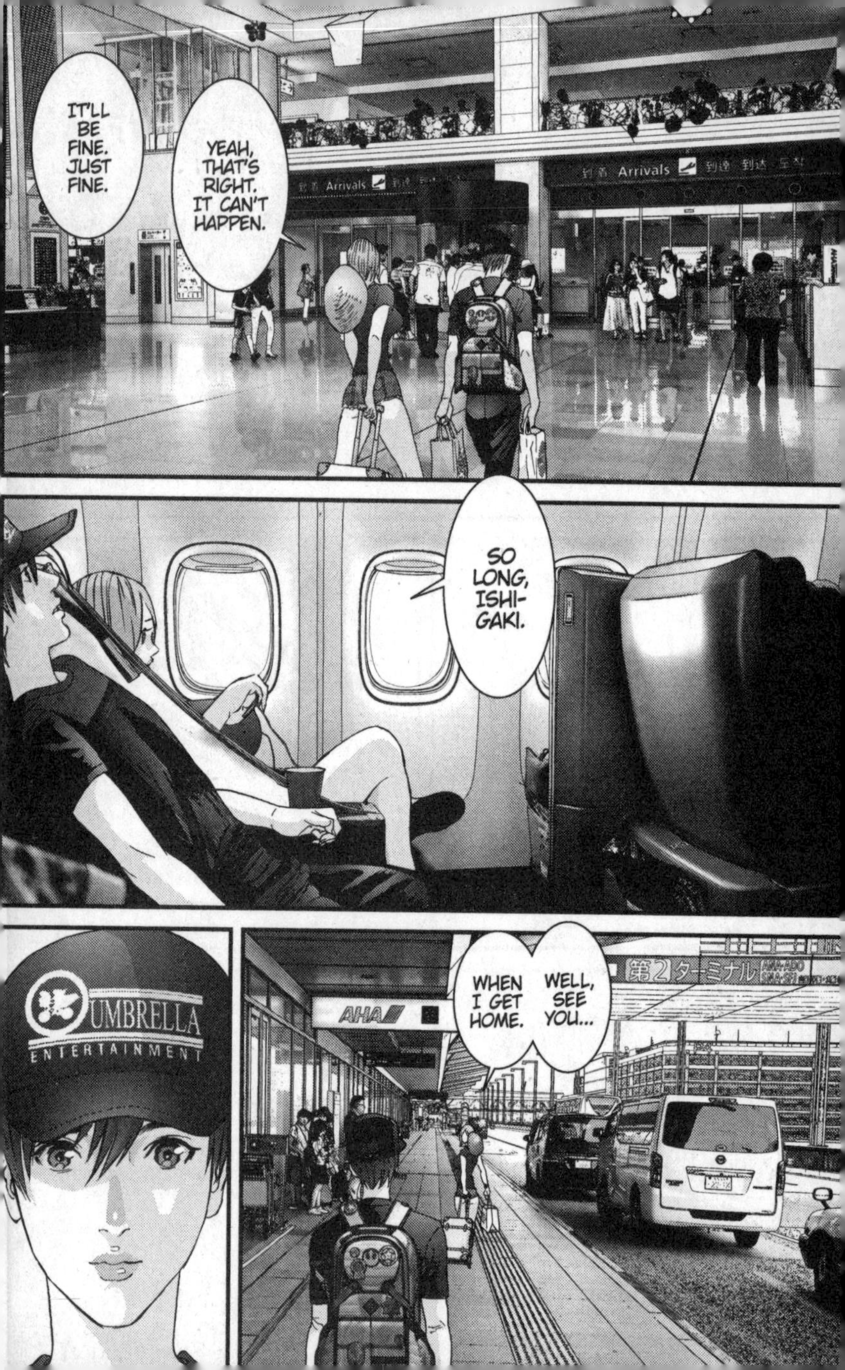
YEAH, THAT'S RIGHT. IT CAN'T HAPPEN.
IT'LL BE FINE. JUST FINE.
Arrivals
Arrivals
SO LONG, ISHI-GAKI.
第2ターミナル
AHA
WELL, SEE YOU...
WHEN I GET HOME.
UMBRELLA
ENTERTAINMENT

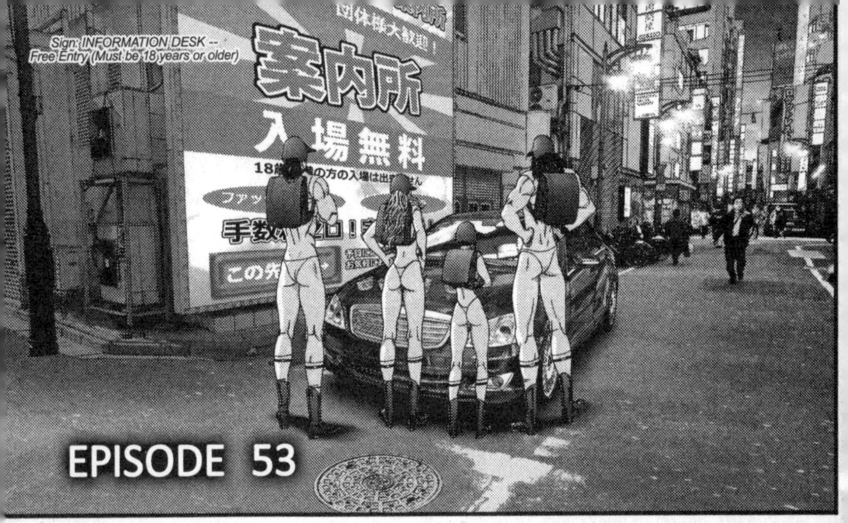
Sign: INFORMATION DESK --
Free Entry (Must be 18 years or older)
案内所
入場無料
EPISODE 53

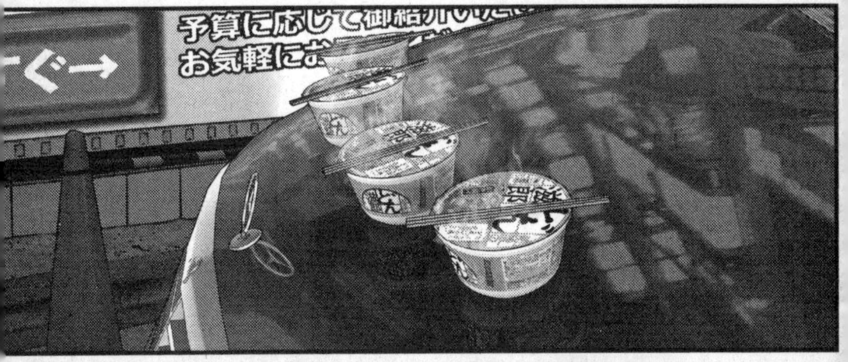

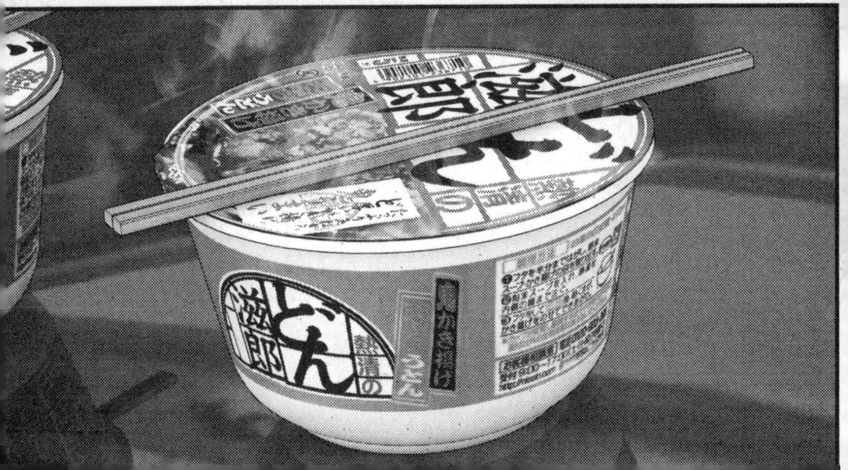

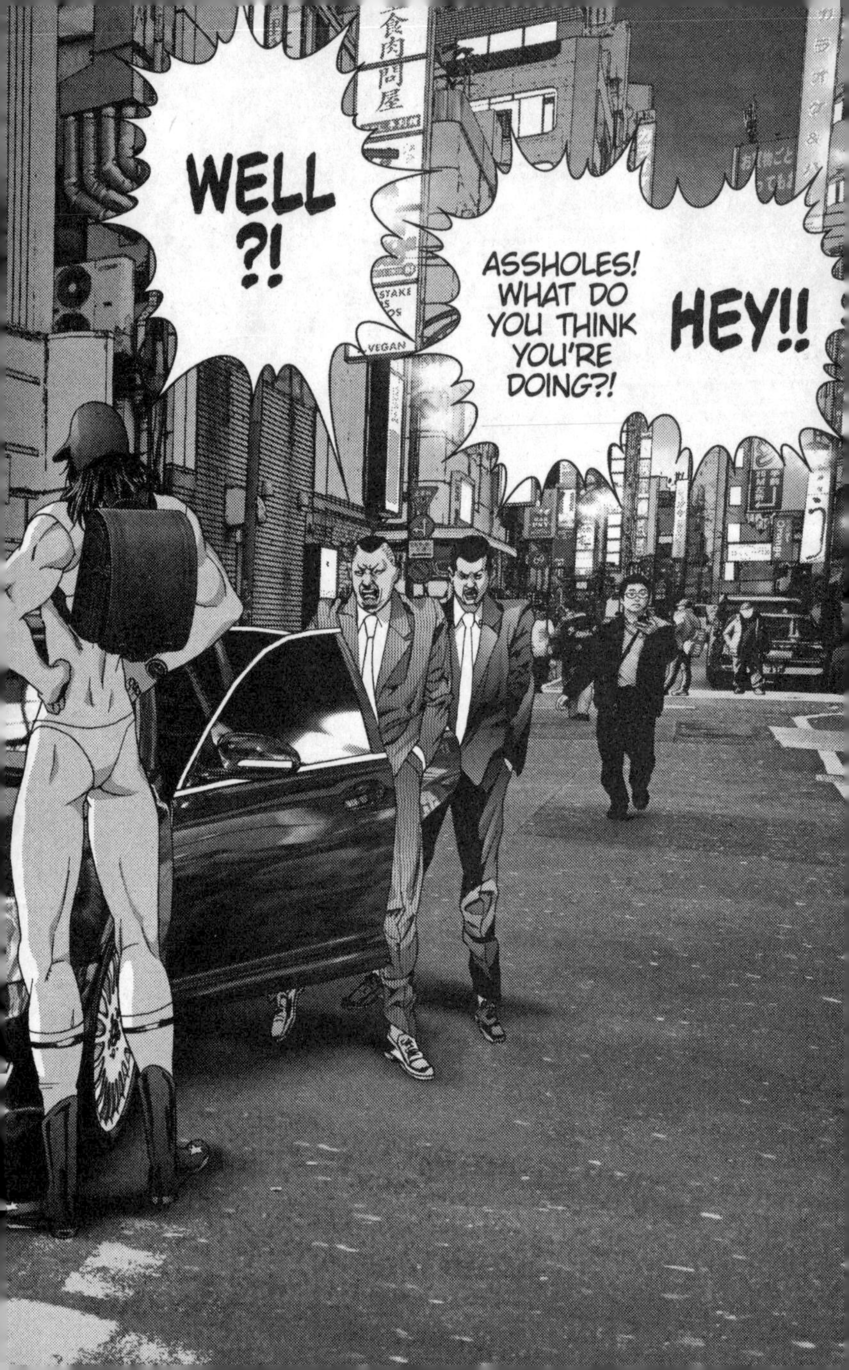
HEY!!
ASSHOLES! WHAT DO YOU THINK YOU'RE DOING?!
WELL ?!
VEGAN

EPISODE 53: ACTIVATION

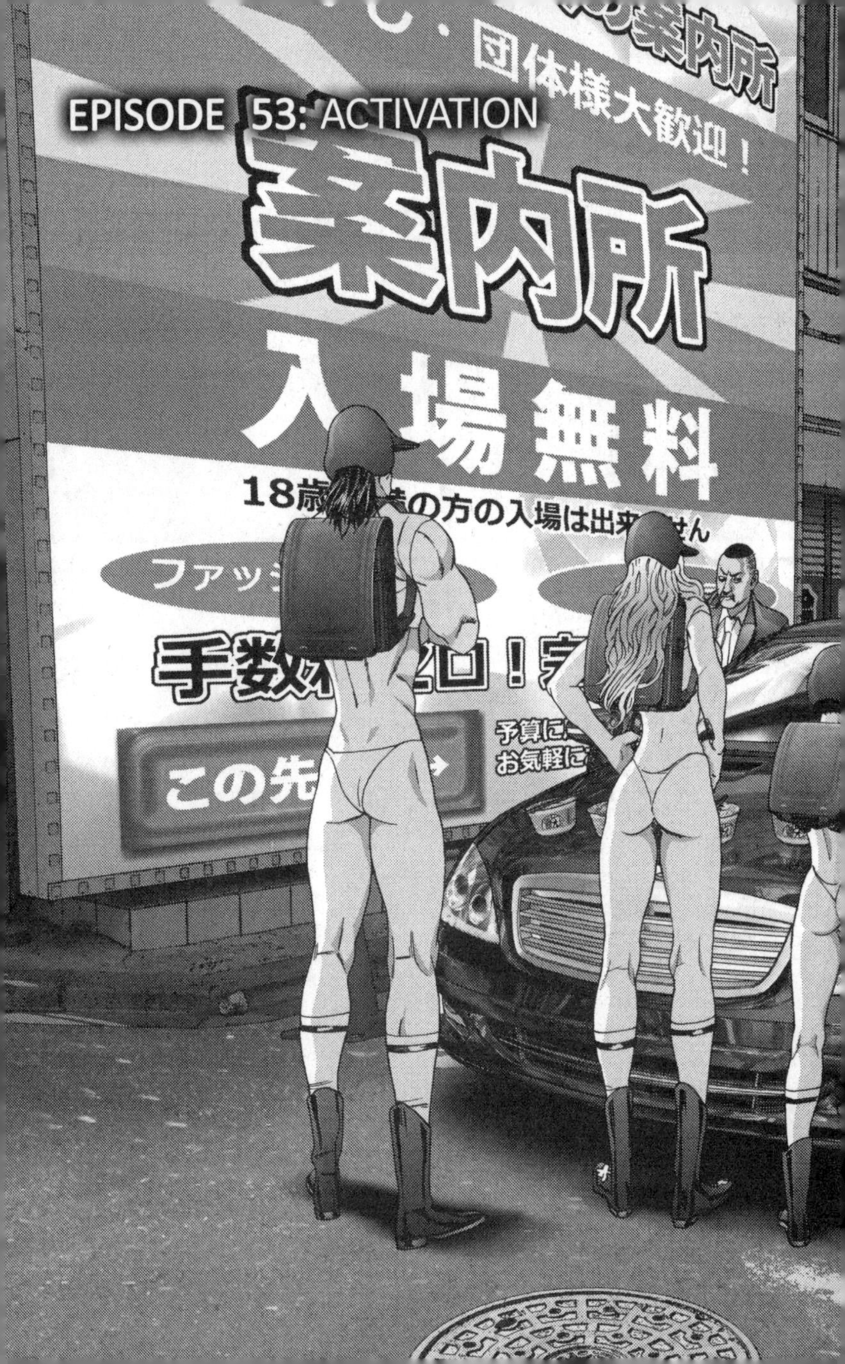

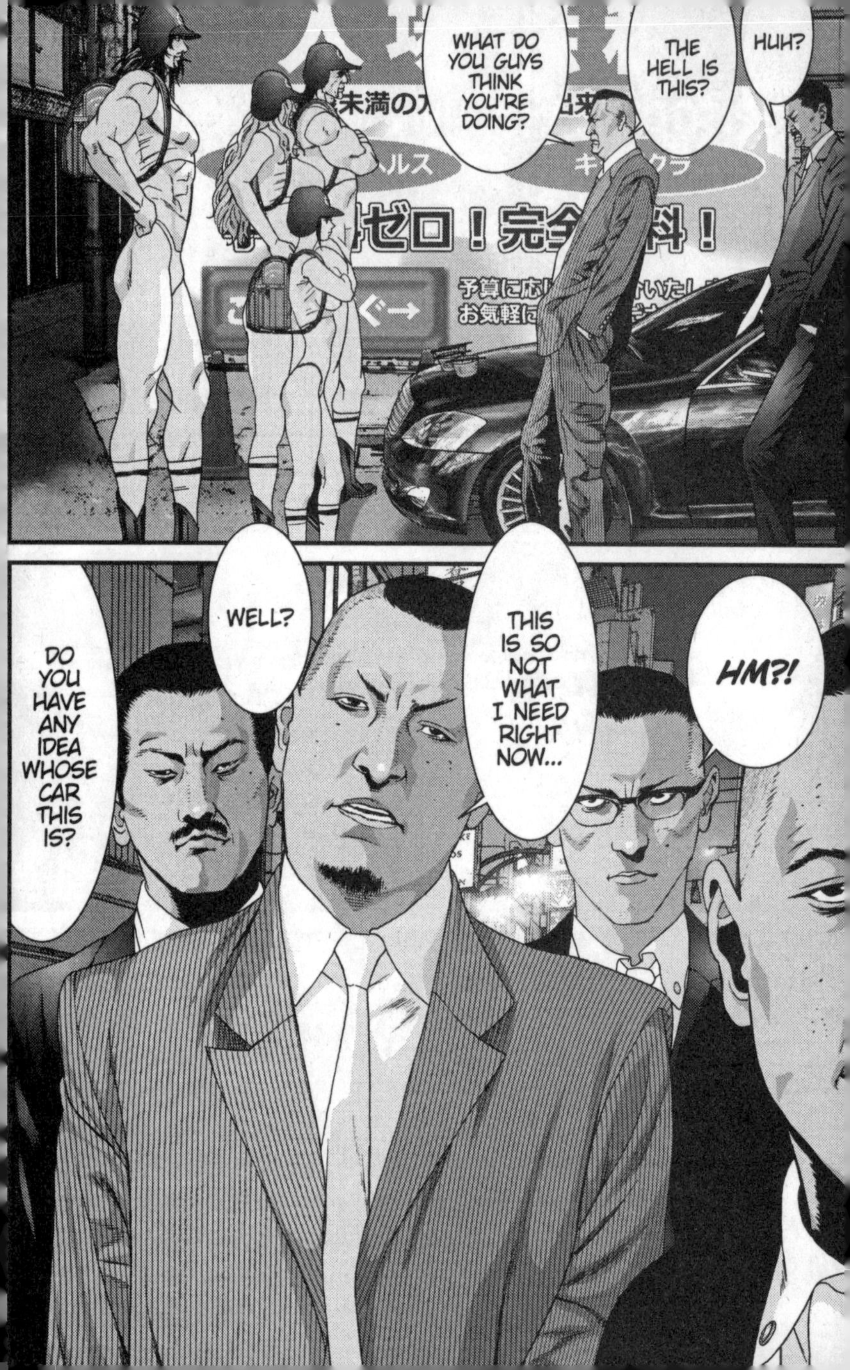
HUH?
THE HELL IS THIS?
WHAT DO YOU GUYS THINK YOU'RE DOING?
HM?!
THIS IS SO NOT WHAT I NEED RIGHT NOW...
WELL?
DO YOU HAVE ANY IDEA WHOSE CAR THIS IS?

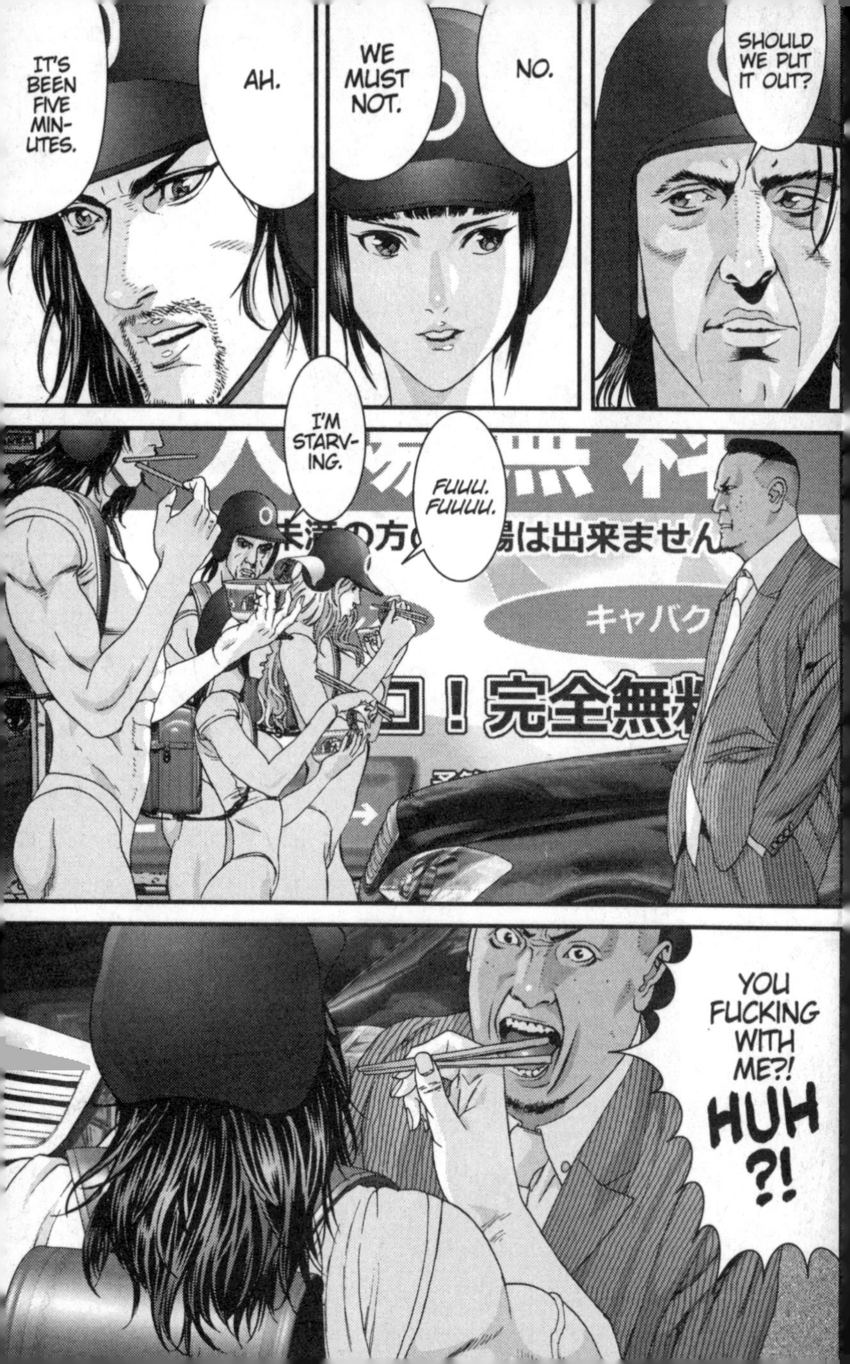
SHOULD WE PUT IT OUT?
NO.
WE MUST NOT.
AH.
IT'S BEEN FIVE MIN-UTES.
FUUU. FUUUU.
I'M STARV-ING.
場は出来ません
キャバク
完全無料
YOU FUCKING WITH ME?! HUH ?!

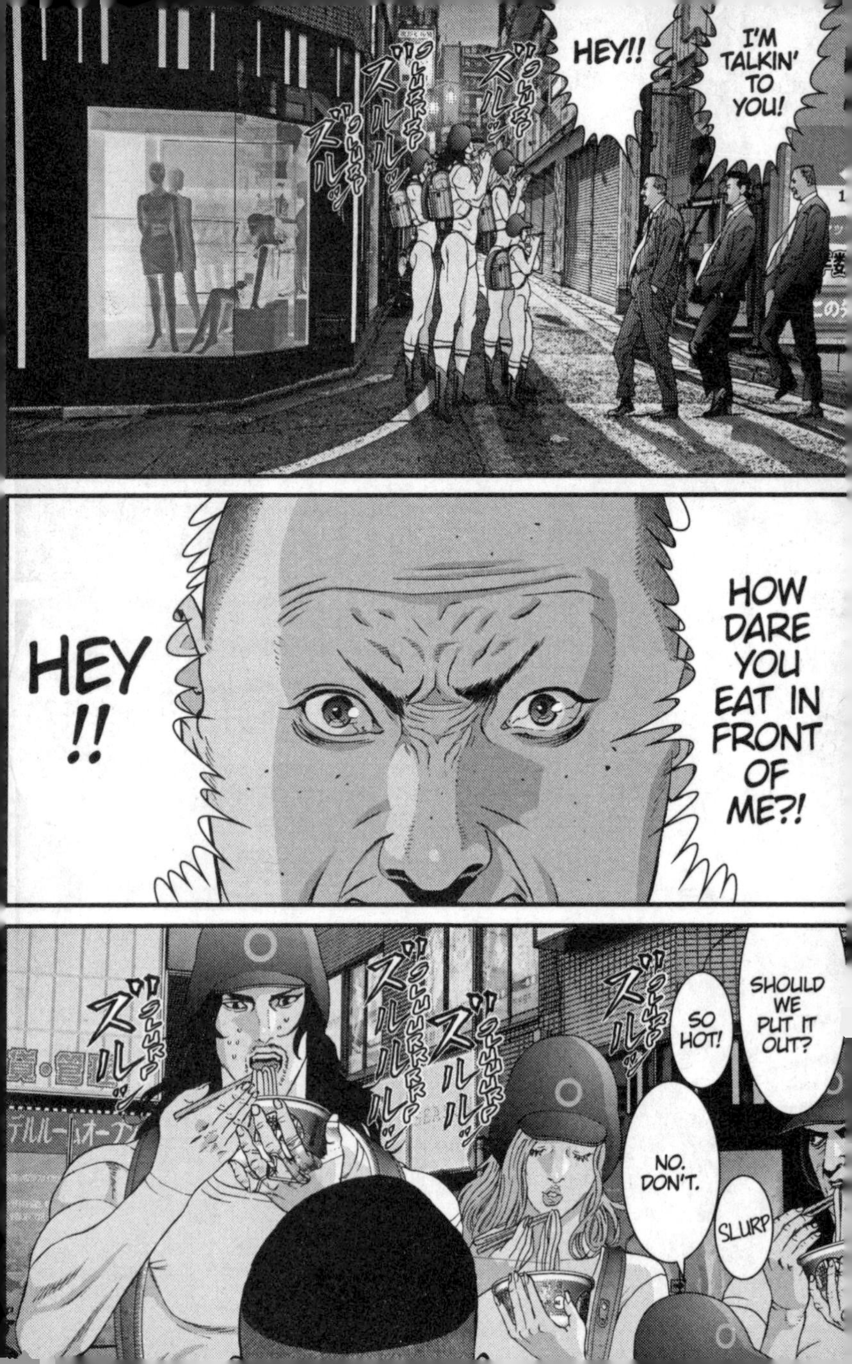
I'M TALKIN' TO YOU!
HEY!!
HOW DARE YOU EAT IN FRONT OF ME?!
HEY!!
SHOULD WE PUT IT OUT?
SO HOT!
NO. DON'T.
SLURP

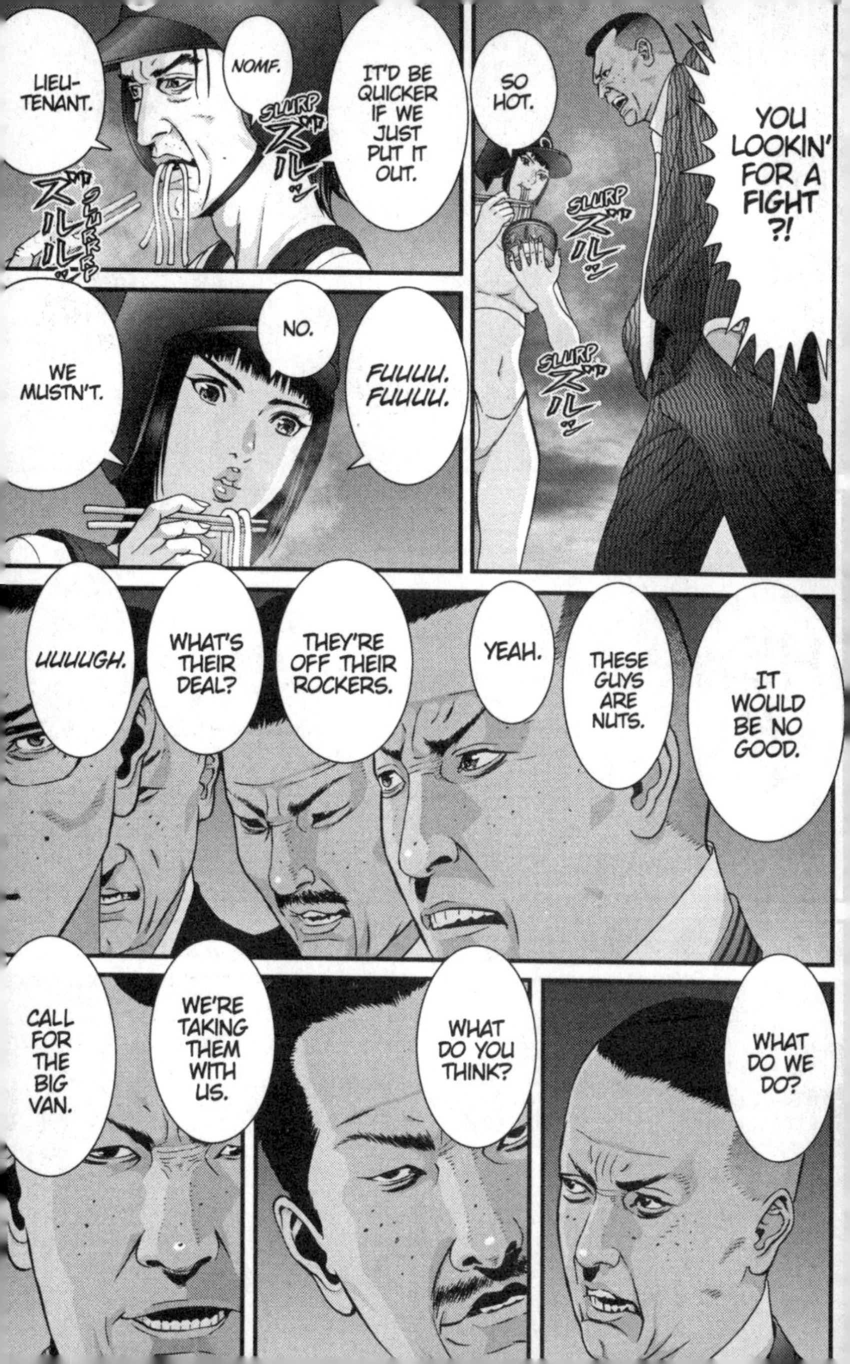
YOU LOOKIN' FOR A FIGHT?!
SLURP
SLURP
SO HOT.
IT'D BE QUICKER IF WE JUST PUT IT OUT.
SLURP
NOMF.
LIEU-TENANT.
SLURP SLURP
FUUUU. FUUUU.
NO.
WE MUSTN'T.
IT WOULD BE NO GOOD.
THESE GUYS ARE NUTS.
YEAH.
THEY'RE OFF THEIR ROCKERS.
WHAT'S THEIR DEAL?
UUUUGH.
WHAT DO WE DO?
WHAT DO YOU THINK?
WE'RE TAKING THEM WITH US.
CALL FOR THE BIG VAN.

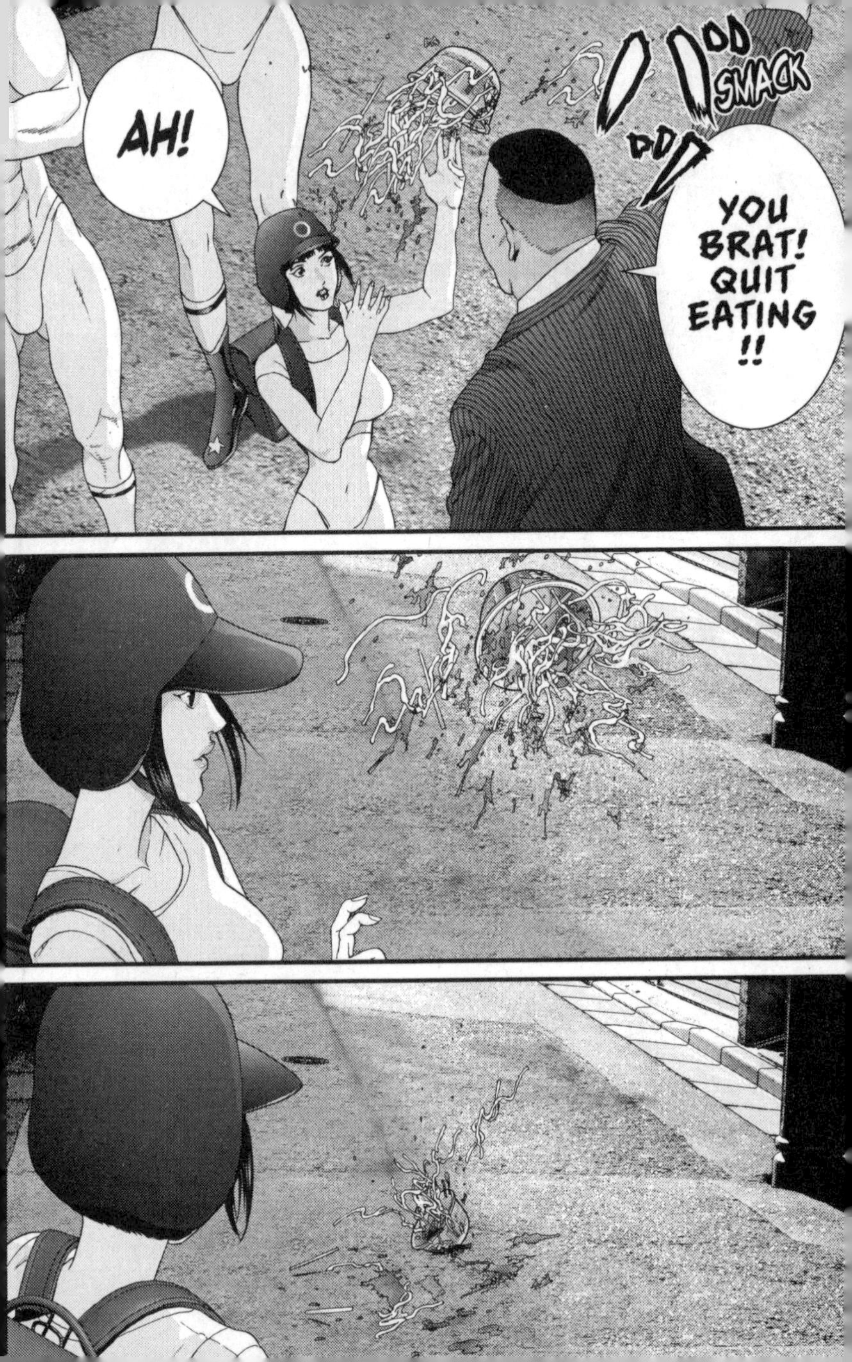
SMACK
YOU BRAT! QUIT EATING !!
AH!

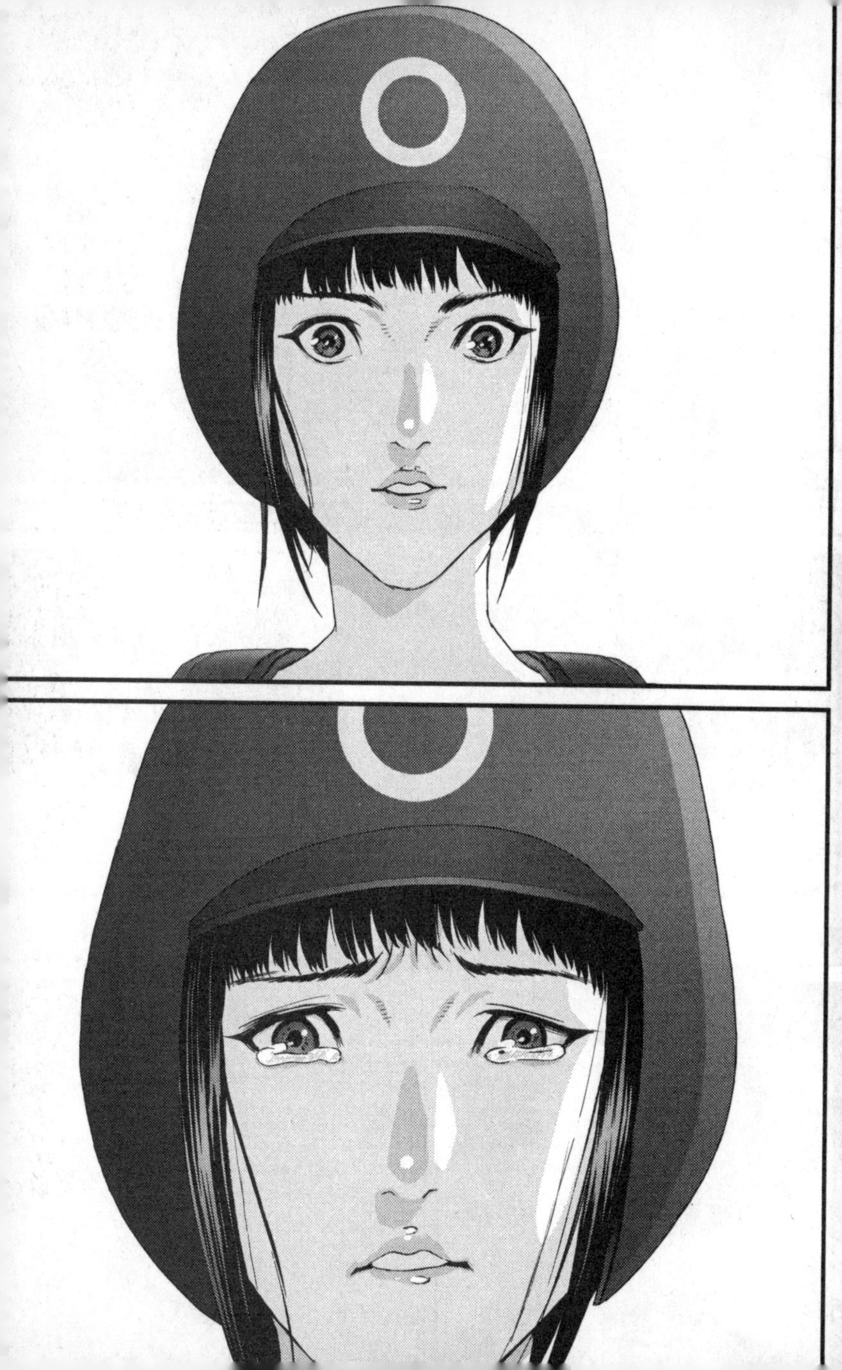

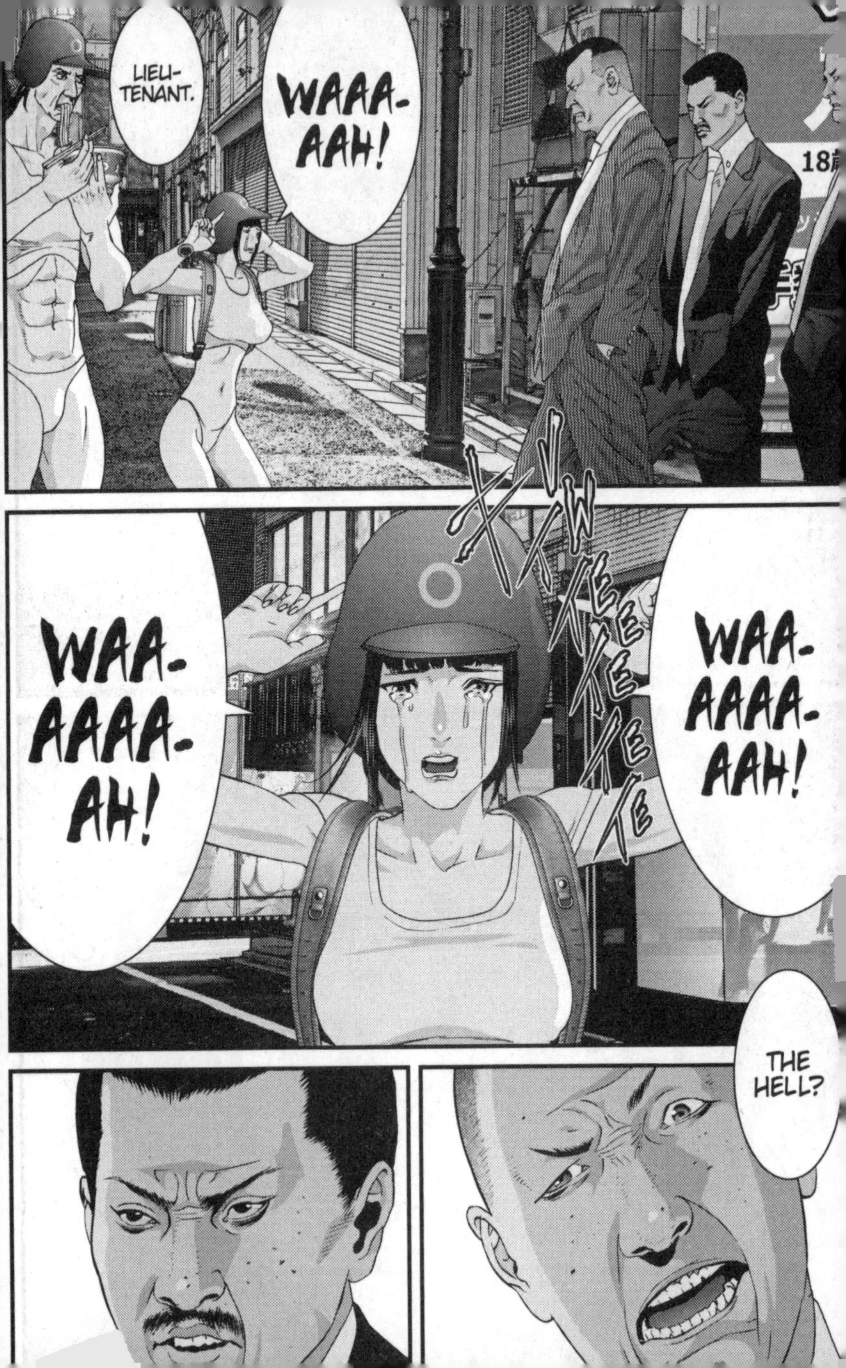
WAAAA-AAH!
LIEU-TENANT.
WAA-AAAA-AAAH!
WAA-AAAA-AH!
THE HELL?

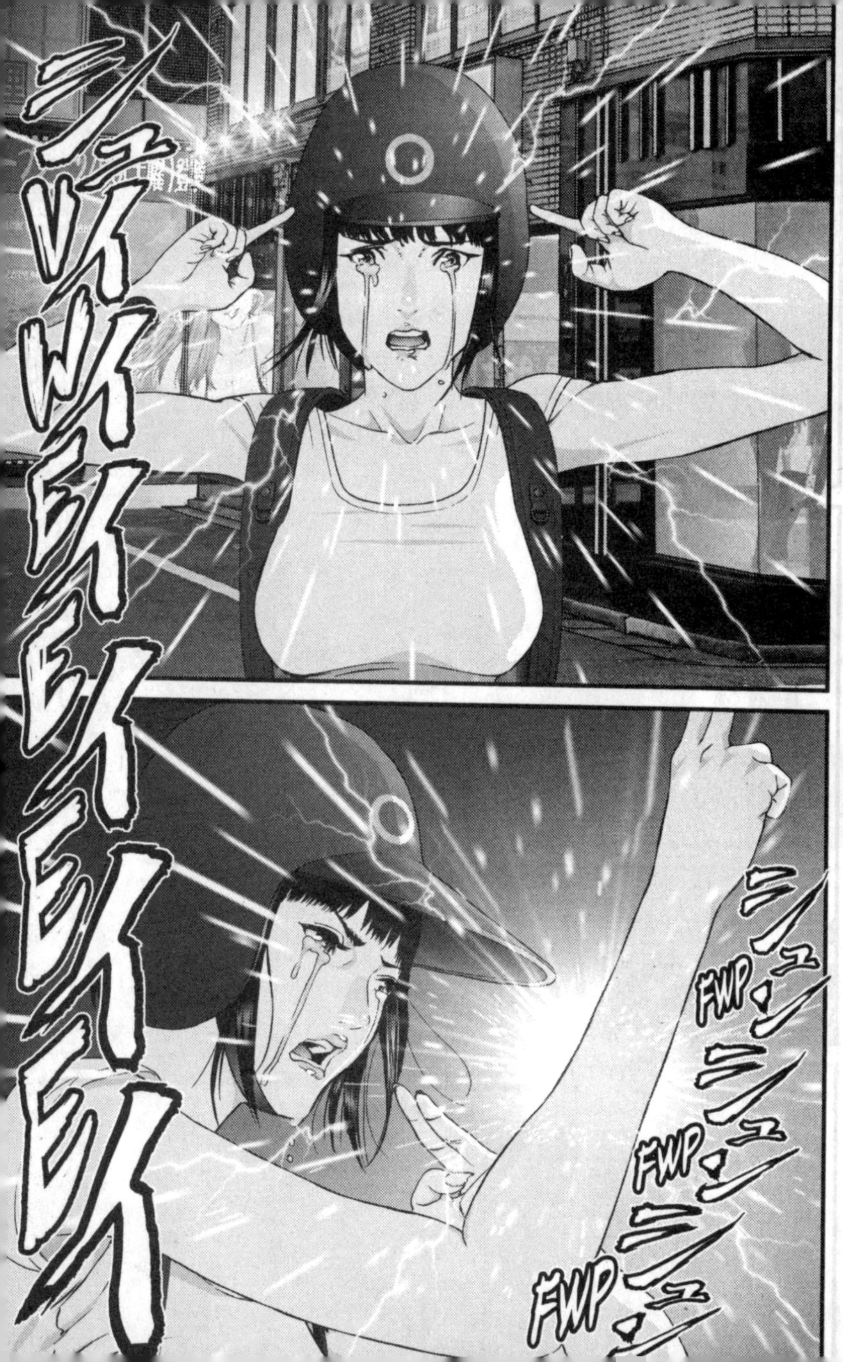
ミュンミュンミュン
FWP
FWP
FWP

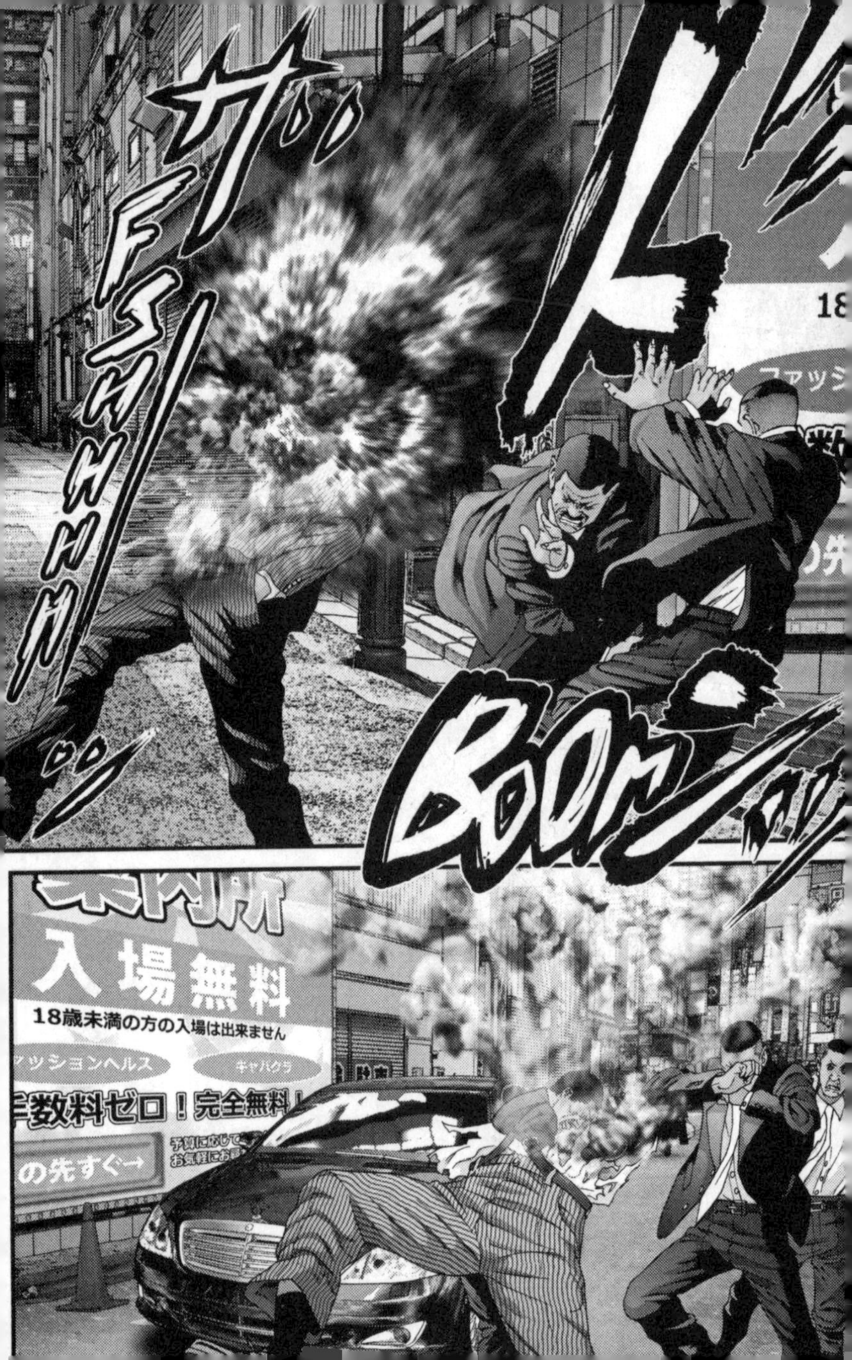
BOOM
入場無料
18歳未満の方の入場は出来ません
キャバクラ
数料ゼロ！完全無料
の先すぐ→

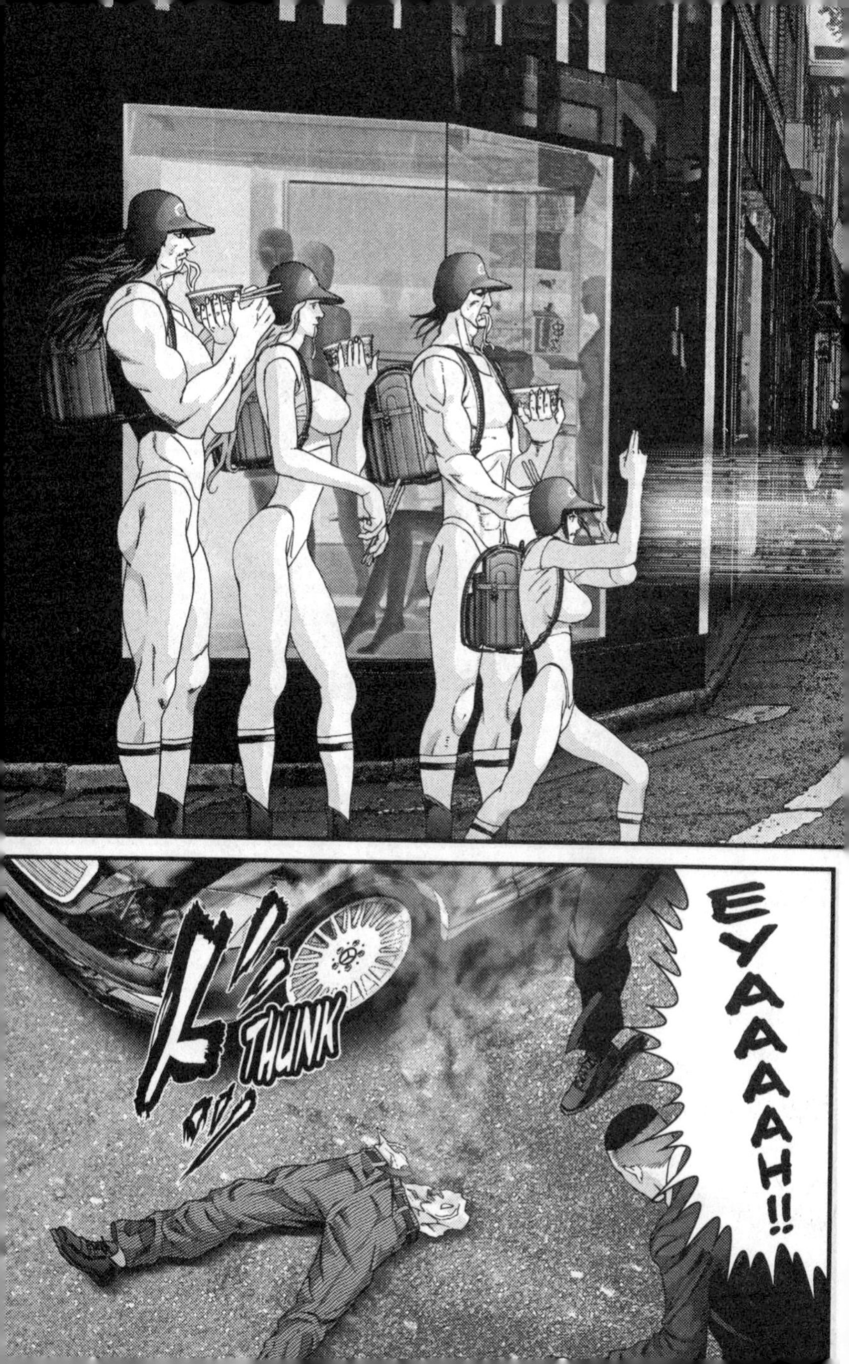
EYAAAAAH!!
THUNK

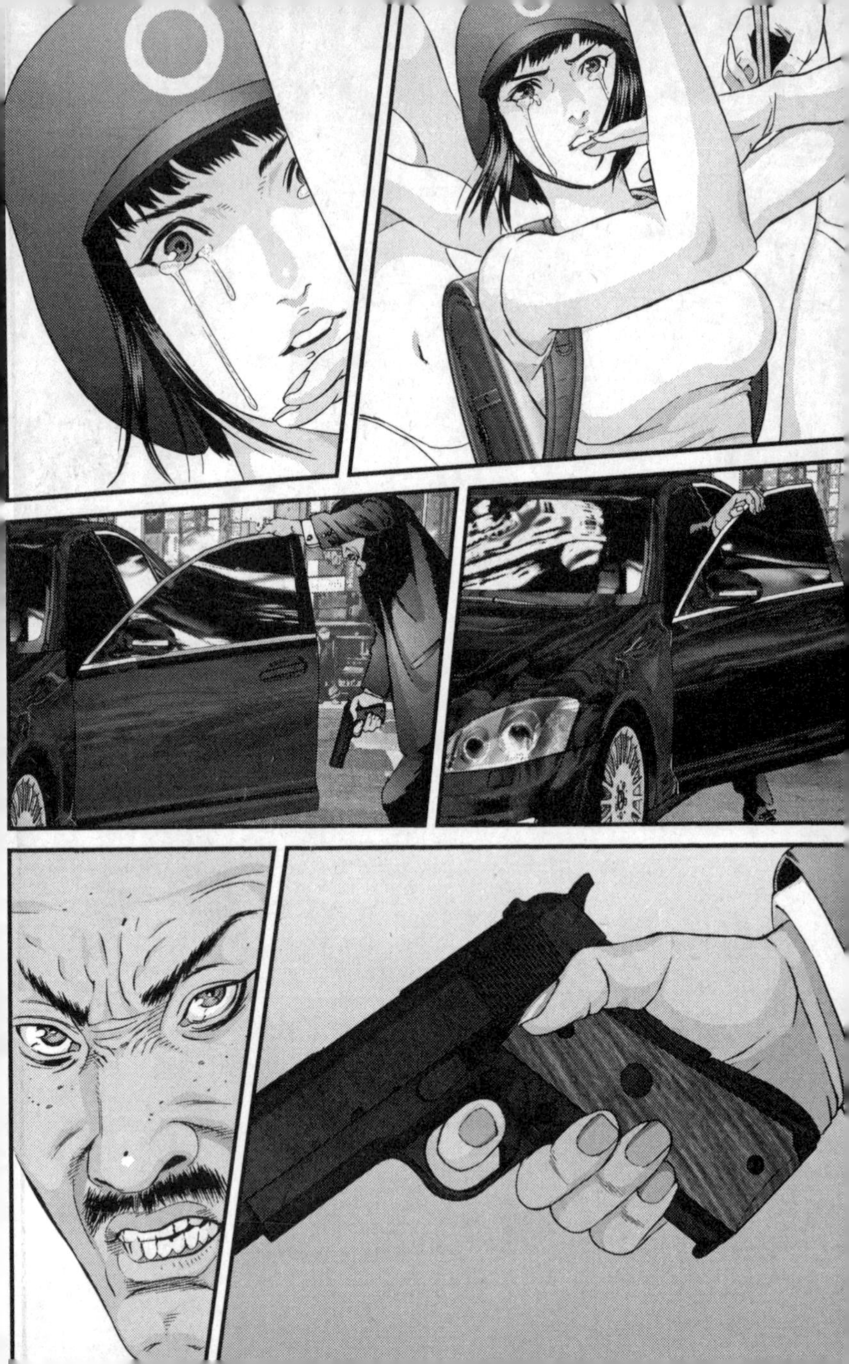

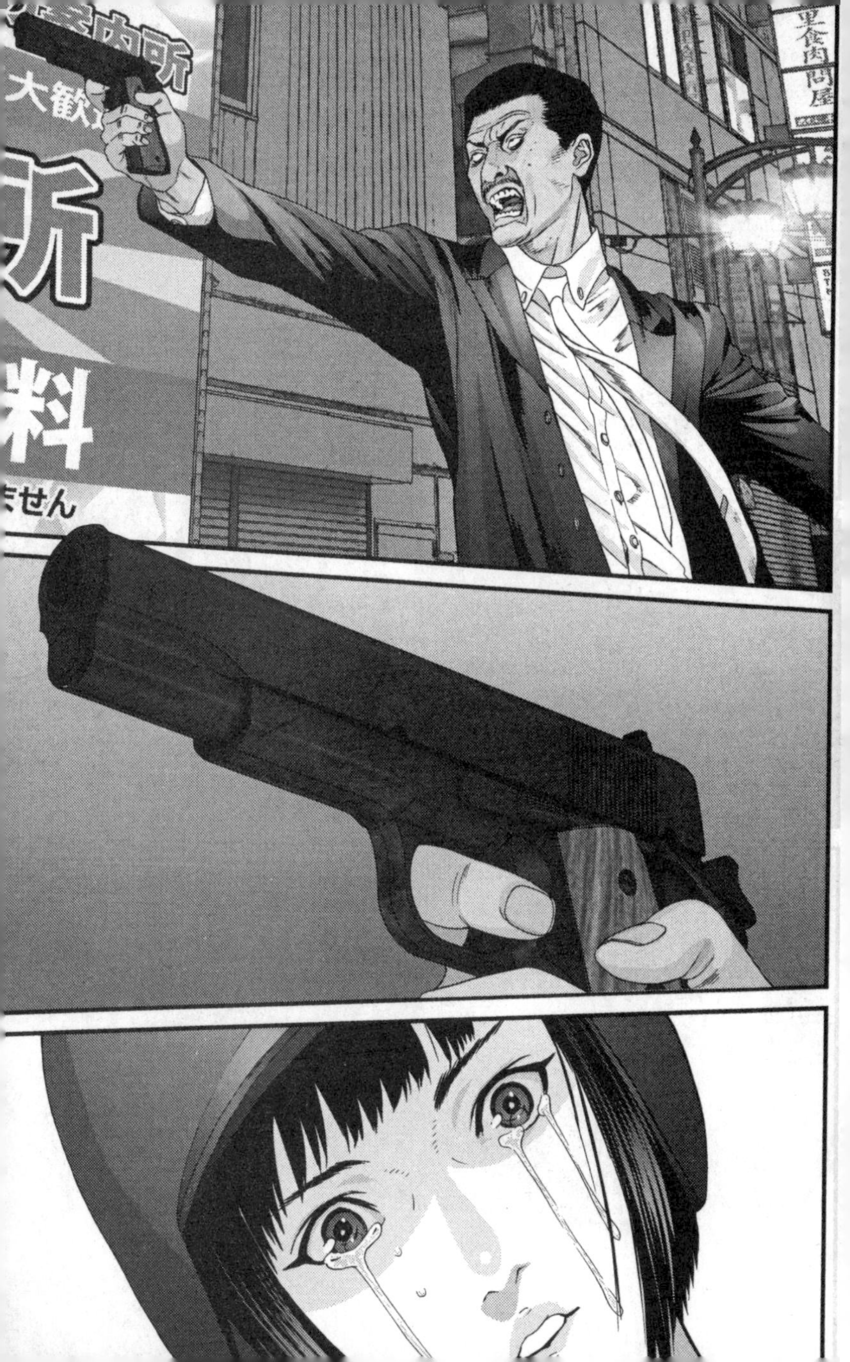
内所
大歓
所
料
せん
食肉問屋

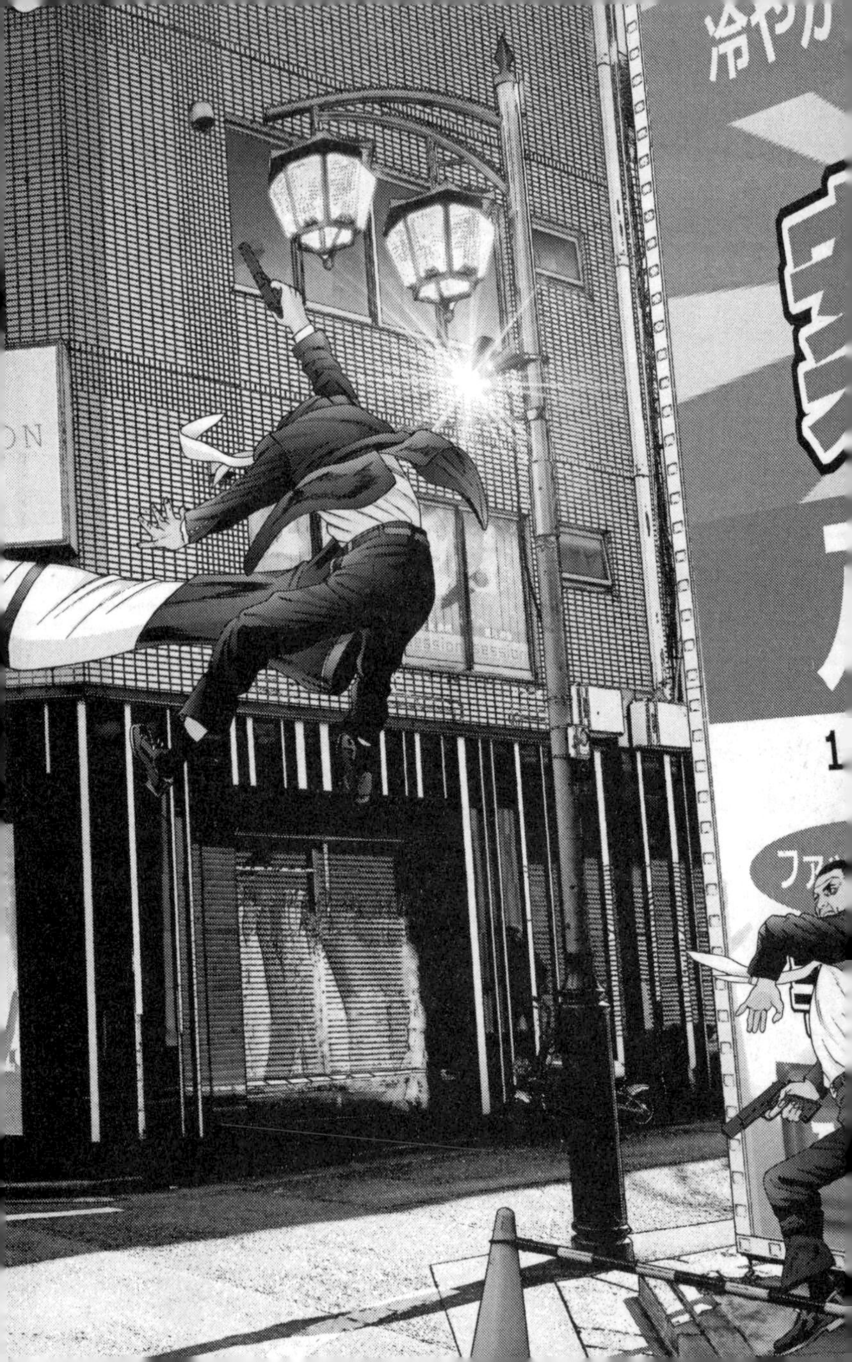
冷やか
ON
ファ

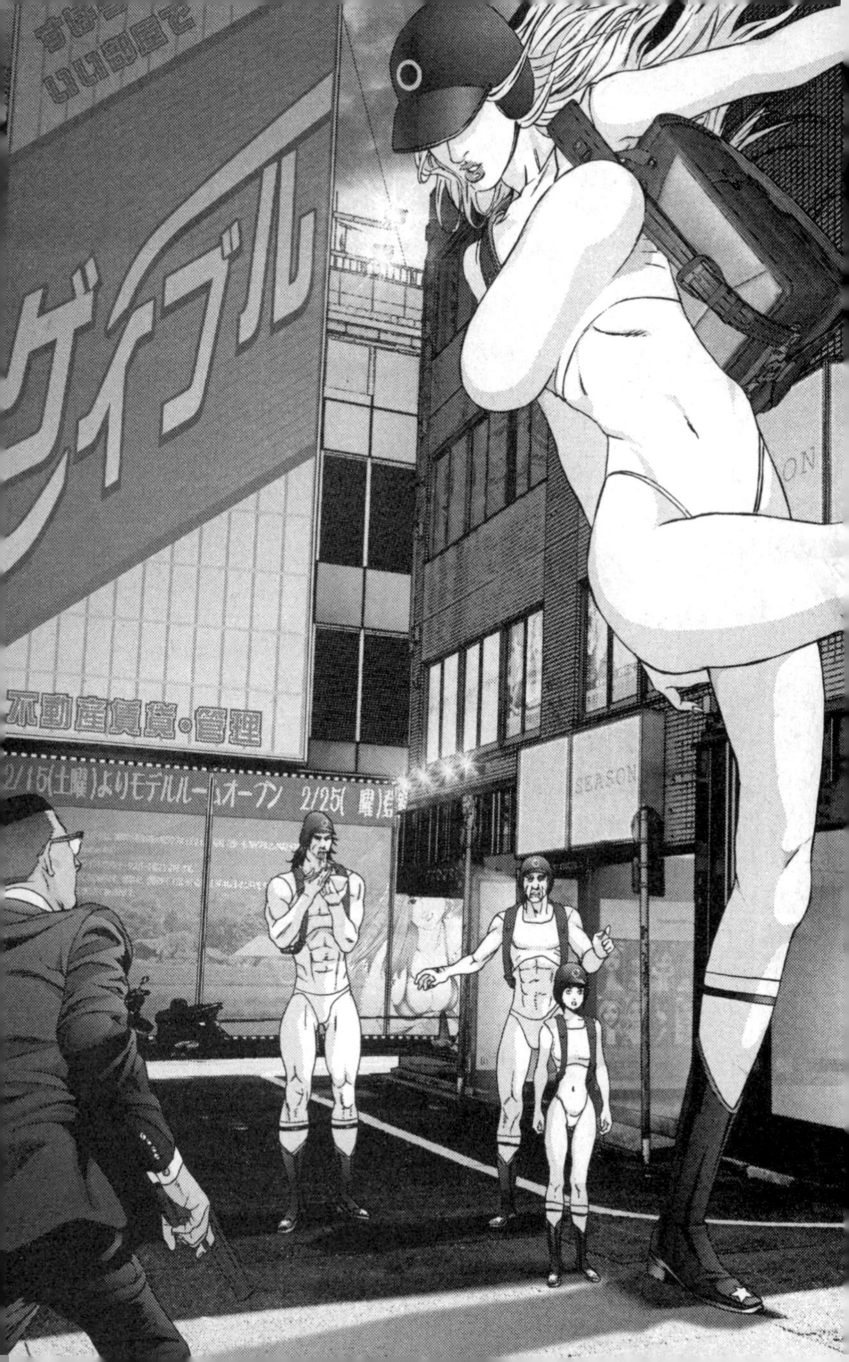
いい部屋で
イブル
不動産賃貸・管理
2/15(土曜)よりモデルルームオープン
SEASON

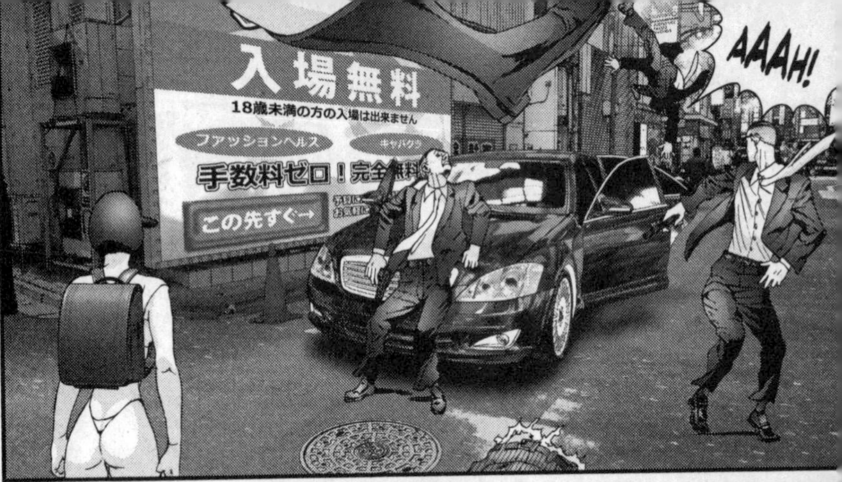
入場無料
18歳未満の方の入場は出来ません
ファッションヘルス
キャバクラ
手数料ゼロ！完全無料
この先すぐ→
AAAH!

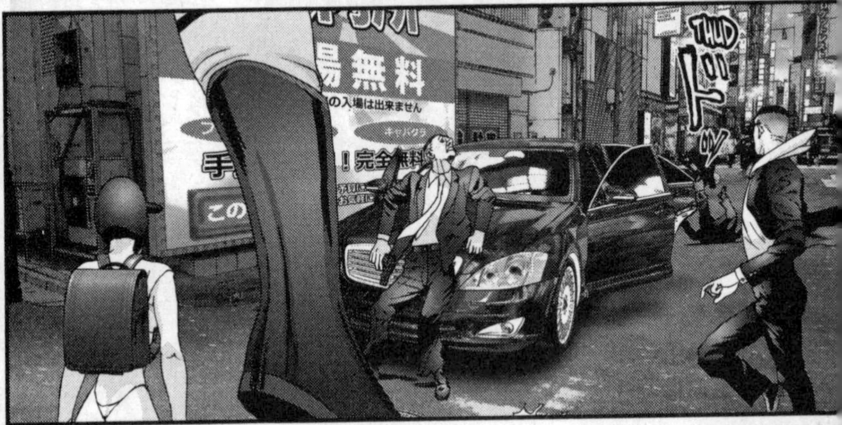
THUD
ドッ

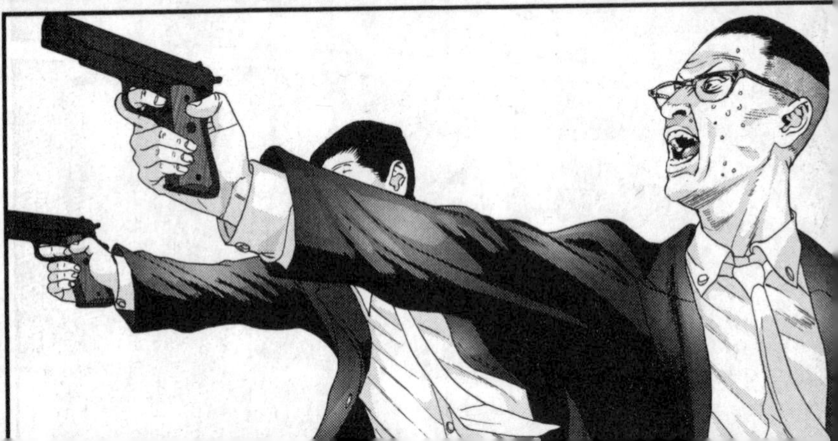

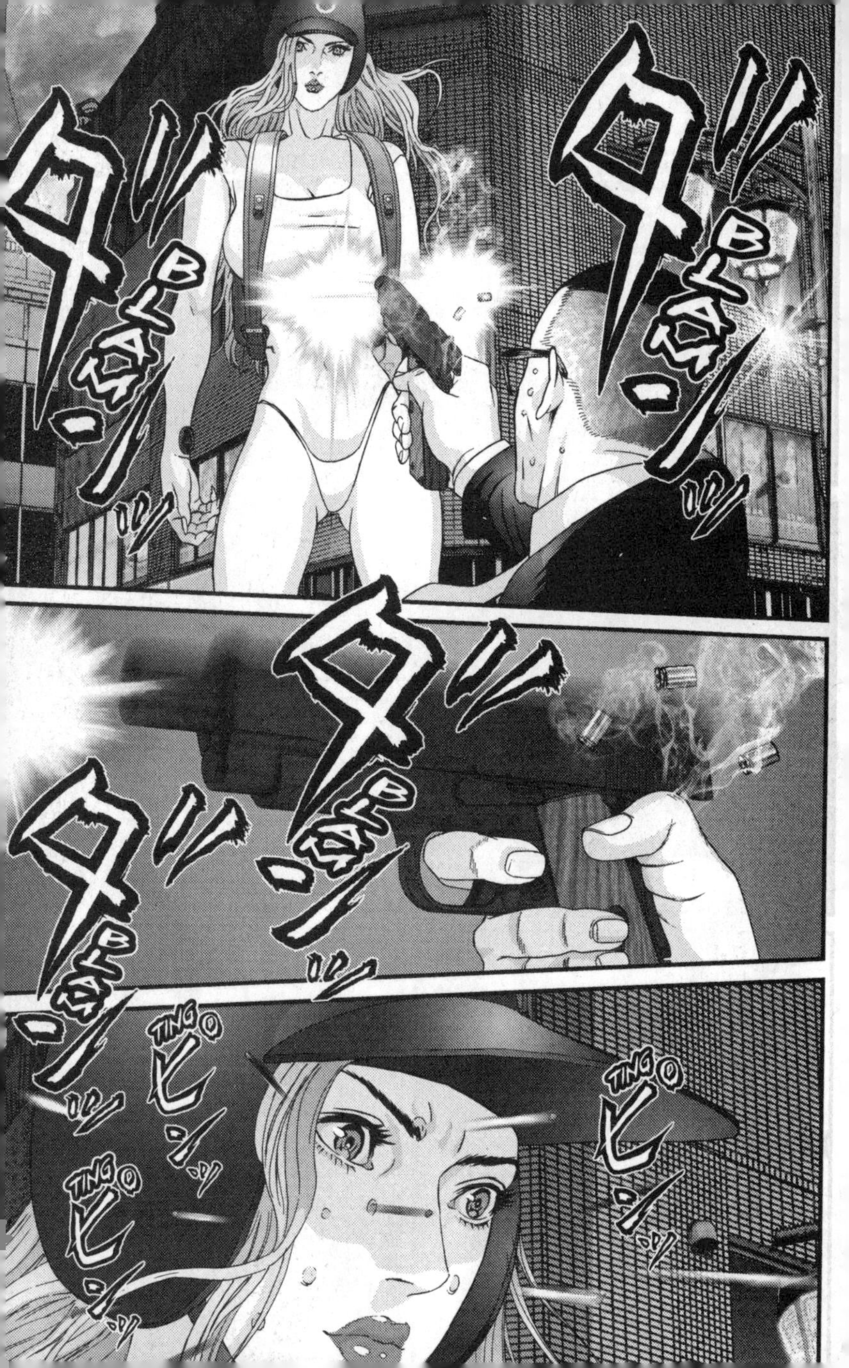
タッ
BLAM
タッ
BLAM
タッ
BLAM
タッ
BLAM
ピン
TING
ピン
TING
ピン
TING

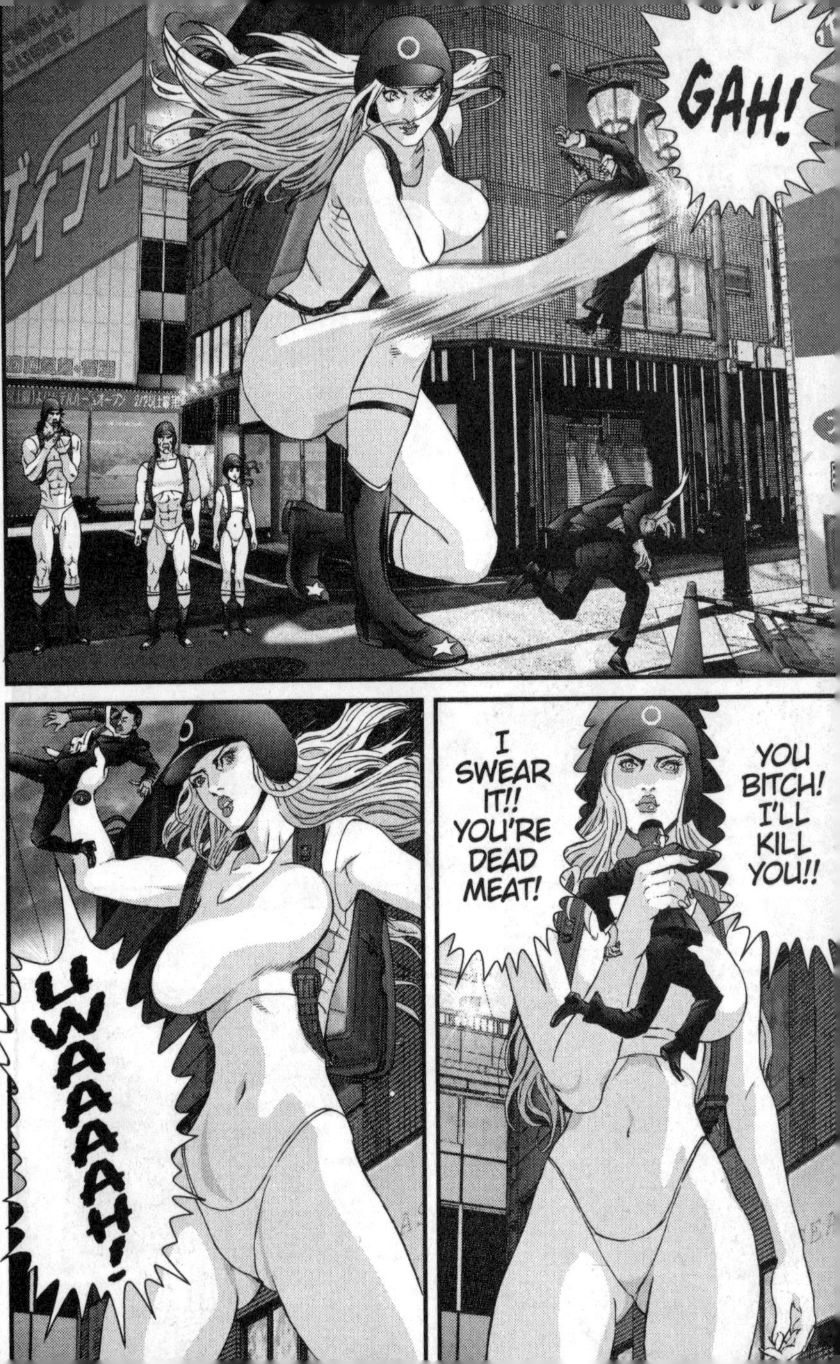
GAH!
YOU BITCH! I'LL KILL YOU!!
I SWEAR IT!! YOU'RE DEAD MEAT!
UWAAAAAH!

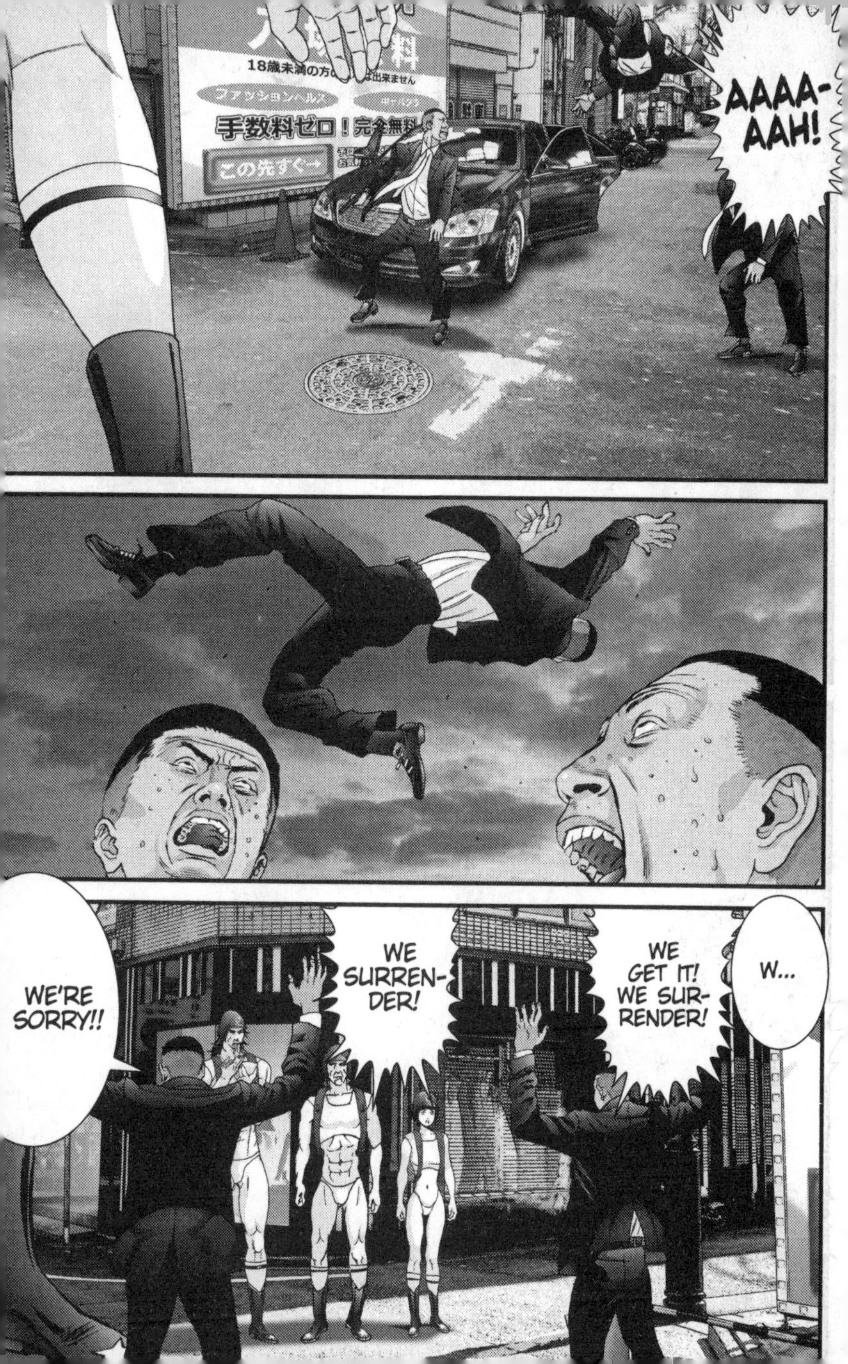
手数料ゼロ！
この先すぐ→
AAAA-AAH!
W...
WE GET IT! WE SURRENDER!
WE SURRENDER!
WE'RE SORRY!!

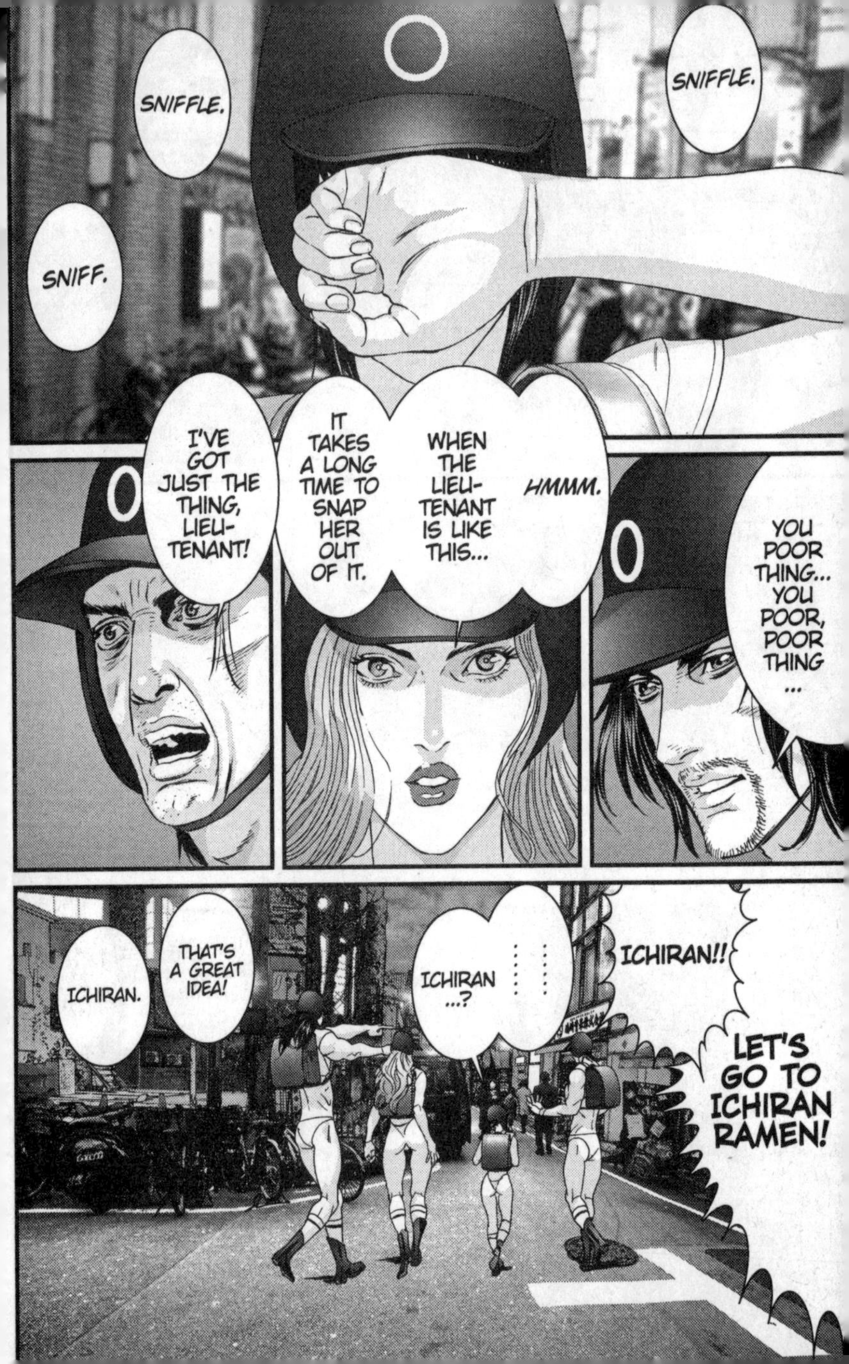

SNIFFLE.
SNIFFLE.
SNIFF.
YOU POOR THING... YOU POOR, POOR THING ...
HMMM.
WHEN THE LIEUTENANT IS LIKE THIS...
IT TAKES A LONG TIME TO SNAP HER OUT OF IT.
I'VE GOT JUST THE THING, LIEUTENANT!
ICHIRAN!!
LET'S GO TO ICHIRAN RAMEN!
... ...
ICHIRAN ...?
THAT'S A GREAT IDEA!
ICHIRAN.

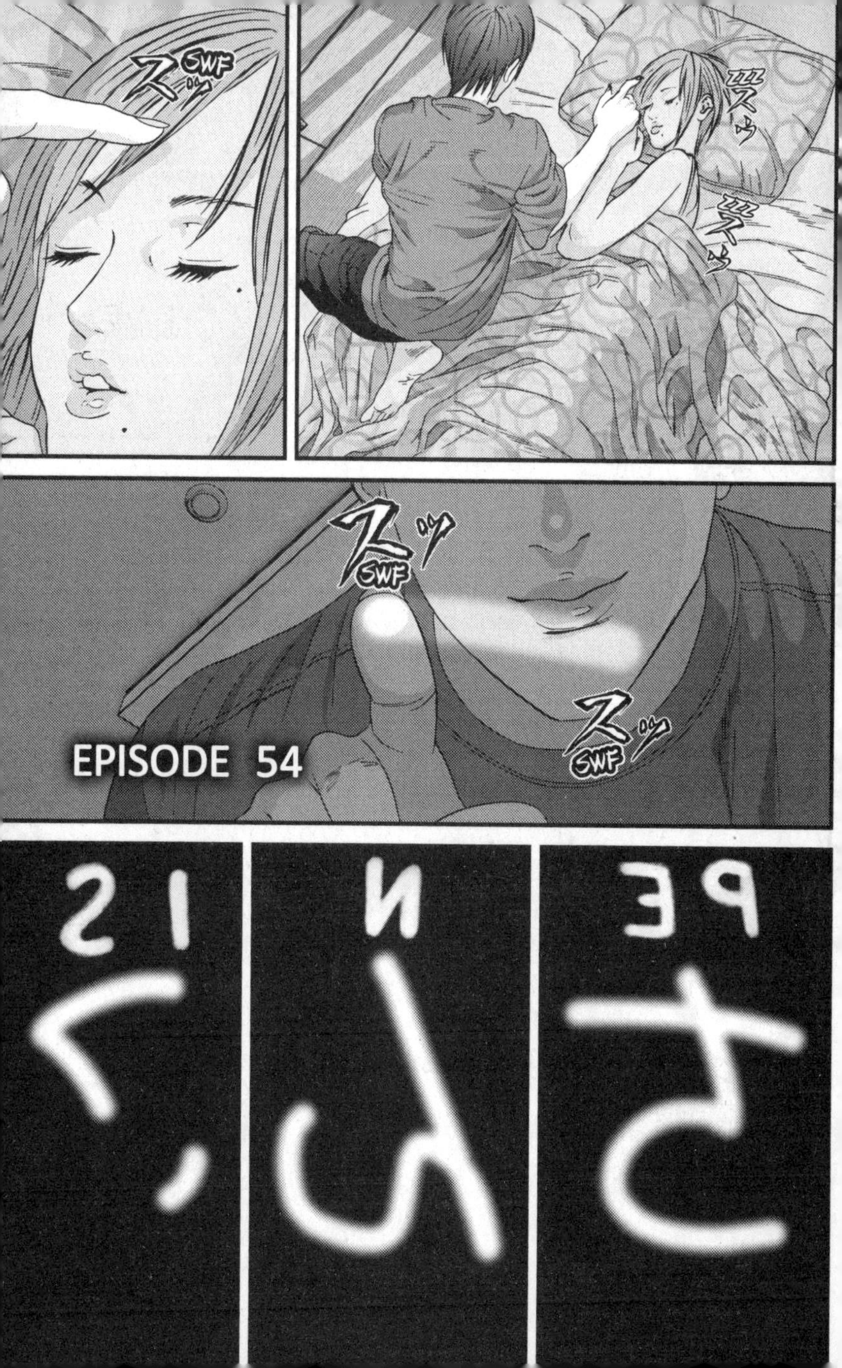
ZZZ
ZZZ
SWF
SWF
SWF
EPISODE 54
PE
N
IS

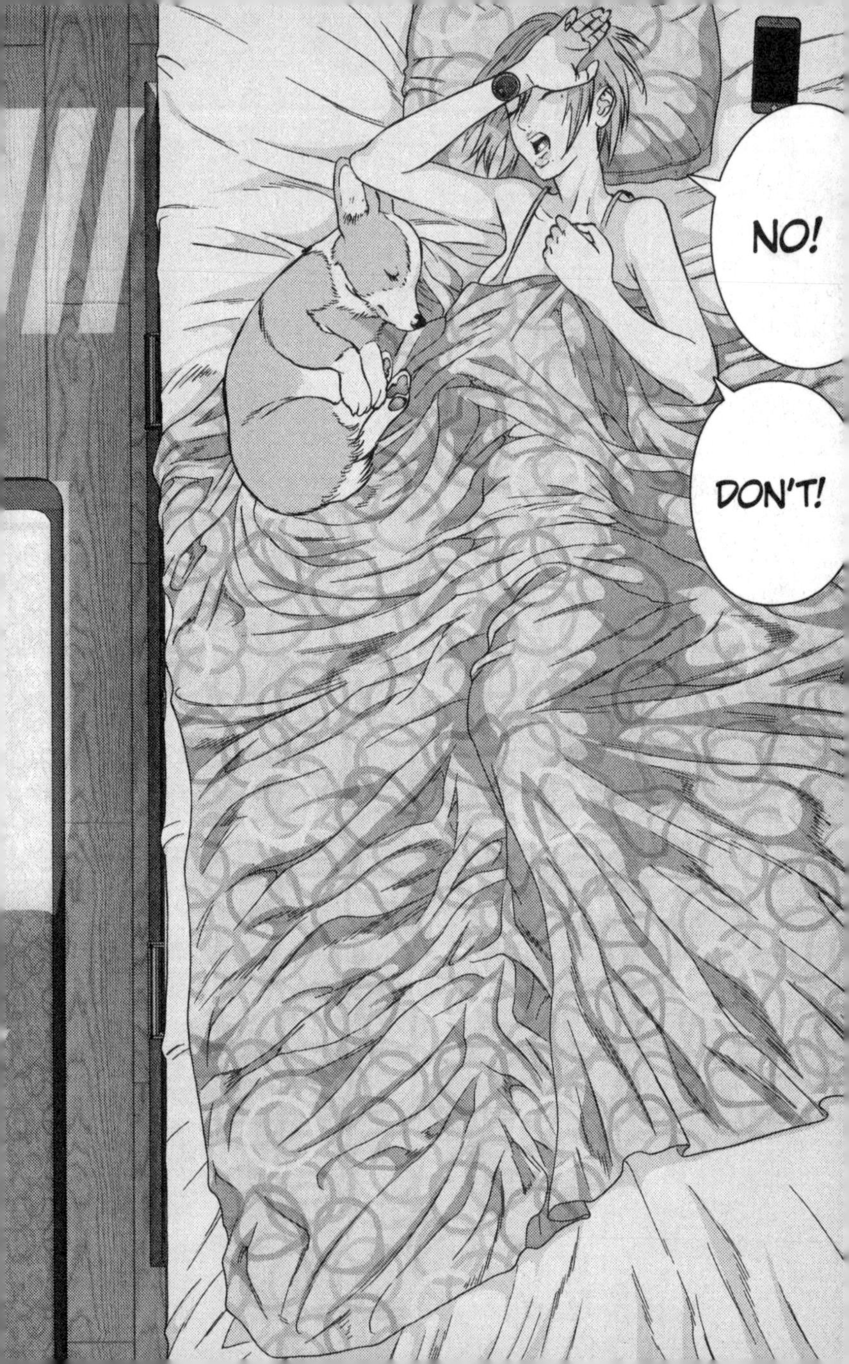
NO!
DON'T!

EPISODE 54: BOYFRIEND

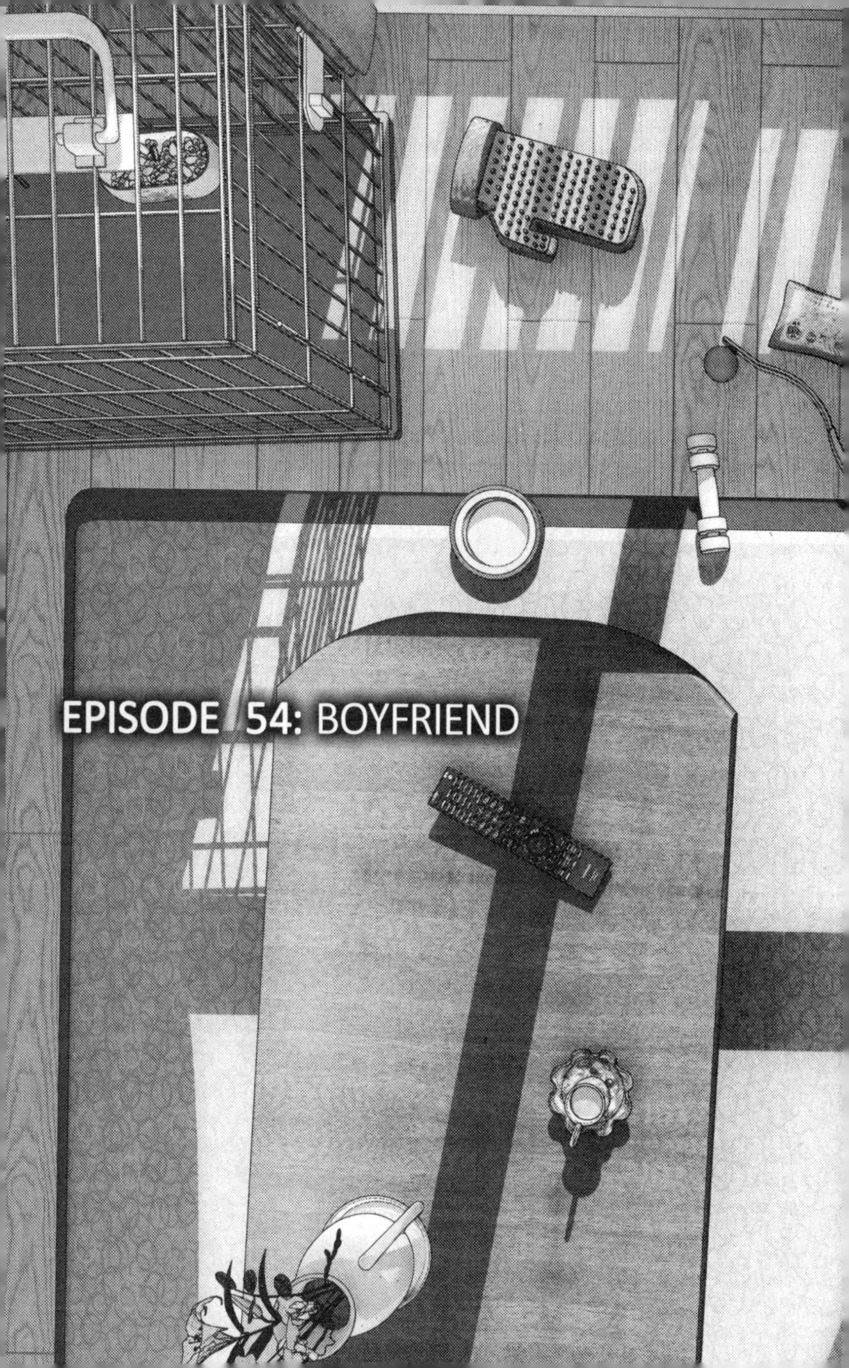

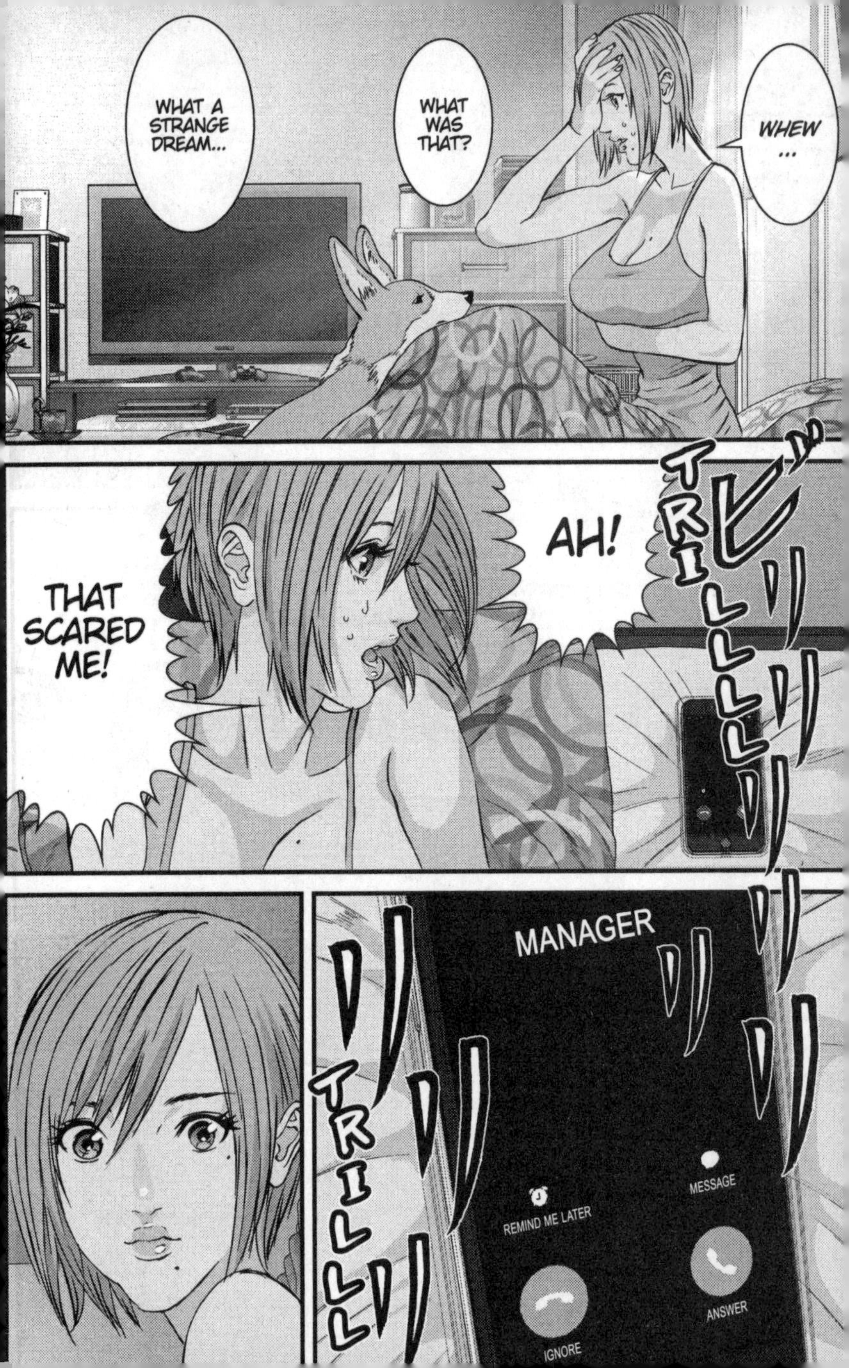
WHEW ...
WHAT WAS THAT?
WHAT A STRANGE DREAM...
TRILLLLL
AH!
THAT SCARED ME!
MANAGER
MESSAGE
REMIND ME LATER
ANSWER
IGNORE
TRILLL

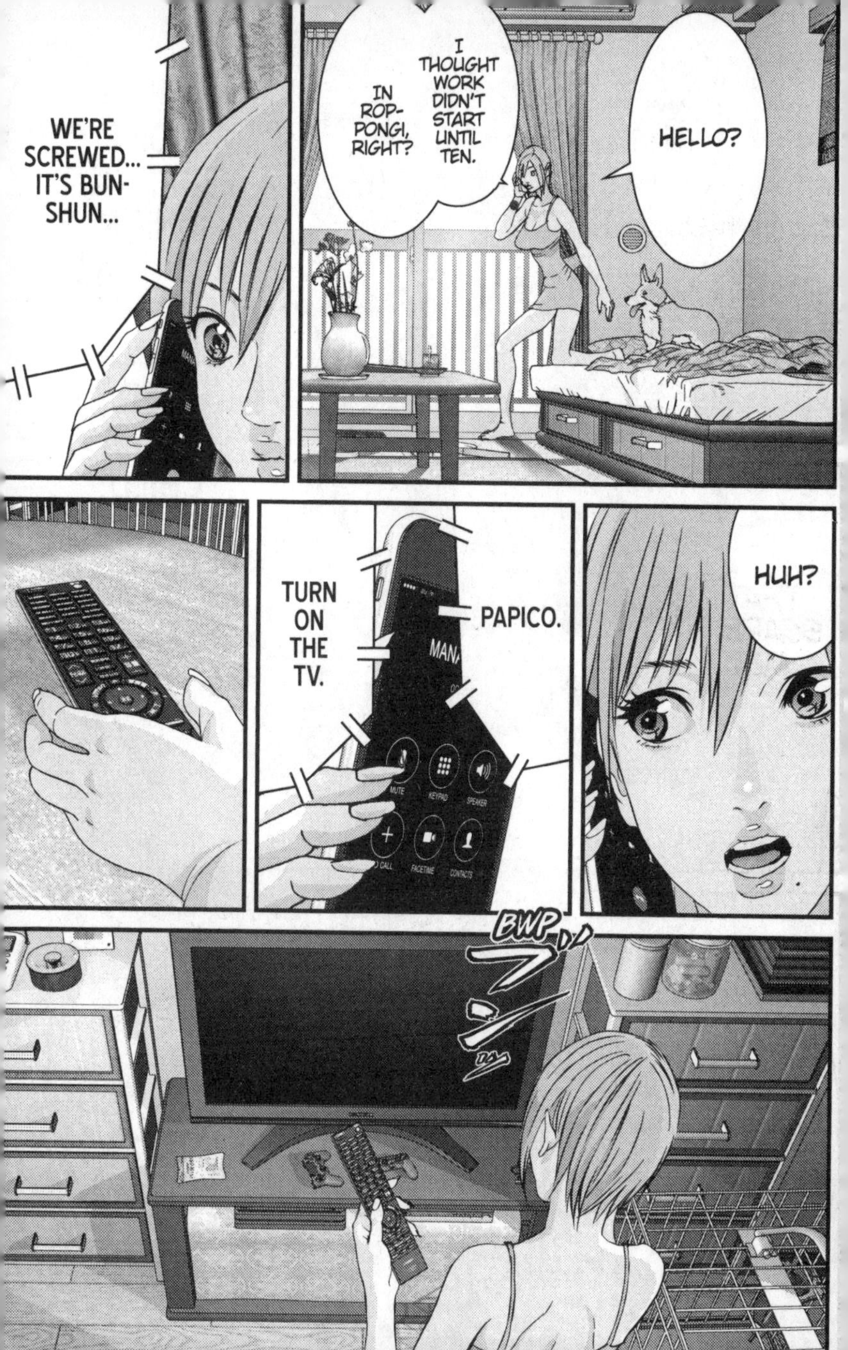
HELLO?
I THOUGHT WORK DIDN'T START UNTIL TEN.
IN ROP-PONGI, RIGHT?
WE'RE SCREWED... IT'S BUN-SHUN...
HUH?
PAPICO.
TURN ON THE TV.
BWP

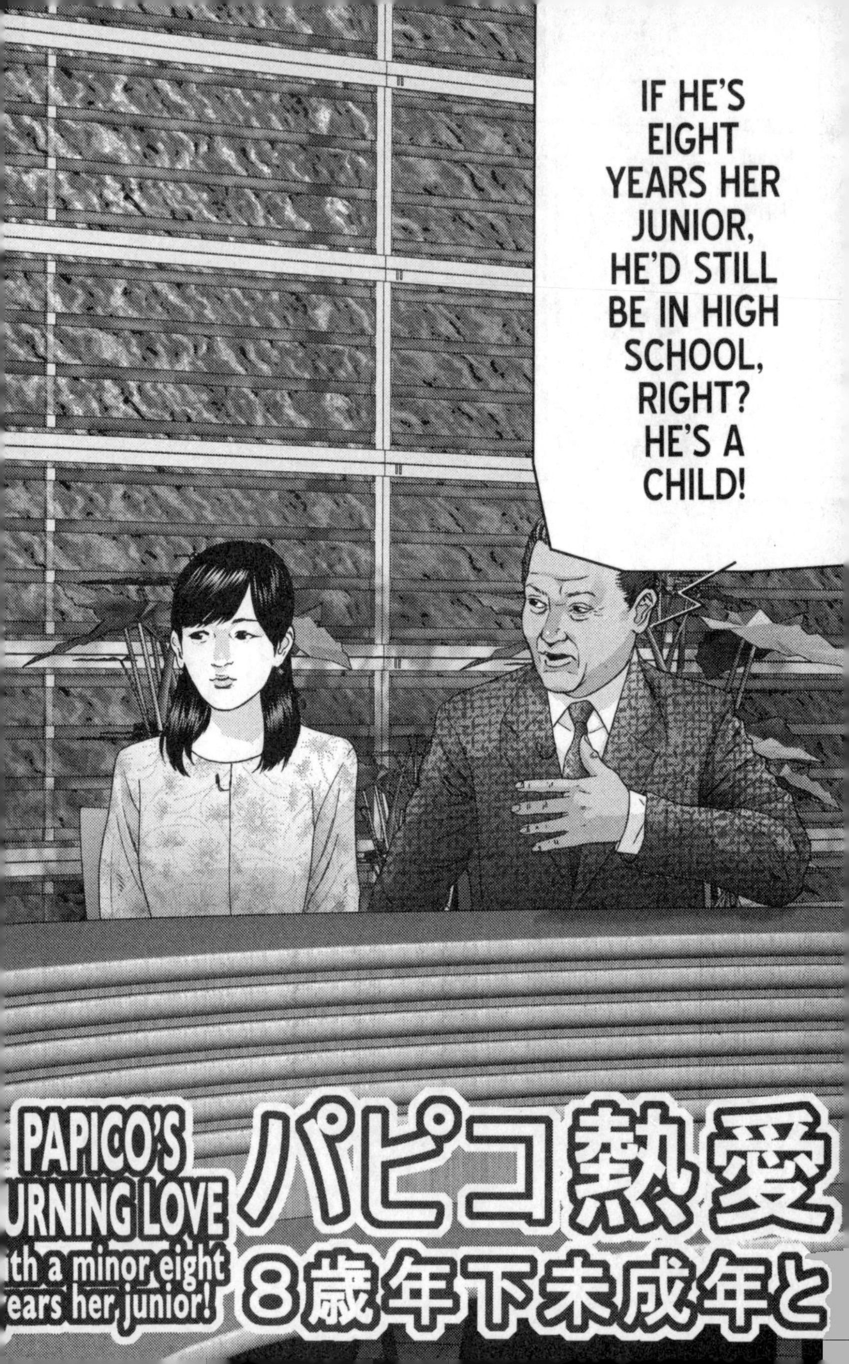
IF HE'S EIGHT YEARS HER JUNIOR, HE'D STILL BE IN HIGH SCHOOL, RIGHT? HE'S A CHILD!
PAPICO'S
URNING LOVE
th a minor eight
ears her junior!
パピコ熱愛
8歳年下未成年と

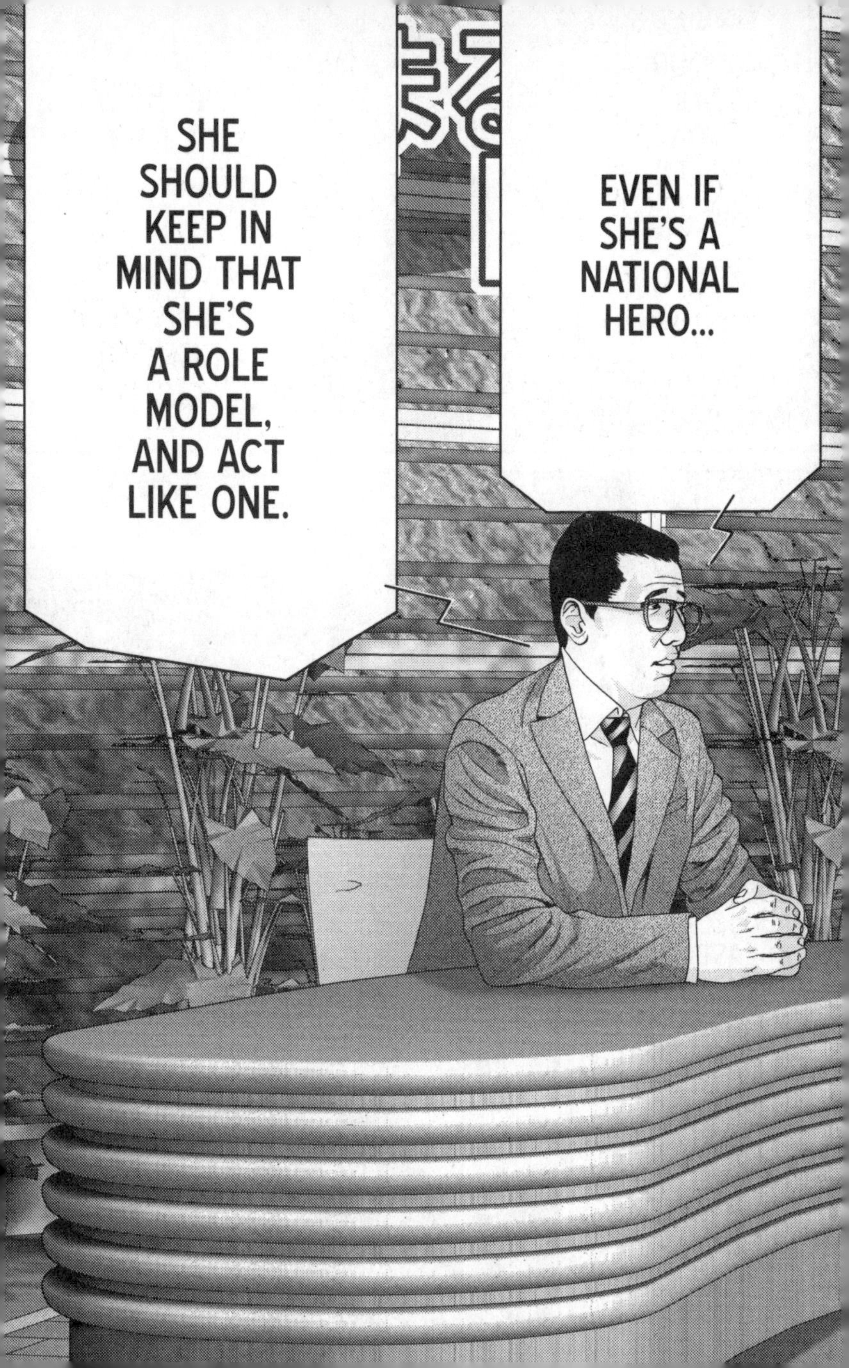
EVEN IF SHE'S A NATIONAL HERO...
SHE SHOULD KEEP IN MIND THAT SHE'S A ROLE MODEL, AND ACT LIKE ONE.

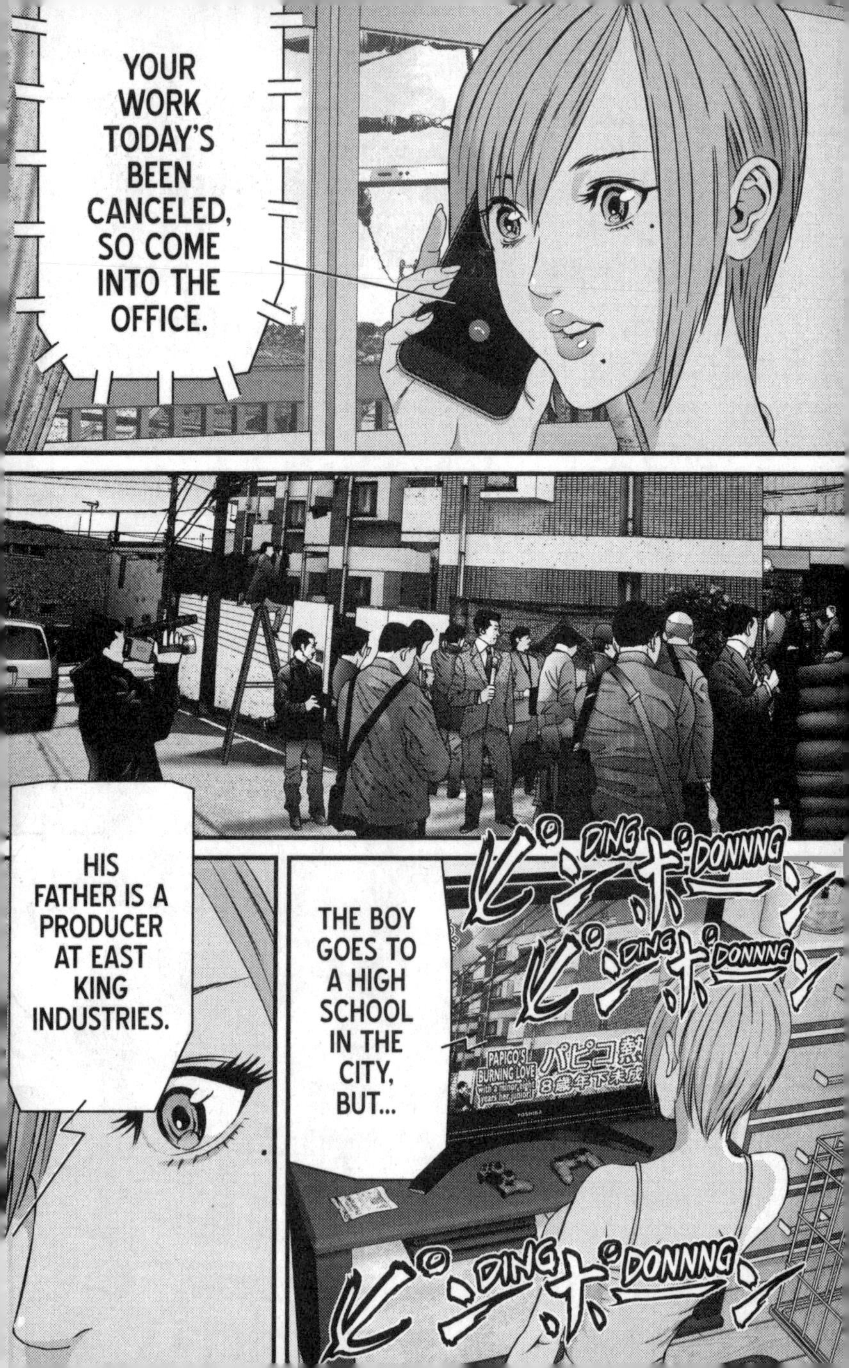
YOUR WORK TODAY'S BEEN CANCELED, SO COME INTO THE OFFICE.
ピンポーン DING DONNNG
ピンポーン DING DONNNG
THE BOY GOES TO A HIGH SCHOOL IN THE CITY, BUT...
PAPICO'S BURNING LOVE with a minor eight years her junior
ピンポーン DING DONNNG
HIS FATHER IS A PRODUCER AT EAST KING INDUSTRIES.

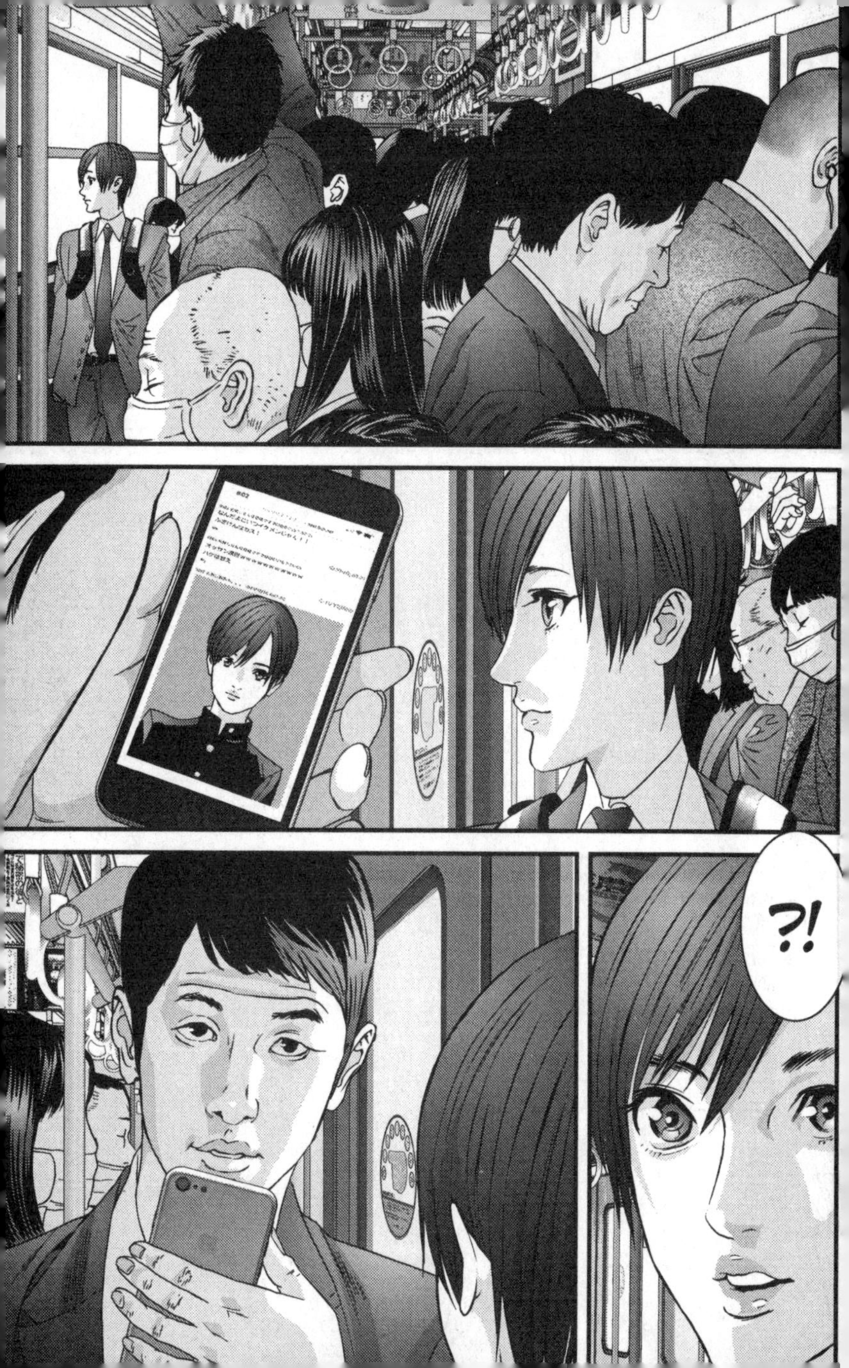
#02
なんだよこいつイケメンじゃん！！
ふざけんなカス！
ハゲは甘え
?!

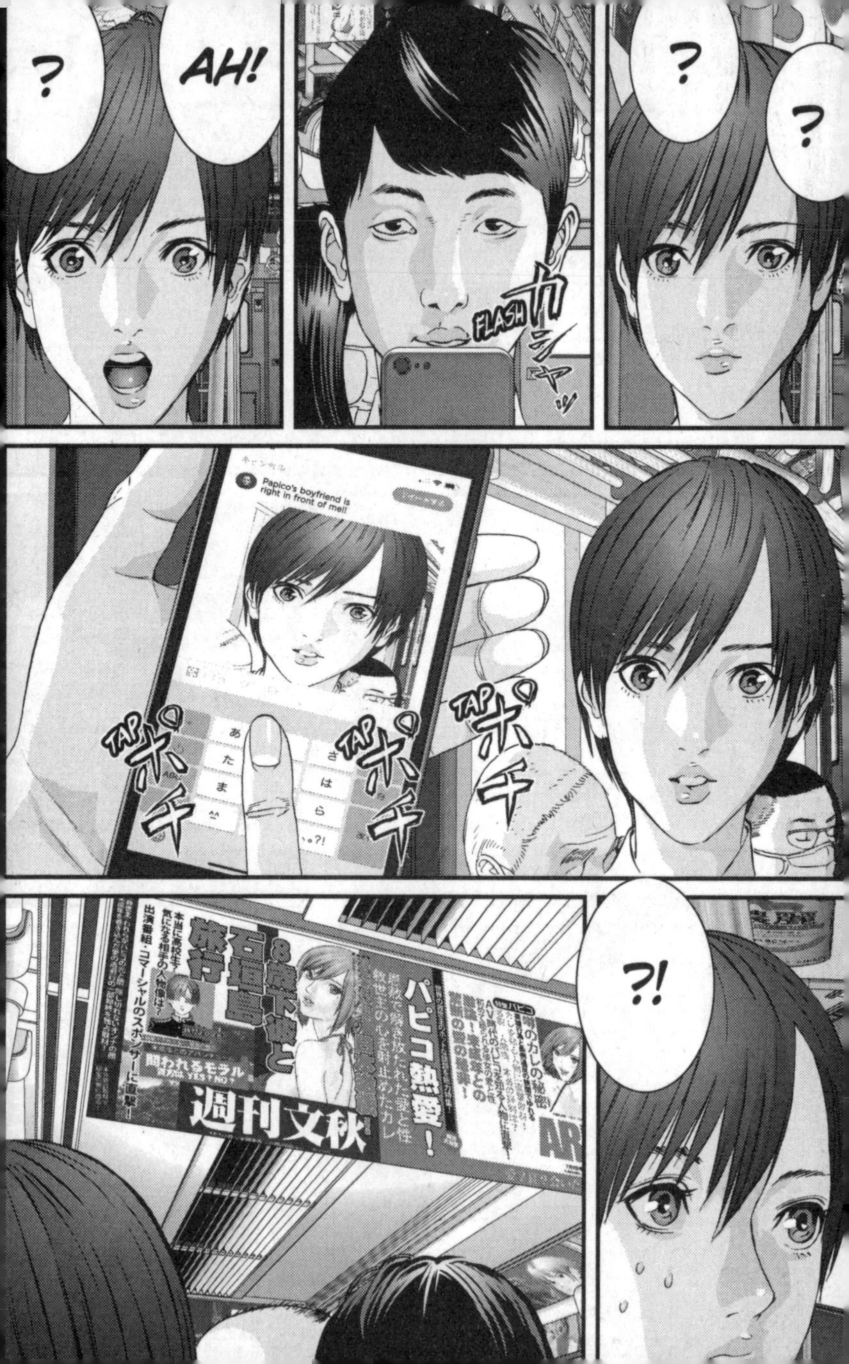
?
?
FLASH カシャッ
AH!
?
Papico's boyfriend is right in front of me!!
TAP ポチ
TAP ポチ
TAP ポチ
?!
パピコ熱愛！
本当に高校生？気になる相手の人物像は？
出演番組・コマーシャルのスポンサーに直撃！
週刊文秋

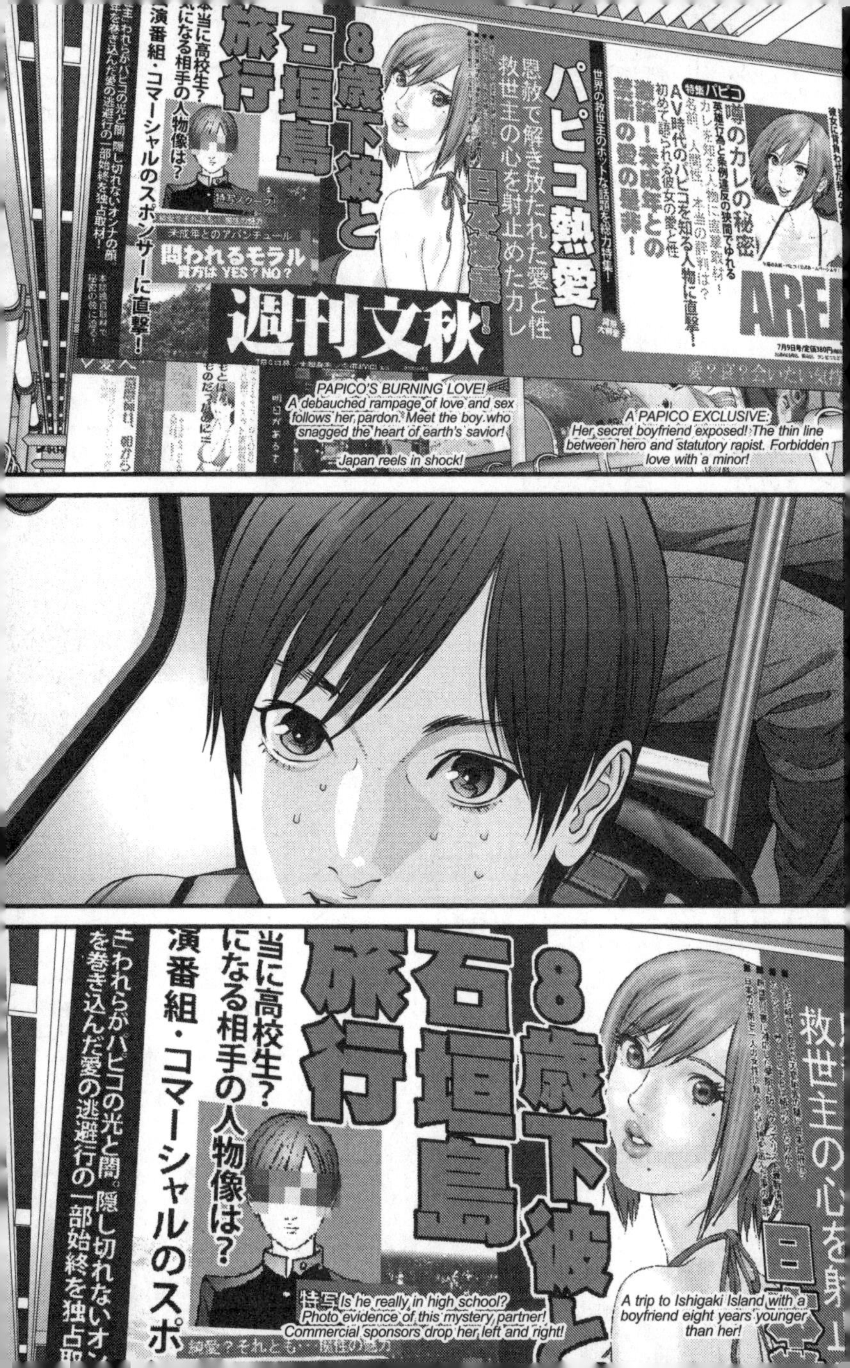
特集パピコ
噂のカレの秘密
A PAPICO EXCLUSIVE:
Her secret boyfriend exposed! The thin line between hero and statutory rapist. Forbidden love with a minor!
世界の救世主のホットな話題を総力特集!
パピコ熱愛!
恩赦で解き放たれた愛と性
救世主の心を射止めたカレ
PAPICO'S BURNING LOVE!
A debauched rampage of love and sex follows her pardon. Meet the boy who snagged the heart of earth's savior!
Japan reels in shock!
週刊文秋!
8歳下彼と
石垣島旅行
本当に高校生?
気になる相手の人物像は?
未成年とのアバンチュール
問われるモラル
貴方は YES? NO?
8歳下彼と
石垣島旅行
当に高校生?
になる相手の人物像は?
A trip to Ishigaki Island with a boyfriend eight years younger than her!
Is he really in high school?
Photo evidence of this mystery partner!
Commercial sponsors drop her left and right!

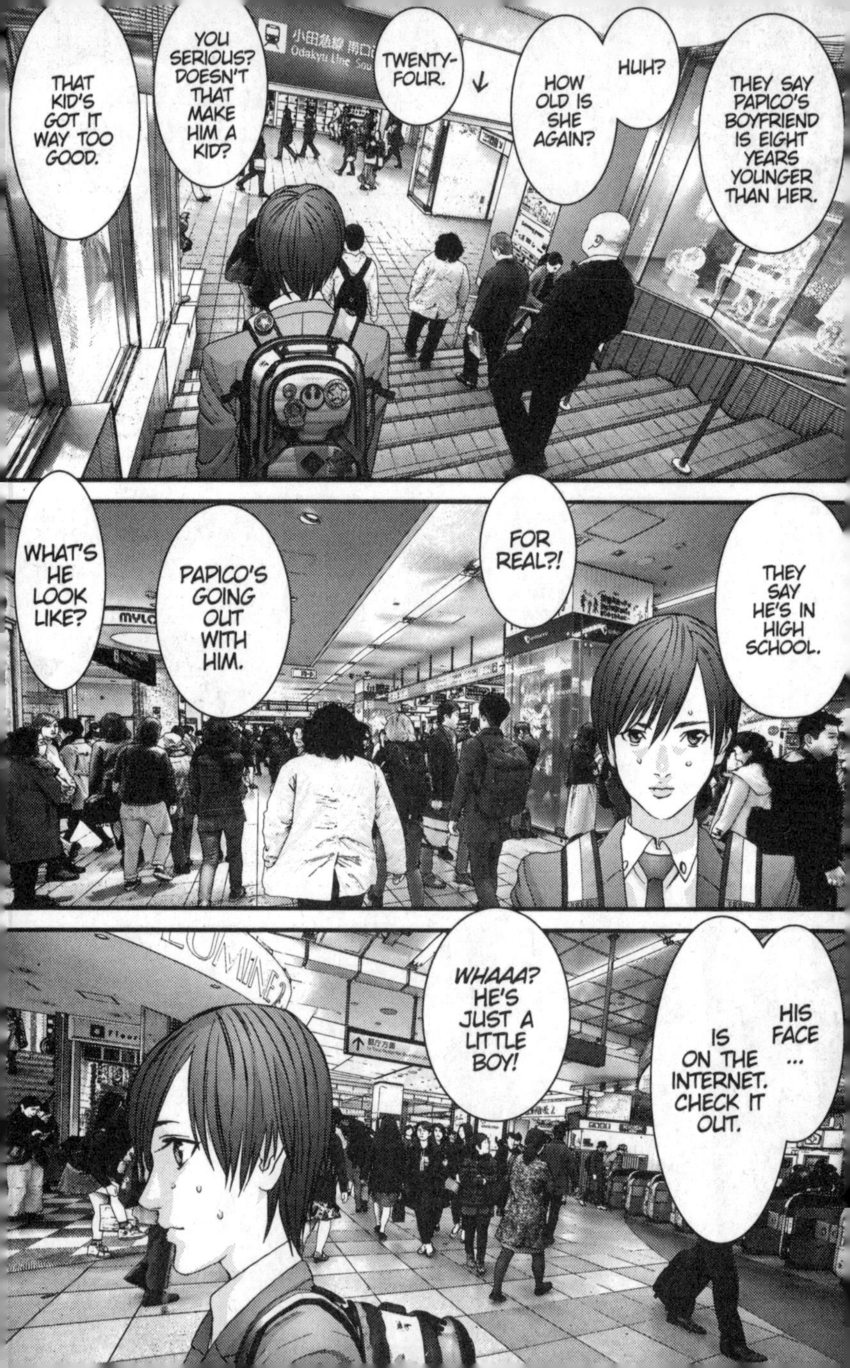
THEY SAY PAPICO'S BOYFRIEND IS EIGHT YEARS YOUNGER THAN HER.
HUH?
HOW OLD IS SHE AGAIN?
TWENTY-FOUR.
YOU SERIOUS? DOESN'T THAT MAKE HIM A KID?
THAT KID'S GOT IT WAY TOO GOOD.
THEY SAY HE'S IN HIGH SCHOOL.
FOR REAL?!
PAPICO'S GOING OUT WITH HIM.
WHAT'S HE LOOK LIKE?
HIS FACE ... IS ON THE INTERNET. CHECK IT OUT.
WHAAA? HE'S JUST A LITTLE BOY!

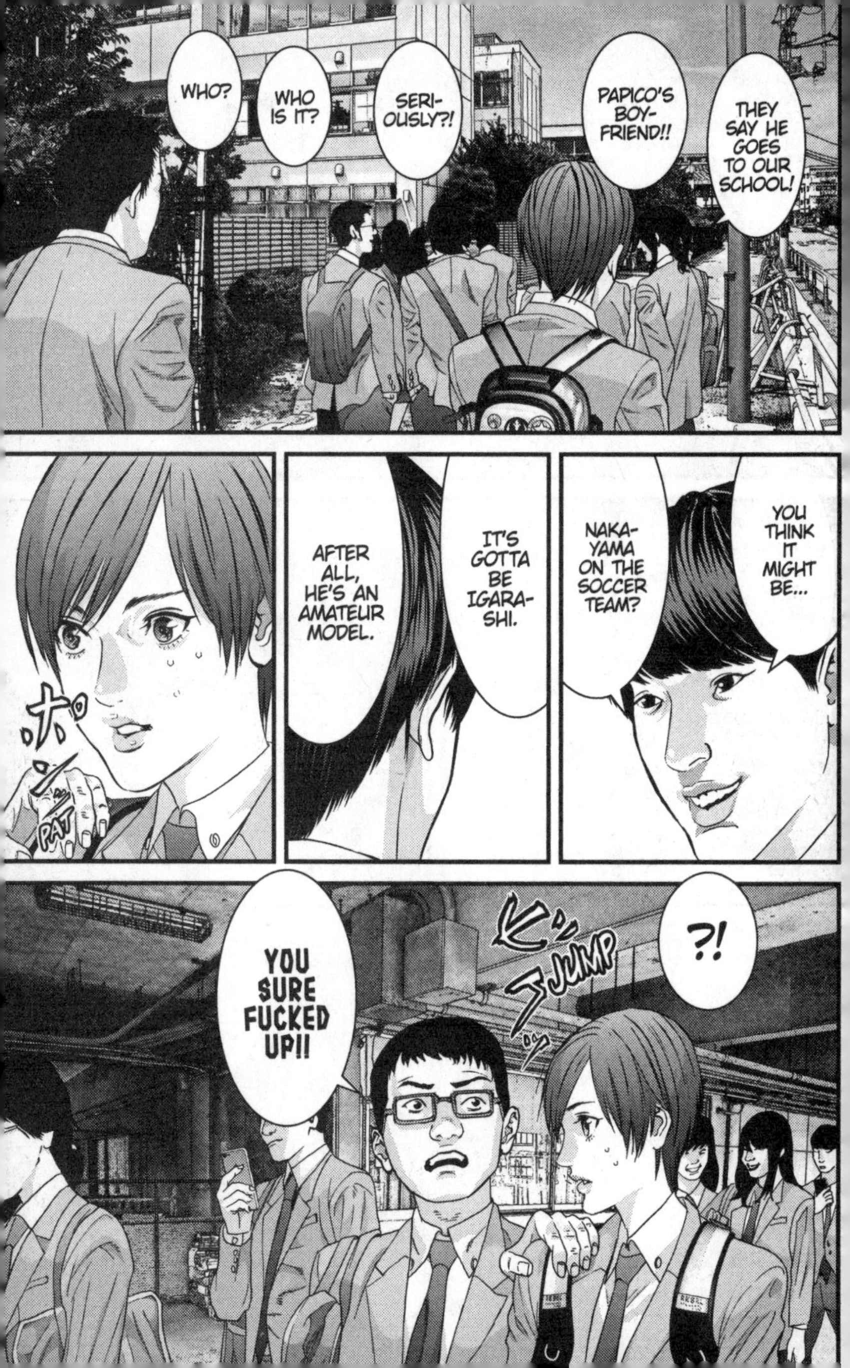
THEY SAY HE GOES TO OUR SCHOOL!
PAPICO'S BOY-FRIEND!!
SERI-OUSLY?!
WHO IS IT?
WHO?
YOU THINK IT MIGHT BE...
NAKA-YAMA ON THE SOCCER TEAM?
IT'S GOTTA BE IGARA-SHI.
AFTER ALL, HE'S AN AMATEUR MODEL.
PAT
?!
JUMP
YOU SURE FUCKED UP!!

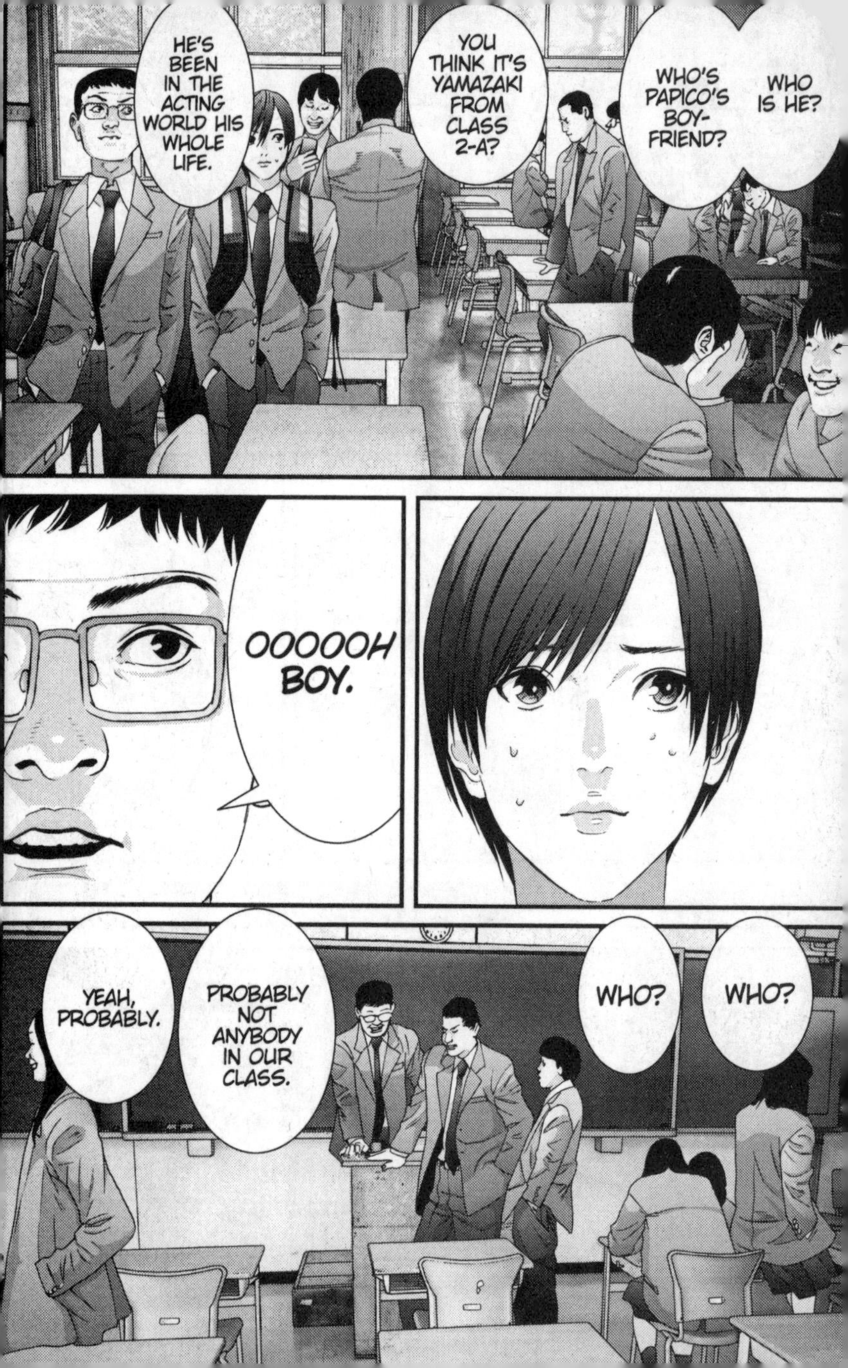
WHO IS HE?
WHO'S PAPICO'S BOY-FRIEND?
YOU THINK IT'S YAMAZAKI FROM CLASS 2-A?
HE'S BEEN IN THE ACTING WORLD HIS WHOLE LIFE.
OOOOOH BOY.
WHO?
WHO?
PROBABLY NOT ANYBODY IN OUR CLASS.
YEAH, PROBABLY.

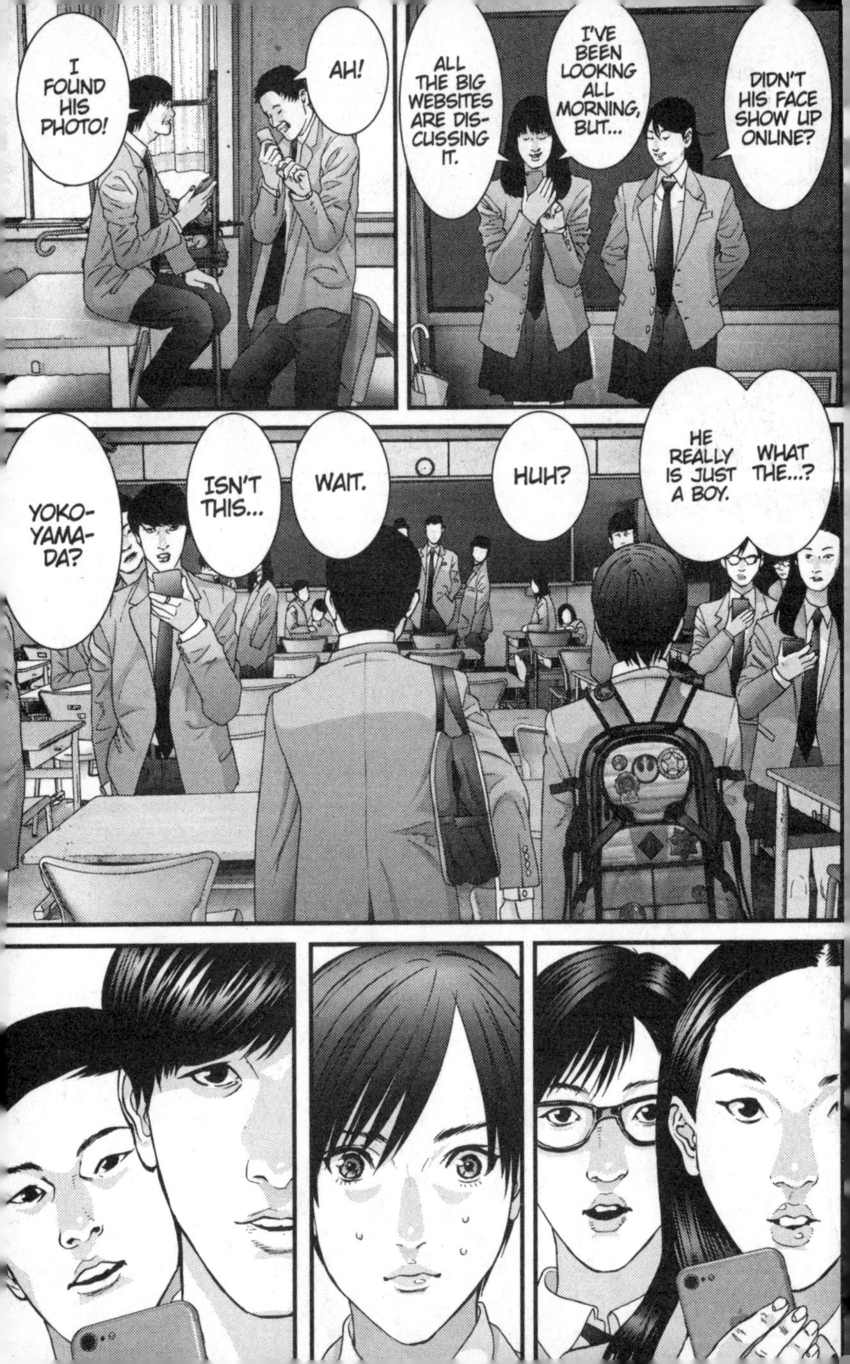
DIDN'T HIS FACE SHOW UP ONLINE?
I'VE BEEN LOOKING ALL MORNING, BUT...
ALL THE BIG WEBSITES ARE DIS-CUSSING IT.
AH!
I FOUND HIS PHOTO!
WHAT THE...?
HE REALLY IS JUST A BOY.
HUH?
WAIT.
ISN'T THIS...
YOKO-YAMA-DA?

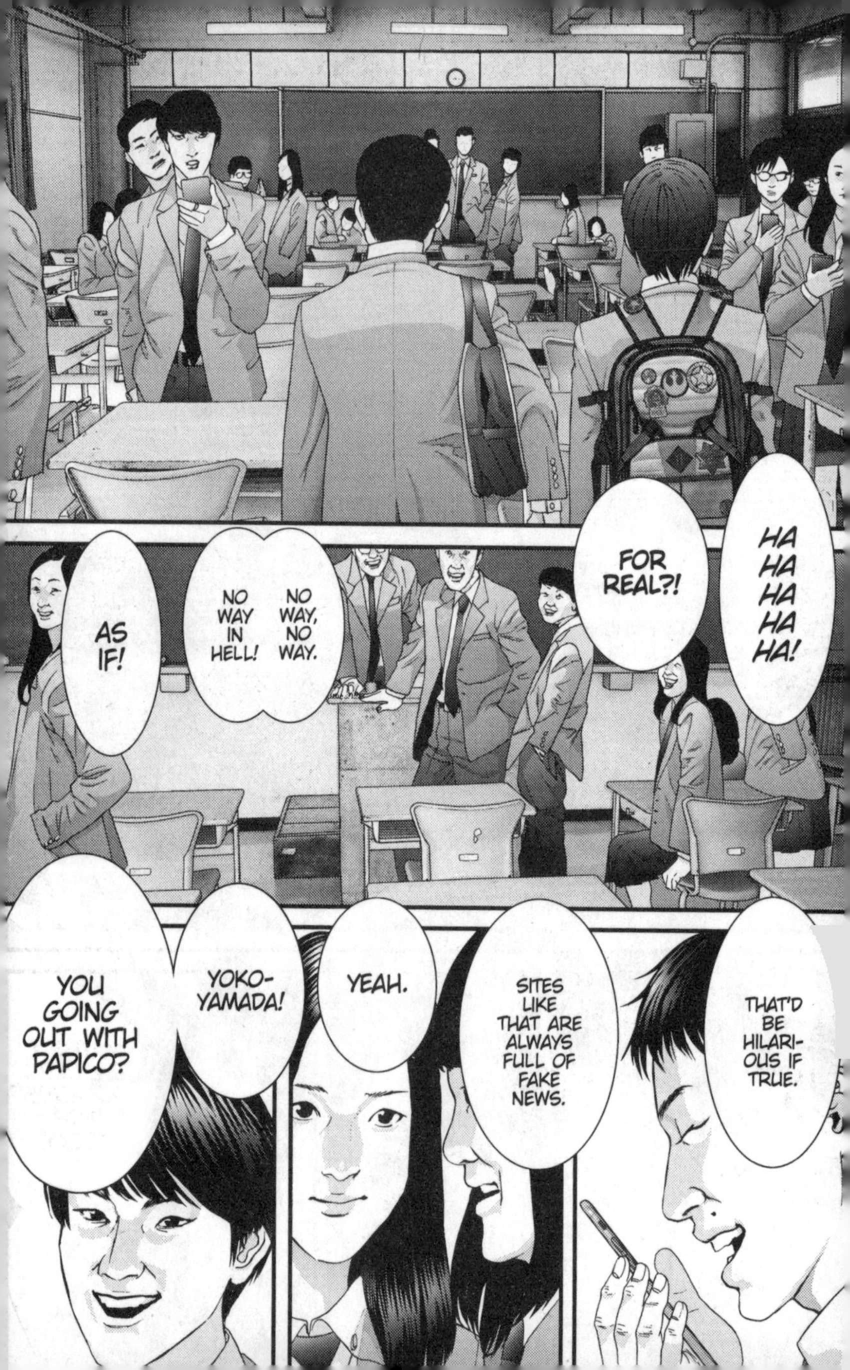
HA HA HA HA HA!
FOR REAL?!
NO WAY, NO WAY.
NO WAY IN HELL!
AS IF!
THAT'D BE HILARI-OUS IF TRUE.
SITES LIKE THAT ARE ALWAYS FULL OF FAKE NEWS.
YEAH.
YOKO-YAMADA!
YOU GOING OUT WITH PAPICO?

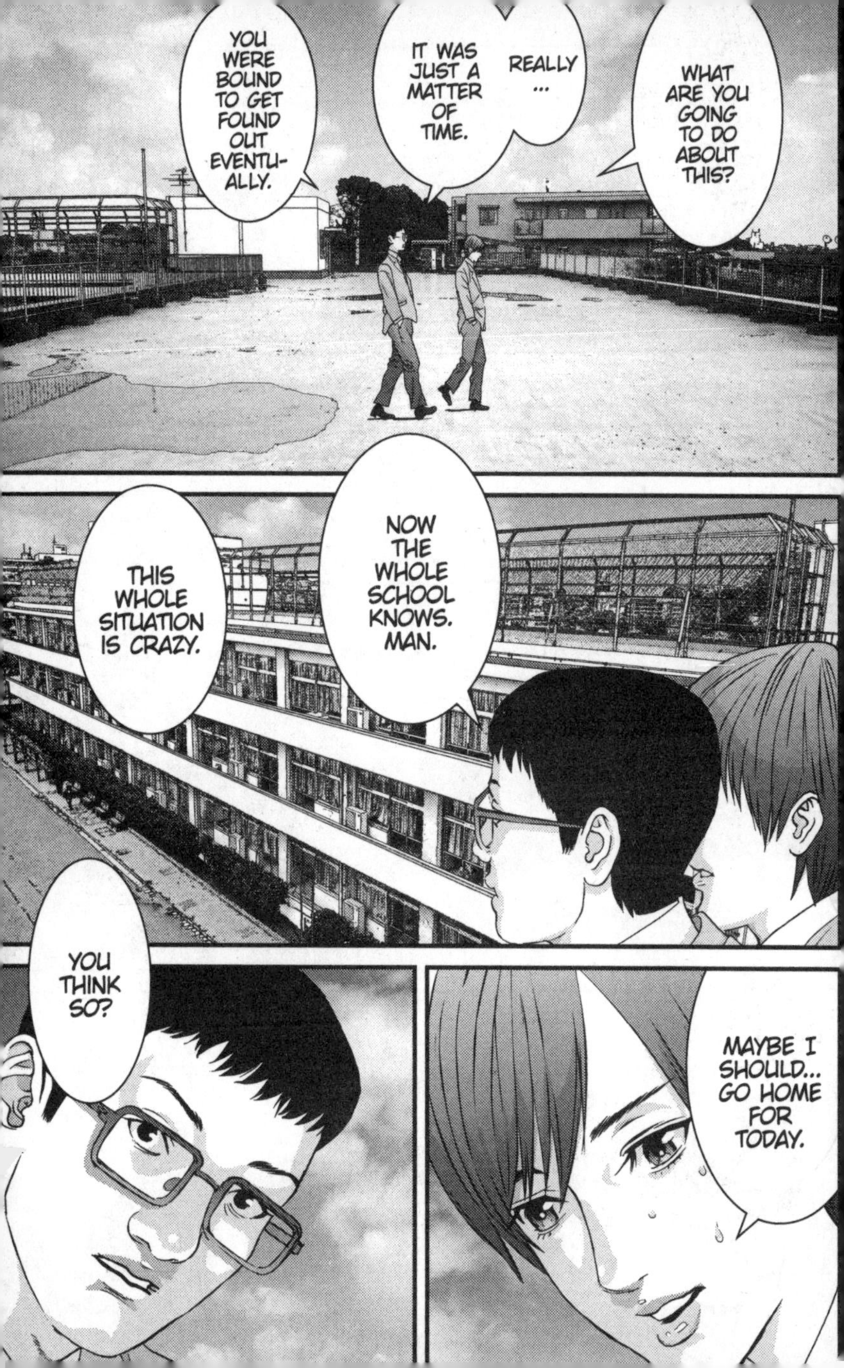
WHAT ARE YOU GOING TO DO ABOUT THIS?
REALLY ...
IT WAS JUST A MATTER OF TIME.
YOU WERE BOUND TO GET FOUND OUT EVENTU-ALLY.
NOW THE WHOLE SCHOOL KNOWS. MAN.
THIS WHOLE SITUATION IS CRAZY.
MAYBE I SHOULD... GO HOME FOR TODAY.
YOU THINK SO?

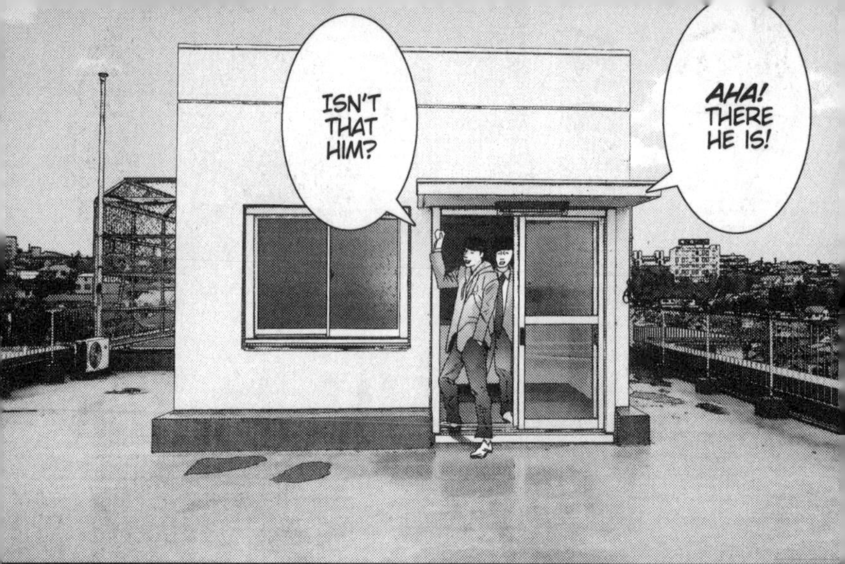
AHA! THERE HE IS!
ISN'T THAT HIM?
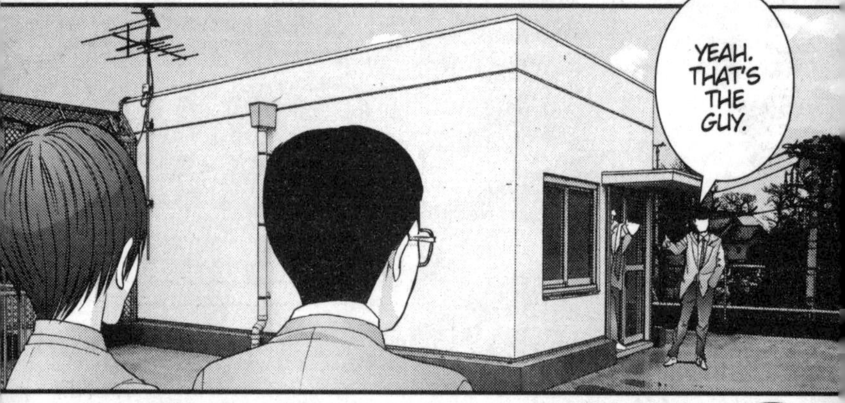
YEAH. THAT'S THE GUY.
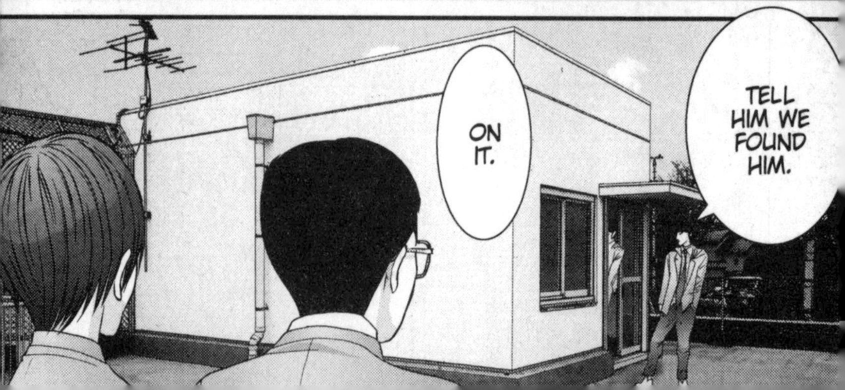
TELL HIM WE FOUND HIM.
ON IT.

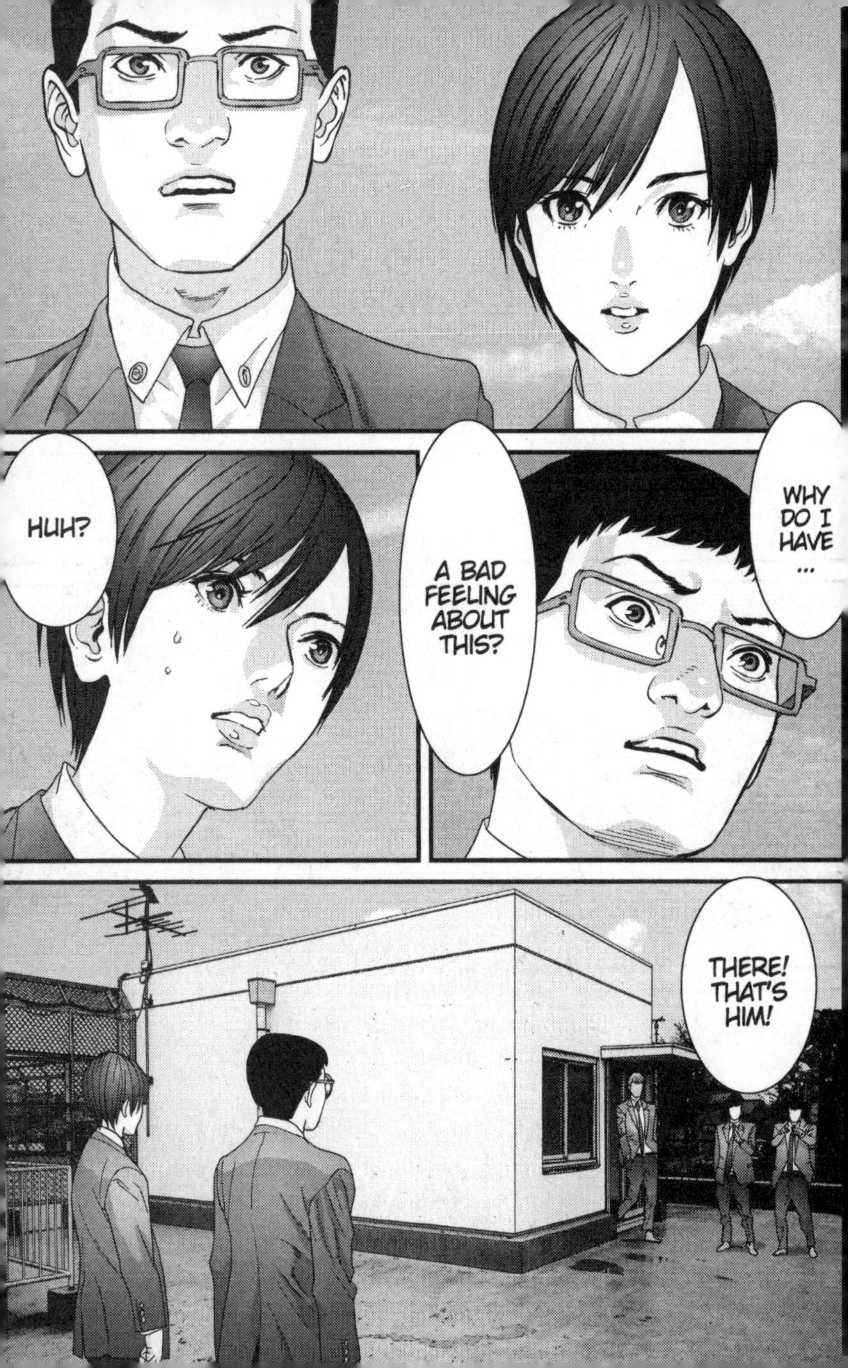
WHY DO I HAVE ...
A BAD FEELING ABOUT THIS?
HUH?
THERE! THAT'S HIM!

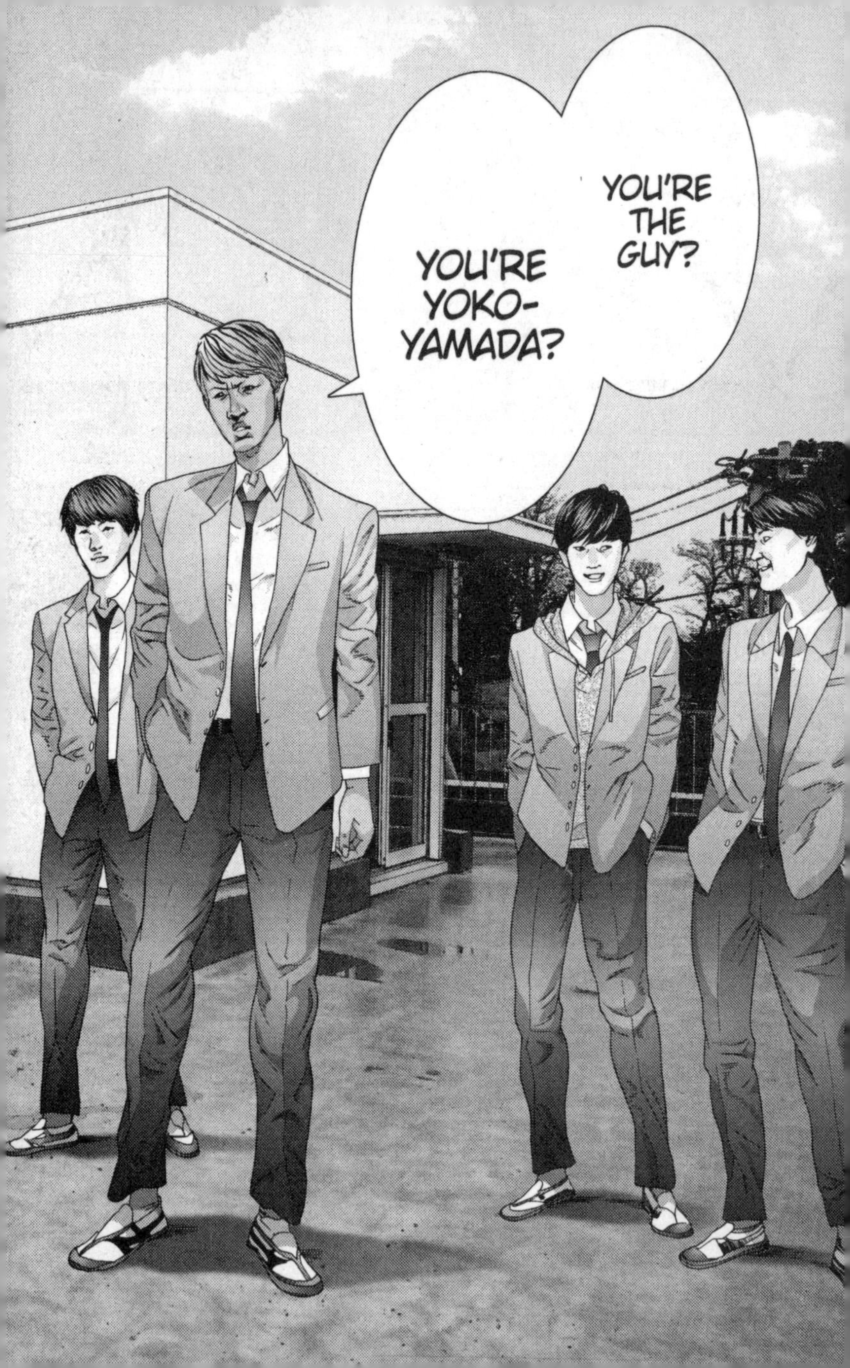
YOU'RE THE GUY?
YOU'RE YOKO-YAMADA?

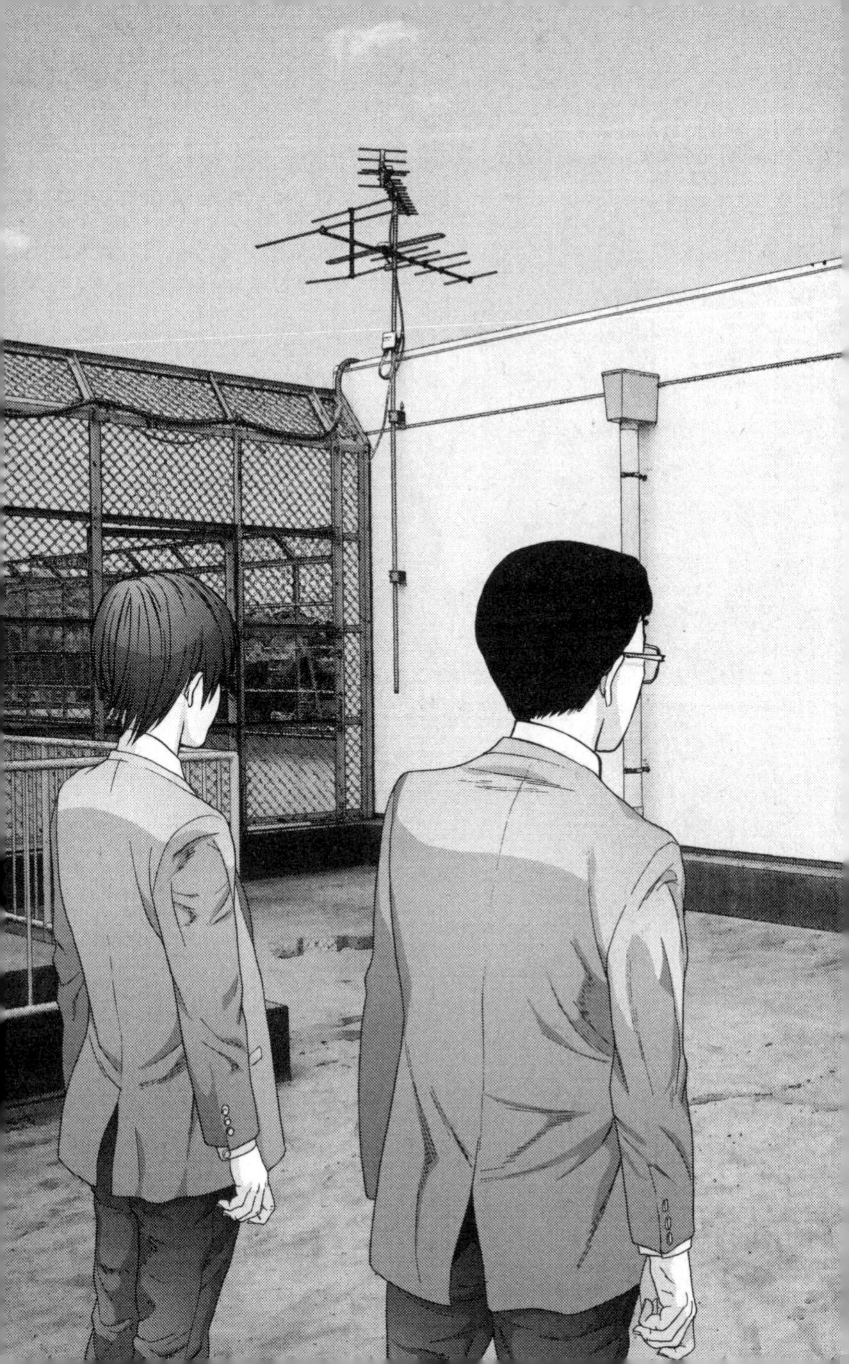

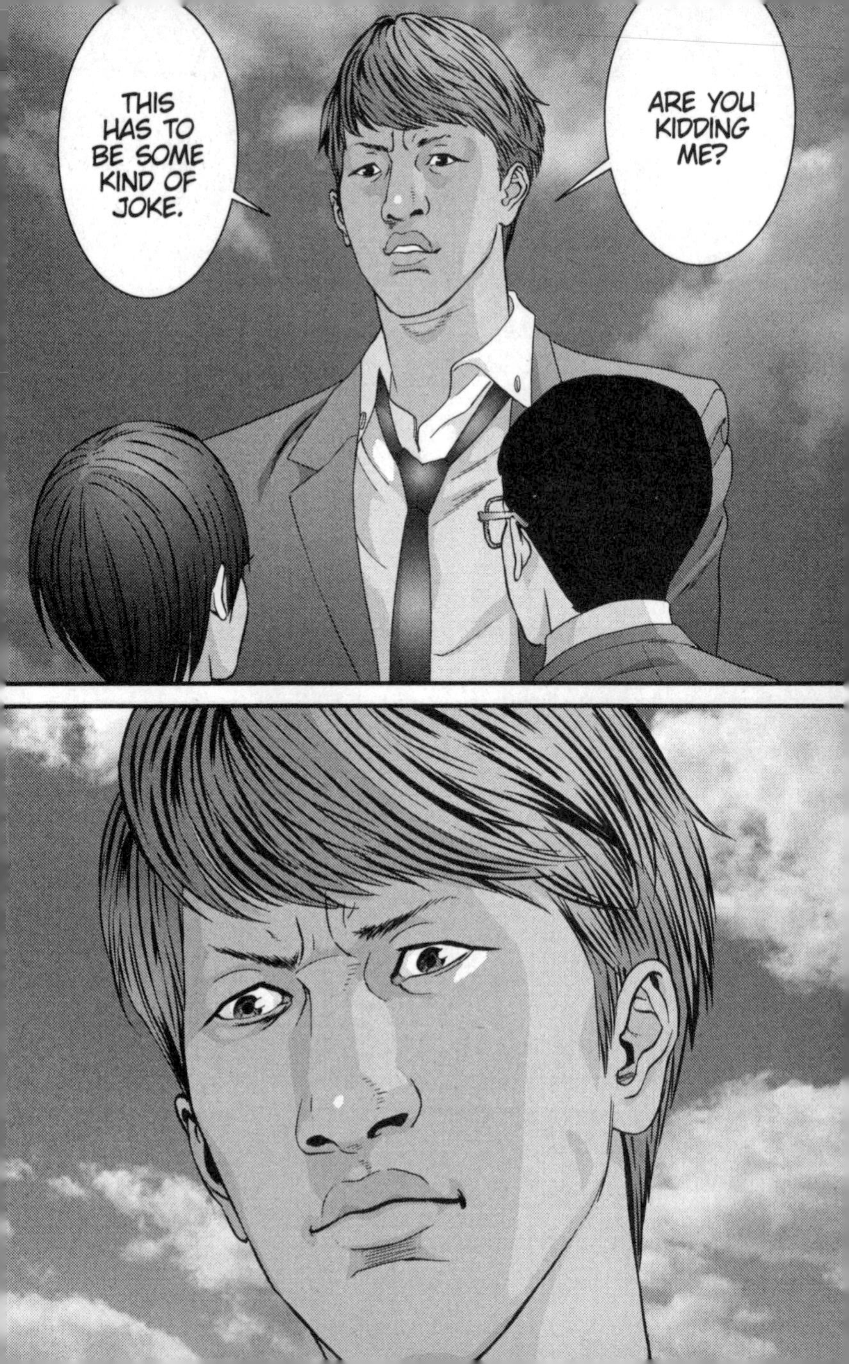
ARE YOU KIDDING ME?
THIS HAS TO BE SOME KIND OF JOKE.

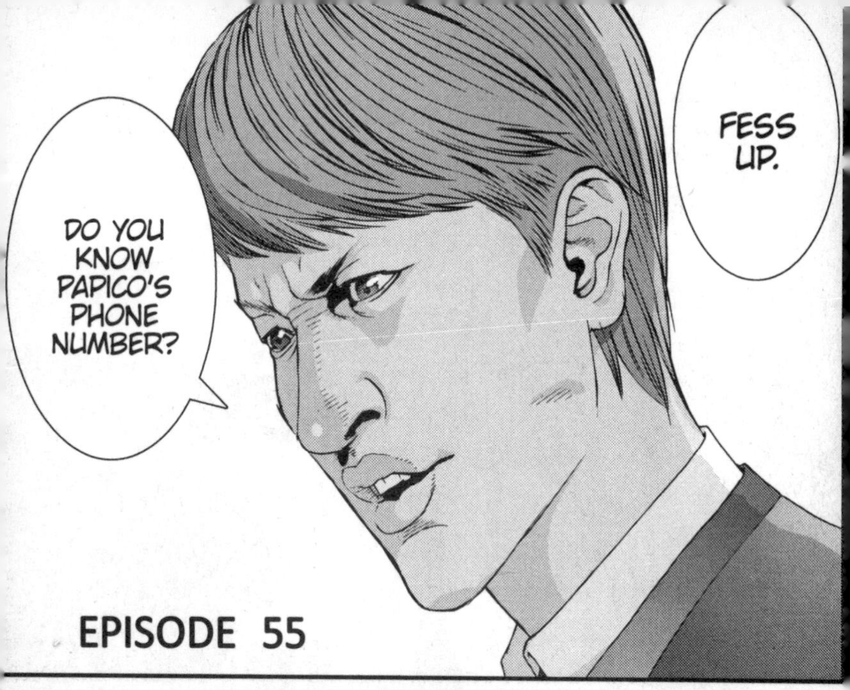
FESS UP.
DO YOU KNOW PAPICO'S PHONE NUMBER?
EPISODE 55

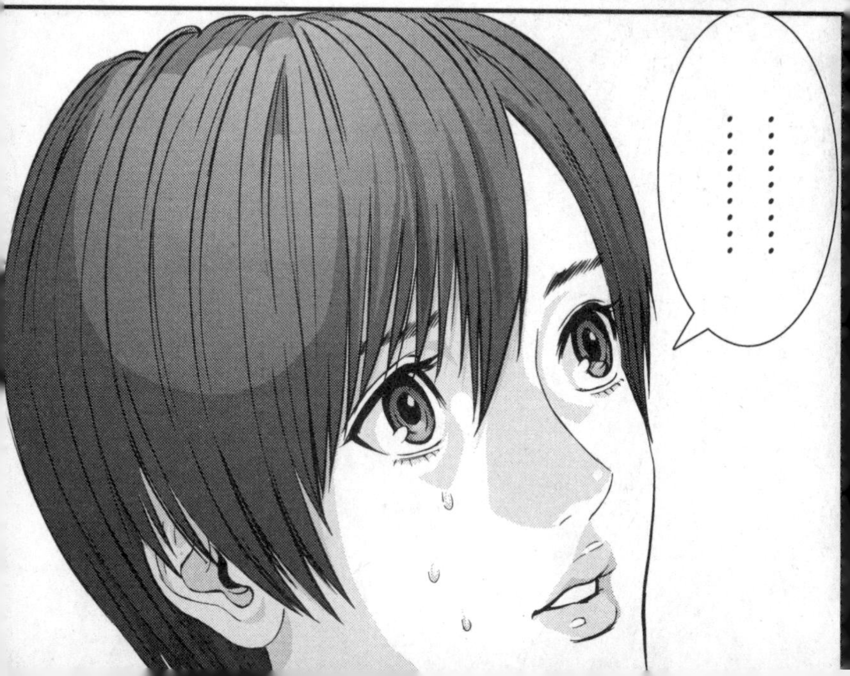
......

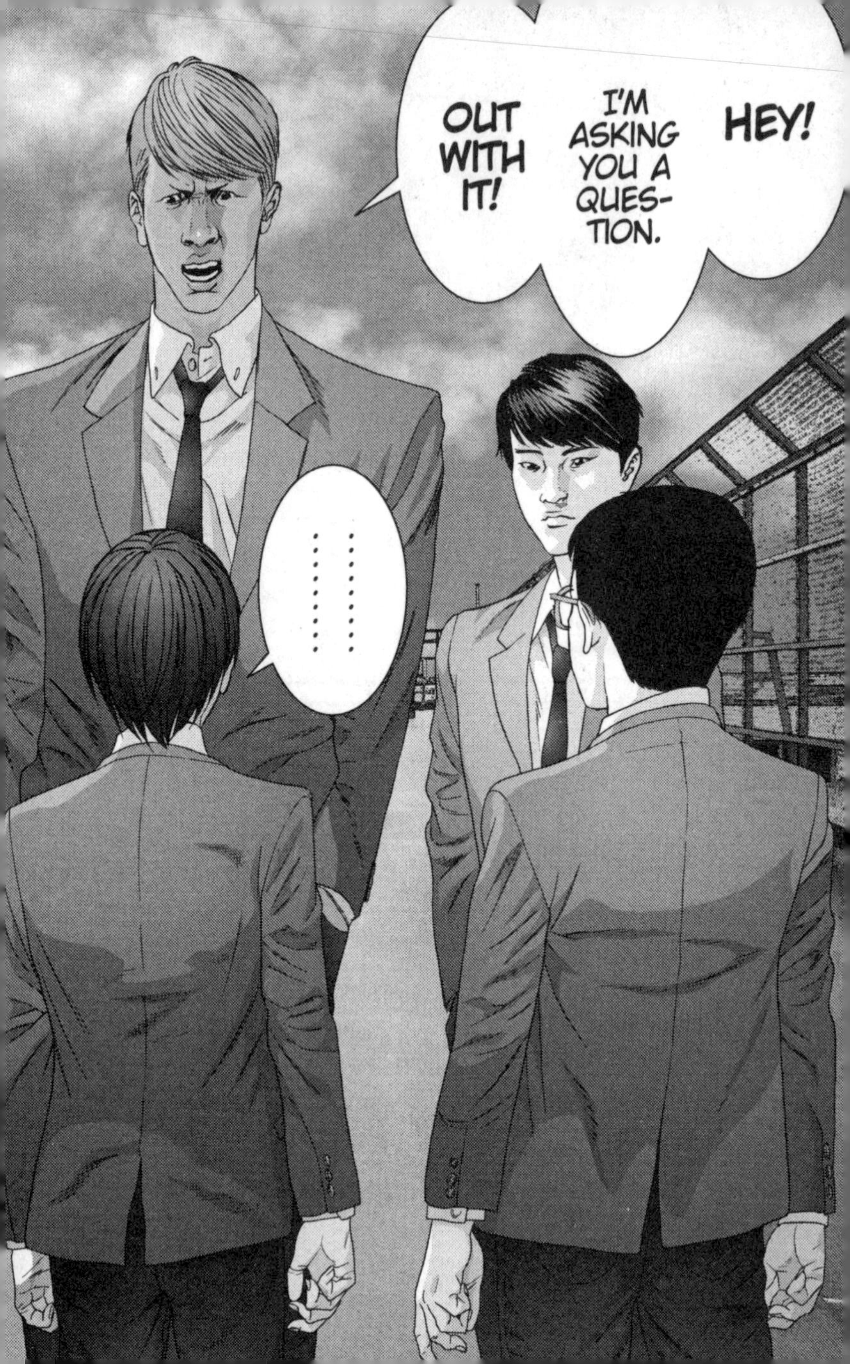
HEY!
I'M ASKING YOU A QUES-TION.
OUT WITH IT!
......

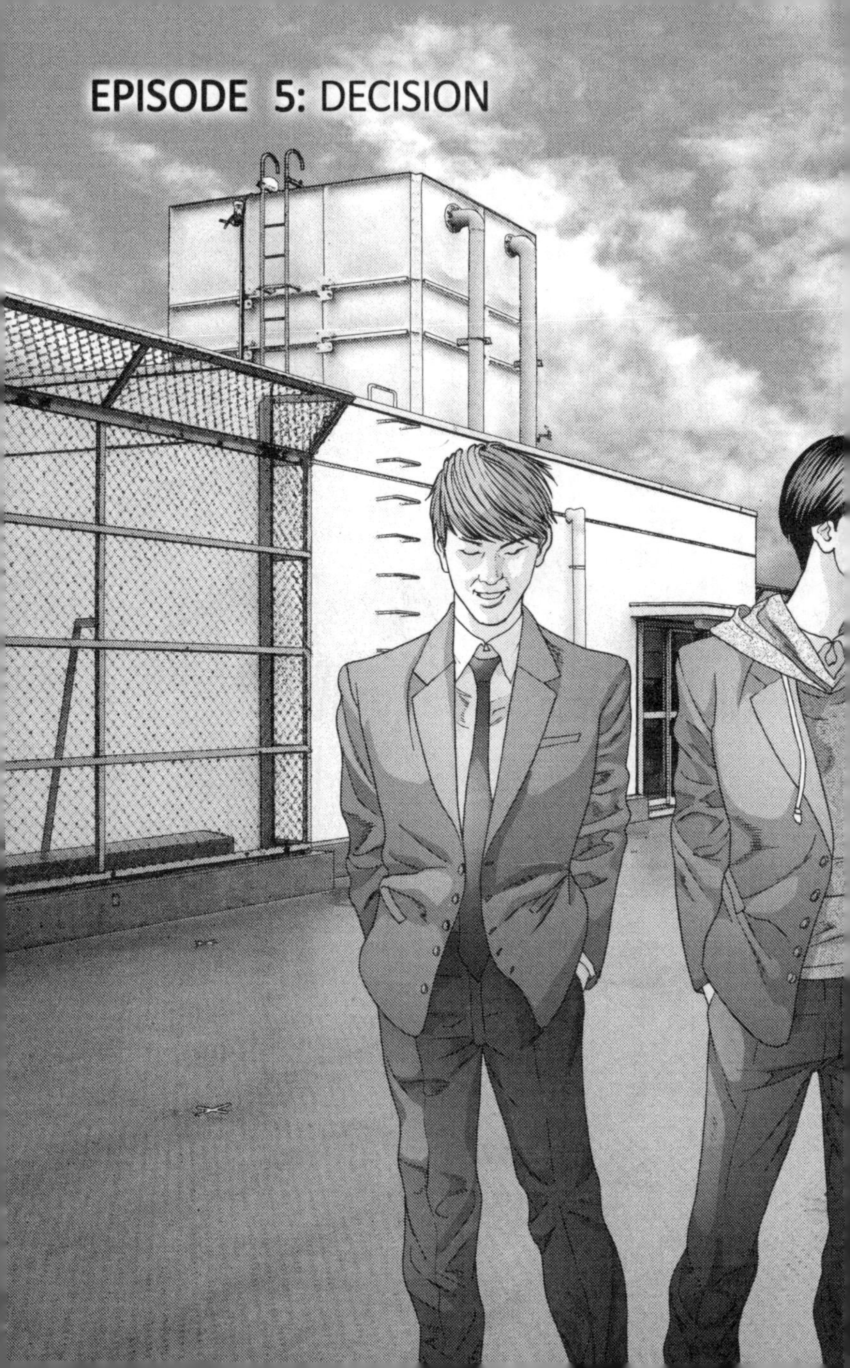
EPISODE 5: DECISION

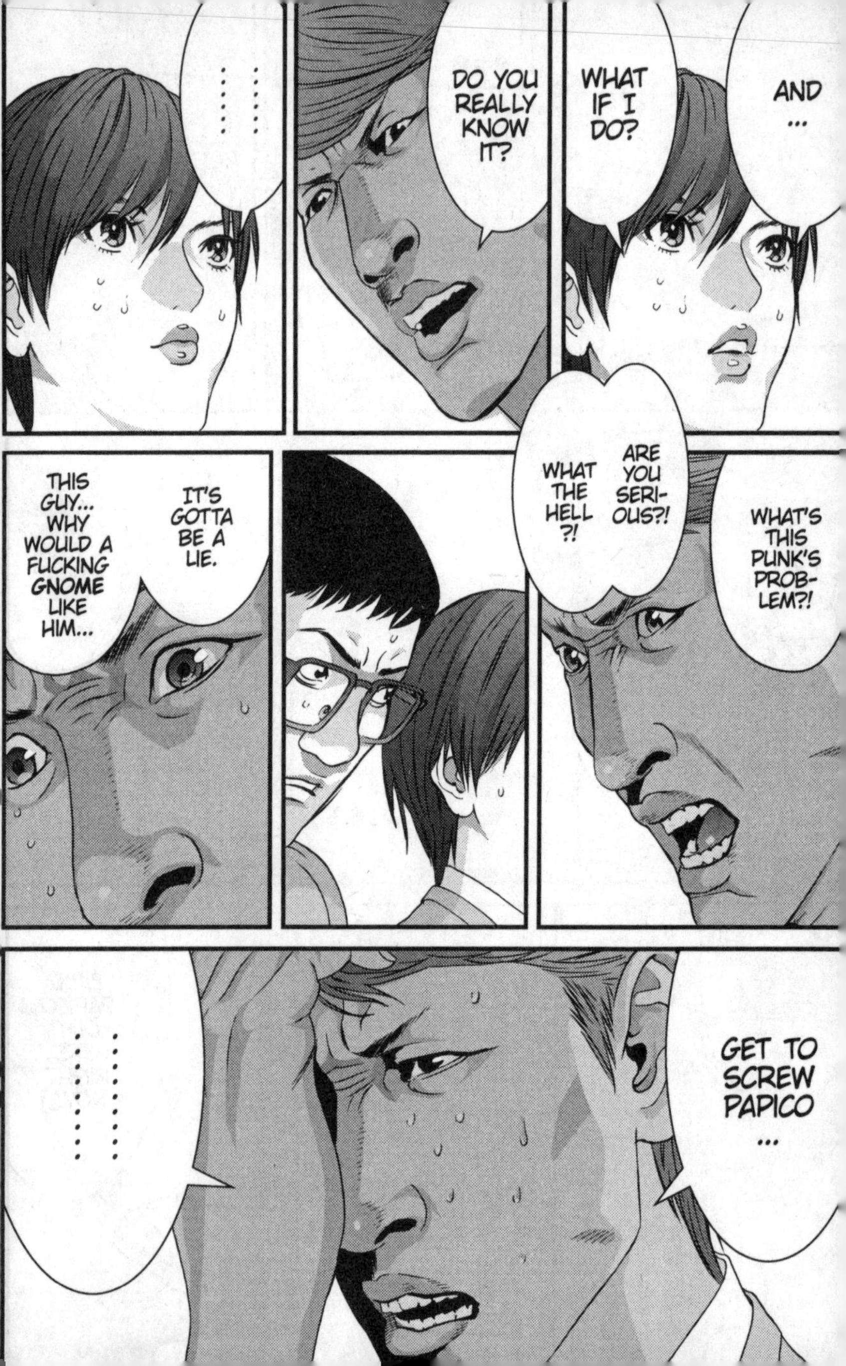
AND ...
WHAT IF I DO?
DO YOU REALLY KNOW IT?
......
WHAT'S THIS PUNK'S PROB-LEM?!
ARE YOU SERI-OUS?!
WHAT THE HELL ?!
IT'S GOTTA BE A LIE.
THIS GUY... WHY WOULD A FUCKING GNOME LIKE HIM...
GET TO SCREW PAPICO ...
......

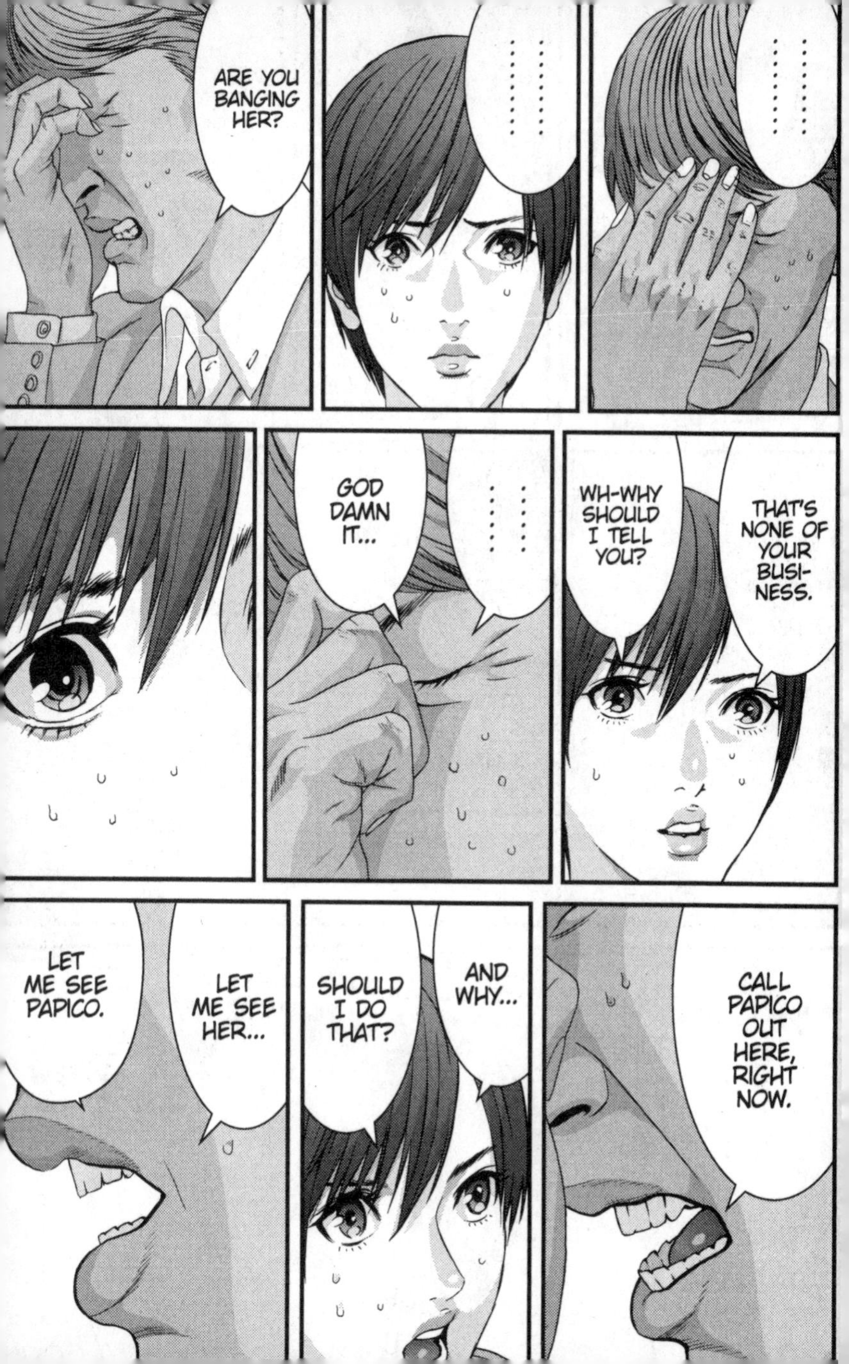
......
......
ARE YOU BANGING HER?
THAT'S NONE OF YOUR BUSINESS.
WH-WHY SHOULD I TELL YOU?
......
GOD DAMN IT...
CALL PAPICO OUT HERE, RIGHT NOW.
AND WHY...
SHOULD I DO THAT?
LET ME SEE HER...
LET ME SEE PAPICO.

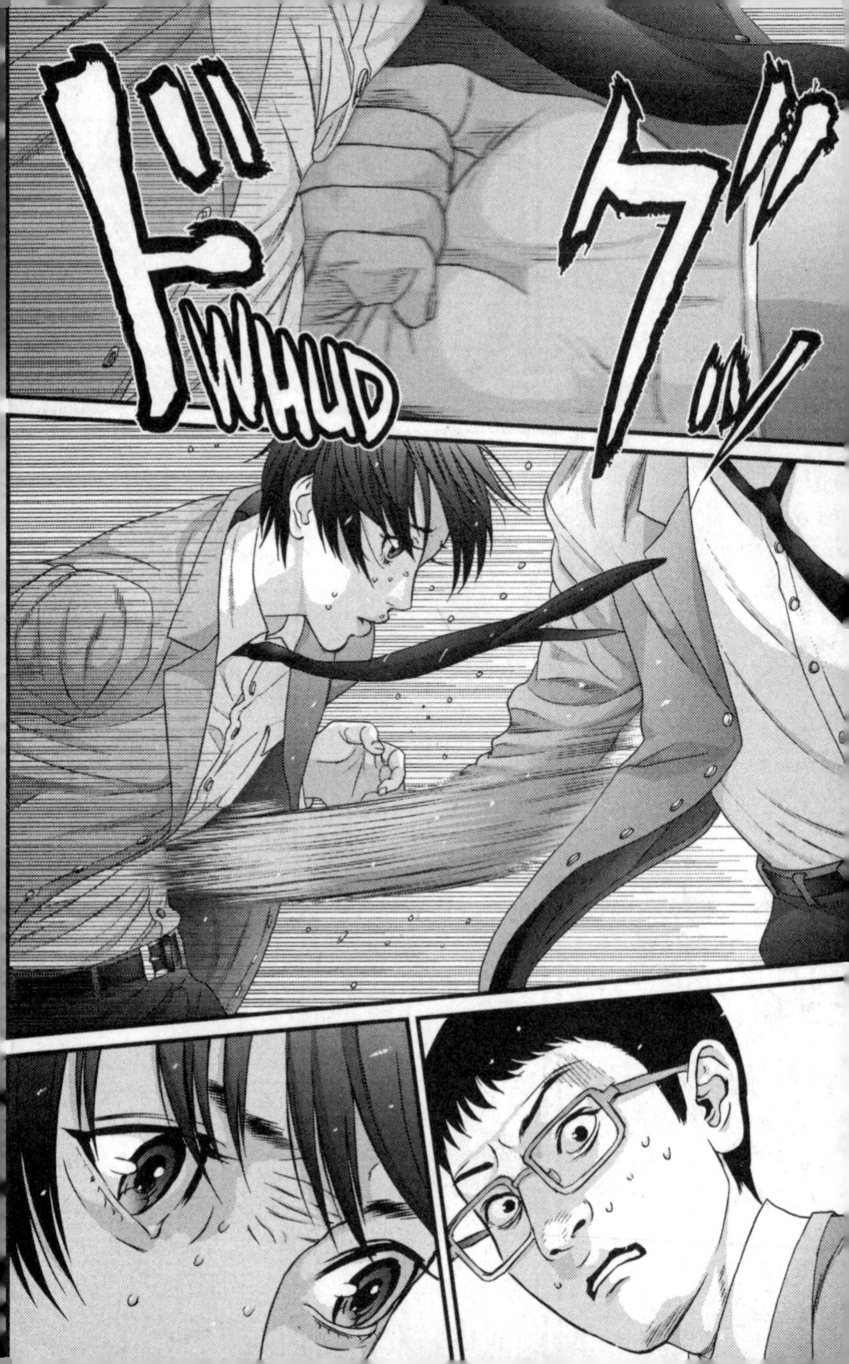
グ
ド
WHUD

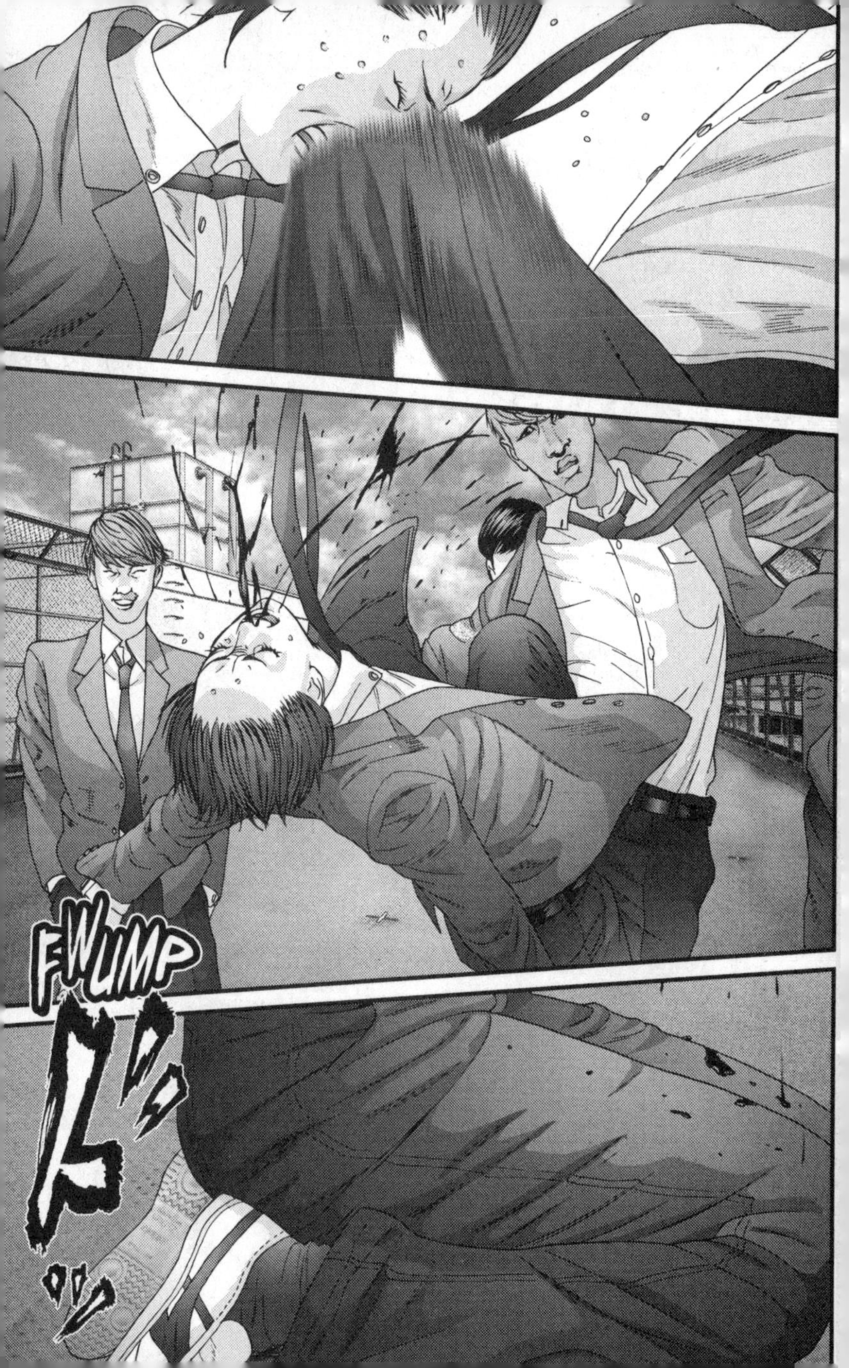
FWUMP

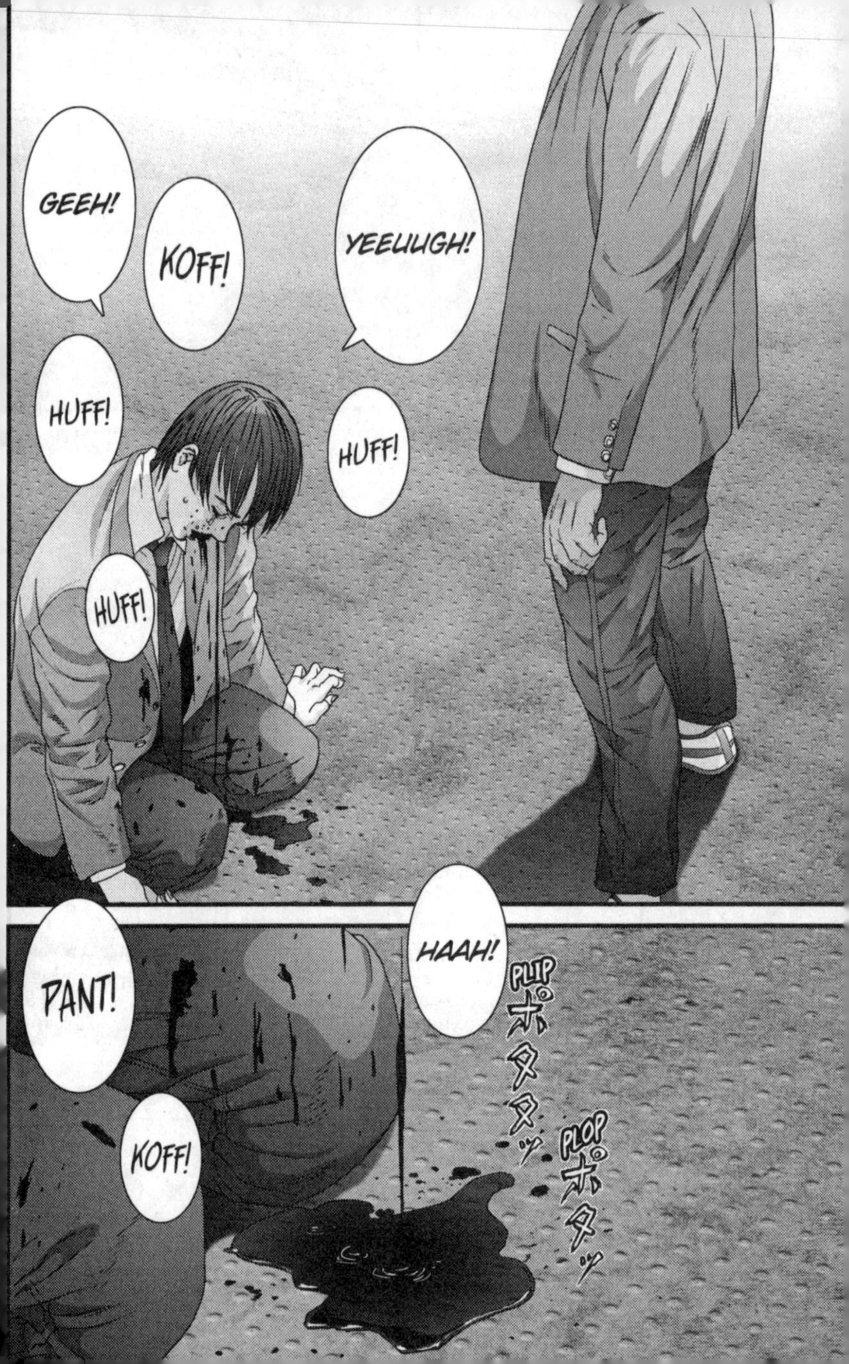
YEEUUGH!
KOFF!
GEEH!
HUFF!
HUFF!
HUFF!
PLOP
ポタッ
PLIP
ポタタッ
HAAH!
PANT!
KOFF!

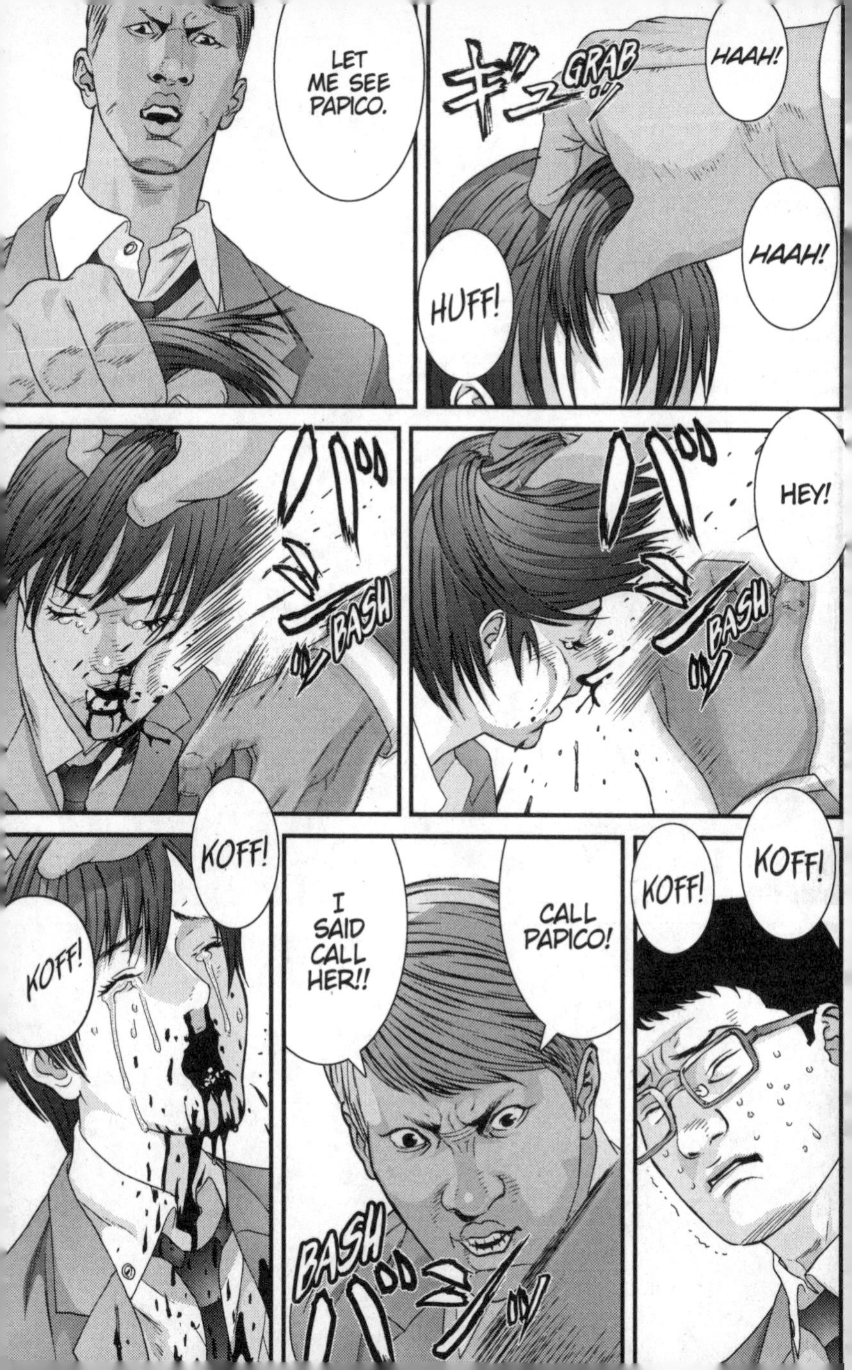
GRAB
HAAH!
HAAH!
HUFF!
LET ME SEE PAPICO.
HEY!
BASH
BASH
KOFF!
KOFF!
CALL PAPICO!
I SAID CALL HER!!
BASH
KOFF!
KOFF!

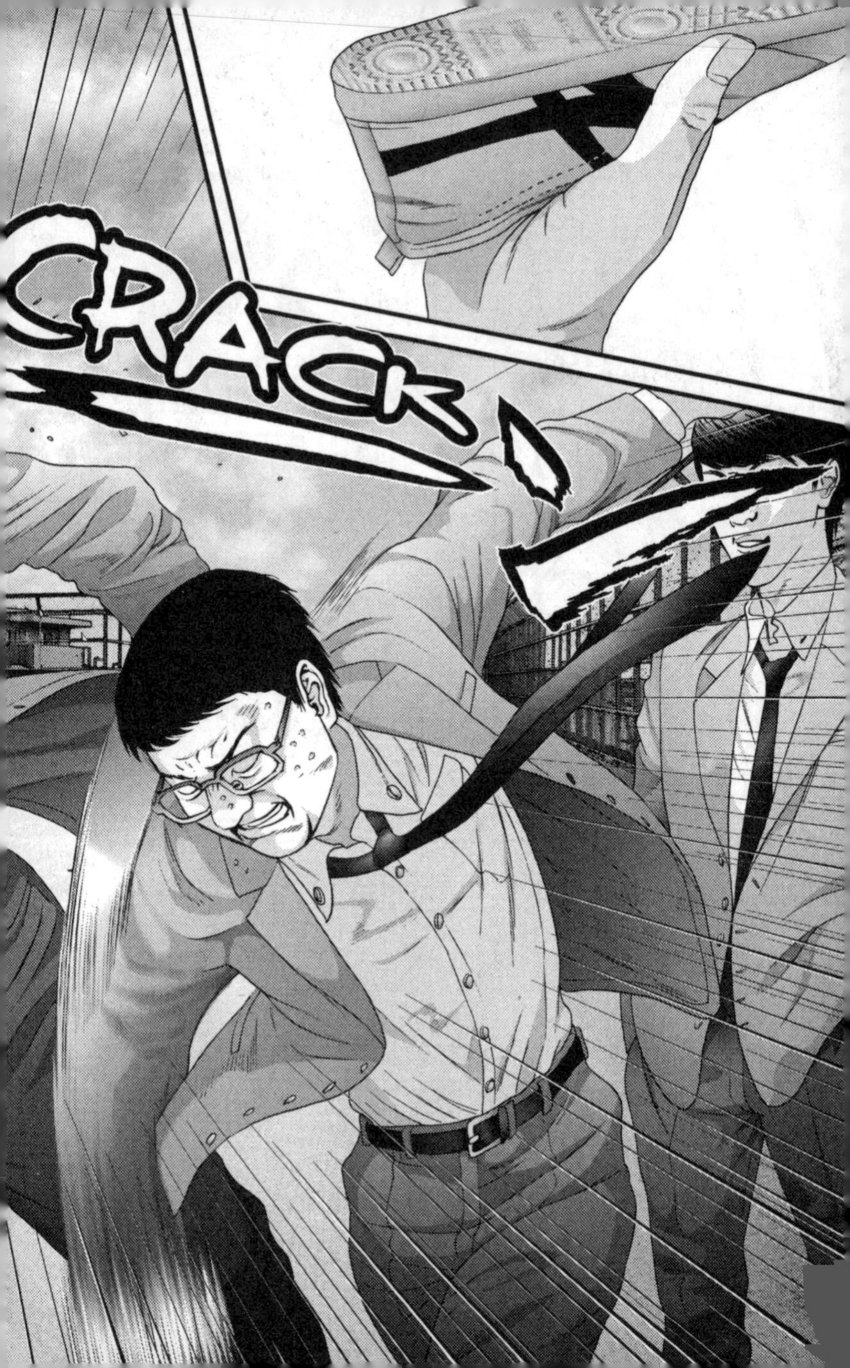
CRACK

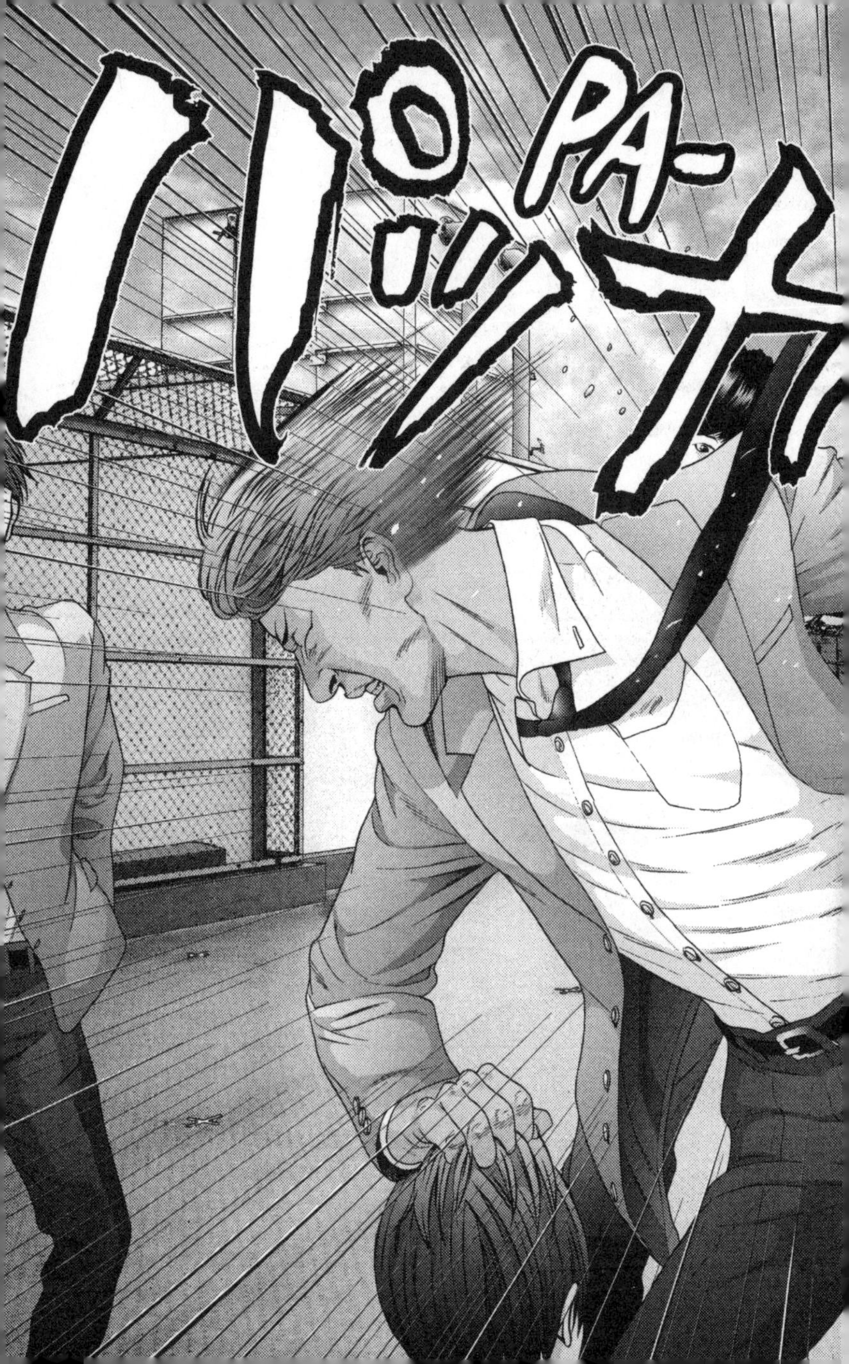
PA-

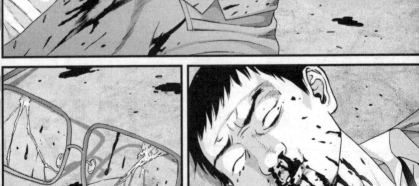

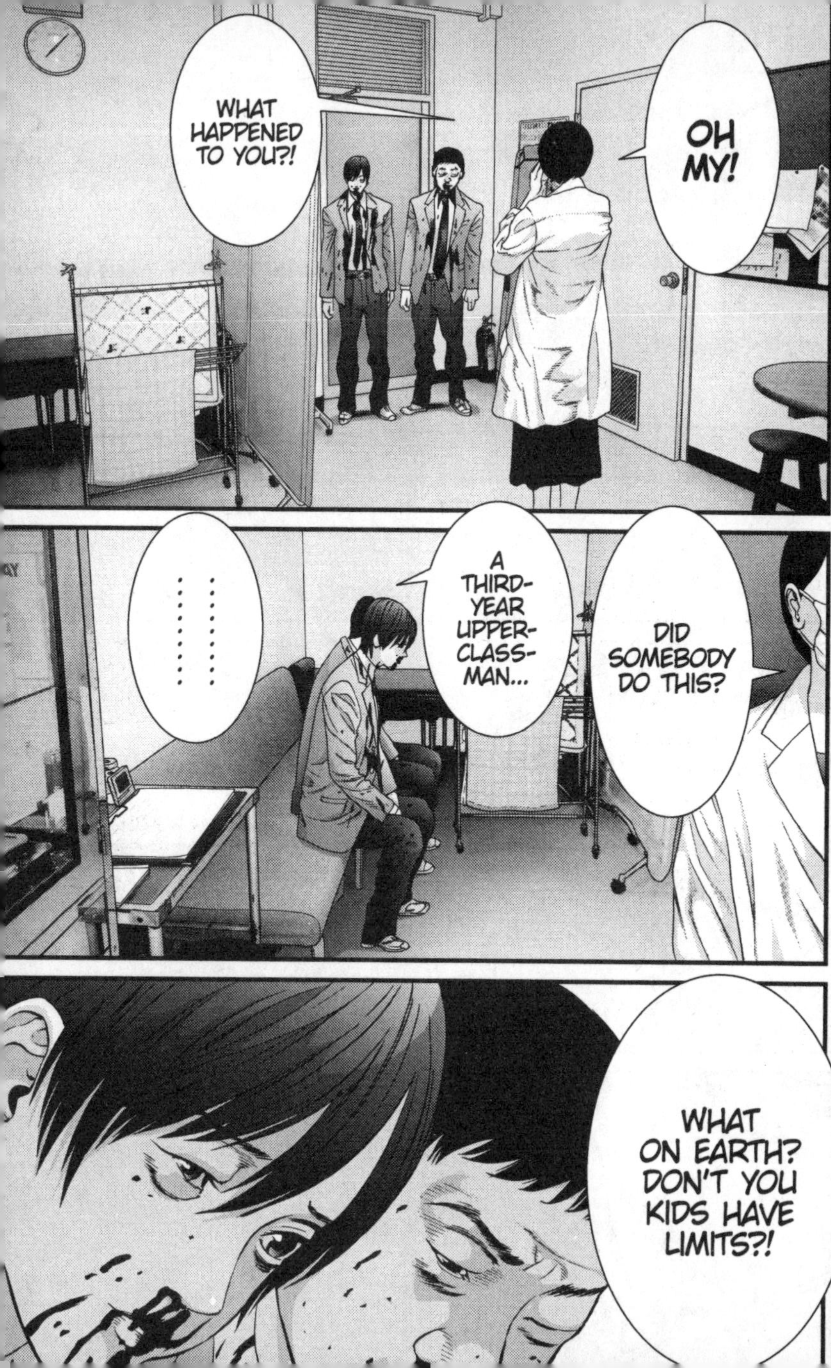
OH MY!
WHAT HAPPENED TO YOU?!
DID SOMEBODY DO THIS?
A THIRD-YEAR UPPER-CLASSMAN...
......
WHAT ON EARTH? DON'T YOU KIDS HAVE LIMITS?!

YEAH.

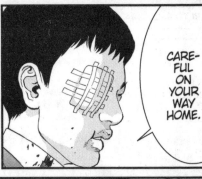

CARE-
FUL
ON
YOUR
WAY
HOME.

PeiPay Pays as you Use
See more >
Papico Gets Illicit with a Minor!! The Bashing Gets Radical
Daily Bugle DB.com
Photos of her romantic trip to Ishigaki Island run in Weekly Bunshun. Partner outed on social media.
PaPiCo
Trending
Latest
Users
Images
Tass @ttttt_tas - 1 min ago
I used to be a fan of Papico, but this latest scandal has made me change my tune. I mean, she got with a 16yo kid. Gross..
3 2 6
Irangar @irangar444 - 2 min ago
Nobody thinks of her as a hero. She got too full of herself. She's nothing but a porn star when all's said and done All she thinks about is kiddy dicks
3 3 11
★Kotonyan Congrats on 3 years
Damn that Yokoyamada (grr) I wish I had a Death Note to use on him
3 1 3
Papico
@papico0209
Awwww, I got to rest sooo much!! What a fulfilling three days~
Can't wait to give it my all starting tomorrow!!
16:48, 2019/09/15 Twitter for iPad
235465 Retweets 981 Likes
World Protester Man @justi - 1 min
Slut!! How could you have a sex romp with a child?! You freak!!
1 3 4
★KYOO★ @honey_bb2 - 2 min ago
Was that kid's dick really that tasty?! #slut #papico
1 2

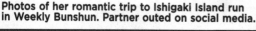

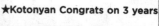

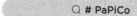

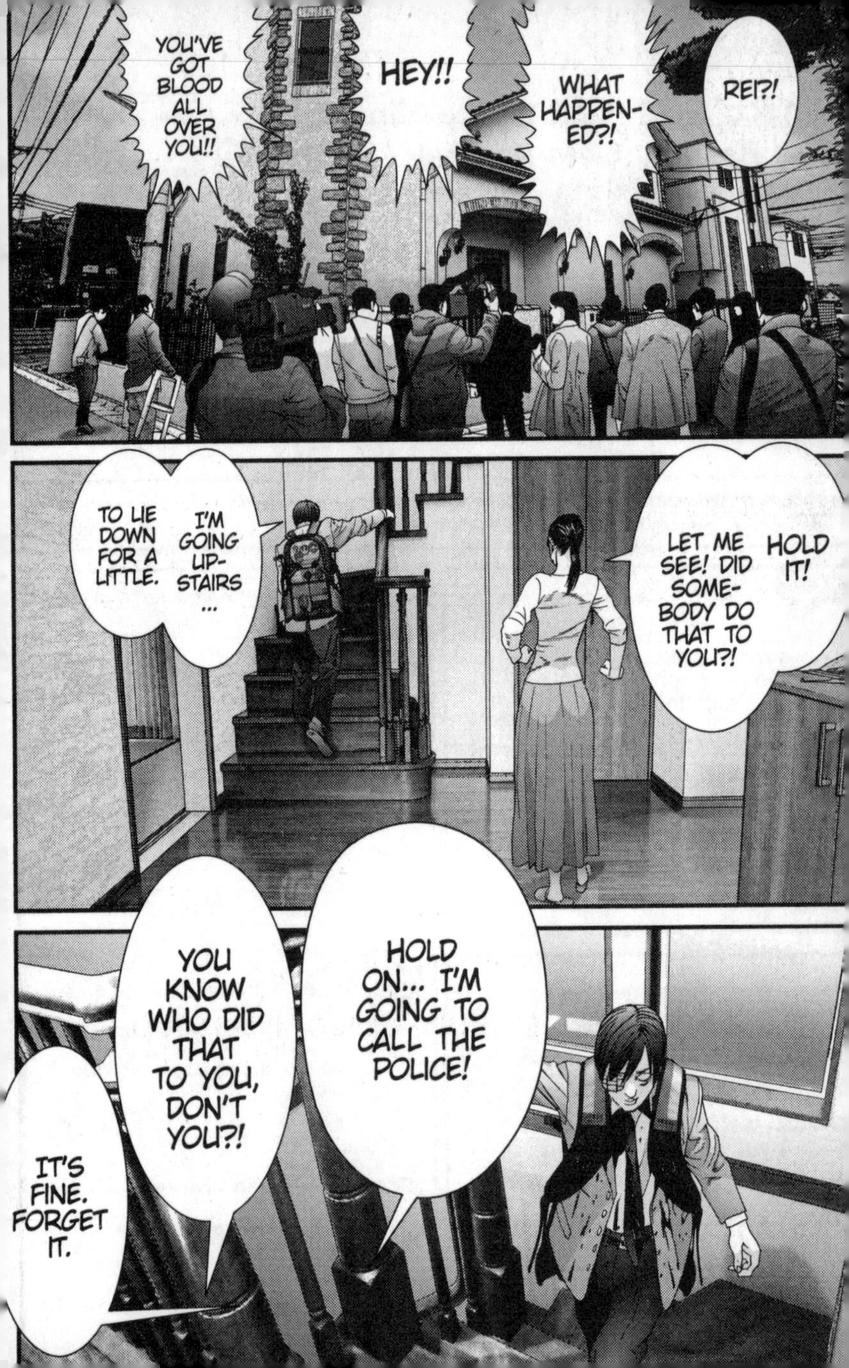
REI?!
WHAT HAPPENED?!
HEY!!
YOU'VE GOT BLOOD ALL OVER YOU!!
HOLD IT!
LET ME SEE! DID SOMEBODY DO THAT TO YOU?!
I'M GOING UPSTAIRS...
TO LIE DOWN FOR A LITTLE.
HOLD ON... I'M GOING TO CALL THE POLICE!
YOU KNOW WHO DID THAT TO YOU, DON'T YOU?!
IT'S FINE. FORGET IT.

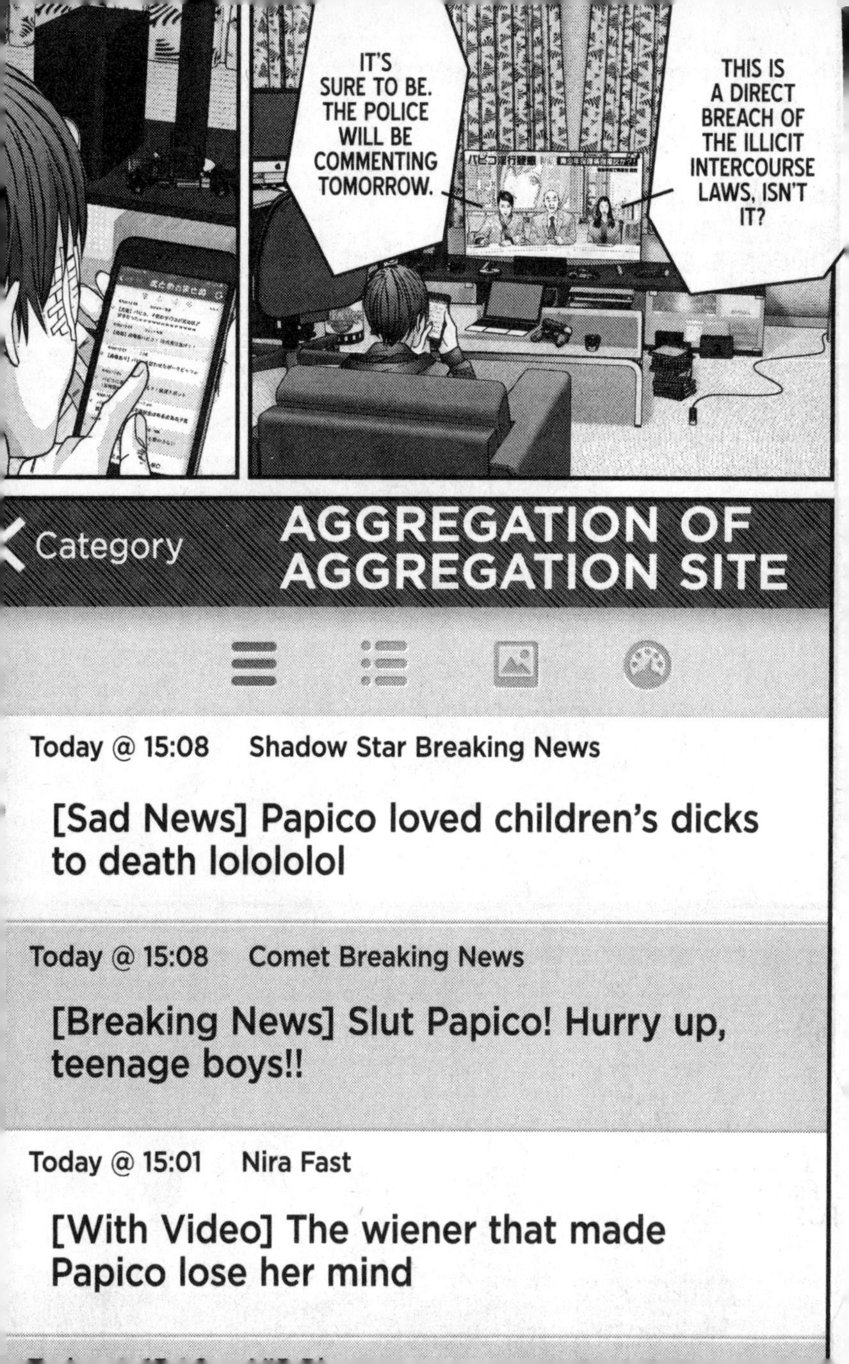
THIS IS A DIRECT BREACH OF THE ILLICIT INTERCOURSE LAWS, ISN'T IT?
IT'S SURE TO BE. THE POLICE WILL BE COMMENTING TOMORROW.
Category
AGGREGATION OF AGGREGATION SITE
Today @ 15:08 Shadow Star Breaking News
[Sad News] Papico loved children's dicks to death lolololol
Today @ 15:08 Comet Breaking News
[Breaking News] Slut Papico! Hurry up, teenage boys!!
Today @ 15:01 Nira Fast
[With Video] The wiener that made Papico lose her mind

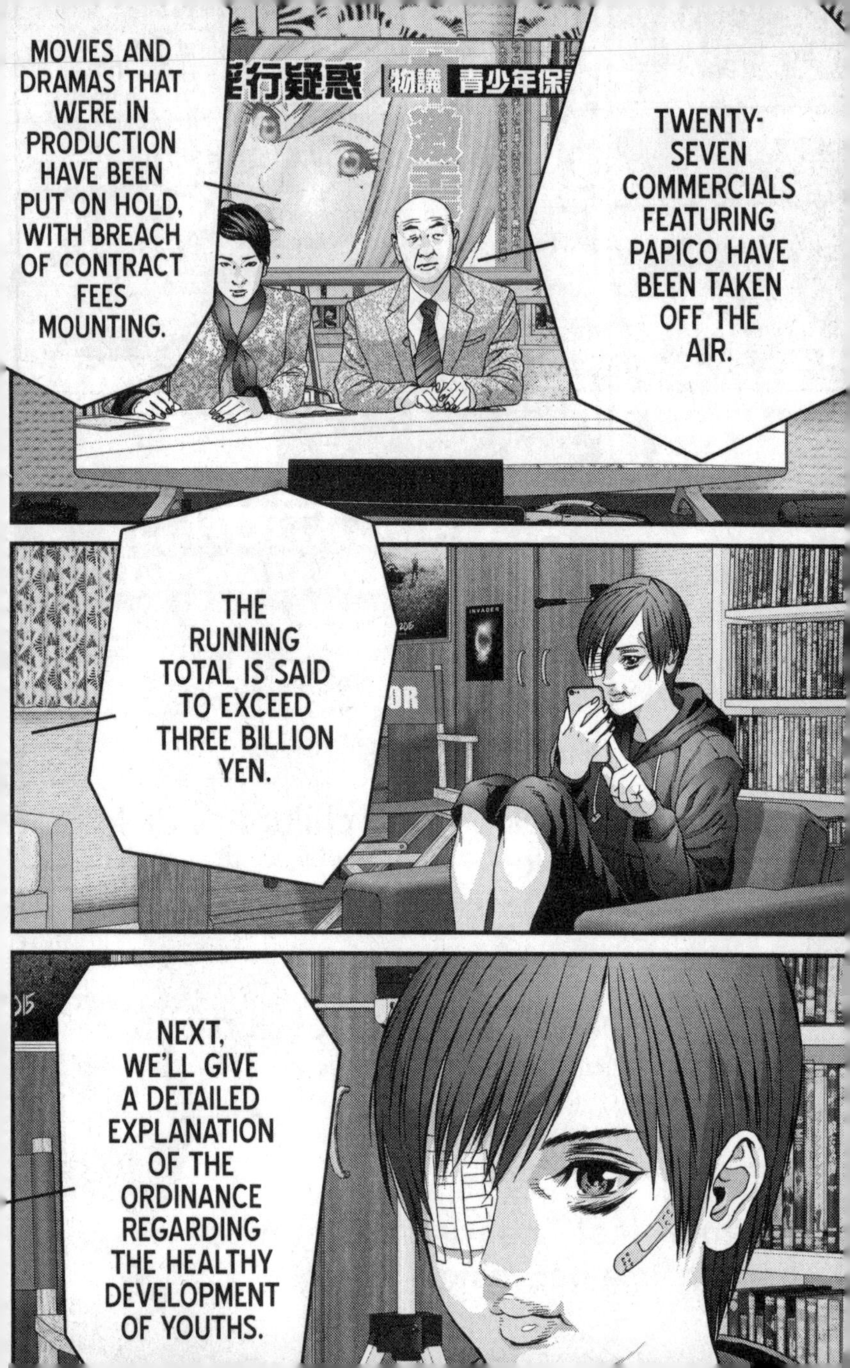
TWENTY-SEVEN COMMERCIALS FEATURING PAPICO HAVE BEEN TAKEN OFF THE AIR.
MOVIES AND DRAMAS THAT WERE IN PRODUCTION HAVE BEEN PUT ON HOLD, WITH BREACH OF CONTRACT FEES MOUNTING.
THE RUNNING TOTAL IS SAID TO EXCEED THREE BILLION YEN.
NEXT, WE'LL GIVE A DETAILED EXPLANATION OF THE ORDINANCE REGARDING THE HEALTHY DEVELOPMENT OF YOUTHS.

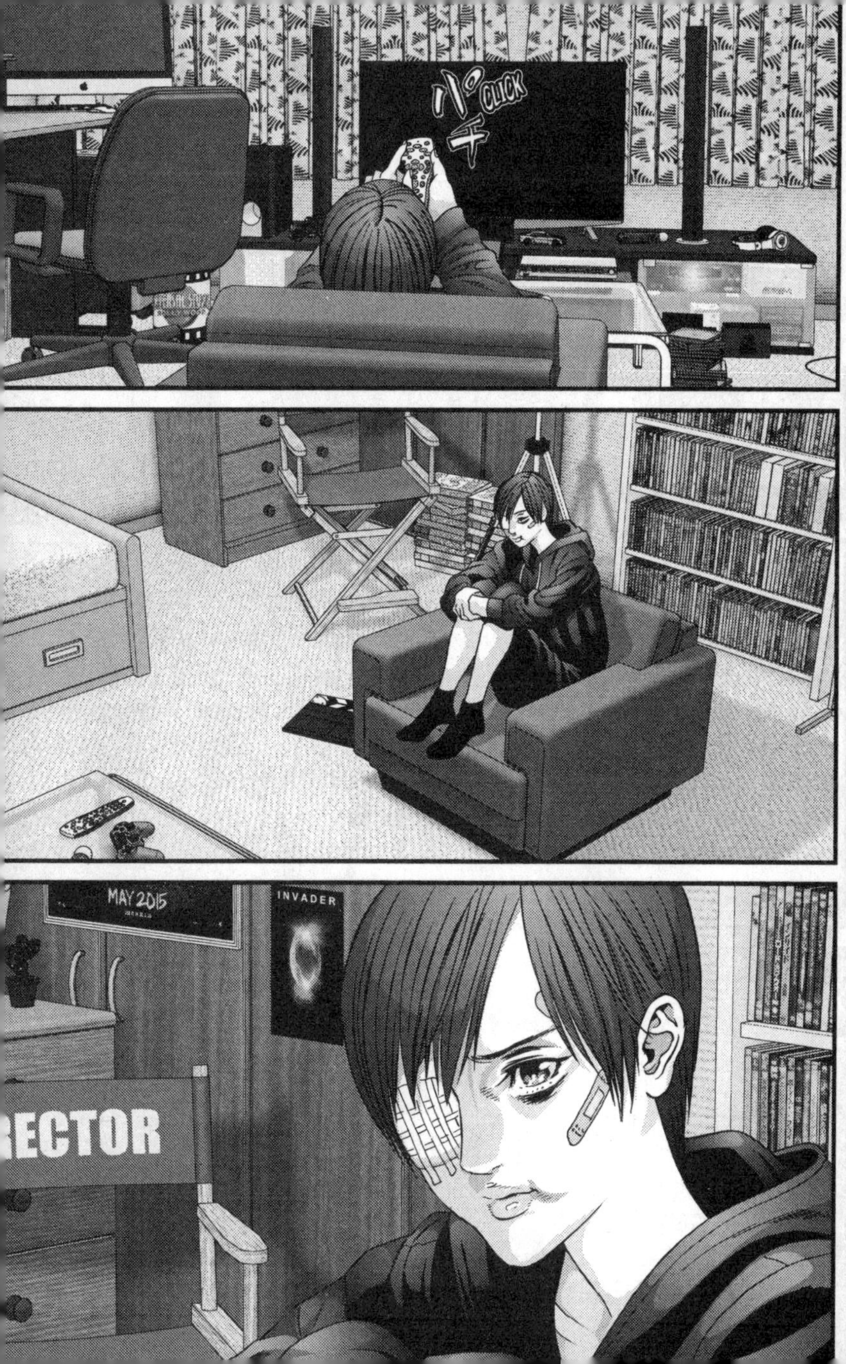
パチ
CLICK
MAY 2015
INVADER
RECTOR

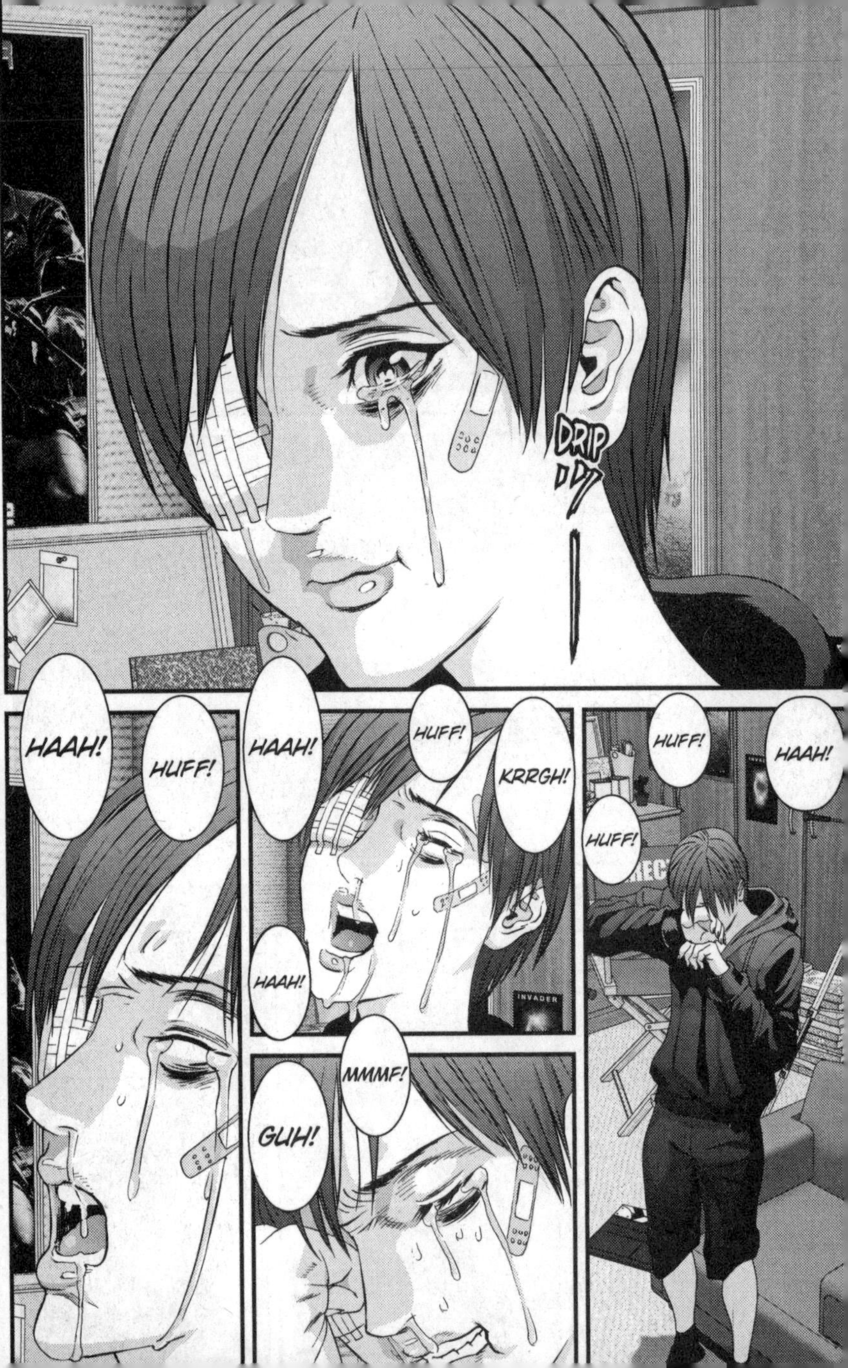
DRIP
HAAH!
HUFF!
HUFF!
KRRGH!
HUFF!
HAAH!
HAAH!
MMMF!
GUH!
HUFF!
HAAH!

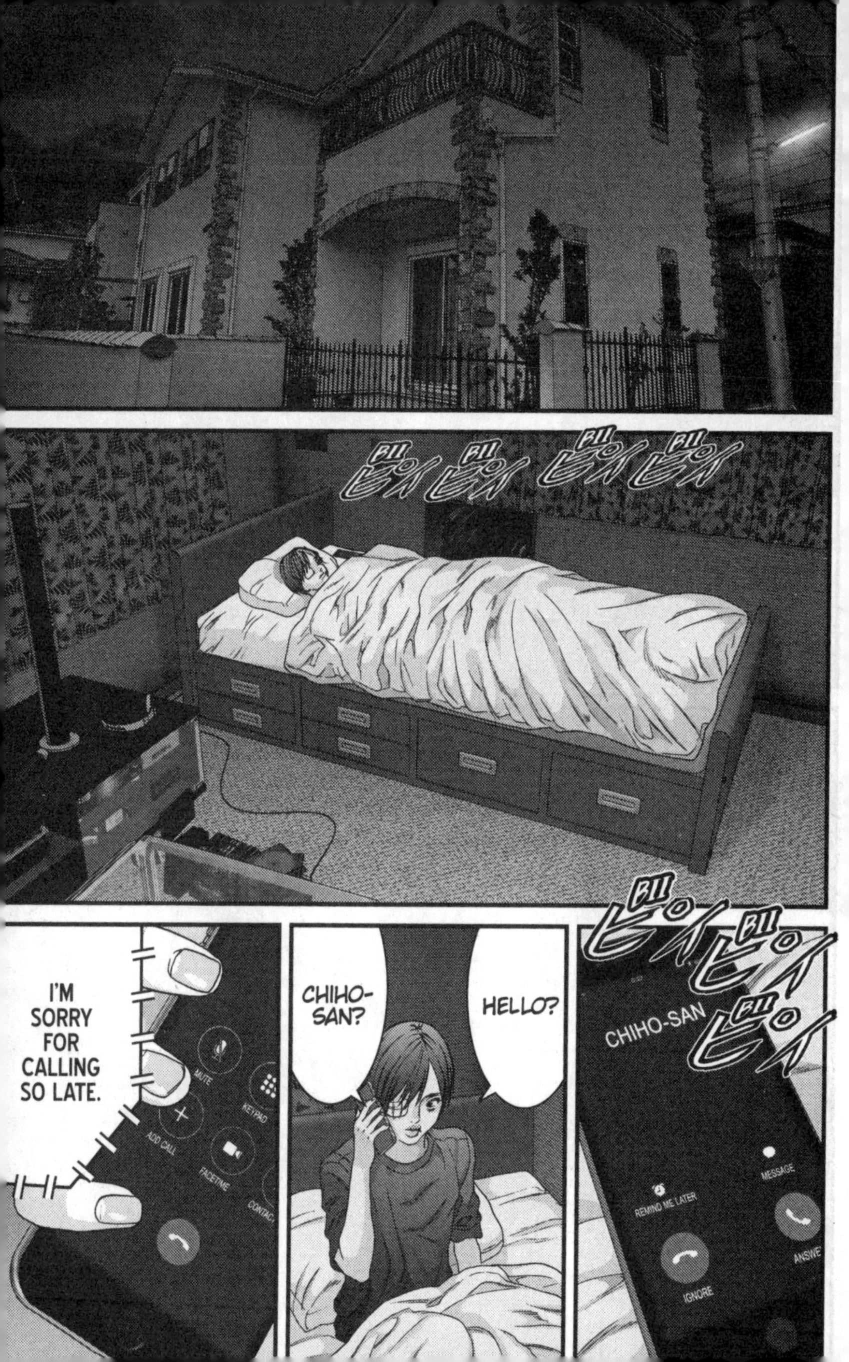
BII BII BII BII
BII BII BII
CHIHO-SAN
MESSAGE
REMIND ME LATER
IGNORE
HELLO?
CHIHO-SAN?
I'M SORRY FOR CALLING SO LATE.
MUTE
KEYPAD
ADD CALL
FACETIME

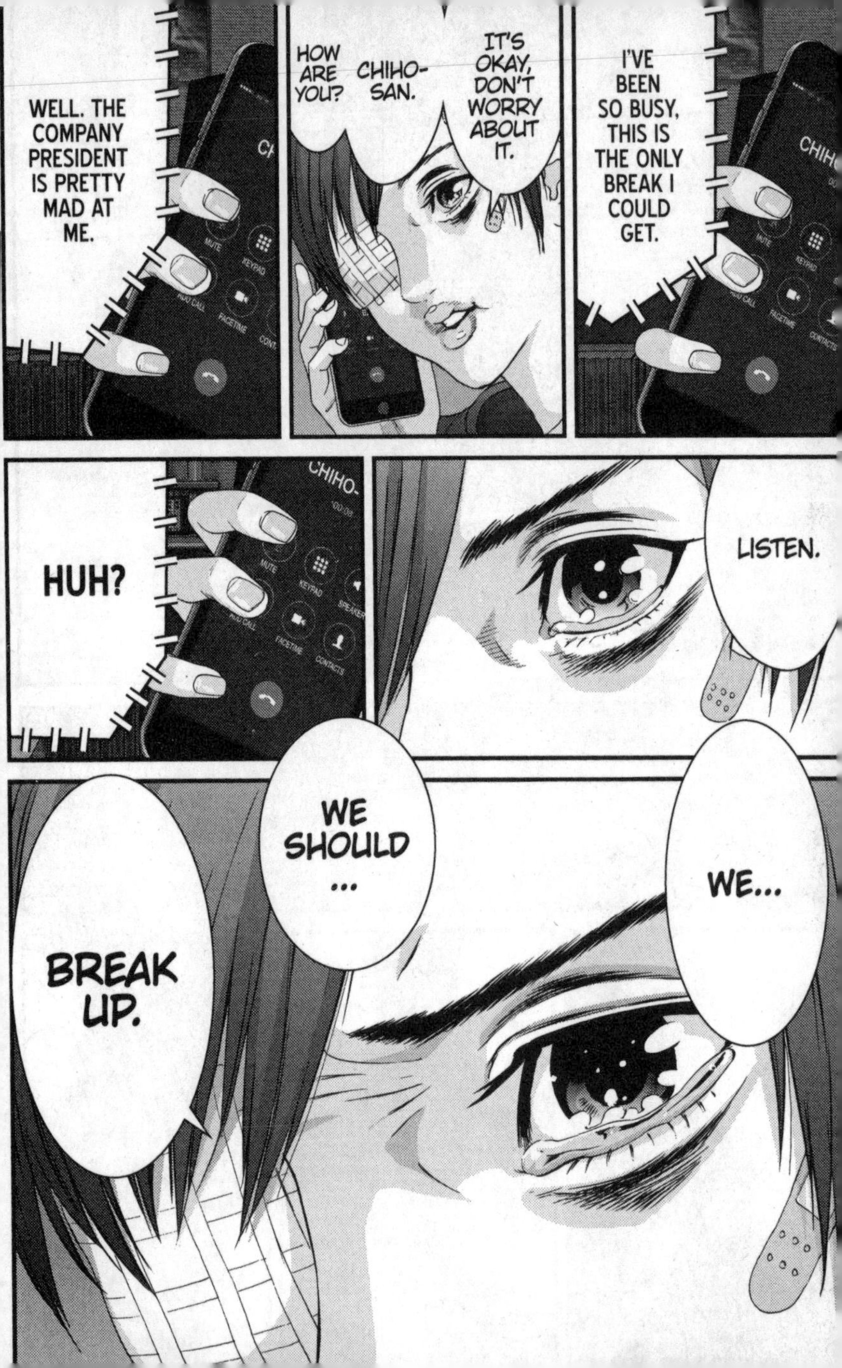
I'VE BEEN SO BUSY, THIS IS THE ONLY BREAK I COULD GET.
IT'S OKAY, DON'T WORRY ABOUT IT.
CHIHO-SAN.
HOW ARE YOU?
WELL. THE COMPANY PRESIDENT IS PRETTY MAD AT ME.
LISTEN.
HUH?
WE...
WE SHOULD ...
BREAK UP.

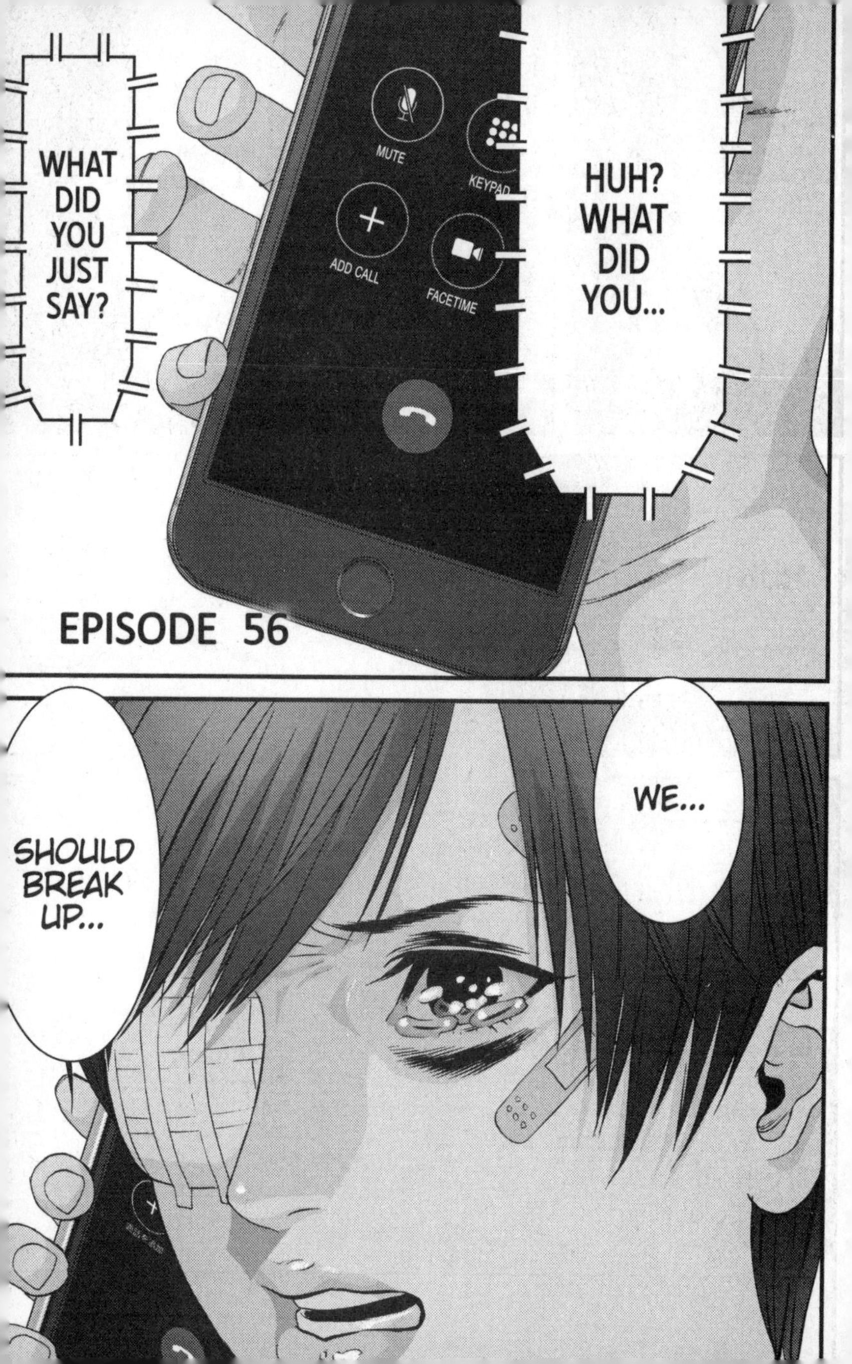
HUH? WHAT DID YOU...
WHAT DID YOU JUST SAY?
MUTE
KEYPAD
ADD CALL
FACETIME
EPISODE 56
WE...
SHOULD BREAK UP...

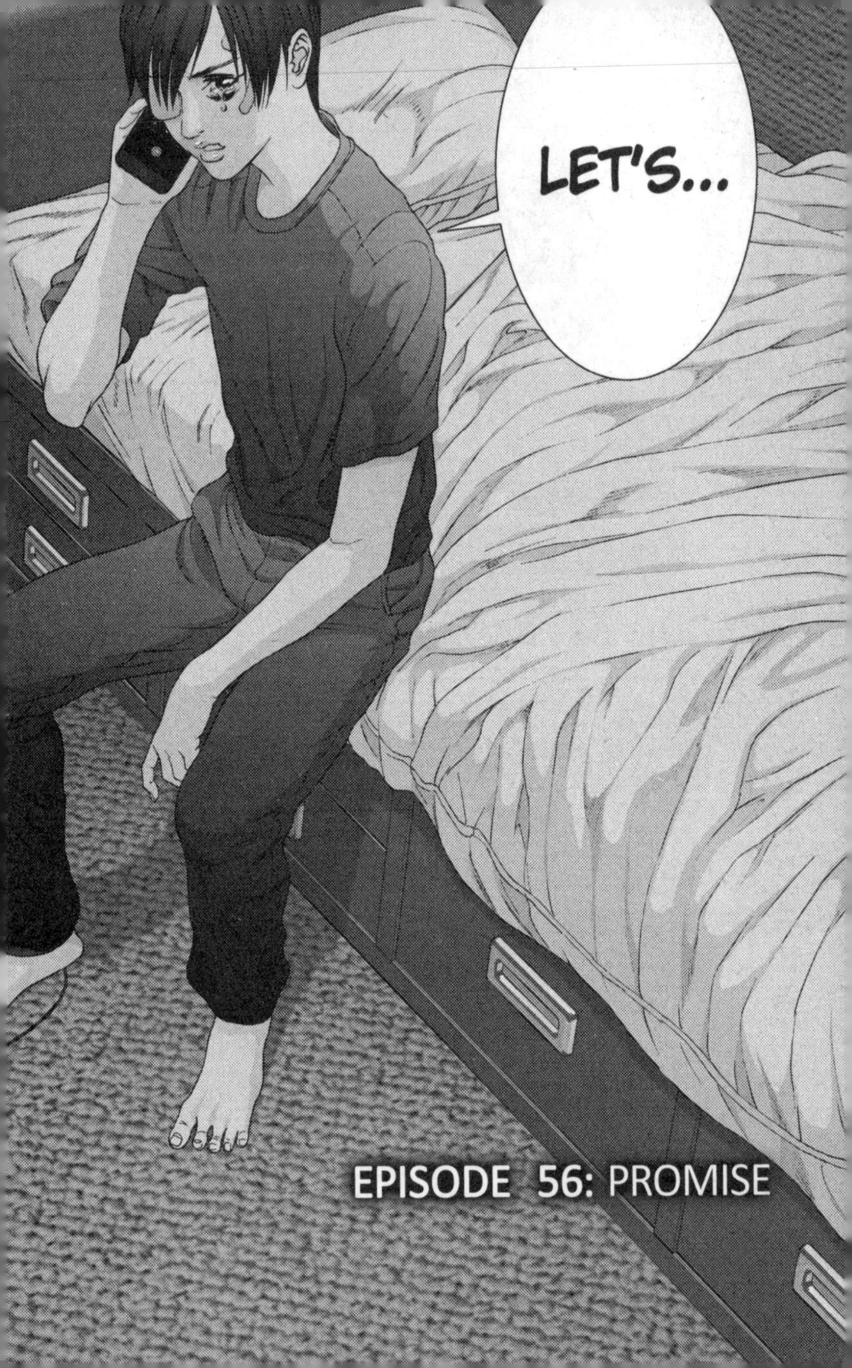
LET'S...
EPISODE 56: PROMISE

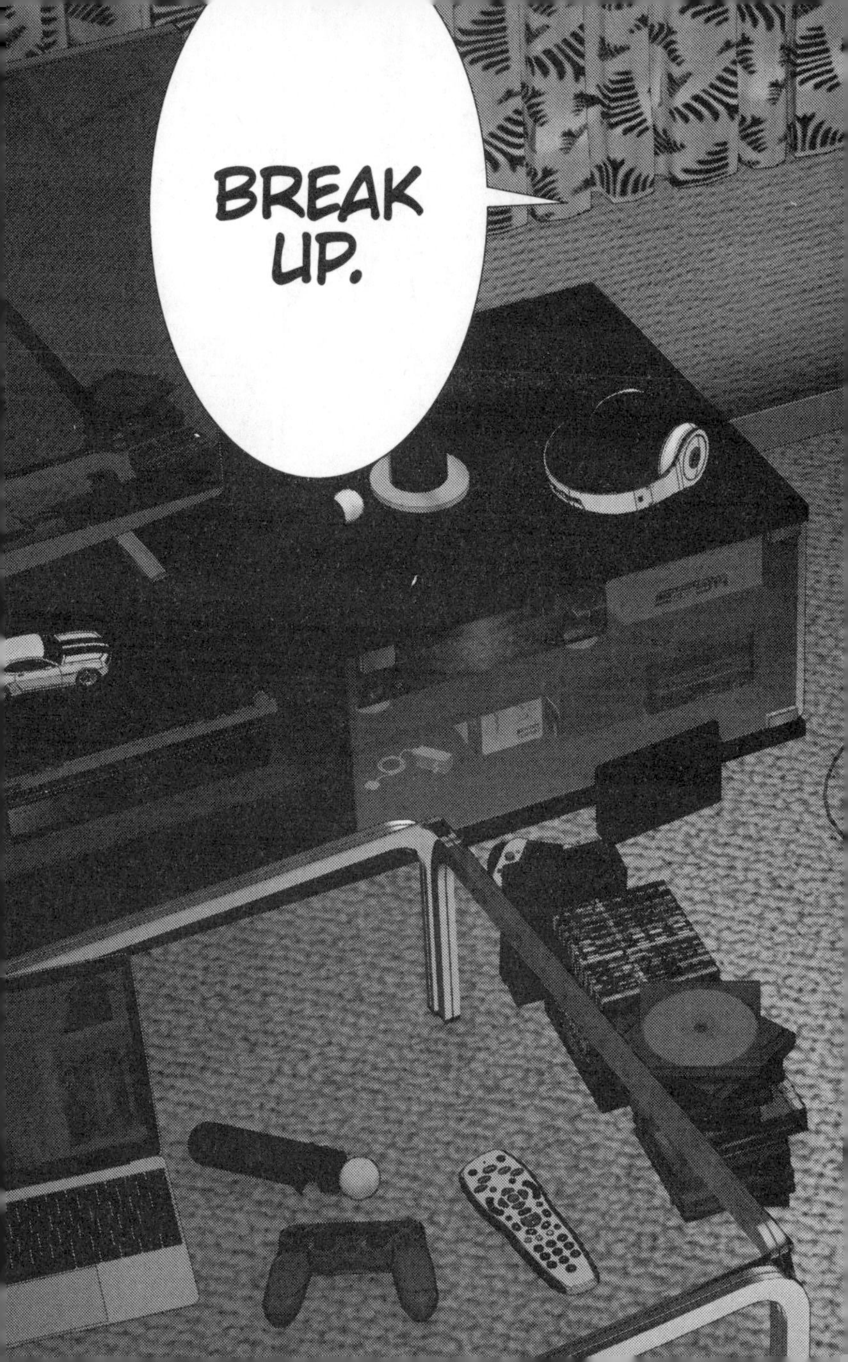
BREAK UP.

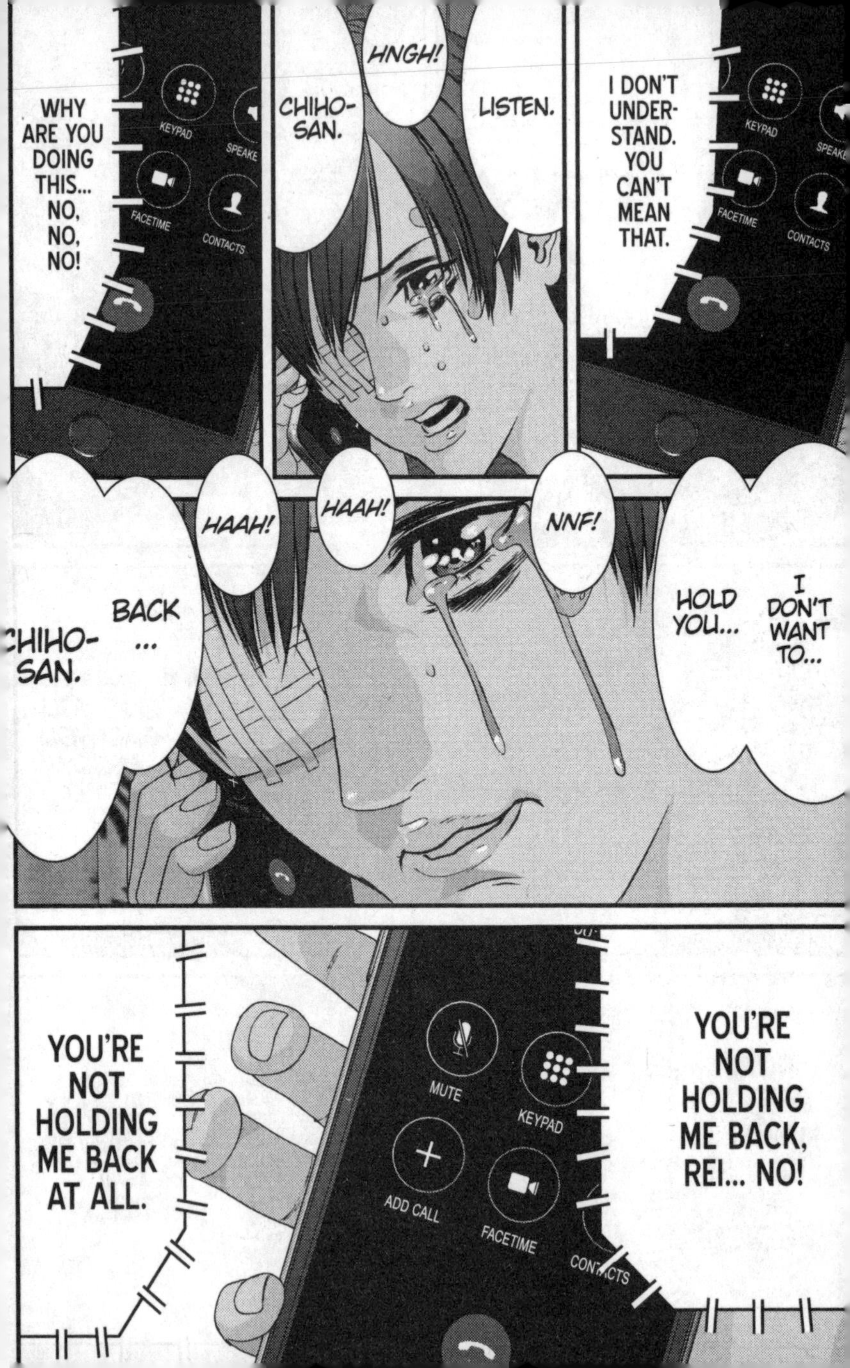
I DON'T UNDERSTAND. YOU CAN'T MEAN THAT.
KEYPAD
SPEAKE
FACETIME
CONTACTS
LISTEN.
HNGH!
CHIHO-SAN.
WHY ARE YOU DOING THIS... NO, NO, NO!
KEYPAD
SPEAKE
FACETIME
CONTACTS
I DON'T WANT TO...
HOLD YOU...
NNF!
HAAH!
HAAH!
BACK...
CHIHO-SAN.
YOU'RE NOT HOLDING ME BACK, REI... NO!
MUTE
KEYPAD
ADD CALL
FACETIME
CONTACTS
YOU'RE NOT HOLDING ME BACK AT ALL.

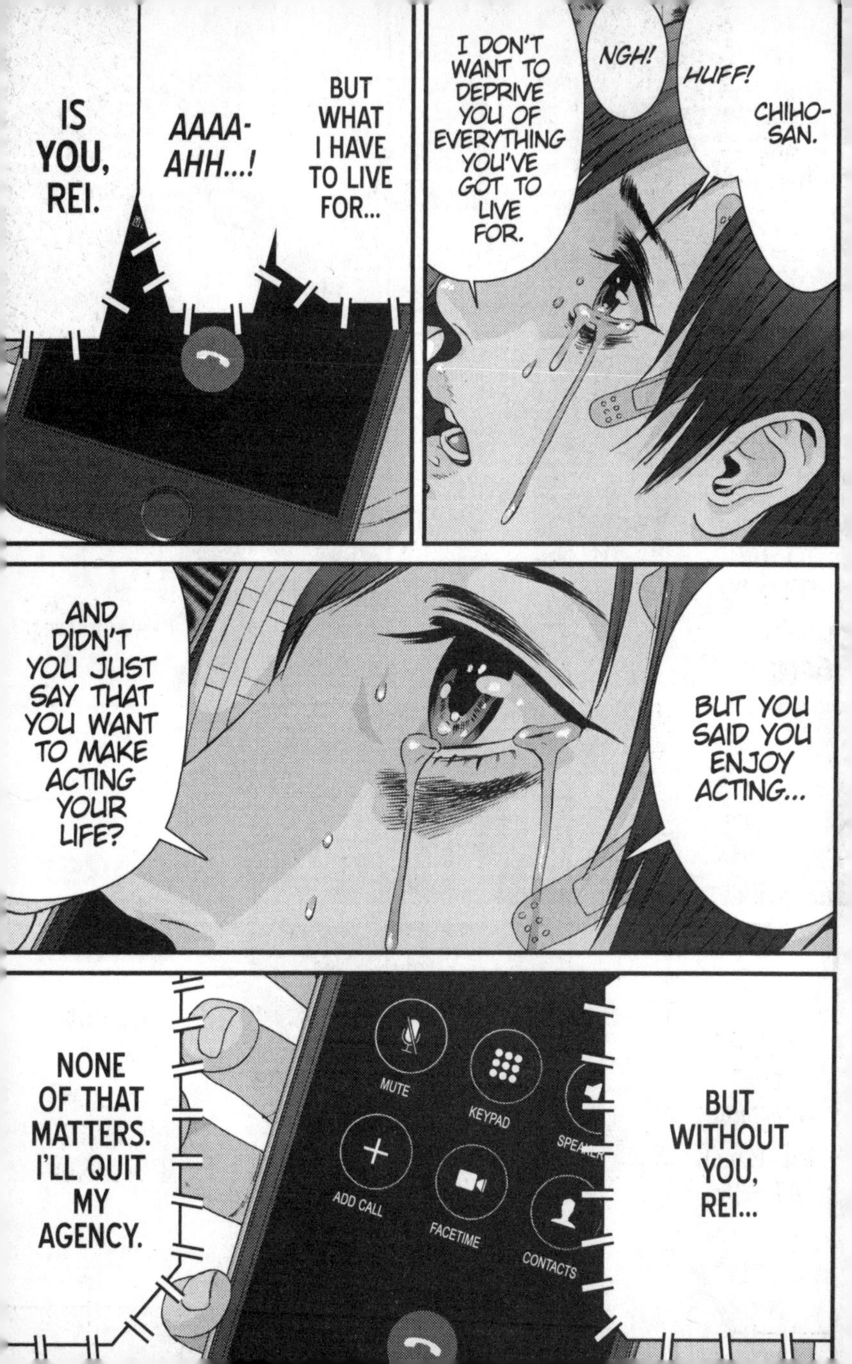
HUFF!
CHIHO-SAN.
NGH!
I DON'T WANT TO DEPRIVE YOU OF EVERYTHING YOU'VE GOT TO LIVE FOR.
BUT WHAT I HAVE TO LIVE FOR...
AAAA-AHH...!
IS YOU, REI.
BUT YOU SAID YOU ENJOY ACTING...
AND DIDN'T YOU JUST SAY THAT YOU WANT TO MAKE ACTING YOUR LIFE?
BUT WITHOUT YOU, REI...
MUTE
KEYPAD
ADD CALL
FACETIME
CONTACTS
NONE OF THAT MATTERS. I'LL QUIT MY AGENCY.

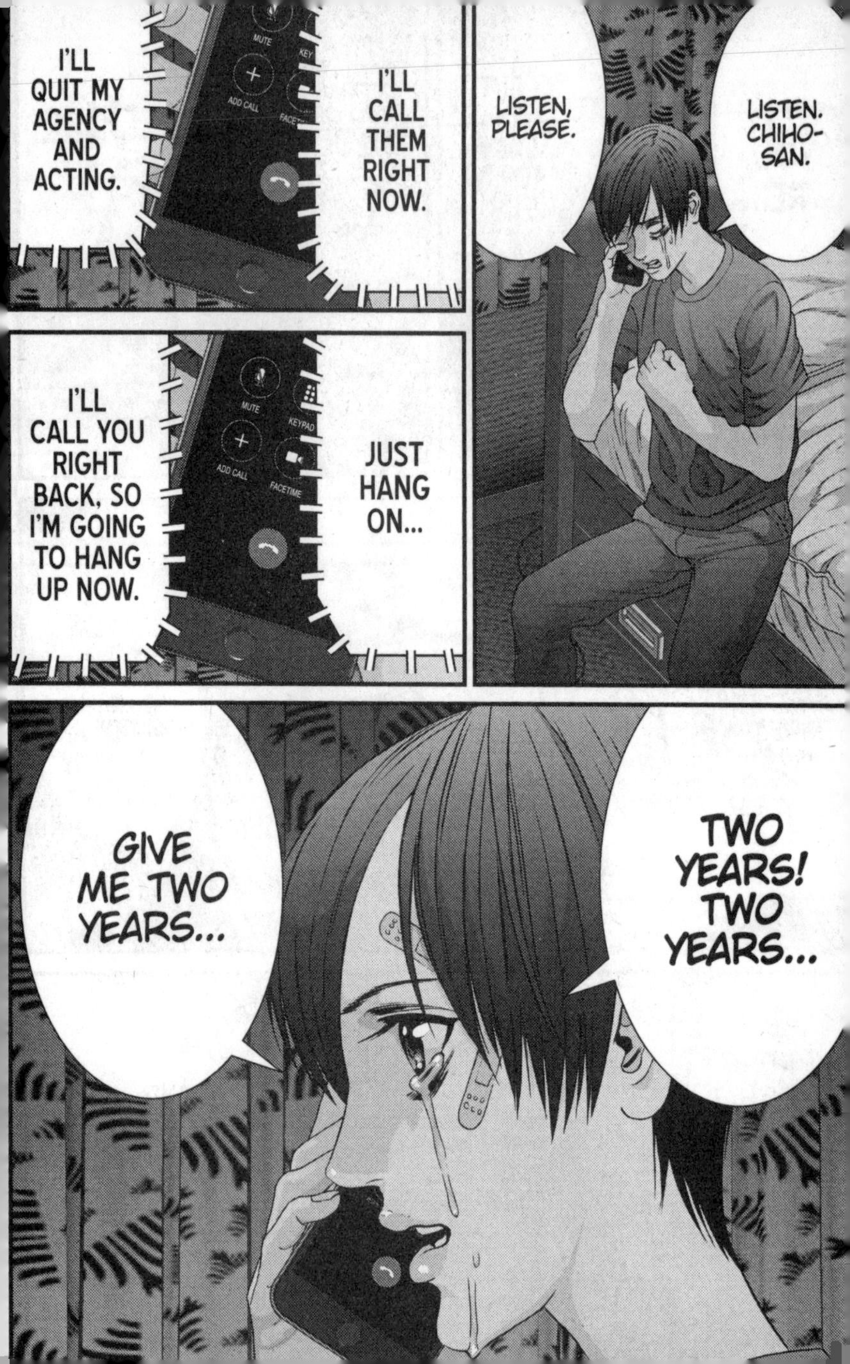
LISTEN. CHIHO-SAN.
LISTEN, PLEASE.
I'LL CALL THEM RIGHT NOW.
I'LL QUIT MY AGENCY AND ACTING.
JUST HANG ON...
I'LL CALL YOU RIGHT BACK, SO I'M GOING TO HANG UP NOW.
TWO YEARS! TWO YEARS...
GIVE ME TWO YEARS...

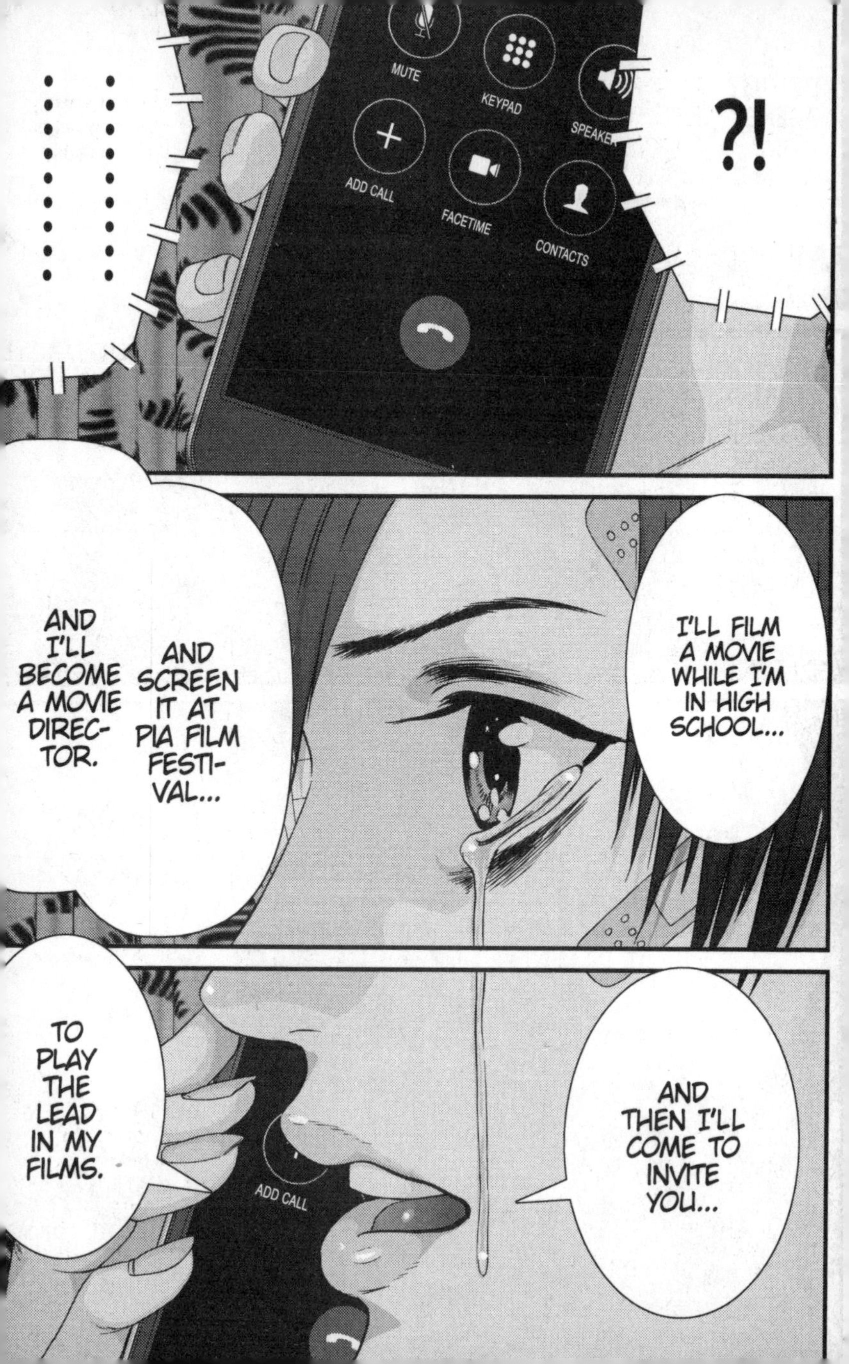
?!
MUTE
KEYPAD
SPEAKER
ADD CALL
FACETIME
CONTACTS
......
I'LL FILM A MOVIE WHILE I'M IN HIGH SCHOOL...
AND SCREEN IT AT PIA FILM FESTI-VAL...
AND I'LL BECOME A MOVIE DIREC-TOR.
AND THEN I'LL COME TO INVITE YOU...
ADD CALL
TO PLAY THE LEAD IN MY FILMS.

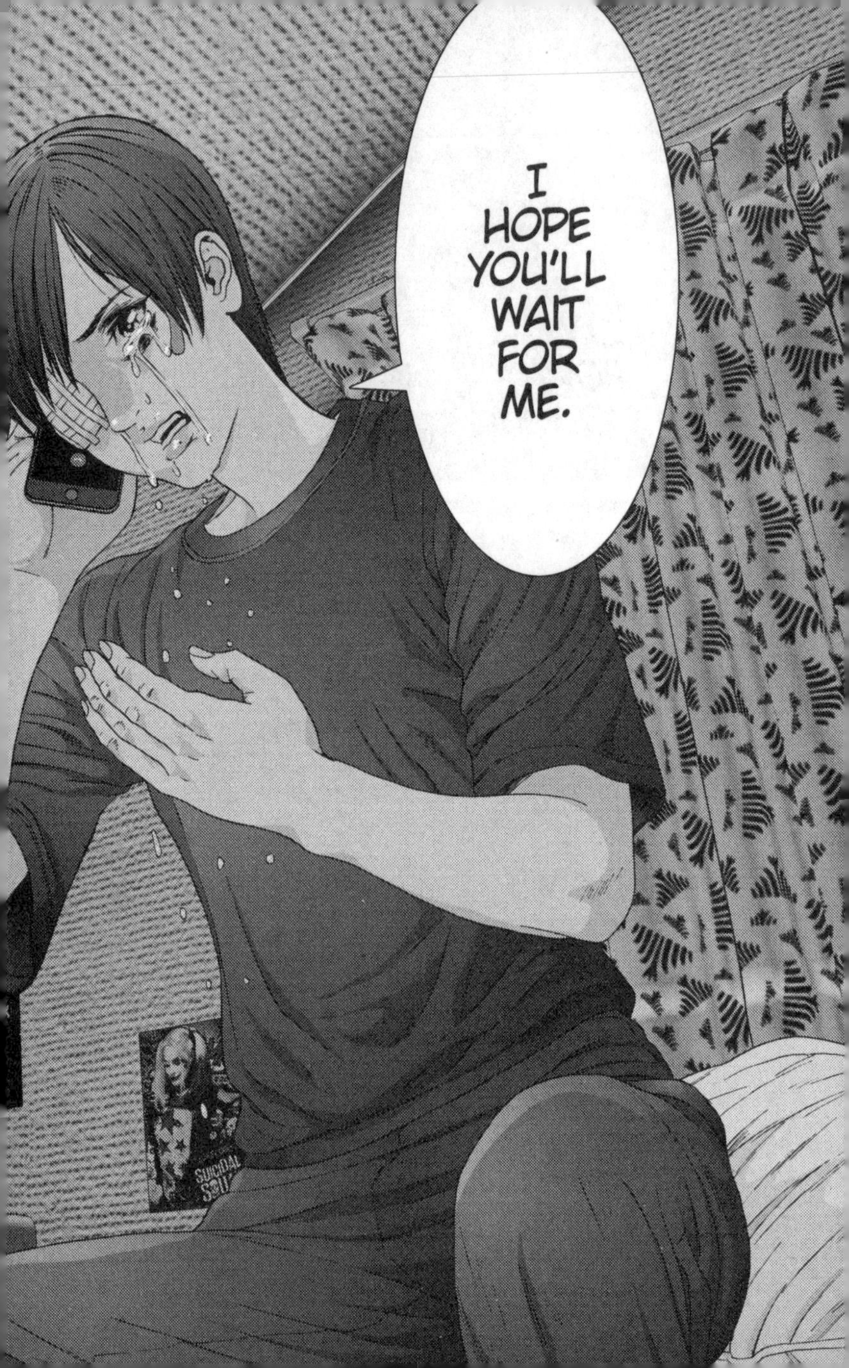
I HOPE YOU'LL WAIT FOR ME.

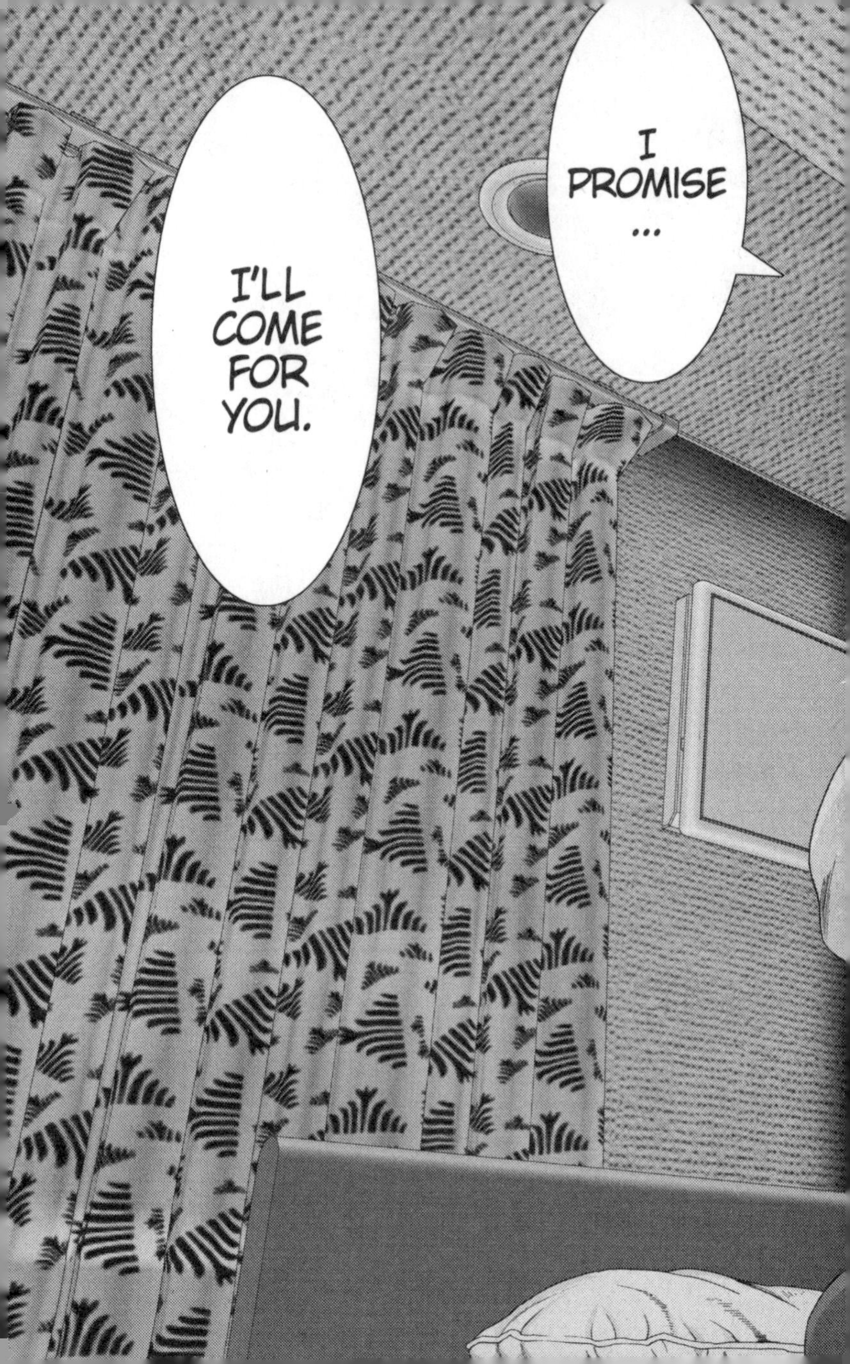
I PROMISE ...
I'LL COME FOR YOU.

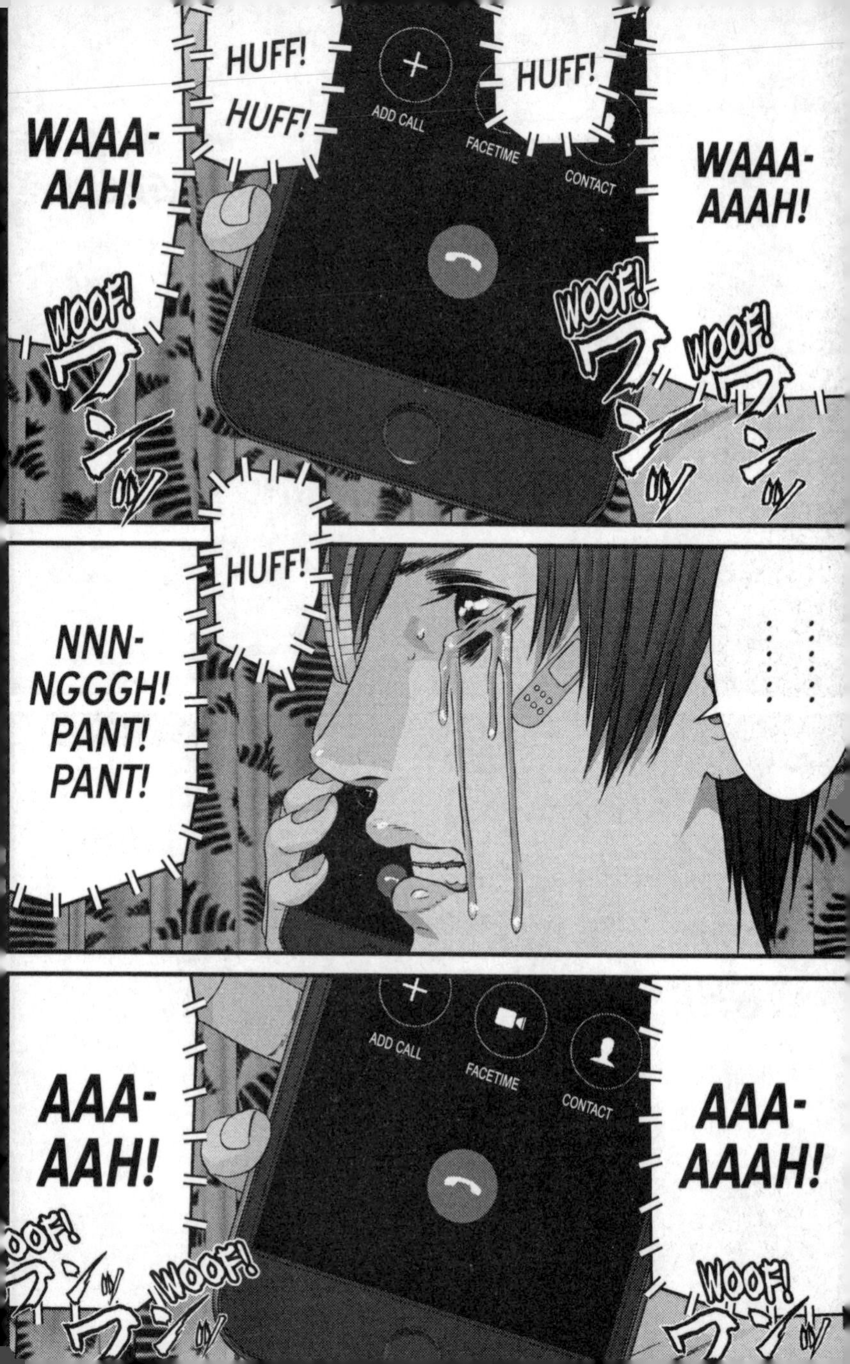
WAAA-AAAH!
WOOF!
WOOF!
HUFF!
CONTACT
FACETIME
ADD CALL
HUFF!
HUFF!
WAAA-AAH!
WOOF!
......
HUFF!
NNN-NGGGH! PANT! PANT!
AAA-AAAH!
WOOF!
CONTACT
FACETIME
ADD CALL
AAA-AAH!
WOOF!
OOF!

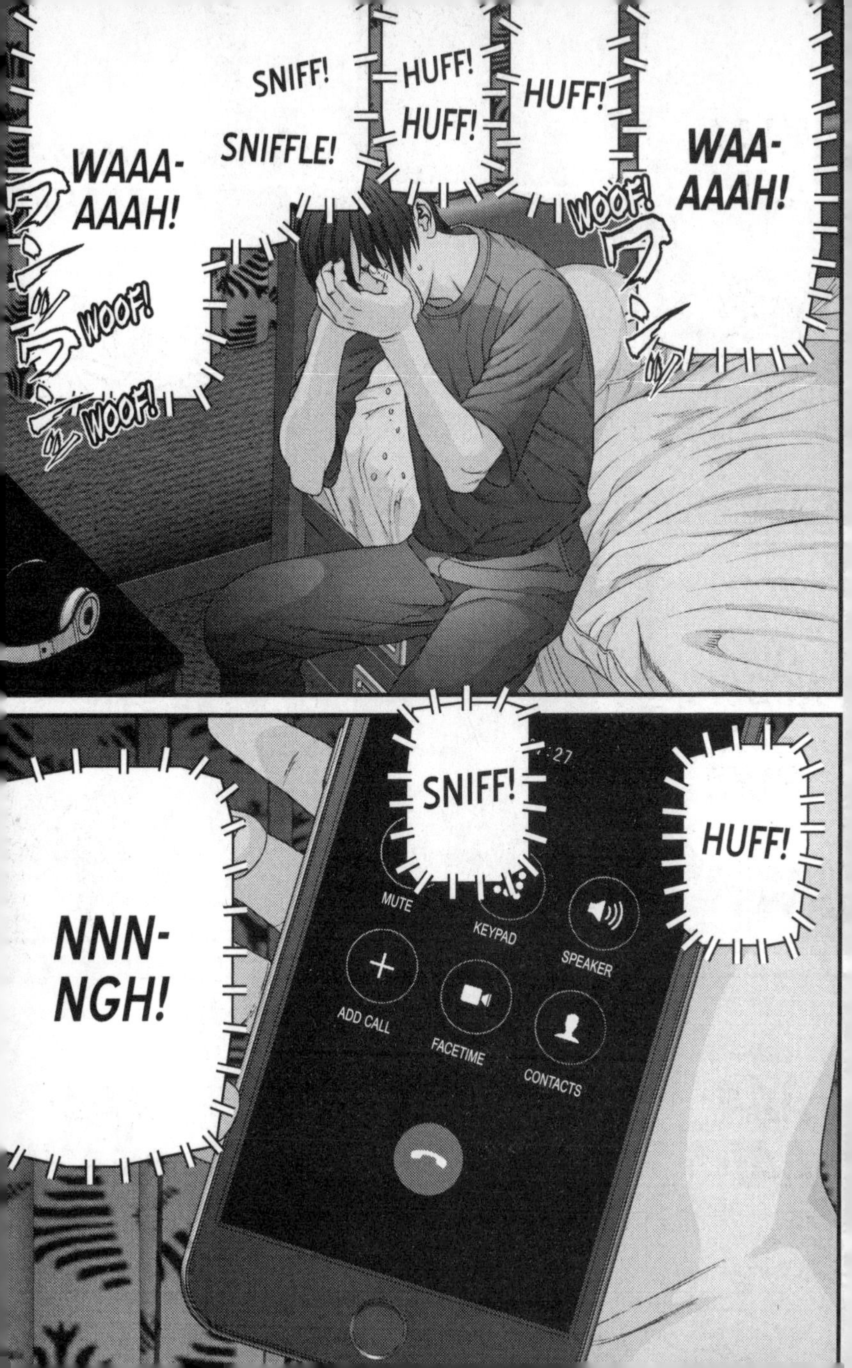
WAA-
AAAH!
WOOF!
HUFF!
HUFF!
HUFF!
SNIFF!
SNIFFLE!
WAAA-
AAAH!
WOOF!
WOOF!
HUFF!
SNIFF!
SPEAKER
KEYPAD
MUTE
CONTACTS
FACETIME
ADD CALL
NNN-
NGH!

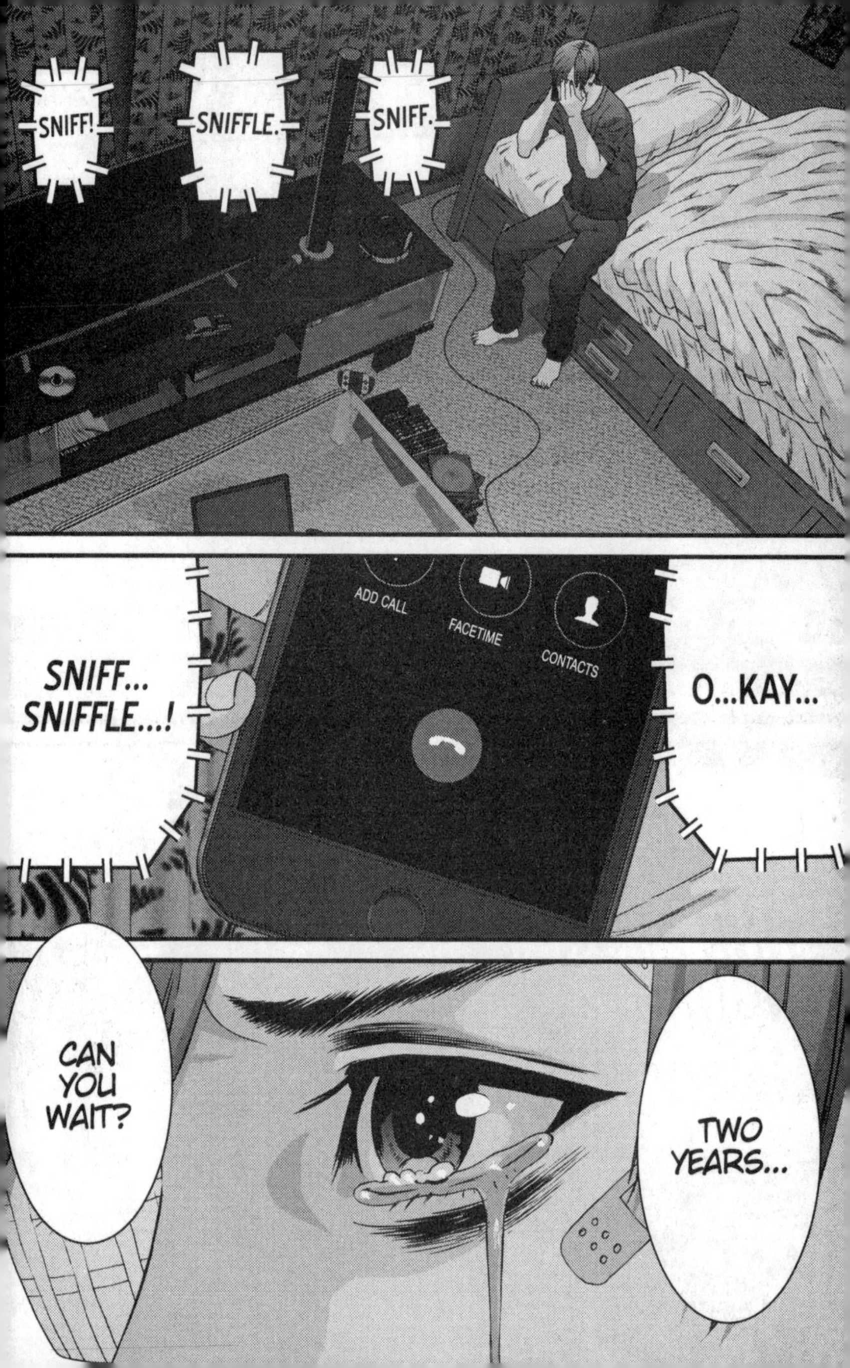
SNIFF.
SNIFFLE.
SNIFF!
ADD CALL
FACETIME
CONTACTS
O...KAY...
SNIFF... SNIFFLE...!
TWO YEARS...
CAN YOU WAIT?

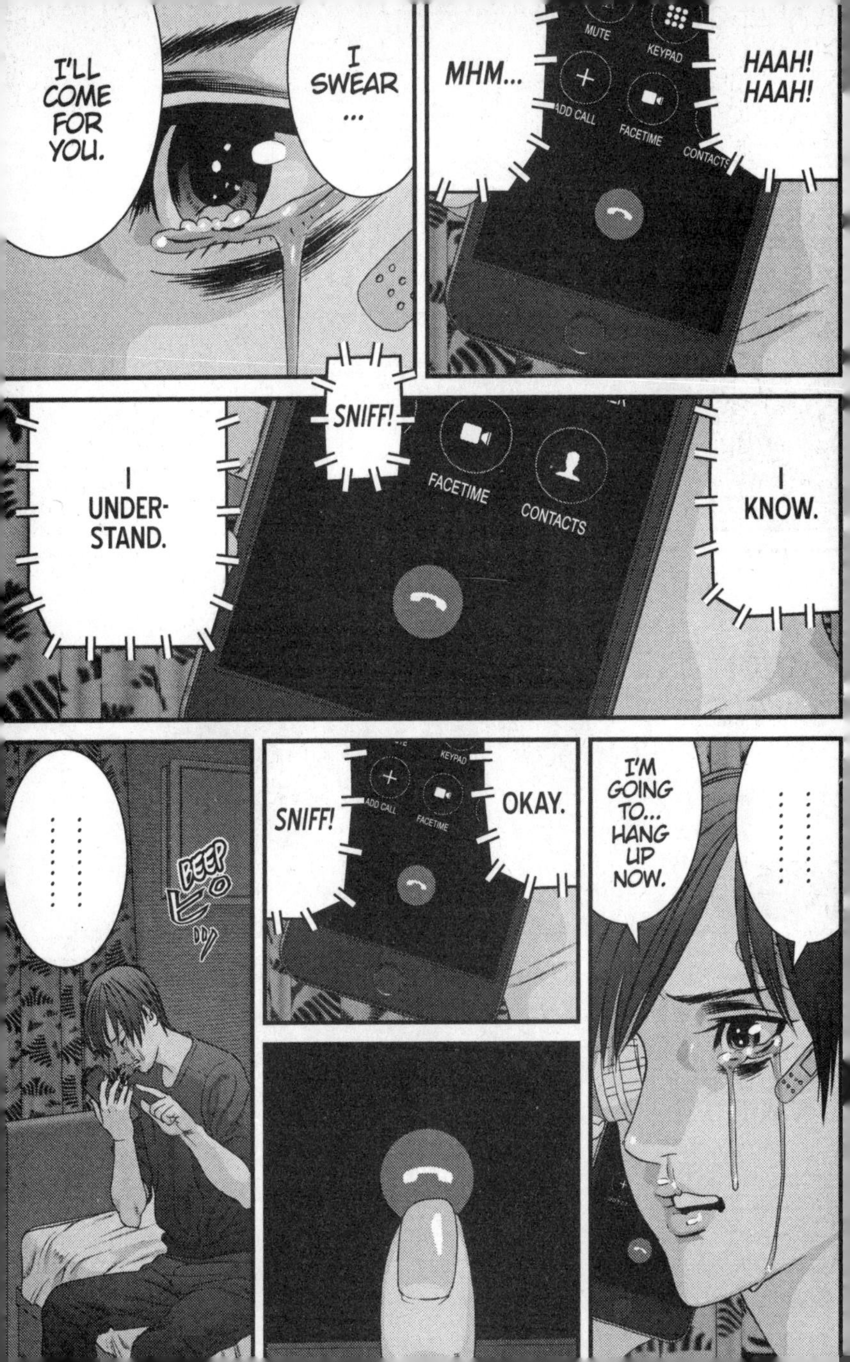
HAAH! HAAH!
MUTE
KEYPAD
ADD CALL
FACETIME
CONTACTS
MHM...
I SWEAR ...
I'LL COME FOR YOU.
I KNOW.
FACETIME
CONTACTS
SNIFF!
I UNDER-STAND.
......
I'M GOING TO... HANG UP NOW.
KEYPAD
ADD CALL
FACETIME
OKAY.
SNIFF!
BEEP
......

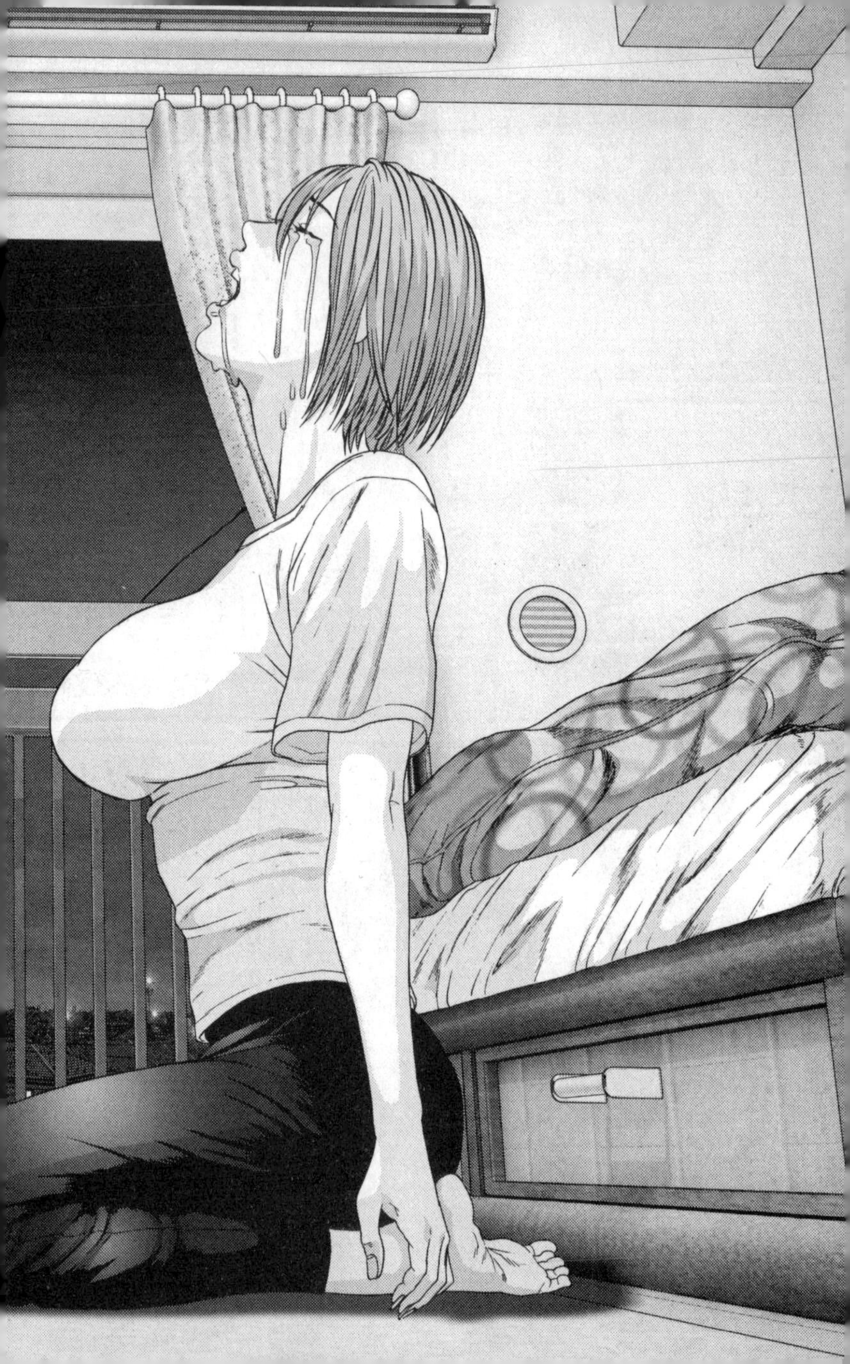

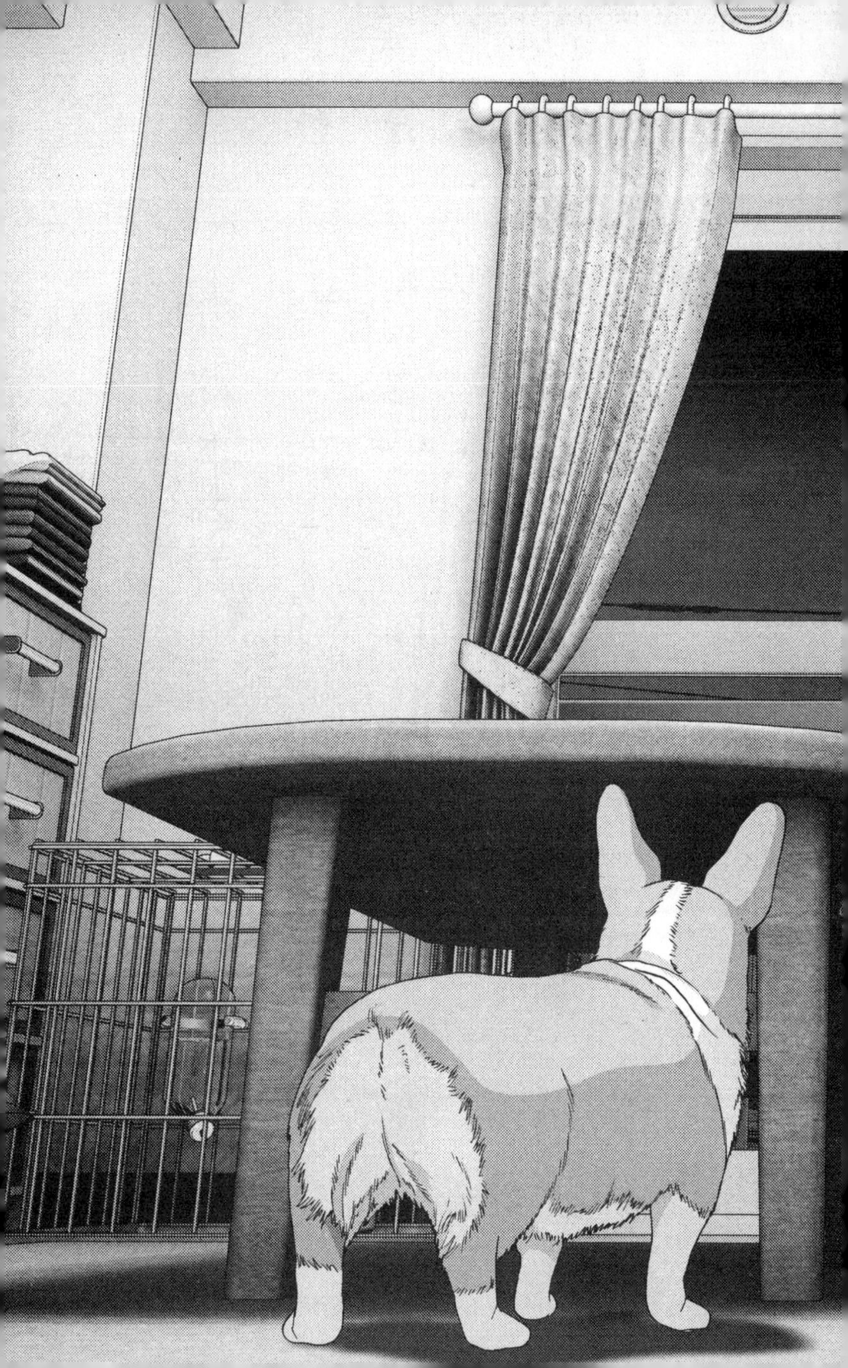

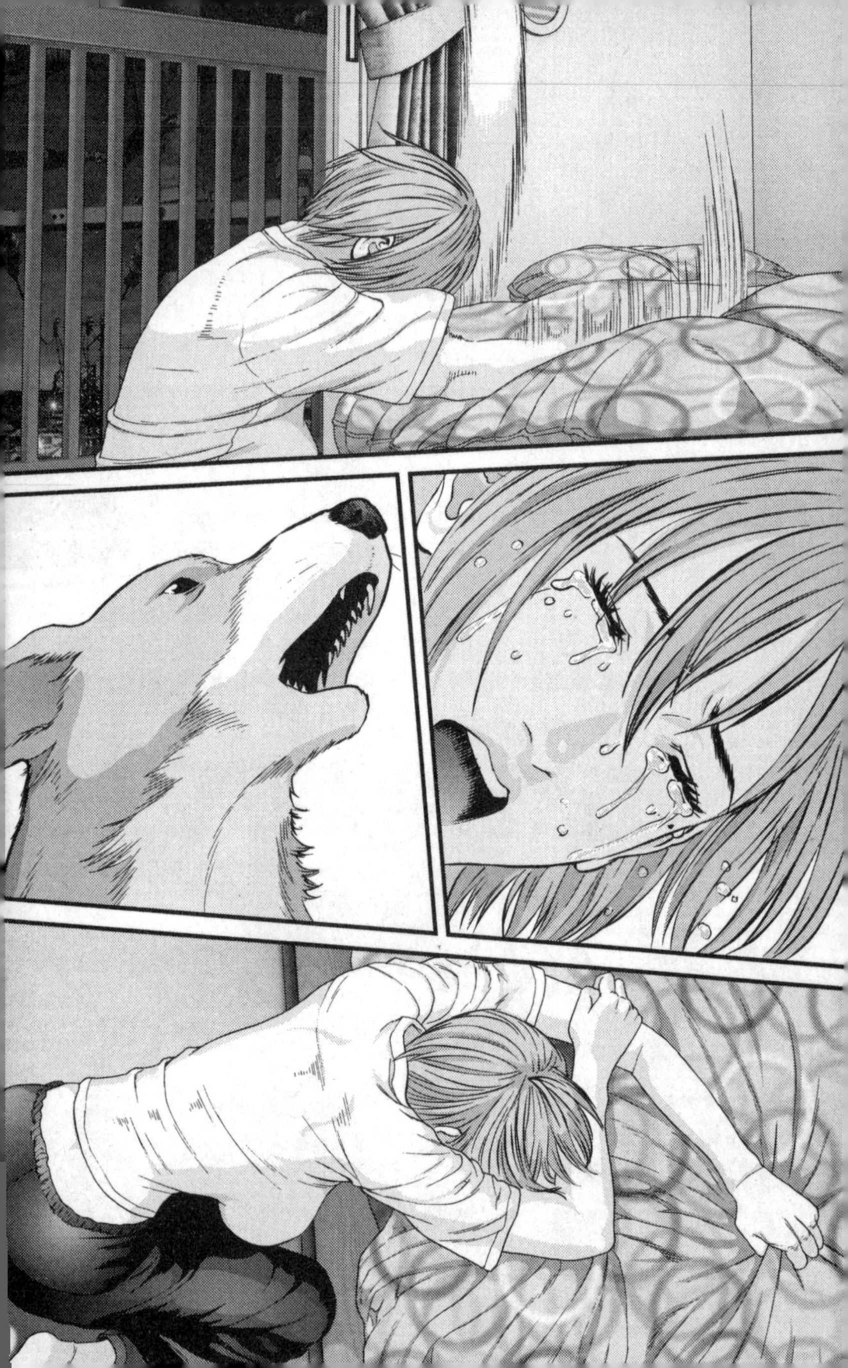

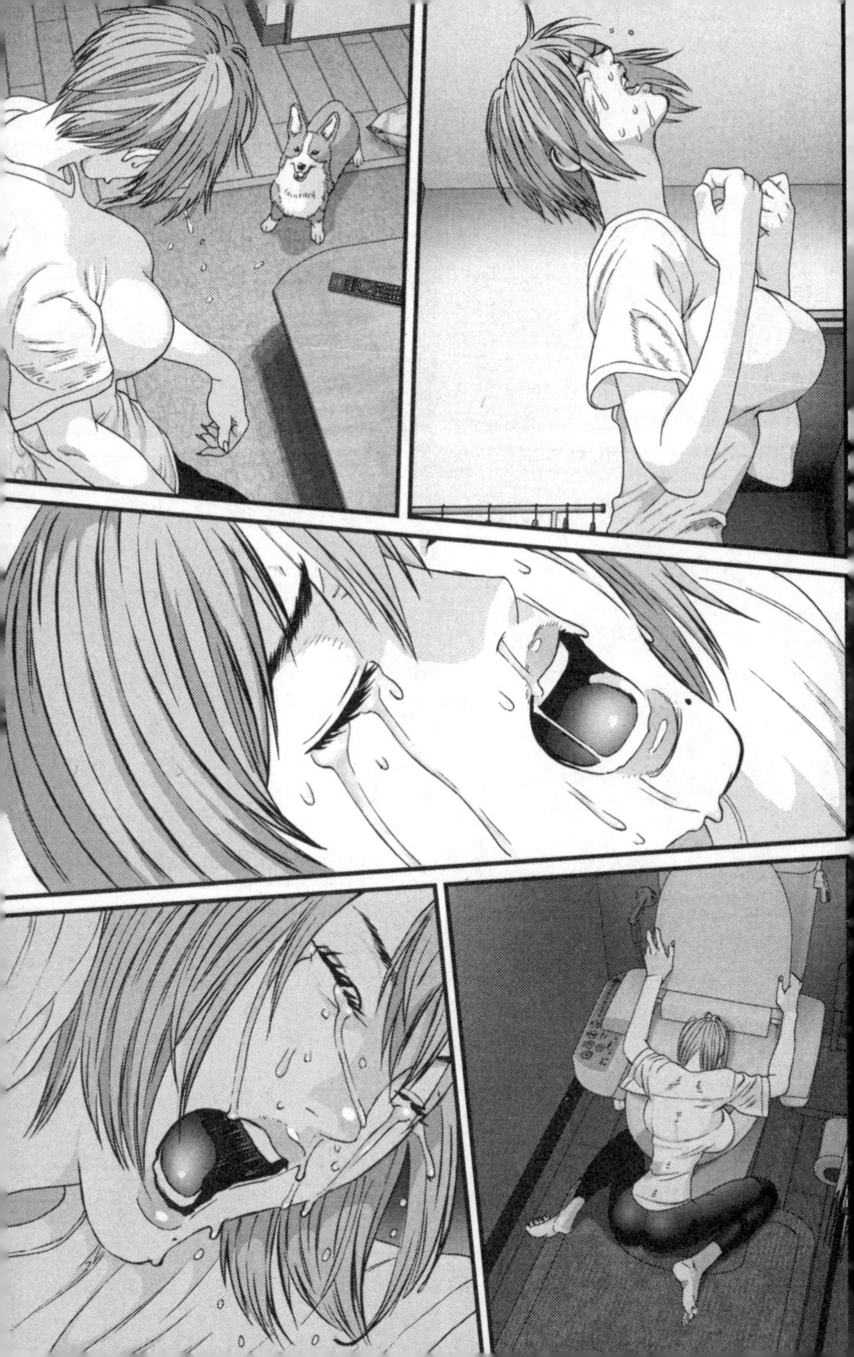

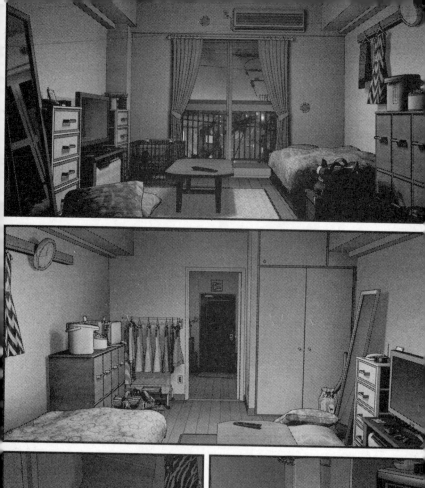
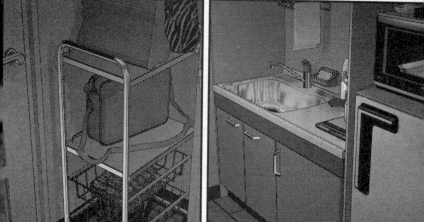

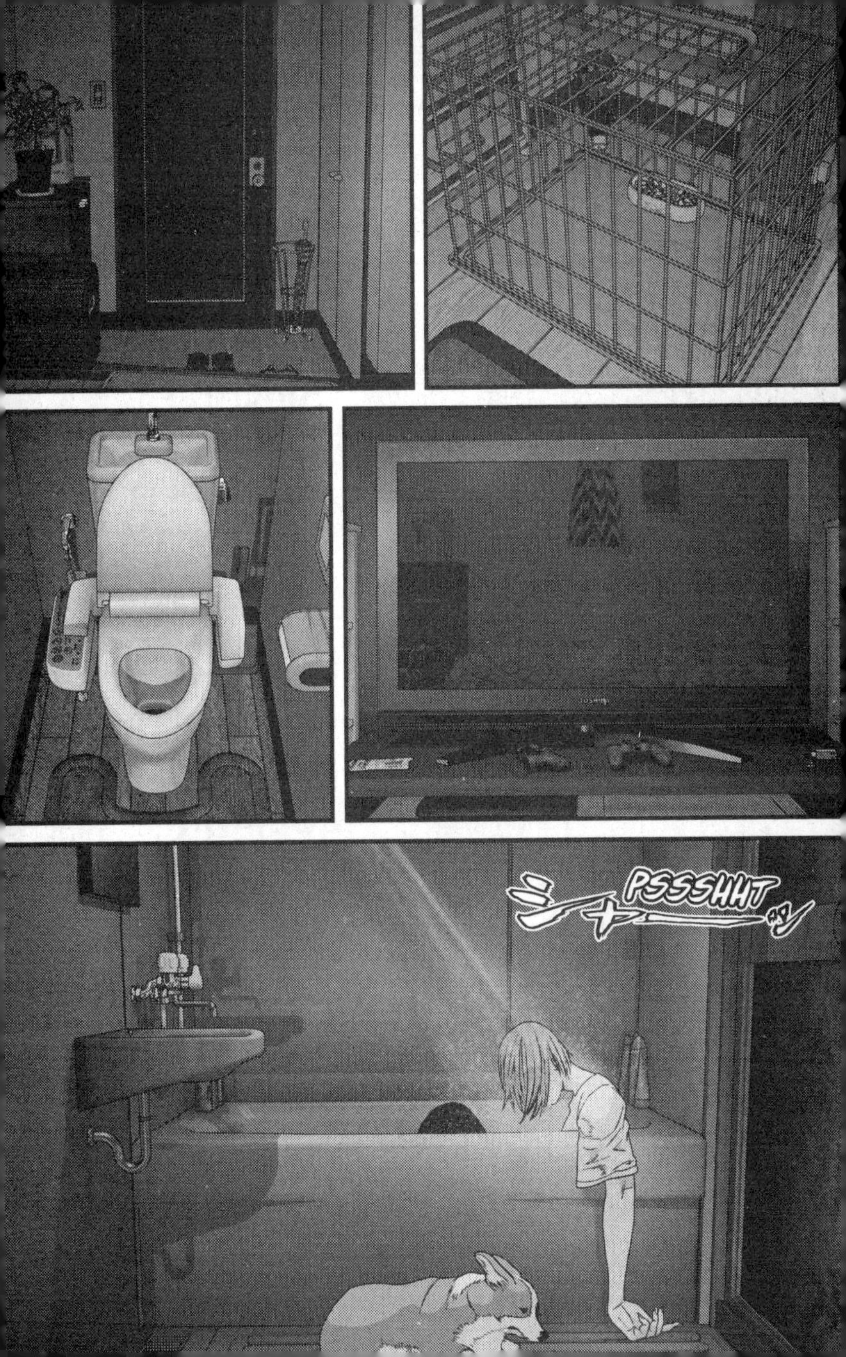
PSSSHHT

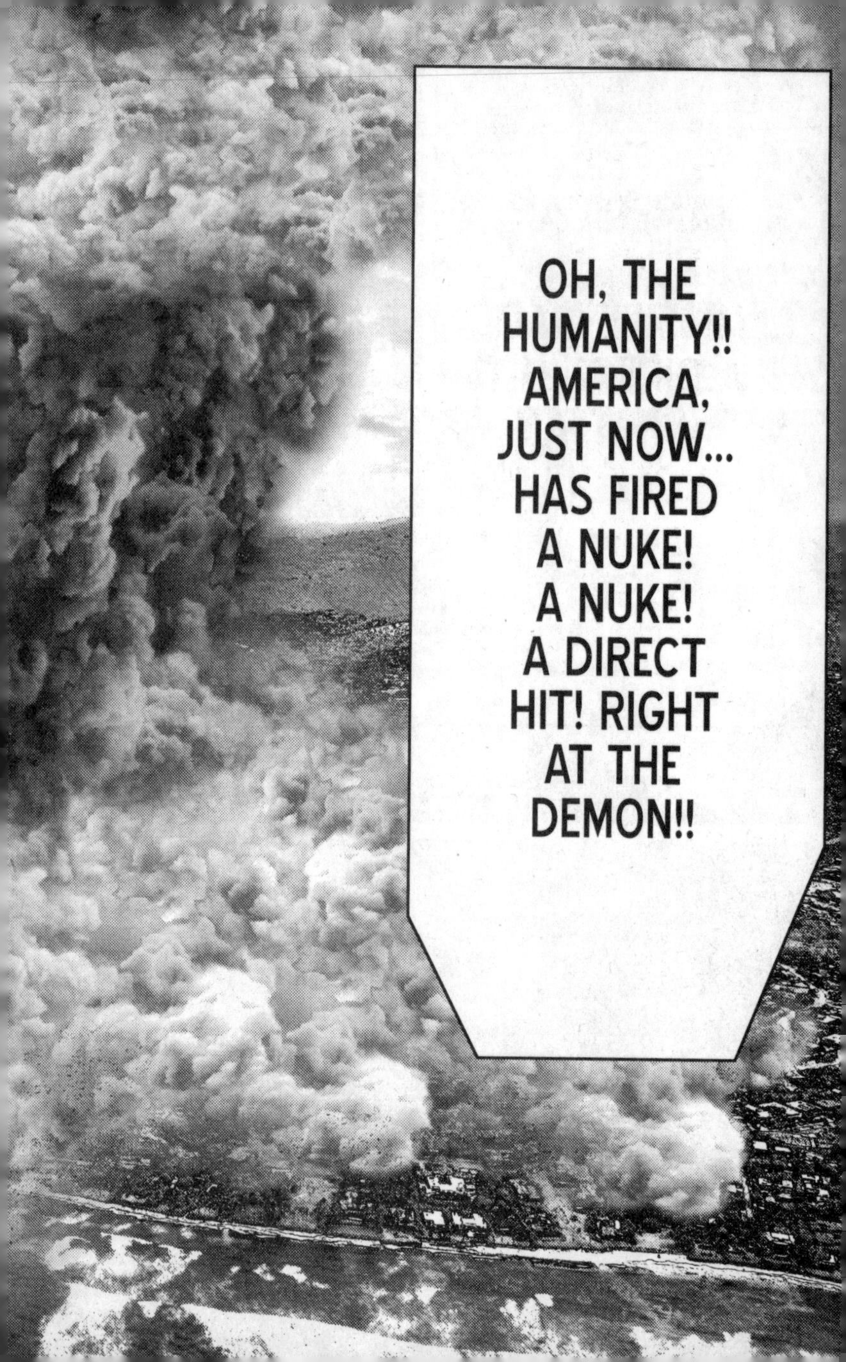
OH, THE HUMANITY!! AMERICA, JUST NOW... HAS FIRED A NUKE! A NUKE! A DIRECT HIT! RIGHT AT THE DEMON!!

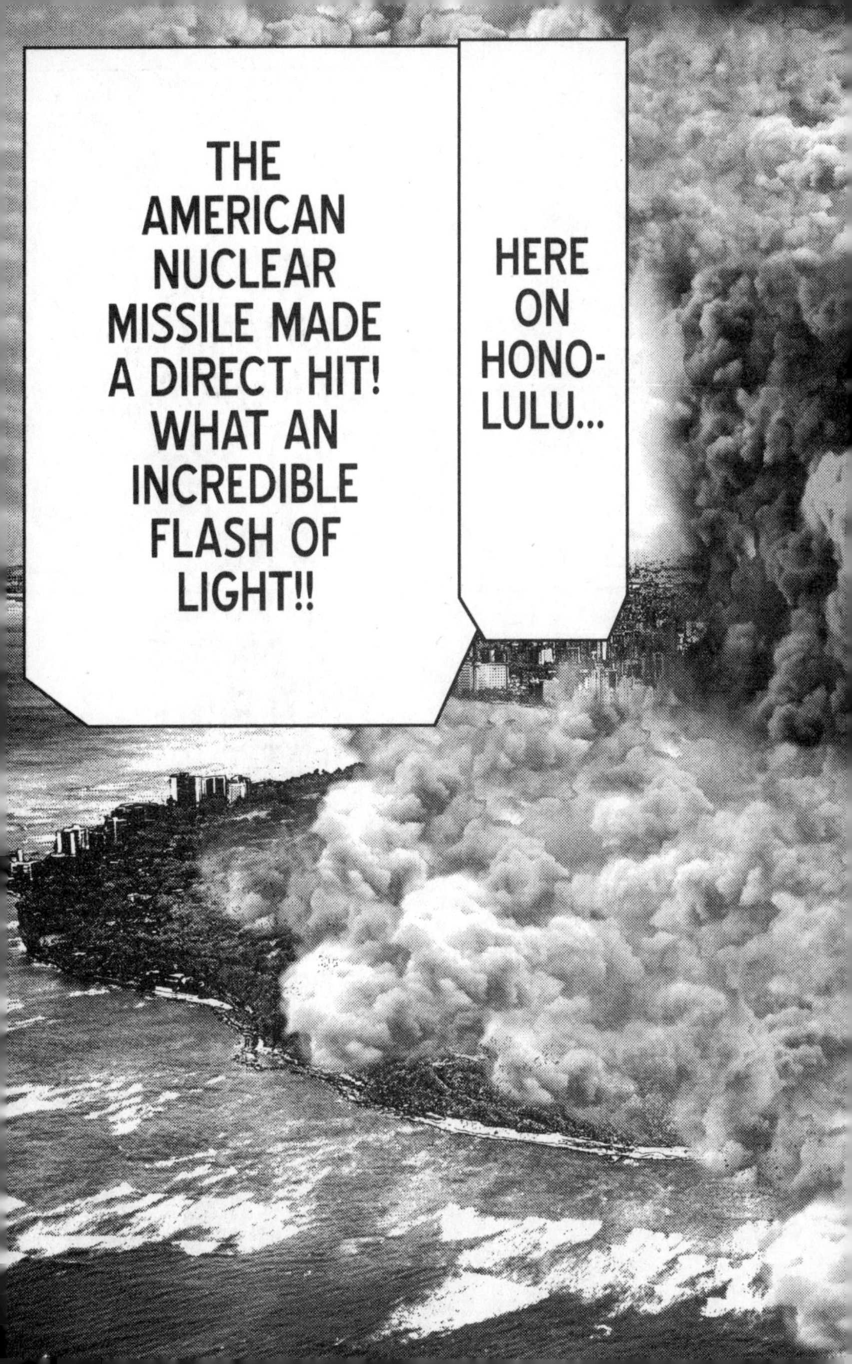
HERE ON HONO-LULU...
THE AMERICAN NUCLEAR MISSILE MADE A DIRECT HIT! WHAT AN INCREDIBLE FLASH OF LIGHT!!

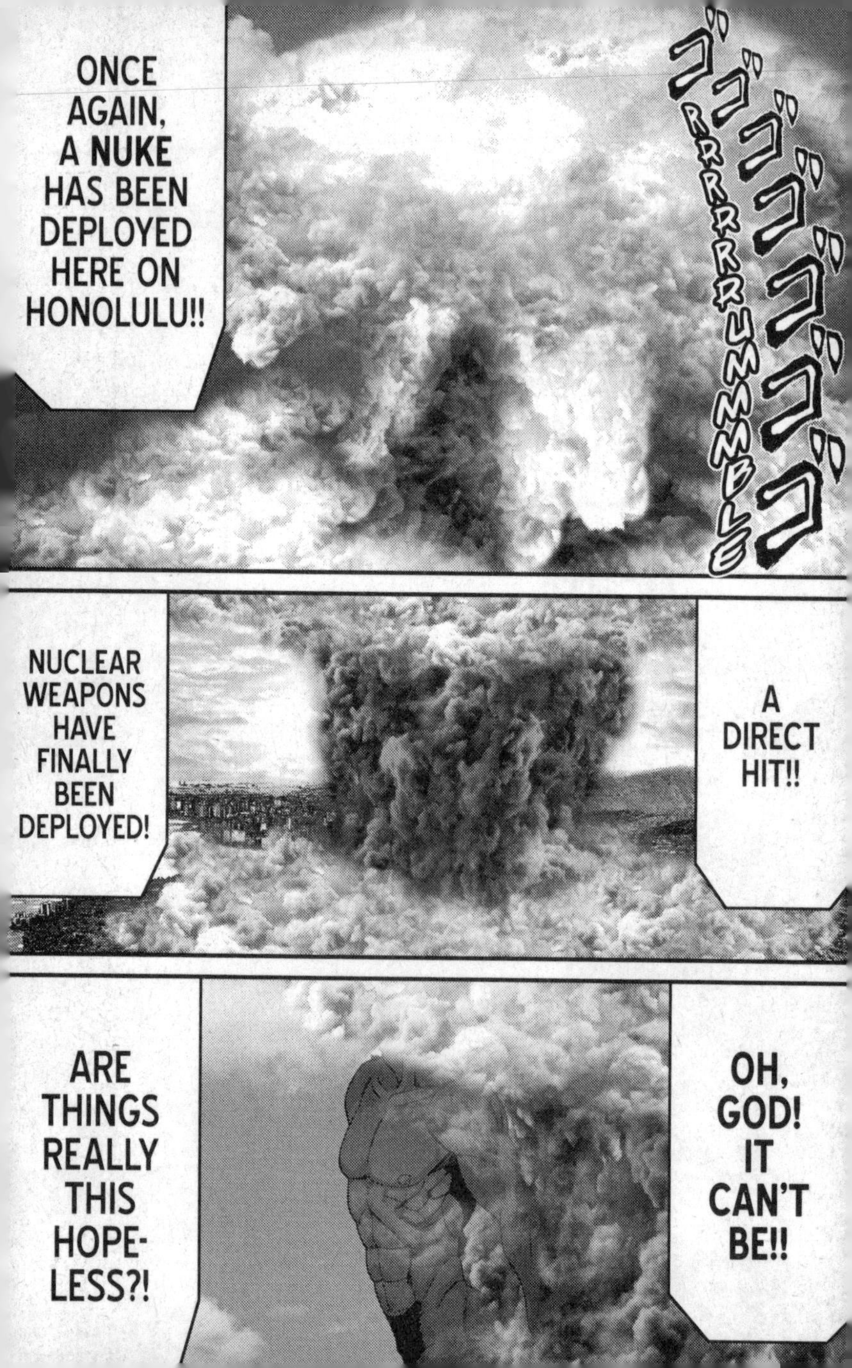
ゴゴゴゴゴゴゴ
RRRRRRUMMMBLE
ONCE AGAIN, A **NUKE** HAS BEEN DEPLOYED HERE ON HONOLULU!!
A DIRECT HIT!!
NUCLEAR WEAPONS HAVE FINALLY BEEN DEPLOYED!
OH, GOD! IT CAN'T BE!!
ARE THINGS REALLY THIS HOPE-LESS?!

"GIGANT" CHAPTER SIX : END   TO BE CONTINUED _

SEVEN SEAS ENTERTAINMENT PRESENTS

GIG∧NT

story and art by HIROYA OKU   VOLUME 6

TRANSLATION
Christine Dashiell

ADAPTATION
Jamal Joseph Jr.

LETTERING
Ray Steeves

ORIGINAL COVER DESIGN
BALCOLONY.
(ei Sometani and Hinano Honda)

IN COOPERATION WITH
Guillaume Hennequin

COVER DESIGN
Nicky Lim

PROOFREADER
Dawn Davis

EDITOR
J.P. Sullivan

PREPRESS TECHNICIAN
iannon Rasmussen-Silverstein

PRODUCTION ASSOCIATE
Christa Miesner

PRODUCTION MANAGER
Lissa Pattillo

MANAGING EDITOR
Julie Davis

ASSOCIATE PUBLISHER
Adam Arnold

PUBLISHER
Jason DeAngelis

GIGANT VOLUME 6
by Hiroya OKU
© 2018 Hiroya OKU
All rights reserved.
Original Japanese edition published by SHOGAKUKAN.
English translation rights in the United States of America, Canada, and the United
Kingdom arranged with SHOGAKUKAN through Tuttle-Mori Agency, Inc.

Seven Seas press and purchase enquiries can be sent to Marketing Manager Lianne
Sentar at press@gomanga.com. Information regarding the distribution and purchase of
digital editions is available from Digital Manager CK Russell at digital@gomanga.com.

Seven Seas and the Seven Seas logo are trademarks of
Seven Seas Entertainment. All rights reserved.

ISBN: 978-1-64827-348-3
Printed in Canada
First Printing: October 2021
10 9 8 7 6 5 4 3 2 1

////// READING DIRECTIONS //////

This book reads from *right to left*,
Japanese style. If this is your first time
reading manga, you start reading from
the top right panel on each page and
take it from there. If you get lost, just
follow the numbered diagram here.
It may seem backwards at first,
but you'll get the hang of it! Have fun!!

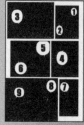

Follow us online: www.SevenSeasEntertainment.com